Measurement and Evaluation in Physical Education

Measurement and Evaluation in Physical Education

D. Allen Phillips
University of Northern Colorado

James E. Hornak
Central Michigan University

John Wiley and Sons
New York Chichester Brisbane Toronto

To Doran and Tina
To Joan, Mom and Dad Hornak

Library of Congress Cataloging in Publication Data:

Phillips, D. Allen, 1942-
Measurement and evaluation in physical education.

Includes index.

1. Physical fitness — Testing. I. Hornak, James E., 1943- joint author. II. Title.
GV436.P52 613.7'076 79-12977
ISBN 0-471-04962-X

Printed in the United States of America

10 9 8 7 6 5 4 3 2 1

Preface

Physical educators spend a substantial amount of their time and effort in measuring and evaluating students. This text is designed to give students in measurement and evaluation the tools to make intelligent decisions regarding all phases of the measurement and evaluation process.

Our main purpose in writing this book is to help the student of measurement and evaluation to be able to design, develop, administer, and evaluate valid and reliable measuring instruments. Few tests have been included in the book. Our view is that once an understanding of the underlying principles of measurement and evaluation is gained, the students will be able to construct tests and test items that fit their teaching situations. The tests that have been included use little or no equipment and do not require special training to be administered. They serve as examples rather than as recommended tests or test items.

Because we feel that objectives are paramount in importance in the measurement and evaluation process, we have initiated each chapter with a list of competencies that the student should have after reading and studying the content in that chapter. Each chapter is followed by study questions to help the students assess their mastery of objectives.

Chapter 1 introduces the terminology and identifies the purposes of measurement and evaluation. Chapter 2 presents the historical and philosophical perspectives. A table of milestones in measurement and a simplified model of instruction highlight this chapter. Chapter 3 presents the essential statistical techniques necessary in the evaluation process and includes a discussion on the use of the computer. Chapter 4 identifies the various types of norms and their uses. Chapter 5 discusses validity, reliability, and economy, all important factors associated with the selection and construction of tests. Chapter 6 explains the importance of behavioral objectives and identifies procedures necessary in writing objectives for the cognitive, affective, and psychomotor domains. Chapter 7 introduces the test blueprint and shows how test items can be written for each domain of behavior. Chapter 8 is concerned with the administrative aspects of testing while Chapter 9 describes various methods of grading. Chapter 10 is a unique chapter and discusses the various sources of information used to locate and evaluate tests.

Chapters 11 to 14 define anthropometric traits, basic performance traits, multiple performance traits, the domains of behavior, and present examples in many of the test areas. Several appendixes supplement the text with additional pertinent information. We have given the student sound philosophical, statistical, and measurement principles that can be used in constructing, selecting, administering, and evaluating tests.

We thank our families for their patience and consideration during the writing of the manuscript. Also we are grateful to the publishers cited in the text for permission to reprint copyrighted material.

D. Allen Phillips
James E. Hornak

Contents

Figures

Tables

CHAPTER 1

Introduction to Measurement and Evaluation in Physical Education

After you have read and studied this chapter you should be able to:
1. *Define the terms test, measurement, and evaluation.*
2. *Distinguish the differences among the terms test, measurement, and evaluation.*
3. *Identify the purposes of measurement and evaluation in physical education.*

Teachers must make decisions about students on a daily basis. Some decisions are objective and appear quite easy to make. Others, however, are based on teachers' value systems and are generally subjective and difficult to make.

The various processes of measurement and evaluation more easily and objectively enable the physical educator to make decisions about students and their performances. *Tests* must be administered, *measures* must be assigned, and *evaluations* must be made regularly by every teacher. These three terms provide the entire philosophical basis for making decisions about student characteristics.

DEFINITIONS

A test is commonly defined as a tool or instrument of measurement that is used to obtain data about a specific trait or characteristic of an individual or group. Motor fitness is measured by tests such as the AAHPER Youth Fitness Test. Personality might be measured by tests such as the Cattell Sixteen Personality Factor Questionnaire or the Minnesota Multiphasic Personality Inventory. A teacher might measure the extent to which instructional objectives have been achieved with a teacher-made test.

A measure is the score that has been assigned on the basis of a test. This, of course, implies that measures may be recorded only as a numerical value. No decision can be made concerning the quality of a score by itself. This can be done only in the form of an evaluation, which is discussed below.

Evaluation is a complex term that often is misused by both teachers and students. It involves making decisions or judgments about students based on the extent to which instructional objectives are achieved by them. These decisions may involve the use of both quantitative (measures) and qualitative data. In an evaluation of a student, judgments should be made in a thorough, systematic manner by using the best and most comprehensive measurement program available. Remember that evaluations must be made in light of the teachers' instructional objectives that should have been previously identified. Evaluation may involve qualitative measures when decisions relative to the instructional objectives are made. In other words, evaluative decisions may be based on either quantitative or qualitative measures depending on the type of test involved and the type of information that the teacher desires from the test. The terms tests, measures, and evaluations are clearly distinct but related. Teachers obtain measures from tests in order to make fair evaluations about specific traits or characteristics of their students. Tests and measures are entities in themselves and involve no decisions or extra considerations. Evaluation, on the other hand, is totally a decision-making process.

Before listing and discussing the purposes of measurement and evaluation in physical education, remember that the total student is never evaluated or in fact tested. Only specific characteristics or traits — strength, speed, and knowledge, for instance — are observed and evaluated at one time. For this reason it is inappropriate to discuss evaluation of a student rather than the evaluation of a characteristic of the student.

PURPOSES OF MEASUREMENT AND EVALUATION IN PHYSICAL EDUCATION

Unfortunately, few students clearly understand the objectives or purposes of measurement and evaluation in the typical school setting. Most students feel that the assignment of grades is the only real purpose of evaluation. This thinking is too limited; there are numerous functions that a good program of measurement and evaluation, if properly understood and administered, can serve.

Placement

Before teachers begin a unit of study they must assess the skill level of each student. Based on the results of the preassessment, the teacher may want to classify students and place them into smaller homogeneous groups that will perhaps increase the rate of learning. The placement of students with similar skills into a learning group allows the teacher to individualize the instruction within that group. More skilled students can be challenged with objectives and the development of advanced techniques. Students with fewer skills are also challenged with objectives and skill development that are tailored to their initial status.

Diagnosis of Learning Problems

Diagnostic evaluation searches for underlying causes of learning problems that commonly confront teachers of physical education. Diagnostic evaluation is quite complex. It involves thorough testing of a particular characteristic of a student. It generally involves the formulation of a plan for corrective action. For example, if a student continues to experience failure in the execution of a certain skill after considerable effort by the teacher, a detailed diagnostic testing procedure might be necessary. Evaluation of the tests would lead to a solution of the problem and a plan for short- and long-term corrective action.

Progress During Instruction

It is important for both the student and teacher to keep abreast of the student's daily progress during instruction. A special type of evaluation called *formative evaluation*, which consists largely of self-testing exercises with continuous feedback, is used to provide this vital information. Formative evaluation will be discussed in later chapters. The feedback received by the students provides instant reinforcement of the successful completion of a task and a basis for identifying and correcting specific individual problems. Although any form of testing instrument will serve this purpose of measurement, most teachers have found that teacher-made check lists or observational techniques are most satisfactory. However, most tests that measure progress are directed toward improvement of the student and generally are not utilized in the assignment of unit grades.

Achievement After Instruction

Evaluation for achievement at the end of an instructional unit is designed to quantify the extent that the behavioral objectives have been met by each student. This is accomplished by *summative evaluation* which assigns unit grades or course grades and certifies student competency in terms of achievement of the behavioral objectives. Summative evaluation usually involves teacher-made unit tests or various types of standardized tests, discussed later. The assignment of grades and certification of competency must not be taken lightly by the teacher. These grades often become an integral part of each student's permanent records and therefore must be arrived at through well-developed, summative evaluation programs. In addition to grade assignment and certification, this form of evaluation helps the teacher to determine whether the behavioral objectives and instructional procedures are appropriate for the instructional unit.

Determination of Improvement

To many teachers of physical education, a measure of student improvement over short or long periods of time is essential. There are many forms of evaluation that enable the teacher to determine student improvement such as check lists of objectives, teacher-made formative tests, or certain forms of unit tests administered before and after instruction. A certain amount of caution must be exercised in the interpretation of improvement measures. Students whose skills are relatively poor in a specific unit can improve greatly, sometimes with little effort. In contrast, only small improvements can be made by highly skilled students within the same unit. Despite these cautions the knowledge of a student's improvement can be very important in the total learning situation. Some form of improvement evaluation is necessary and should be attempted by the classroom teacher even though precise interpretation may be difficult.

Motivation of Students Through Feedback

Research dealing with feedback has shown that students who are aware of how well they are performing and how much they are improving are likely to be motivated more than students who are not receiving feedback. Also, students learn more rapidly and reach higher levels of performance. Certain students who receive no feedback relative to their performance or improvement may become disenchanted with the learning process. Feedback can be provided by numerous evaluation procedures. However, some method of formative evaluation may provide the best results because of accompanying instantaneous reinforcement and the limited pressures concerning grades.

Assessment of Teaching

Perhaps the best consideration when evaluating a teacher is the performance of his or her students. Learning in the classroom does not take place automatically. Teachers must understand their students as well as their own teaching strengths and weaknessess when they formulate objectives. It is then important for teachers to evaluate their own teaching performances, and it is reasonable to assume that evaluation of individual student performance is a good process of determining teacher effectiveness. Teacher evaluation has always been a difficult procedure for supervisors and administrators. Many existing evaluation procedures consist of student ratings of teacher effectiveness and subjective judgments made by supervisors based on limited evidence. On the other hand, it is possible for supervisors to evaluate teachers based on their objectives and methods, and the success of their students in the classroom. If this procedure is followed, student performance can be used to develop objectivity in the process of teacher evaluation.

Assessment of the Curriculum

Curriculum planning is a complex process involving the input of administrators, teachers, students, and parents. Ongoing measurement programs contribute a great deal to this planning process. Teachers can make judgments concerning certain courses or parts of courses based on evaluation of student performances in similar courses. Perhaps new courses might be added or less useful ones deleted from the curriculum based on the performances of students on summative evaluation instruments such as unit tests or standardized tests.

Prediction of Future Success

Evaluation can be used to predict a student's future success in a specific area or skill. There are many similarities of this purpose to that of placement because present status in a particular skill area is used to predict future success in that same area. The difference, however, is that through prediction students can be advised into activities in which they have the greatest chance of success.

Development of Norms

Norms represent the achievement level of a particular group to which obtained scores can be compared. The development of norms involves administering tests, assigning measures, and then transforming the raw score measures into a new set of scores. The norms or transformed scores are then used by teachers to make important and meaningful judgments about the students taking the test. The concept of norms, including the particular types and their specific computations, is discussed in Chapter 4.

Research Tool

Physical education provides many opportunities for conducting valuable basic and applied research. Research is involved in the solving of complex problems. In most instances the problem-solving procedure involves the administration of one or more specific tests. Measures are assigned to the tests, and hypotheses are tested, leading ultimately to conclusions and generalizations made by the researcher. The value or worth of the conclusions is directly related to the effectiveness of the testing instrument. An invalid or unreliable test can render even a good research project useless. Research provides the physical educator with evidence for selecting activities, methods of instruction, measuring instruments, and measurement techniques.

Summary

A test is a tool of measurement and evaluation. A measure is a score assigned to the performance on a test, whereas an evaluation is a judgment made about a student based on the measure and some predetermined criteria. Measurement and evaluation serve many purposes in physical education. Students may be evaluated and placed in appropriate groups to enhance learning. Another purpose of the measurement and evaluation program during the unit of instruction and achievement after the unit involves the use of formative and summative evaluation procedures respectively. The improvement of students can be measured and evaluated by using proper procedures. Also, students can be motivated with a measurement and evaluation program that provides them with immediate feedback. Another purpose discussed in this chapter is to provide a sound basis for evaluation of teachers and the curriculum. Teachers can use evaluation to develop norms as well as to help predict future success of their students in specific skills. Finally it was shown that measurement and evaluation are important in the process of research.

Study Questions

1. Define these terms: test, measure, and evaluation. Give several examples of each of these.
2. Which of the following represent a test? A measure? An evaluation?
   (a) 40-Yard dash.
   (b) 95-Percent on a rules examination.
   (c) Softball throw for distance.
   (d) An A grade on a skills test.
3. Which purpose of measurement and evaluation deals with how a student is performing on a day-to-day basis? What types of tests might be used in this form of evaluation?
4. Which purpose of measurement best describes the assignment of test grades? Do you feel that this is a justifiable purpose of measurement and evaluation in physical education?
5. How might teachers be evaluated by using measures from their students' test results?
6. We have identified 11 purposes of a measurement and evaluation program in physical education. Give an example of how each of these might be used in a testing program. Can you identify other possible purposes?

CHAPTER 2

Historical and Philosophical Perspectives

After you have read and studied this chapter you should be able to:

1. *Understand the importance of a knowledge of the history of measurement and evaluation.*
2. *Summarize the developments in each of the major topical areas of measurement in physical education.*
3. *Recall the approximate dates of emphasis of the topical areas of measurement in the development of the scientific era of measurement in physical education.*
4. *Identify the eminent contributors in measurement and evaluation in physical education.*
5. *Draw the simplified model of instruction and describe the components of the model.*
6. *Identify various attempts at defining and constructing objectives in education and physical education.*
7. *Summarize the functions and importance of feedback in the simplified model of instruction.*

The major thrust of evaluation, as defined earlier, is to promote and improve learning. Measurement, a technique of evaluation, provides an avenue and a basis for evaluation to occur. Obviously, evaluation and measurement are not recent occurrences. Human beings have always used some type of measurement and evaluation to maintain control over their environment. This control has increased as methods of measurement have advanced. The first part of this chapter gives the *history of measurement and evaluation* in physical education. The second part discusses a *philosophical model of instruction.* Measurement and evaluation, integral parts of the model, are the vehicles through which learning is monitored.

HISTORICAL PERSPECTIVES

The history of measurement in physical education almost follows the development of measurement in education. Physical education is a distinct and important phase of total education; it has a unique area to measure and an equally rich heritage in measurement and evaluation. A knowledge of the history of measurement and evaluation in physical education will help us obtain:

1. A better understanding of measurement and evaluation in physical education.

2. An appreciation of the measurement and evaluation efforts of predecessors in the profession of physical education.
3. An understanding of the changing role of physical education in American society.
4. An insight into many areas that comprise physical education.
5. A basis for prediction of future developments and emphasis in measurement.

History can be studied from two perspectives. We may attempt a chronological study of the developments in measurement and evaluation. Additionally, we might make a topical study of the subareas within physical education that historically have been measured. Because of its importance to physical educators, the history of measurement in physical education will be discussed from both perspectives with major emphasis on topical areas.

A summary of the major milestones in the history of physical education measurement is shown in Table 2.1. The milestones of physical education closely parallel those of educational measurement. An excellent discussion of the history of educational measurement including a Table of Milestones, can be found in Ebel (1972). The remainder of the historical discussion will be devoted to brief comments on many of the physical education milestones included in the following topical areas.

Topical Areas	*Approximate BeginningDate*
Anthropometric traits	1860
Basic performance traits	
Strength tests	1875
Cardiovascular tests	1900
Multiple performance traits	
Motor or athletic ability tests	1900
Motor fitness tests	1940
Domains of behavior	
Sports skills or psychomotor tests	1925
Social-psychological or affective tests	1930
Knowledge or cognitive tests	1940

Table 2.1 Milestones of Physical Education Measurement

Date	*Leader*	*Development*	*TopicalArea*
766 B.C.	Greeks	Olympics	Sports skills or psychomotor
400 B.C.	Hippocrates	Body types	Anthropometry
1820	Rostan	Body types	Anthropometry
1861	Edward Hitchock, MD	Anthropometric Measurements	Anthropometry

Date	*Leader*	*Development*	*TopicalArea*
1873-80	Dudley Sargent, MD	Intercollegiate Strength Test Physical Measurement program	Anthropometry Strength
1884	Angelo Mosso	Ergograph	Cardiovascular
1885	Association for Advancement of Physical Education (Now AAHPER)	Professional Association	Anthropometry now all areas
1894	Turners (Normal School of Gymnastics)	Motor Ability Test	Motor ability
1896	J. H. Kellogg	Universal dynamometer	Strength
1902	Dudley Sargent, MD	Universal Test for Strength, Speed and Endurance of the Human Body	Basic performance traits
1905	C. W. Crampton	Cardiac Function Test	Cardiovascular
1910	J. H. McCurdy	Heart Rate Test	Cardiovascular
1912	Indiana University	Sigma Delta Psi Fraternity	Motor ability
1913	Playground and Recreation Association of America	Athletic Badge Test	Motor ability
1921	Dudley Sargent, MD	Sargent Jump	Motor ability
1924	David Brace	Basketball Skill Test	Sports skills or psychomotor
1925	Frederick Rand Rogers	Physical Fitness Index Strength Index	Motor fitness
1925	E. Kretschmer	Body types	Anthropometry
1927	David Brace	Motor Ability Test	Motor ability
1928	Edwin R. Elbel	Isometric training	Strength
1928	Van Buskirk	Behavior Rating Scale	Social-psychological or affective
1929	Frederick W. Cozens	Cozens Athletic Ability Test	Motor ability
1929	J. G. Bliss	Basketball Knowledge Test	Knowledge or cognitive
1930	AAHPER	Research Quarterly	All areas
1931	Waid Tuttle	Pulse-Ratio Test	Cardiovascular
1931	Charles McCloy	Iowa Revision-Brace Test	Motor ability

Date	*Leader*	*Development*	*TopicalArea*
1935	Joanna Dyer	Tennis Backboard Test	Sports skills or psychomotor
1935	Edith Hyde	Archery	Sports skills or psychomotor
1936	B. E. Blanchard	Behavior Rating Scale	Social-psychological or affective
1940	Thomas De Lorme	Modern isotonic training	Strength
1940	William Sheldon	Somatotypes	Anthropometry
1940-41	M. Gladys Scott	Swimming, tennis badminton	Knowledge or cognitive
1943	Esther French	French Knowledge Tests	Knowledge or cognitive
1943-44	Karl Bookwalter	Indiana Motor Fitness Tests	Motor fitness
1943	Lucien Brouha	Harvard Step Test	Cardiovascular
1947	B. E. Phillips	JCR Test	Motor fitness
1947	Thomas Cureton	University of Illinois Motor Fitness Test	Motor fitness
1954	Charles McCloy	McCloy General Motor Ability Test	Motor ability
1954	H. Harrison Clarke	Use of cable tensio-meter	Strength
1954	Hans Kraus-Ruth Hirschland	Kraus-Weber Tests	Motor fitness
1955	Carlos Wear	Wear Attitude Scale	Social-psychological or affective
1956	Dwight D. Eisen-hower	President's Council on Youth Fitness	Motor fitness
1957	Harold M. Barrow Test	Barrow Motor Ability	Motor ability
1957	AAHPER	AAHPER Youth Fitness Test	Motor fitness Cardiovascular
1958	Charles Cowell	Social Behavior Trend Trend Index	Social-psychological or affective
1966-7-9	AAHPER	AAHPER Skill Tests	Sports skills or psychomotor
1968	Gerald Kenyon	Attitude Scales	Social-psychological or affective

Date	*Leader*	*Development*	*TopicalArea*
1968-70	Kenneth Cooper	Aerobics	Cardiovascular
1971-75	Barbara Heath J. E. Lindsay Carter	Anthropometric Somatotyping	Anthropometry
1974	Robert J. Sonstroem	Attitude Scales	Social-psychological or affective

Anthropometric Traits

The measurement of the structure and proportions of the body is called anthropometry. Measurement of man originated in ancient India, Egypt, and Greece. The Greek, Hippocrates, was one of the first known measurement experts. In the fourth century B.C. he designated two fundamental body types, *phthisic habitus* (long and thin) and the *apoplectic habitus* (short and thick), and studied them for medical reasons. These two body types, comprising a dichotomy, are the basis for later classifications.

In America, emphasis on anatomical measurements began at the time of the Civil War. In 1861, Edward Hitchcock, a medical doctor, began collecting measurements such as height, weight, age, girths of chest, arm, and forearm, lung capacity, and strength of the upper arm. He then performed the tests on the students at Amherst College, and developed, over the course of 20 years, standard body proportions of college males. These anthropometric measures initiated the era of *scientific measurement* in physical education.

During the time Hitchcock was gathering his data, Dr. Dudley A. Sargent at Harvard University began a comprehensive anthropometric testing program consisting of 40 measurements. In 1893, he published percentile tables indicating standards based on anthropometric and strength measures for college men and women. Sargent's testing program was subsequently adopted by the forerunner of the present American Alliance for Health, Physical Education, and Recreation for use in schools and colleges.

In the early twentieth century, D. W. Hastings of Springfield College conducted a study of the rate of growth of the human body from age 5 to 21. His findings were later published in a manual. Others studied the relationship of height, weight, and body type. Street developed the concept of height-weight index. McCloy developed a classification index using weight, height, and age. Helen Pryor of Stanford University developed width-weight tables. Later the Wetzel Grid Technique, (1941) consisting of the same components as McCloy, was used to evaluate growth and development, and Meredith's Height-Weight Chart (1947), which identified normal and abnormal growth patterns, was developed.

The concept of body type was also investigated by Kretschmer and published in 1925. He determined that there were three general body types — the asthenic (thin type), athletic (muscular), and pyknic (fat) — and attempted to relate body type to personality. Sheldon, Stevens, and Tucker (1940) developed the concept of somatotype (body type) and coined the three components now well known. Endomorphy (fatness), mesomorphy (musculoskeletal development), and ectomorphy (linearity) were determined to be present in varying amounts in all body types. Sheldon and his co-workers developed a numerical rating system from 1 to 7. Each somatotype utilized the three components in ½ units in this order: endomorphy 1-7, mesomorphy 1-7, ectomorphy 1-7. Low first component ratings describe physiques with little nonessential fat while high numerical ratings signify high degrees of nonessential fat. Low second component ratings signify little musculoskeletal development while high ratings indicate marked development in these areas. Low third component ratings signify short extremities while high ratings mean linearity of body segments and of the body as a whole. For instance, an extreme endomorph has a 7-1-1 somatotype. The majority of somatotypes of males were found to hover close to the arithmetic center 4-4-4. Figure 2.1 gives examples of somatotypes using Sheldon's system.

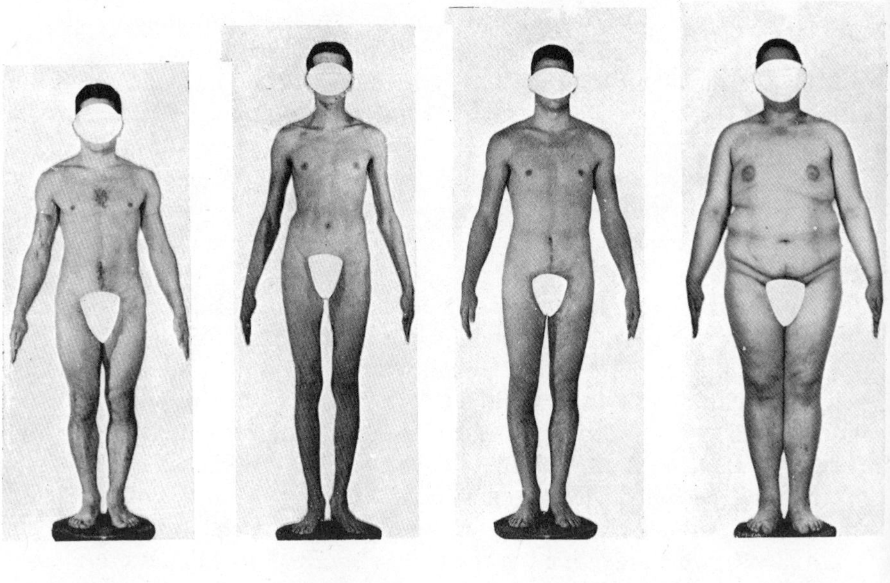

Figure 2.1. The mesomorph, ectomorph, average body type and endomorph according to Sheldon's classification. William H. Sheldon, *Atlas of Men,* Harper & Brothers, New York, 1954.

Sheldon and his associates first studied men from age 18 to 65 and utilized photography as the measurement technique. The complicated somatotyping evaluation process involves experts ratings and photographs. Using a sample of 46,000 men, Sheldon later published the *Atlas of Men*, which has become a bible of sorts. Sheldon also studied female somatotypes and found a number of differences. For instance, females quite often are more endomorphic and less mesomorphic. It is now more than three decades since Sheldon introduced the concept of somatotyping. Since that time a number of modifications have been made. The first one was by Cureton (1947), which introduced the strength factor into the somatotyping process. Other systems based upon Sheldon's original system have developed. Examples are the Heath Modification, the Damon method, the Parnell method, and most recently, the Heath-Carter Somatotype method (1975). The Heath-Carter method expands the rating scale beyond 1-7 and incorporates photography or anthropometric measures including fat, muscle, and bone in an attempt to limit the subjectiveness of somatotyping.

Basic Performance Traits

The first major effort testing basic performance traits, especially strength, appeared about 1880 as an extension of the scientific era of measurement.

Strength Tests. The measurement of strength, obviously, is not a new concept. References to strength feats can be found in ancient Greek and Roman history of physical education. In the seventeenth century, French anthropologists developed and used dynamometers for measuring strength. Sargent first emphasized measuring strength when he developed the Intercollegiate Strength Test in 1873 while a medical student at Yale. This test was used extensively in the late nineteenth century by universities.

J. H. Kellogg, in the 1890's, made an important contribution to strength testing while studying the importance of exercise as a therapeutic measure. His contribution, the universal dynamometer, was developed and utilized to measure the strength of 25 muscle groups.

With the turn of the century, the emphasis on measuring strength waned for at least two reasons: strength measurement did not take into consideration muscular endurance or heart and lung function, and strength exercises, according to the beliefs of the time, caused overdevelopment of muscles and therefore hindered athletic performance. Thus, for a decade or more, emphasis changed to body efficiency. Interest in strength began its resurgence in 1915 when E. G. Martin recognized the need for a strength test that could be used for comparing normal versus abnormal muscle groups. Martin was studying the after-effects of a polio epidemic in Vermont. The Martin Resistance Test utilized a spring scale and was based on the principle of resistance to a pull rather than voluntary exertion.

Frederick R. Rogers stimulated additional interest in strength testing in 1925 with the development of his Strength Index and the Physical Fitness Index (PFI). His ideas were based on Sargent's Intercollegiate Strength Test but differed in terms of test construction and statistical validation of the test items. Rogers' test is still considered a classic in the field of strength testing although one item of the test battery, lung capacity, is not a measure of muscular strength. Charles H. McCloy, in 1931, revised the Rogers Strength Index, improving such factors as administration, scoring, and validity. In rehabilitating wounded World War II war veterans, in the 1940s, Thomas DeLorme, used strength measurements and isotonic strength building. He is given much credit for formulating modern isotonic training procedures.

H. Harrison Clarke later developed a battery of 38 tests, the Oregon Cable Tension Strength Tests, to measure the strength of individual muscle groups. Two instruments, the goniometer, which determines joint angle, and the cable tensiometer, which measures pulling force on a cable, were used to measure isometric muscle strength at the various joints. Figure 2.2 shows the cable tensiometer developed by Pacific Scientific Company and modified by Clarke for his battery of strength tests.

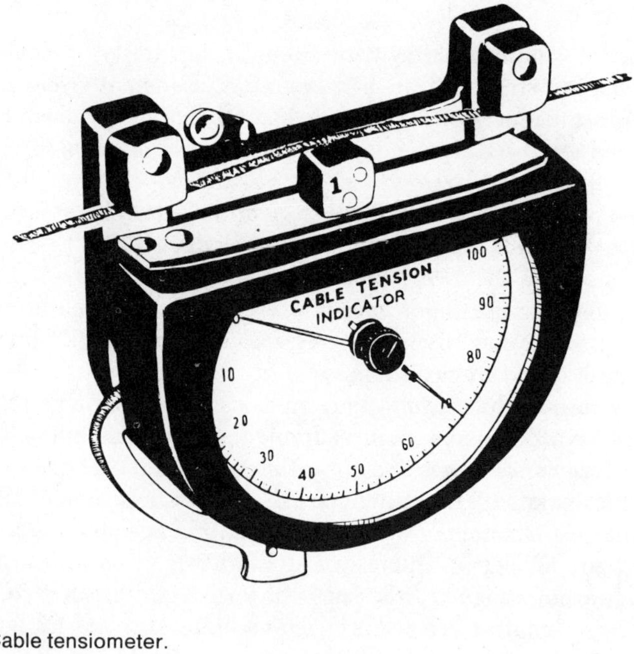

Figure 2.2. Cable tensiometer.

There have been continual scientific innovations in terms of instrumentation for strength testing. Obviously strength training has proved to be a major factor in successful motor performance. Isokinetic strength development is an example of a new kind of strength training. The instrumentation for measuring strength developed by various training methods has been developed by a number of manufacturers. An example of a sophisticated instrument is the Cybex II system manufactured by Lumex, Inc.

Cardiovascular Tests. Tests of cardiac function and circulorespiratory endurance originated in the twentieth century. These tests measure the function of the heart, lungs, and vessels supplying blood to the body, as well as the capillary system, and the oxygen-carrying capacity of the blood. Interest in cardiovascular testing began in 1884 when Angelo Mosso, an Italian physiologist, invented the ergograph to measure work. Mosso observed that the efficiency of the circulatory system affected the performance of muscles. Thus, interest in a new area of measurement began to develop.

In 1905, C. W. Crampton devised the first test of cardiac function by utilizing changes in cardiac rate and blood pressure. Soon after, McCurdy (1910) devised a test of physical condition in which heart rate was the criterion of measurement. At the beginning of World War I, a barrage of cardiac function tests were published by Meylan, Foster, Barach, and Barringer. In 1920, Schneider published a test of physical efficiency that had been used in World War I to assess the fitness of military personnel. In 1925, Campbell developed a cardiovascular test involving breath-holding and recovery after exercise. The test eventually evolved into the Campbell Pulse Ratio Test, which compared resting pulse with pulse after exercise. The most popular test of the time was the Tuttle Pulse Ratio Test, developed in 1931 and influenced by Campbell's work. In the 1930's, Tuttle conducted much empirical research with the test and added to the body of knowledge in this area. The McCloy Test of Present Condition and the McCurdy-Larson Test of Organic Efficiency were also developed in the third decade of the twentieth century.

The next major advancement was the development of the Harvard Step Test by Lucien Brouha at Harvard in 1943. The efficiency of the cardiorespiratory system was tested by noting the rate at which the heart returned to normal after the exercise of bench-stepping was performed. The Harvard Step Test was utilized for many years and heralded as an accurate test of cardiovascular functioning. The treadmill and various sophisticated testing and recording instruments eventually made the Harvard Step Test obsolete in research projects. The most recent developments include utilization of such instruments as the Beckman MMC, a self-contained evaluating instrument that gives a computer-type readout of various cardiorespiratory functions while the subject exercises on a treadmill. Functional cardiorespiratory tests such as the 600-yard run, an item of the AAHPER Youth Fitness Test, and the 12-minute run as proposed by Cooper in *The New Aerobics* (1970) have been utilized and norm systems developed to estimate cardiovascular efficiency.

The development of tests of other basic performance traits (i.e., power, agility, speed, balance, and flexibility) have occurred throughout the twentieth century. Although various tests in these areas have been constructed, the two major basic performance traits of historical significance are strength and cardiovascular endurance. Tests in each of these areas will be identified in Chapter 12.

Multiple Performance Traits

Interest in multiple performance traits began in two distinct waves. Motor ability and athletic ability tests were initiated in the early part of this century, while physical fitness and motor fitness tests are primarily products of the past 50 years.

Motor Ability — Athletic Ability. Along with the emphasis in cardiovascular testing that began at about 1900, interest also developed in athletic or motor ability testing. Early tests involved fundamental movements such as running, jumping, and throwing and were intended to test such factors as speed, power, agility, strength, and endurance. Although not identical, motor educability and motor capacity tests fall within this measurement area.

Athletic (motor) ability was first tested by the Turners (Normal School of Gymnastics) who, in 1894, developed test items to compare athletic performance of students. In 1902, Dudley Sargent, because of his belief that strength tests did not measure endurance and speed, developed a battery of simple exercises to be performed for 30 minutes. Those who completed the test battery were considered athletically fit. Shortly thereafter, Dr. George Meylan of Columbia University developed comprehensive tests of running, jumping, vaulting, and climbing that were later used at many universities for grading and classification. Motor ability tests were utilized in the public schools before universities and in the first decade of the twentieth century these tests were given in New York City, Cleveland, Baltimore, and Cincinnati. In 1913, the forerunner to the present National Recreation and Parks Association (NRPA), the Playground and Recreation Association of America, published the Athletic Badge Test, which included several track and field tests as well as rope climbing and vaulting. Standards for boys and girls were developed and used in public schools throughout the nation.

In 1912, Sigma Delta Psi, the national athletic honorary fraternity for men, was founded at Indiana University. A series of minimum standards in several types of athletic events had to be met for membership into the national fraternity. These tests are currently administered by intramural personnel at most universities. Tests developed at other universities soon followed; the University of California Classification Test and another constructed at the University of Oregon are two examples. Until the 1920s the majority of tests were for men or boys only. Garfiel at Barnard developed the first motor ability test for women in 1925. Later, similar tests for women were developed at Oregon and Wellesley.

Under the supervision of J. H. McCurdy, the chairman of the National Committee on Motor Ability Testing in 1924, general ability tests were developed for football, soccer, field hockey, basketball, and tennis. About the same time, new statistical techniques became available and allowed the development of scientifically constructed tests that had better validity and reliability. In the following years, new and better tests were devised. In 1927, David K. Brace of Texas developed his motor ability test, revised in 1931 by C. H. McCloy of Iowa. McCloy's revision is now called the Iowa Brace test and is considered a test of motor educability. In 1929, Frederick W. Cozens developed the Test of General Athletic Ability, which has been widely used. From 1930 until 1960, general motor ability tests for students of various educational status were developed. However, since 1960 there has been little use of such tests.

Physical Fitness — Motor Fitness. The terms physical fitness and motor fitness are not synonymous. In essence, motor fitness is a limited phase of general motor ability. Motor fitness, however, is more general than physical fitness. The meaning and relationship of these terms is aptly explained by Clarke, "Physical fitness elements are muscular strength, muscular endurance and circulatory endurance. Muscular power, agility, speed, and flexibility are added to compose motor fitness; then, kinesthetic arm-eye foot-eye coordinations are needed for general motor ability."*

Fitness measurement and evaluation has always been done. The ancient Greek philosopher, Socrates, is responsible for the well-known phrase "a sound mind in a sound body." The sound body implies physical fitness.

Fitness tests in the United States are recent occurrences, although hints of fitness testing appeared in the Turnvereins of the East and Midwest during the nineteenth century. Fitness became a national issue during World War I because many inductees could not pass their physicals. The Physical Fitness Index (PFI), published by Frederick R. Rogers in 1925, was the first modern physical fitness test. Actually Rogers' PFI tests muscular strength, muscular endurance, and lung capacity, which are only three of several components that comprise physical fitness. Motor fitness tests were developed initially during World War II, again when emphasis was placed on the fitness of military men. Almost all branches of the armed services developed fitness tests with norms.

*H. Harrison Clarke, *Application of Measurement to Health and Physical Education,* Fifth Edition, 1976, p. 1973. Reprinted by permission of Prentice-Hall, Inc., Englewood Cliffs, New Jersey.

Examples are the Army Physical Efficiency Test and the Navy Standard Physical Fitness Test. A number of other motor or physical fitness tests were created during the war years for college and school groups. In 1943, Karl Bookwalter developed a motor fitness test for college men. Variations for high school boys (1944), girls (1944), and elementary school children (1948) soon followed. The latter adaptations were used in Indiana. In 1945 the National Section on Women's Athletics (now NAGWS) of the AAHPER proposed a motor fitness test for high school girls that was widely used for years.

In 1947, B. E. Phillips published the JCR (jump, chin, 100-yard shuttle-run) Test in the *Research Quarterly,* which proved to be popular. In the same year, T. K. Cureton of Illinois published a fourteen- and an eighteen-item motor fitness test. Subsequently, a seven-item test, which is more administratively feasible, was developed.

In 1954, about a decade after the end of World War II, the nation received startling news regarding the relative fitness of its youth. Kraus and Hirschland (1954) examined 4458 students from the eastern United States and 3157 Swiss, Austrian, and Italian children on six tests of minimum muscular fitness popularly known as the Kraus-Weber tests. The tests were designed to indicate the level of strength and flexibility for certain key muscle groups and were graded on a pass-fail basis. Results revealed that 57.9 percent of U. S. children and only 8.7 percent of the European children failed one or more test items. Figure 2.3 shows the flexibility test, which produced the greatest number of failures. Although the scoring and validity of the Kraus-Weber test were later questioned, they rekindled interest in fitness development and testing.

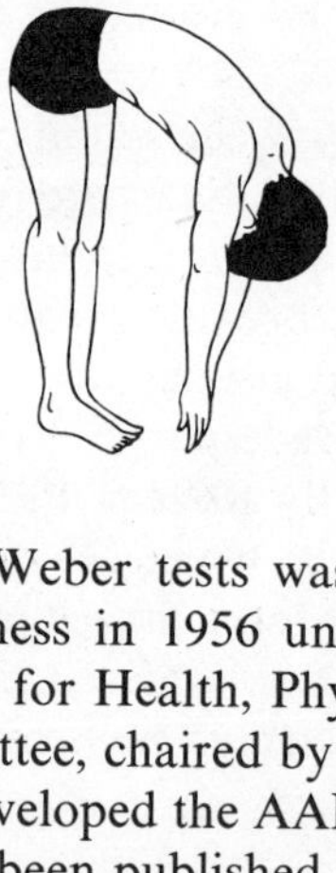

Figure 2.3. Kraus-Weber flexibility test.

A direct result of the Kraus-Weber tests was the establishment of the President's Council on Youth Fitness in 1956 under President Eisenhower. The AAHPER (American Alliance for Health, Physical Education, and Recreation) appointed a special committee, chaired by the late Paul Hunsicker of the University of Michigan, that developed the AAHPER Youth Fitness Tests in 1957. Revisions of the test have been published in 1965 and 1975. It is undoubtedly the most widely used fitness test in the United States. The *AAHPER Youth Fitness Test* has been officially adopted by the President's Council on Physical Fitness and Sports. The President's Physical Fitness

Award has been established as a motivational technique and is distributed to all boys and girls who achieve the 85th percentile or better on all the tests. The test manual is available from AAHPER in Washington, D.C. (1976). The AAHPER Youth Fitness Test is currently under revision. The items on the new revision will emphasize health-related fitness. The four items will include: sit-up test, sit-and-reach flexibility test; a test of cardiorespiratory function (9 min. or 1 mile run); and body composition measures (skinfolds). The new manual for testing will be published in 1980.

Many other physical or motor fitness tests have been developed, for example, by universities, states, and armed services.

A major consideration of most modern fitness tests has been to test as simply, easily, and economically as possible. Modern instrumentation and innovations such as Cooper's *The New Aerobics* (1970) have made fitness and fitness testing remain in the forefront of measurement in physical education programs. Such innovations as adult and family fitness programs with prescribed exercises have added to the body of knowledge in the areas of physical and motor fitness as well as cardiovascular fitness testing.

Domains of Behavior

Bloom and his associates (1956) have categorized behavior in three broad areas: the cognitive, affective, and psychomotor domains. However, published tests of knowledge (cognitive), social-psychological traits (affective), and skills (psychomotor) in physical education have been utilized for the past 50 years.

Sports Skills: The Psychomotor Domain. Sports and athletics provide the basis for the development of numerous elaborate and extensive skill tests. Skill evaluation of sorts has always been done. For example, in the ancient Greek and Roman narratives of gymnastic events, the pentathlon, boxing, chariot races, running events, and other sport activities have been reported. Results of the ancient Olympics have been documented in several historical texts in physical education.

In America, nineteenth-century physical education was characterized by gymnastics and calisthenics. In the late 1800s a battle developed over which gymnastics system should be adopted — the German Turner system or the Swedish system — although both systems had regional popularity. Eventually, in the early twentieth century, the foreign gymnastic systems were rejected in favor of games and sports. As early as 1913 the Athletic Badge Tests were published by the Playground and Recreation Association of America. Emphasis on the sports and games in the physical education curriculum created a similar interest in the evaluation of the skills of those games and sports, especially in the 1920s.

Brace developed skill tests in basketball in 1924. They were revised by him and included in a publication with achievement tests in indoor baseball and soccer. Beall continued the pioneer work in skill testing, but in a different sport. She devised a test in tennis to measure selected qualities deemed essential for success in that sport. Bliss, who also published an early knowledge test in basketball, developed early sports technique tests in basketball and baseball for junior high students.

Although economic conditions made the 1930s a dismal decade for physical education, the proliferation of sports skill tests continued. In 1934, Johnson developed a basketball test for high school boys while Young and Moser composed a test of basketball ability for women. In 1935, Dyer published her widely used Tennis Backboard Test, and Hyde established a scale of Archery Achievement for college women. In 1937, Borleski developed a test to measure the ability to play touch football. A test in volleyball skills was created by French and Cooper in 1937 and, shortly after, the Russell-Lange Volleyball Test was published in the *Research Quarterly*.

In the 1940s the interest continued in the development of several skill tests in badminton, basketball (the Knox Basketball Test), field hockey, handball, rhythm and dance, swimming, table tennis, volleyball, and others. Since 1950, tests in a wide range of sport, recreational, and athletic activities have been developed. Interest has moved toward the development of national norms for a wide range of sport activities. This project has been undertaken by the AAHPER Research Council under the direction of Frank A. Sills. To date, tests and test manuals have been developed in archery (1967), basketball for boys (1966), basketball for girls (1966), and volleyball (1969). Percentile norms for all test items are available from the AAHPER for each sex from age 10 to 18.

Social-Psychological Measurements: The Affective Domain. Social and psychological measurements developed in physical education as identification of objectives of the profession became clear. An example is Jay B. Nash's emotional-impulsive developmental objective. However, in early physical education, the attitudinal changes, character development, and the like, were considered concomitants inherent in the process of physical education. Because the social-psychological aspect was usually considered a major objective, the need became apparent for measurement of progress toward meeting that objective. The first scale in the social area was Van Buskirk's character rating scale in 1928. Another early attempt (1931) in this area was made by McCloy with the publication of a behavior rating scale. It included statements that measured development in leadership, active qualities, attitude, self-control, cooperation, sportsmanship, ethics, efficiency, and sociability. Blanchard, in 1936, developed a behavior rating scale for measuring character and personality, using McCloy's scale as a basis. E. W. O'Neal published a similar scale simultaneously with Blanchard. From 1930 until after World War II, social and psychological investigations in physical education utilized the above scales or those developed for testing in other educational areas.

Interest in the affective domain was revived at mid-century. Carlos Wear constructed equivalent forms of an attitude scale that were published in 1955 and became a popular tool to measure attitudes toward physical education. More recently, Kenyon (1968) developed two forms of an attitude inventory utilizing six dimensions: social experiences, health and fitness, pursuit of vertigo, aesthetic experience, catharsis, and ascetic experience. Sonstroem (1974) recently constructed Physical Estimation and Attraction Scales, using Kenyon's scale as a guide. Additional scales have been developed by Edington (1968) and Adams (1963). In 1969, Johnson published Sportsmanship scales.

Social behavior measurement has also received much emphasis in the past two decades. Charles Cowell developed the Social Behavior Trend Index in 1958, utilizing 10 pairs of positive and negative behavior trends. H. Harrison Clarke and others associated with the Medford Boys Growth Studies have done several research studies in the social measurement area. A number of personality inventories not specifically developed for measurement in physical education have been utilized in an increasing number of studies. Examples are the Bell Adjustment Inventory, the very popular Cattell Sixteen Personality Factor Questionnaire, the Edwards Personality Inventory, and the Tennessee Self-Concept Scale.

Within the past decade, there has been an increased effort to understand the sociological dimensions of sport and physical education. Instruments have been developed to evaluate whether sport builds character, whether socialization occurs by participation in sport and physical education, whether social mobility occurs through participation in sports as well as many other things. Thus, many sociopsychological instruments, previously unknown to most physical educators, are now considered important in developing a body of knowledge in this area of physical education.

Knowledge Tests: The Cognitive Domain. Cognitive domain testing in physical education has occurred as long as there have been physical education programs. All of the early tests and many of current ones are teacher-made tests. Many published knowledge tests in physical education have become outdated.

Yet, there have been numerous successful attempts at the development of standardized tests in specific areas of physical education. The first published knowledge test is supposed to be a basketball test constructed by Bliss in 1929. Heath and Rogers developed knowledge and skill tests for fifth- and six-grade boys in sports of soccer and playground baseball in the early 1930s. In 1940 and 1941, Gladys Scott published knowledge tests for swimming, tennis, and badminton in the *Research Quarterly*. Many of the published knowledge tests have been developed for use with college women — Scott's tests, for instance. French constructed knowledge tests in 1943, which also were designated for women and, specifically, for physical education majors. These tests included many sport and activity areas. Marjorie Phillips, in 1946, developed a standardized badminton knowledge test for college women. Examples of measurement of the cognitive domain for the college age level were prolific in the *Research Quarterly* and *JOHPER* during the 1940s and 1950s.

Standardized tests of knowledge have been published for men by Waglow and Stephens (1953) (1955), Gershon (1957), and Winn (1957) in the activities of softball, golf, gymnastics, and soccer. In 1966, Hooks developed comprehensive knowledge tests for men in the sports of volleyball, badminton, softball, and tennis.

The majority of cognitive tests in physical education have been developed exclusively for men or for women, although the reason is somewhat questionable. Some of the most recent tests, published in physical education, are not specifically for either sex — Hewitt's Comprehensive Tennis Knowledge Test (1965) and a test of physical fitness knowledge by Mood (1971).

Certainly the construction of a good knowledge test is a difficult task. Standardized tests, if current, are a valuable teacher aid. The search continues for objective, valid tests that can be applied easily to the local situations.

PHILOSOPHICAL PERSPECTIVES

Education and physical education are concerned with the development of human beings. Sometimes the concern is for the specific individual, such as why a student is having so much difficulty in performing a simple motor skill. In other instances, the concern is for groups of individuals, such as why so many more American students failed one item of the Kraus-Weber Test of Minimum Muscular Efficiency than did the youth of Sweden, Austria, and Italy. In still other instances the concern is with students as universal representatives of mankind such as when research is done to determine whether there is a relationship between socioeconomic background and motor ability. Measurement and evaluation provide a scientific and objective basis for understanding the qualities of the individual, the group, or mankind as a whole. Progress in the educational process is directly related to and dependent on effective measurement and evaluation.

Measurement and evaluation are the modes used to determine the realization of the objectives and aim of the physical education program. Relevant knowledge is gathered through measurement and its evaluation; sound decisions arise from that information. In reality, to know an individual means to be able to describe him or her as accurately and totally as possible. Measurement and evaluation provide a basis for determining where to begin in teaching a particular activity and enable the physical educator to monitor experiences that lead toward realizing the outcomes of that teaching.

Evaluation is an integral facet of the educational process and underlies all successful teaching and learning. The goal of education is to bring about permanent behavior changes through practice and experience. In formal education, the schools attempt to determine the extent to which general and specific objectives have been attained. Since planned evaluation implies the presence of objectives, it becomes the vehicle through which this information can be obtained.

Simplified Model of Instruction

Instructional or behavioral objectives are related to measurement and evaluation through teaching. A model of instruction provides a useful guide for designing, implementing, evaluating, and improving instruction. Kibler and his colleagues (1974) have developed a general model of instruction that is applicable to all levels of education, all subject-areas, and any length of instructional unit. An adaptation of this model is presented in Figure 2.4.

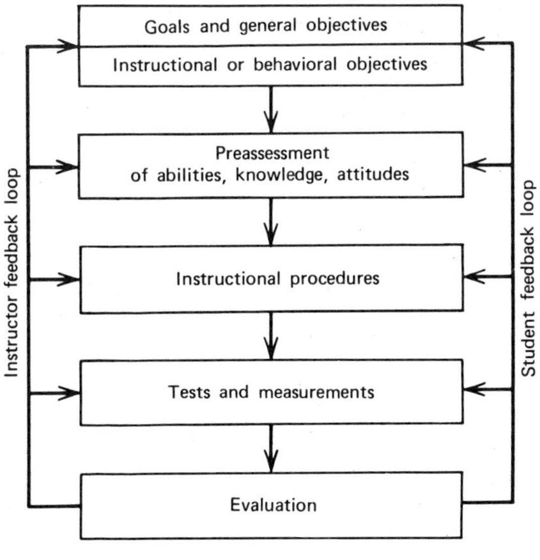

Figure 2.4. Simplified model of instruction.

The simplified model of instruction serves as a guide that the instructor can use in making decisions regarding *instructional objectives, preassessment, instruction, measurement,* and *evaluation.* This chapter will identify and discuss each component in the simplified model of instruction.

Goals, Instructional and Behavioral Objectives. The most important component of the model is the first one in which the instructor determines what is to be achieved in the unit of instruction. Instructional objectives in physical education should reflect the general objectives of education as well as those of the profession. Instructional objectives may be defined as statements that describe what students will be able to do after completing a prescribed unit of instruction. The terms *instructional objectives* and *behavioral objectives* have similar meanings and will be used interchangeably in this test. The term behavioral objective is popular because objectives are most appropriately specified in terms of expected behavior. A resumé of the general objectives of education and those of physical education serve as guidelines and boundaries for the development of instructional or behavioral objectives.

Educational Objectives. An early attempt at developing general educational objectives was made in 1919 with the publication of the Cardinal Principles of Secondary Education. They are:

1. Health.
2. Command of fundamental processes.
3. Worthy home membership.
4. Vocation.
5. Citizenship.
6. Worthy use of leisure.
7. Ethical character.

These seven cardinal principles provide a broad direction for what formal education in America should accomplish. Later, the Educational Policies Commission (1938) stated four major objectives and identified specific goals under each objective. The four objectives are:

1. Self-realization.
2. Human relationships.
3. Economic efficiency.
4. Civic responsibility.

These objectives represented a restatement of the Cardinal Principles. In 1961 the Educational Policies Commission published *The Central Purpose of American Education* (1961), which indicated that the major purpose of education should be the development of the rational powers of man. It also reaffirmed that the 1918 and 1938 statements were valid objectives and that American schools must be concerned with the accomplishment of such objectives.

Most attempts at stating specific instructional objectives have emanated from the comprehensive effort by Bloom and his co-workers (1956). The Taxonomy of Educational Objectives attempted to reduce vagueness in the statements of educational goals.

Three domains of behavior were identified from Bloom's work: the cognitive, the affective, and the psychomotor. Within each of these behavioral areas, it is possible to classify objectives in an orderly arrangement. The values of the taxonomies, according to their formulators, are:

1. *To clarify and tighten the language of educational objectives.*
2. *To provide a convenient system for describing and ordering test items, examination techniques, and evaluation.*
3. *To provide a framework for comparing and studying educational programs.*
4. *To select principles of classifying educational outcomes which reveal a real order among these outcomes . . . something beyond a simple classification scheme.**

Bloom and his associates (1956) completed the cognitive domain taxonomy in 1956. Later Krathwohl and others (1964) published the affective domain taxonomy; most recently, Harrow (1972) completed the project by publishing the taxonomy of the psychomotor domain. These taxonomies will be considered in Chapter 6.

It is apparent that the goals and objectives of physical education and general education are similar. In each of the statements of educational objectives outlined in this chapter, physical education contributes either directly or indirectly to their accomplishment. It is one of many subject areas within the school curriculum that contributes to the accomplishment of educational goals. However, physical education is also unique because it is the only subject area in the school curriculum that can accomplish these goals through physical activity.

General Objectives of Physical Education. Physical education is specifically concerned with the development of psychomotor abilities such as skill; cognitive abilities such as knowledge and application of facts and concepts; and affective abilities such as attitudes, values, and appreciations.

In addition to the completed Taxonomy of Educational Objectives project, several taxonomies of the motor domain have been developed. Examples are those of Simpson (1966) and Jewett (1971). Before the development of taxonomies, the objectives of physical education, although more specific than those of education, served as general guidelines for physical education programs. The traditional objectives for the physical education profession are as follows.

1. Organic development and physical fitness.
2. Neuromuscular skill development.
3. Development of knowledge and understanding.
4. Socioemotional development.

One obvious limitation of stating objectives in such general terms is that teachers often feel no sense of responsibility for accomplishing anything specifically. The modern taxonomies of objectives have attempted to alleviate this limitation by providing attention to detail in the development of the goals.

We attach considerable importance to the establishment of behavioral objectives in physical education. Chapter 6 specifically discusses the identification and writing of behavioral objectives for physical education. It is only when objectives have been specified clearly that instruction, measurement, and evaluation procedures can be meaningful and useful. Regardless of the varying terminology, the major purpose of measurement and evaluation in physical education is to determine whether instruction has been successful in meeting the stated objectives.

Preassessment of Skills and Abilities. Before initiating a unit of instruction, the skills, knowledge, and attitudes of students should be preassessed in light of the stated behavioral objectives. Preassessment is most important when instructors initiate a unit in which they are unfamiliar with students' skills, knowledges, and attitudes. Information should be gathered regarding: (1) how much of what is to be learned during the instructional unit is already known; (2) whether students are capable of achieving the objectives of the unit; and (3) the instructional activities that should be prescribed for each student. Feedback from the preassessment should provide the instructor with information to modify behavioral objectives, if necessary. The information can also help to determine whether any students need remedial work because of a lack of prerequisite skills and which instructional methods should be utilized.

The instruments used in preassessment of basic physical traits such as strength, endurance, flexibility, and of multiple traits such as motor fitness, physical fitness, and psychomotor skills may be the same ones used to assess student achievement after instruction. However, several other preassessment procedures such as interviews or informal class discussion might also be utilized. Cognitive traits often cannot be effectively preassessed with standardized instruments. In some cases, however, standardized tests of affective traits are useful in assessing attitudes before instruction. But often, standardized instruments do not relate closely enough to the stated behavioral objectives. Therefore, instructors of physical education are often required to develop their own preassessment tests.

When courses are organized in a hierarchy, (i.e., beginning, intermediate, advanced), preassessment can often be made by examining the behavioral objectives of the preceding course. If these behavioral objectives are not available, a preassessment test should be developed by analyzing the behaviors students should possess in order to benefit from instruction.

Instructional Procedures. When students have been preassessed and any necessary adjustments made, the instructional procedures are implemented. They involve selecting an effective method that will enable students to attain the behavioral objectives. Some of the various methods of teaching physical education are lecture, discussion, laboratory activity, demonstration, independent study, reading, and the use of audiovisual materials. A discussion of these methods is beyond the scope of this text. The model of instruction does not prescribe the methods of instruction that should be used. Since behavioral objectives for classes vary, the methods of instruction to achieve those objectives will also vary. For example, many activity-oriented classes in physical education are classified according to skill level. In an advanced class a teacher is apt to have different behavioral objectives and utilize different methods of instruction than for a beginning class in the same activity. Research, one of the purposes of measurement and evaluation, has identified numerous principles of instruction. For example, specific feedback should be given as close to the time of performance as possible. These principles can provide the instructor of physical education with much insight into the optimum use of the various instructional methods.

The final step in the instructional procedure involves implementing the plan of instruction. The purpose of the instructional process is to help students achieve the selected behavioral objectives.

Tests and Measurements. Measurement procedures consist of locating, selecting, and obtaining published tests or developing such instruments to measure the degree of accomplishment of the stated behavioral objectives. Chapters 7 and 10 discuss these tasks in detail. It is crucial that the instruments accurately measure the same behaviors as those specified in the objectives. The instruments generally used measure the acquisition of knowledge, skills, or attitudes. They may be administered during instruction to monitor learning progress and to diagnose any learning difficulties experienced by students, or they may be administered as a comprehensive test after the instructional unit has been completed to assess the attainment of the objectives.

Evaluation. During the instructional process, periodic measures should be obtained to assess the students' progress relative to the accomplishment of the objectives (formative evaluation). Similarly, a summative evaluation of student achievement should be made after the unit has been completed done by analyzing the results of carefully selected or prepared measuring instruments. The major focus of evaluation is on student mastery of the behavioral objectives. In addition to the evaluation of students through the analysis of student accomplishment of objectives, instruction and the instructional methods can also be evaluated. This final component of the simplified model of instruction can be utilized for many other purposes that were identified in Chapter 1 such as the prediction of future performance and as a research tool.

Feedback. In Figure 2.4, two feedback loops are illustrated. Feedback or knowledge of results is inherent in the simplified model of instruction and is provided for the student or the instructor. One feedback loop informs the instructor that components of the model might need modification. This feedback can be utilized by the instructor at any level of the model; that is, before, during, and after instruction.

For example, assessment of student knowledge, skills, and attitudes prior to an instructional unit in physical education might give the instructor insight that might change the behavioral objectives or modify the instructional or measurement methods. As another example, formative evaluation of students can provide the instructor with information about the progress of students in the achievement of behavioral objectives. This evaluation can also provide information for subsequent changes in behavioral objectives, methodology, or testing instruments. Likewise, summative evaluation of the terminal behaviors after a unit of instruction might necessitate changes in any or all of the first four components in the model. In other words, feedback can be obtained from each component in the simplified model of instruction, which can help the instructor improve behavioral objectives, preassessment procedures, instructional methodology, and tests and measurements.

A second feedback loop provides the students with knowledge of the results of their progress toward accomplishment of the behavioral objectives. Feedback can be provided before instruction has begun by evaluation of preässessment measures or later, through formative and summative statements of progress. Empirical research has consistently supported the use of feedback as a method of accelerating learning. If the students are provided with immediate feedback during the instructional unit, they receive knowledge about their degree of mastery of the objectives and can then concentrate on activities that will help them overcome their deficiencies.

Summary

Measurement and evaluation in education and physical education have a rich heritage. A review of the past helps to explain current conditions and provides a basis for future developments in measurement and evaluation.

Many milestones in physical education measurement have occurred in several waves of emphasis since the beginning of the scientific era, which was initiated with anthropometric testing at Amherst in 1861. In the final quarter of the nineteenth century, Dudley Sargent began the thrust toward strength testing. Early in the present century, the interest in measuring strength waned and was replaced by cardiovascular and motor ability testing. By 1925 the new physical education utilizing sports and games had gained adoption, and sports-skill tests were developed. With the acceptance of major objectives of physical education, behavior rating scales and character inventories were developed to assess achievement in the affective domain. As World War II approached, emphasis returned to fitness, with tests of motor fitness. Later the famous Kraus-Weber tests, the development of the President's Council on Youth Fitness, and Cooper's aerobics continued the emphasis on fitness. The final major measurement area, cognitive testing, received much attention in the 1940s.

Many specific tests are reported in the *Research Quarterly* and *JOPER* publications of the AAHPER. By consulting these periodicals, we see that early measurement in all the areas mentioned was rather crude and relatively simple by today's standards. Major breakthroughs have been made in every topical area of physical education measurement — a fine tribute to the contributors, since all future accomplishments are based on a knowledge of the past.

The ultimate goal of educational instruction is to change student behavior in the desired direction. Measurement and evaluation play important and specific roles in assessing learning and performance. Through the use of well-constructed objectives, meaningful evaluation can occur.

A simplified model of instruction was presented. The major components of the model are (1) goals, instructional objectives, and behavioral objectives; (2) preassessment of knowledge, skills, and attitudes; (3) instructional procedures; (4) tests and measurements; and (5) evaluation. Feedback is evident throughout the model.

A very important component in the model is the establishment of behavioral objectives. This task has been made easier by general statements of objectives and by the *Taxonomy of Educational Objectives*, which demonstrated that most learning occurs in the cognitive, affective, and psychomotor domains. Taxonomies have been developed for each of the domains, and these classifications have given direction to the development of specific behavioral objectives. Evaluation involves making judgments on teaching and learning based on the results of measurement. However, the focus is usually on the student's achievement of objectives.

Study Questions

1. What developments have caused the changes in the emphasis of measurement in physical education from 1860 to present?
2. Why is the study of the history of measurement in physical education important?
3. How have wars affected measurement and evaluation in physical education?
4. Which major topical areas within physical education have had much measurement emphasis? Little emphasis?
5. What is the difference between motor ability and motor fitness? Historically which was measured first? Why?
6. Why are objectives important in the process of evaluation?

7. What are the Cardinal Principles of Secondary Education? To how many of these does physical education specifically contribute? Indirectly contribute?
8. Identify the general objectives of physical education.
9. Draw the simplified model of instruction and summarize each component of the model.
10. Which component of the simplified model of instruction is the most important? Give rationale for your choice.
11. Why is feedback important throughout the instructional model?

CHAPTER **3**

Statistical Techniques Essential to Measurement

After you have read and studied this chapter you should be able to:

1. *Organize test scores for more efficient analysis.*
2. *Identify and define the measures of central tendency.*
3. *Compute the mode, median, and mean.*
4. *Identify and define the measures of variability.*
5. *Compute the range, quartile deviation, and standard deviation.*
6. *Interpret measures of central tendency and variability.*
7. *Define skewness and kurtosis.*
8. *Define correlation.*
9. *Compute correlations using Pearson product-moment and Spearman rank-difference procedures.*
10. *Interpret correlation coefficient.*
11. *Understand basic computer design.*
12. *Understand introductory programming procedures.*
13. *Recognize the availability of packaged computer programs.*

Statistics is a branch of mathematics that deals primarily with the analysis of scores for individuals or groups of individuals. It is a fundamental aspect of any course in measurement and evaluation. Without at least a passing acquaintance of statistics the student of measurement and evaluation is unable adequately to classify or interpret test scores.

This chapter deals with the statistical tools or techniques that are considered essential for the student and teacher of tests and measurements. The information in this section is not intended to be a substitute for a general statistics textbook; rather it is a presentation of the statistical tools and methods that will help students and teachers better organize and interpret test data. Only those statistics that directly serve this function are included.

One area of concern to the teacher when using statistical tools as an aid in the interpretation of test scores is *organizing the data*, the first process that will be identified and developed. Second, the teacher must become familiar with the *essential statistical techniques* that are most commonly utilized in the interpretation of test scores. Finally, an introduction to the *computer* and a cursory discussion of *programming* the typical computer will be presented in this chapter.

ORGANIZING THE DATA

Table 3.1 includes the raw scores of 50 students in one psychomotor and two cognitive tests from an instructional unit in golf. These sets of scores are similar to those that confront teachers of physical education almost daily. The measures are found in a random order and are difficult to interpret or to utilize efficiently.

Table 3.1 Raw Scores for Golf Instructional Unit (N = 50)

Student	*Skill Application*	*Mechanics Application*	*Rules Application*
1	80	38	50
2	37	22	33
3	57	46	59
4	45	33	40
5	58	34	41
6	60	39	52
7	67	34	52
8	81	41	48
9	59	40	50
10	42	20	20
11	48	20	25
12	56	36	40
13	47	30	29
14	56	44	51
15	40	16	22
16	62	31	30
17	75	31	28
18	68	31	41
19	51	21	20
20	53	26	40
21	61	45	56
22	42	20	22
23	56	39	31
24	61	24	36
25	67	39	36
26	70	40	37
27	68	30	32
28	57	38	56
29	57	21	30
30	49	20	24
31	64	30	39

Student	Skill Application	Mechanics Application	Rules Application
32	72	28	42
33	65	20	30
34	55	46	26
35	40	20	26
36	46	28	24
37	53	41	52
38	48	33	41
39	59	28	46
40	57	30	40
41	52	40	57
42	50	36	38
43	71	32	41
44	63	24	37
45	64	20	30
46	70	31	36
47	60	43	52
48	54	21	22
49	68	22	32
50	72	35	40

Before analyzing any set of scores, it is best to organize them in some manner so that they are more easily understood and more efficiently used.

The method of score organization that will be presented utilizes the raw scores as presented in Table 3.1. Traditionally, measurement experts have argued that working with ungrouped data is somewhat more time-consuming and less efficient than the grouped methods, which involve the use of frequency tables, because of repetition in the mathematical computations. However, with the increased availability of calculators and computers and the simplification of some raw score formulas, the ungrouped procedures presented here are considered to be preferred techniques for working with test scores. Currently the use of the hand calculator is becoming widespread in all fields including physical education. Recent technological advances have decreased the prices of the calculator to the point that almost every student entering high school or university has access to one. In addition, recent advances have allowed manufacturers to develop calculators that are extremely advanced and very rapid and efficient in their work. Hand calculators are available that can compute means, standard deviations, and even correlations: one merely reads in the scores by the keyboard and then pushes a single key designed to calculate a specific function.

As easy as the computations are with modern desk calculators, we feel that a basic understanding of the ungrouped data formulas and interpretations of the basic descriptive statistics essential to measurement is important to the student and teacher of physical education. These computational techniques, formulas, and interpretations are presented in this chapter, using only the standard ungrouped calculation techniques. For students who may be interested in the grouped procedures for handling test scores, Appendix E has been developed and will adequately fulfill their needs.

The process for organizing data is routinely simple. The scores are ranked from high to low for a golf skills test (Table 3.2).

Table 3.2 Ungrouped Organization of Scores from a Golf Skills Test ($N = 50$)

Score	*Rank*	
81	1	
80	2	
75	3	
72	4.5	Score 72 is tied for
72	4.5	Ranks 4 and 5
71	6	
70	7.5	Score 70 is tied
70	7.5	for ranks 7 and 8
68	10	Score 68 is tied
68	10	for ranks 8, 10,
68	10	and 11
67	12.5	Score 67 is tied for
67	12.5	Ranks 12 and 13
65	14	
64	15.5	Scores 64 is tied for
64	15.5	Ranks 15 and 16
63	17	
62	18	
61	19.5	Score 61 is tied for
61	19.5	Ranks 19 and 20
60	21.5	Score 60 is tied for
60	21.5	Ranks 21 and 22
59	23.5	Score 59 is tied for
59	23.5	Ranks 23 and 24
58	25	
57	27.5	Score 57 is
57	27.5	tied for
57	27.5	Ranks 26, 27,
57	27.5	28, and 29
56	31	Score 56 is tied
56	31	for ranks 30,
56	31	31, and 32
55	33	
54	34	
53	35.5	Score is tied for

Score	*Rank*	
53	35.5	Ranks 35 and 36
52	37	
51	38	
50	39	
49	40	
48	41.5	Score 48 is tied
48	41.5	for ranks 41 and 42
47	43	
46	44	
45	45	
42	46.5	Score 42 is tied
42	46.5	for ranks 46 and 47
40	48.5	Score 40 tied
40	48.5	for ranks 48 and 49
37	50	

Notice from the table that ranks are included and are averaged in the case of ties in the raw scores.

Certain simple interpretations can be made from this ranking procedure such as high score, low score, and the range. More important, however, the scores are now organized so that the ungrouped statistical procedures, presented later in this chapter, can be applied.

ESSENTIAL STATISTICAL TECHNIQUES

In the field of measurement and evaluation there are four computational procedures that are considered essential to analyzing and interpreting test scores. A measure of *central tendency* is usually the first statistical technique used when the teacher begins to analyze test scores. In addition any thorough analysis of the measures achieved by students must include the computation and interpretation of the *variability* of the distribution. The transformation and interpretation of *norms* is also an essential statistical technique but will be presented in detail in Chapter 4. Finally an understanding of the meaning and uses of relationship or *correlation* is very important to teachers of physical education who hope to incorporate a sound measurement program into their instructional units.

Central Tendency

This term is defined as a single measure that represents all of the other measures in the distribution. The three measures of central tendency, in ascending order of sophistication and usefulness, are the *mode*, the *median*, and the *mean*. In the following section each of these measures is defined, computed, and interpreted.

Mode. The mode is the measure that occurs most often in a distribution. If the data are presented graphically, the mode is identified by the highest point of the curve. However, this definition fits the mode only when the data are analyzed by using ungrouped techniques. When using grouped procedures as presented in Appendix E, the identity of the individual scores is lost, and therefore it is impossible to determine which score actually occurs most often in the distribution. The definition that must be applied in this situation is the midpoint of the step interval that contains the most scores. This is also true if the data are presented graphically. Occasionally a distribution of scores will have two, three, or even more modes. If this occurs, the distribution is called *bimodal, trimodal*, or the appropriate modal term.

Computation of the Mode. By referring to the test scores in Table 3.2, we see that the score 57 occurs four times and no other score has the same or more frequencies. The score 57 is therefore the mode for the set of golf skill test scores.

Interpretation of the Mode. The mode is considered the least reliable of the central tendency measures and is often used only as an early estimate. As a statistic, the mode is of limited value. It does not lend itself to algebraic manipulation because its calculating does not rely on particular score values of the characteristics or their numerical order, but only on the frequency of occurrence. In certain kinds of nominal or labeling data, the mode is the only measure of central tendency that can be used. However, in more usable types of data involving typical test scores where the mean or median can be computed, the mode is seldom utilized in any final evaluation. An example using the data from Table 3.2 will exemplify the crudeness of utilizing the mode as a representative score in the distribution. The mode of the distribution is 57, which occurred four times. If the 57 had occurred one less time and the 68 one more time, the ungrouped mode would change 11 score units from 57 to 68. This example demonstrates the care that must be taken by the teacher when using the mode in interpreting or making evaluations of a set of test scores based on the mode as the measure of central tendency.

Median. The median is the middle score in a distribution or the point on a scale such that half the measures are above it and half the measures are below. It is the 50th percentile point. If the distribution is represented graphically, the median divides the total area under the curve into two equal parts. If the number of scores in the distribution is even, the median is halfway between the two middle scores. Of course, if the number of measures is odd, the median is the exact middle score.

Computation of the Median. The median (Mdn) is often called a counting measure of central tendency. For ungrouped data it is computed by counting up from the lowest score to the midpoint of the set of scores. To obtain this score we use

$$\text{Mdn} = \frac{N + 1}{2}$$

This procedure is shown in Table 3.3 where Mdn = position of the median in the distribution, and N = the number of scores in the distribution.

Table 3.3 Measures of Central Tendency and Variability Computed from Ungrouped Golf Skills Test Scores (N = 50)

	Scores (X)	
	81	
	80	
	75	
	72	
	72	
	71	
	70	
↑	70	
	68	
	68	
	68	
50 percent of scores	67	$Q_3 = 67$
	67	
	65	
	64	
↓	64	
	63	
	62	
	61	
	61	
	60	
	60	
	59	
	59	
	58	

	Scores (X)	
Median = 57.5	57	
	57	mode = 57
	57	
	57	
	56	
	56	
	56	
	55	
	54	
	53	
	53	
	52	
	51	
50 percent of scores	50	$Q_1 = 50.5$
	49	
	48	
	48	
	47	
	46	
	45	
	42	
	42	
	40	
	40	
	37	

$$\overline{X} = \frac{\Sigma X}{N} = \frac{2913}{50} = 58.26$$

$$s = \sqrt{\frac{\Sigma(X - \overline{X})^2}{N}} = \sqrt{107.11} = 10.35 \quad R = (H - L) + 1 = (81 - 37) + 1 = 45$$

The number of scores in the distribution is 50. The score that represents the median is found by adding 1 to the 50 and dividing by 2. The result is 25.5, which indicates that the median is a point halfway between the two middle scores. By counting we find that the 25th score is 57, and the 26th score is 58. The point halfway between the two is 57.5, which is the median for the distribution.

Interpretation of the Median. The median is a much better measure of central tendency than the mode and in certain instances may be more useful than the mean to represent a set of scores. The median is called an ordinal statistic; it only takes into account the frequencies in the distribution and not the distances between the frequencies. In other words, the median does not use the numerical value of each score in the distribution. This fact makes the median useful in distributions with extremely high or low scores. If two of three extremely low scores occur in a distribution, the arithmetic mean may appear considerably lower than it should. Since the median does not consider the numerical value of the scores (only the frequencies), it is often used as the measure of central tendency when such atypical scores are present. In a normally distributed set of scores the median generally coincides with the mean. Because the computation of the median does not consider the numerical value of the scores, it is not commonly used in further statistical procedures. Certain nonparametric tests utilize the median.

Mean. The mean ($\overline{X}$) is frequently called the arithmetic average. Another definition refers to the mean as the sum of a set of measures divided by the number of measures in the distribution. If the distribution is presented graphically the mean is a point on the horizontal axis which is the center of gravity.

Computation of the Mean. This procedure is relatively simple. We sum or add all the measures and divide the sum by the number of measures in the distribution. The formula and an example of computing the mean from the golf skills test scores in Table 3.3 are shown below where:

$$\overline{X} = \frac{\Sigma X}{N}$$

X = mean

X = raw score

Σ = summation

N = number of scores in distribution

Therefore

$$\overline{X} = \frac{2913}{50} = 58.26$$

Interpretation of the Mean. For most populations the mean is a more accurate or efficient measure of central tendency than either the median or the mode. It is rigorously defined, easy to calculate, and used in other statistical calculations. The mean is affected by the numerical value of each score of the distribution of scores. However, it is very stable. Unless there are a number of atypical scores in the distribution, the mean is not changed significantly. Therefore, in normal distributions where the teacher wants to obtain the maximum interpretive uses from the measures of central tendency, the mean is always chosen. The exceptions are in sets of scores that vary greatly from the normal distribution where the median might be selected or in nominal or labeling kinds of data where the mode is the only measure that can be used.

Variability

The variability of a distribution is defined as the spread of the scores around a point. The different measures of variability accurately describe the dispersion of raw scores, information not available if only central measures are used. The measurement and consideration of the variation among individuals on test performances is of utmost concern to the teacher of physical education. It is well known that practically all psychomotor, cognitive, and affective measures utilized by the teacher exhibit considerable variation among individuals. The amount of that variation and how it may be described is the thrust of this discussion. Variability is usually represented by the *range*, the *quartile deviation*, and the *standard deviation*.

Range. This is the simplest and least useful of the measures of variation with respect to meaningful interpretation. The range is the difference between the highest and lowest measures in the distribution. Generally, in determining the range, we add 1 to the difference between the highest and lowest scores to account mathematically for both extreme numbers in the set of scores.

Computation of the Range. The range is computed only from the original set of raw scores. This is done because in grouped data the identities of the scores become lost, and it would be impossible to carry out the computation. The formula and an example of computing the range from the data in Table 3.3 are shown below.

$$R = (H - L) + 1$$

where

R = range

H = highest score in the distribution

L = lowest score in the distribution

1 = constant

Therefore

$$R = (81 - 37) + 1 = 45$$

Interpretation of the Range. Although unsophisticated in statistical terms, the range is used quite often by teachers to determine the spread or variability of scores after a test because it is so quick and easy to compute. The range can provide some helpful insights into the class performance but should not be used as a substitute for the quartile deviation or the standard deviation, discussed later in this section. For one reason, the range is considered unstable as a measure of variability in large samples because of the increased probability of an extreme score. In addition the range is quite closely related to sample size rather than to the actual knowledges and skills of the students.

Quartile Deviation. A better measure of variability is the quartile deviation, which is concerned with the range of scores that include only a specific part of the total set of scores. The quartile deviation is, therefore, defined as the spread or range of the middle 50 percent of the scores around the median. It is based on the range of the middle 50 percent of the scores. The total range is called the *interquartile* range, and the quartile deviation sometimes called the semi-interquartile range is simply one half of this range.

Computation of the Quartile Deviation. The quartile deviation will be computed from data shown in Table 3.3. The student will need to refer to Chapter 4 for a definition and description of quartiles that are used in the final computation of the quartile deviation. The formula for computing the quartile deviation is.

$$Q_D = \frac{Q_3 - Q_1}{2}$$

where

Q_D = quartile deviation

Q_3 = 3rd quartile or 75th percentile

Q_1 = 1st quartile or 25th percentile

2 = constant

From Table 3.3, Q_3 is found to be 67 and Q_1 is 50.5. Therefore, the quartile deviation is

$$Q_D = \frac{67 - 50.5}{2} = 8.25$$

Interpretation of the Quartile Deviation. The quartile deviation indicates the amount that needs to be added to or subtracted from the median to include the middle 50 percent of the scores. This number can then be interpreted as a measure of variability. It is also used in conjunction with the median, since both measures involve counting procedures in their computation.

The quartile deviation may give valuable information about classes of students taking the same examination using the same methodology. If the quartile deviation is much larger in one group, the teacher might conclude that different instructional methods might produce better performance results in the two classes.

Standard Deviation. This deviation is the square root of the average of the squared deviations from the mean. It is usually represented by *s*, *SD*, or the Greek σ. Computation of the standard deviation involves determining the amount that each score deviates from the mean, squaring each deviation, summing the squared deviations, and finally determining the average deviation by dividing by the number of scores in the distribution. Another definition identifies the standard deviation as a score that represents the average difference from the mean. This definition is perhaps more descriptive of standard deviation and more easily understood than the first one.

Computation of the Standard Deviation. The standard deviation will be computed from the golf skills test scores in Table 3.3. The procedure is simple but if the number of scores is large, the task becomes somewhat time-consuming. The computations and formulas are shown below.

$$s = \sqrt{\frac{\Sigma(X - \overline{X})^2}{N}}$$

$$s = \sqrt{\frac{5355.74}{50}} = \sqrt{107.11} = 10.35$$

where

s = standard deviation

Σ = summation

X = raw score

$\overline{X}$ = mean

N = number of scores in distribution

The preceding formula for standard deviation is cumbersome when the mean is not an integer. The following formula is often more useful. The computation follows.

$$s = \sqrt{\frac{\Sigma X^2}{N} - \frac{(\Sigma X)^2}{N^2}}$$

$$s = \sqrt{107.11} = 10.35$$

where

ΣX^2 = sum of squared scores

ΣX = sum of scores

N = number of scores in distribution

Interpretation of the Standard Deviation. The most useful and sophisticated measure of variability is the standard deviation. Often students and teachers lose sight of the meaning of the standard deviation because of the complexity of the computations. Basically it is the average amount that each score differs from the mean. Since the standard deviation depends on the weight of each score in the distribution, it is a more stable measure of variability than either the range or the quartile deviation. Because of its stability the standard deviation is used in numerous formulas for the computation of many types of statistics. One common statistical use is the square of the standard deviation, which is called the variance (s^2).

The standard deviation makes most sense when it is related to a distribution called the *normal* distribution. It is shown as a bell-shaped curve that represents the scores in a large distribution. The bell-shaped curve is nothing more than a graphic representation of the probable outcomes of a set of test or other variable scores. The curve is higher in the middle and flat at the ends, representing the probable scores. There are more ways for scores to occur near the middle and fewer ways for them to occur at the extremes. The normal curve (Figure 3.1) demonstrates this fact with its high center area and lower extremities. In the normal curve the mean, median, and mode coincide.

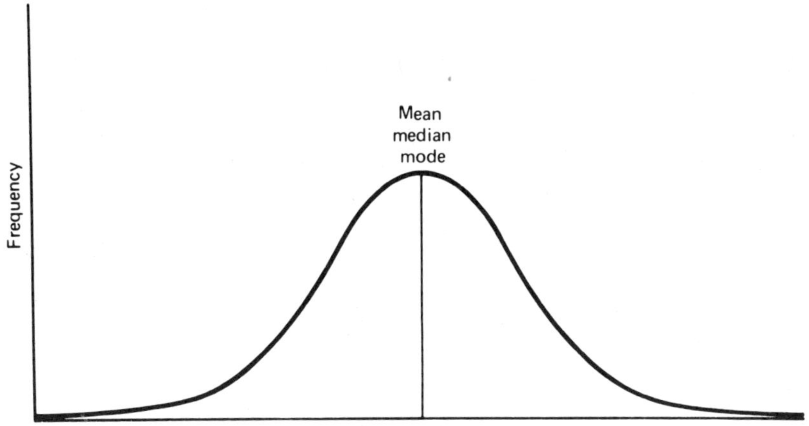

Figure 3.1. The normal curve.

The normal curve has been used as a basis for establishing various norms. If data are normally distributed, interpretation is relatively simple. However, not all distributions of scores conform to the shape of the normal curve. The normal curve in Figure 3.1 is symmetrical; the frequencies are located equally on both sides of the center of the distribution. A curve that is not symmetrical is considered to be *skewed.* In positively skewed distributions the tail of the curve extends toward the right side, where the higher scores are found. Figure 3.2 presents a positively skewed distribution including the relative positions of the mean, median, and mode. In positively skewed curves most of the scores are low, with a few high scores affecting the position of the mean. An extremely difficult test often results in a curve or distribution that is positively skewed. The mean in a positively skewed distribution is always higher than the median.

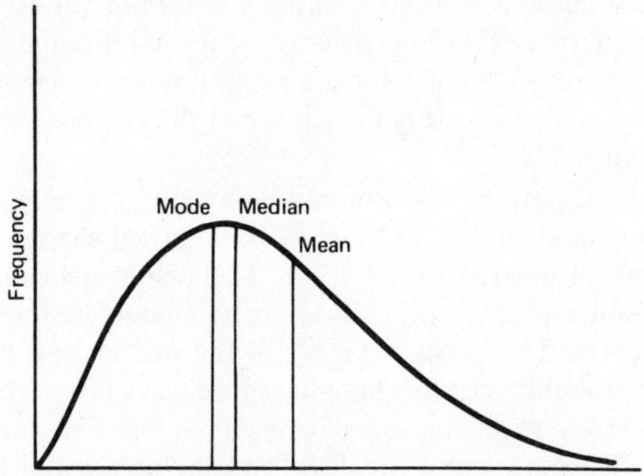

Figure 3.2. Positively skewed distribution.

A distribution in which the tail is toward the left side, where the lower scores are located, is negatively skewed. Figure 3.3 shows the graph of a negatively skewed distribution along with the relative position of the mean, median, and mode. In a negatively skewed distribution, the mean is always lower than the median. Such a distribution might result from a simple test where most scores are high but a few low scores affect the mean.

Even if a curve were symmetrical, it might not be normal. A second variation is termed *kurtosis* and refers to the flatness or peakedness of a distribution when compared to another. In Figure 3.4 the three variations are shown. The normal curve is called *mesokurtic.* If the distribution is more peaked than the normal curve, it is *leptokurtic.* If it is less peaked, it is *platykurtic.* A leptokurtic curve has more average scores than normal, while the platykurtic curve has more extreme scores. Data that are not normal may be normalized by various transformations, although normal distribution allows easier interpretation because skewness and kurtosis remain unchanged. Certain common transformations change the shape of the frequency distribution. As an example, original

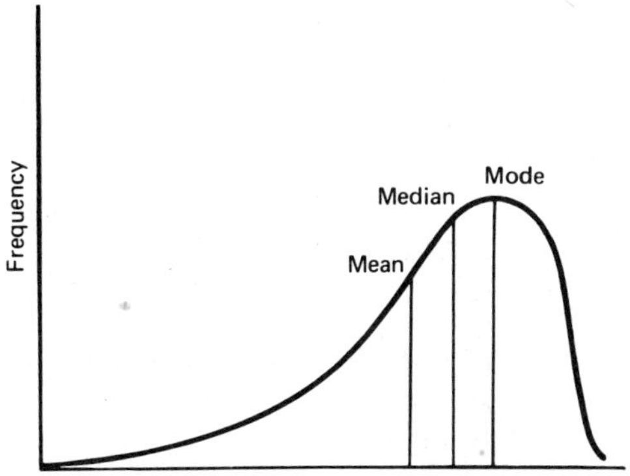

Figure 3.3. Negatively skewed distribution.

data may be negatively skewed and leptokurtic. A normal transformation changes the data so that they are approximately normally distributed. Chapter 4 discusses fully the transformation of measures to norms.

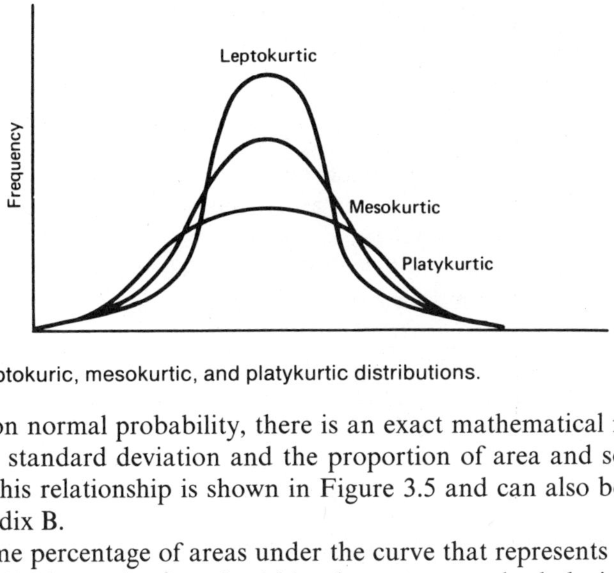

Figure 3.4. Leptokuric, mesokurtic, and platykurtic distributions.

Based on normal probability, there is an exact mathematical relationship between the standard deviation and the proportion of area and scores under the curve. This relationship is shown in Figure 3.5 and can also be computed from Appendix B.

The same percentage of areas under the curve that represents the number of scores will always be found within the same standard deviation limits. Therefore, in any normal curve, 34.13 percent of the scores will fall between the mean and +1.0 standard deviation. Because the curve is symmetrical the same percentage will be found between the mean and −1.0 standard deviation. By adding the percentage shown in Figure 3.5, we can make the following observations about the areas under the normal curve.

1. About two thirds (68.26 percent) of the scores will fall between +1.0 and −1.0 standard deviations.

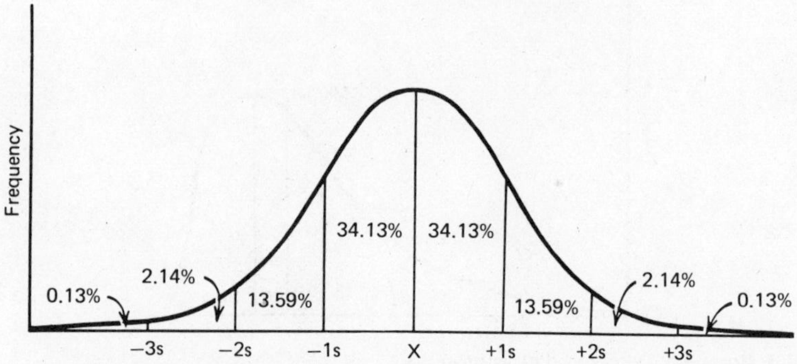

Figure 3.5. The normal curve, with standard deviations and areas.

2. About 95.4 percent of the scores will fall within +2.0 and −2.0 standard deviation.
3. Nearly all scores (99.7 percent) will fall within +3.0 and −3.0 standard deviations.

This relationship of the standard deviation to the distributions of the scores in a normal curve enables the teacher to give the standard deviation a uniform meaning that can be applied to all evaluation situations. Different groups might be compared or the comparative status of an individual may be evaluated. Remember that the typical classroom test does not always conform exactly to the distribution of scores under the normal curve. However, most measures approach the normal curve closely enough so that the meaning and interpretation of the standard deviation can be used without serious problems.

Possibly one of the most meaningful interpretations of the standard deviation for the teacher is that, by knowing the number of standard deviations above or below the mean, the percent of scores normally falling above or below the mean can be expressed. The percent of scores falling below selected standard deviation values on the normal curve is given in Table 3.4. With this table it is easy to translate any score expressed in standard deviation units into the equivalent percentile on the normal curve.

Table 3.4 Percent of Cases Falling Below Selected Standard Deviation Values on the Normal Curve

Deviation in Standard Deviation Units	*Percent of Cases Falling Below*	*Deviation in Standard Deviation Units*	*Percent of Cases Falling Below*
+3.0	99.9	−0.1	46.0
+2.9	99.8	−0.2	42.1
+2.8	99.7	−0.3	38.2

Deviation in Standard Deviation Units	*Percent of Cases Falling Below*	*Deviation in Standard Deviation Units*	*Percent of Cases Falling Below*
+2.7	99.6	−0.4	34.4
+2.6	99.5	−0.5	30.9
+2.5	99.4	−0.6	27.4
+2.4	99.2	−0.7	24.2
+2.3	98.9	−0.8	21.2
+2.2	98.6	−0.9	18.4
+2.1	98.2	−1.0	15.9
+2.0	97.7	−1.1	13.6
+1.9	97.1	−1.2	11.5
+1.8	96.4	−1.3	9.7
+1.7	95.5	−1.4	8.1
+1.6	94.5	−1.5	6.7
+1.5	93.3	−1.6	5.5
+1.4	91.9	−1.7	4.5
+1.3	90.3	−1.8	3.6
+1.2	88.5	−1.9	2.9
+1.1	86.4	−2.0	2.3
+1.0	84.1	−2.1	1.8
+0.9	81.6	−2.2	1.4
+0.8	78.8	−2.3	1.1
+0.7	75.8	−2.4	0.8
+0.6	72.6	−2.5	0.6
+0.5	69.1	−2.6	0.5
+0.4	65.6	−2.7	0.4
+0.3	61.8	−2.8	0.3
+0.2	57.9	−2.9	0.2
+0.1	54.0	−3.0	0.1
+0.0	50.0		

For an example of the procedures discussed in the previous paragraph, select a score of 67 from the golf scores in Table 3.3. By the ungrouped computations the mean was found to be 58.26 and the standard deviation was 10.35. By subtracting the raw score of 67 from the mean (58.26) we see that the raw score exceeds the mean by 8.74 units. This is 8.74/10.35 or .84 of a standard deviation. By referring to Table 3.4 we can expect that a score of 67 will exceed 78.8 percent of the cases. Notice that 0.8 standard deviation was used in the table to make the conversion. If more accurate transformations are desired, Appendix B may be used.

When raw scores are expressed in standard deviation units they have much the same meaning from one distribution to another. Should a student fall 1.0 standard deviation above the mean on the golf skills test and one half of a standard deviation above the mean on the golf rules test, it is obvious that the student is considerably better in skills than in rules relative to the total group completing the two tests. The standard deviation provides the teacher with a unit that can directly compare raw scores from one test to another. This will be discussed in greater detail in the standard score section of Chapter 4.

Correlation

Correlation is used to express the extent of relationship between two or more variables or sets of scores. The degree of relationship is generally called the coefficient of correlation and is represented by all possible numbers between +1.00 and −1.00. An interpretation of correlation will be given later in this chapter. Chapter 5 also discusses the use of correlation for the validation and estimation of reliability for specific tests.

Currently, in the measurement and statistics literature the student and teacher can find numerous correlational techniques that serve various purposes. In this discussion, however, only the *Pearson product-moment* and the *Spearman rank-difference* correlational procedures will be included. These two are the most commonly used methods of computing correlation and will help solve almost any validation or reliability problem that may confront the teacher.

Computation of the Pearson Product-Moment Correlation. The product-moment correlation may be computed from either grouped or ungrouped data. However, grouped methods are extremely inefficient and are now seldom used. Therefore, they are not included in this text. The formula for computing r, the Pearson product-moment is:

$$r = \frac{N\Sigma XY - (\Sigma X)(\Sigma Y)}{\sqrt{[N\Sigma X^2 - (\Sigma X)^2][N\Sigma Y^2 - (\Sigma Y)^2]}}$$

where

r = coefficient of correlation

N = number of students

ΣXY = sum of XY column

ΣX = sum of X column

ΣY = sum of Y column

ΣX^2 = sum of X^2 column

ΣY^2 = sum of Y^2 column

A basketball skills test and rating scale data used in the calculation of the coefficent of correlation are presented in Table 3.5.

Table 3.5 Product-Moment Correlation for Basketball Skills Test and Rating Scale Data (N = 40)

Basketball Skills Test (X)	Basketball Rating Scale (Y)	$(X)^2$	$(Y)^2$	(XY)
71	33	5041	1089	2343
86	43	7396	1849	3698
92	47	8464	2209	4324
66	29	4356	841	1914
74	35	5476	1225	2590
80	39	6400	1521	3120
63	28	3969	784	1764
64	29	4096	841	1856
82	41	6724	1681	3362
57	24	3249	576	1368
84	42	7056	1764	3528
75	36	5625	1296	2700
65	29	4225	841	1885
76	38	5776	1444	2888
80	39	6400	1521	3120
63	27	3969	729	1701
76	36	5776	1296	2736
75	35	5625	1225	2625
85	42	7225	1764	3570
68	31	4624	961	2108
72	33	5184	1089	2376
74	35	5476	1225	2590
73	32	5329	1024	2336
79	38	6241	1444	3002
72	33	5184	1089	2376
71	32	5041	1024	2272
78	38	6084	1444	2964
70	32	4900	1024	2240
69	32	4761	1024	2208
76	36	5776	1296	2736
69	31	4761	961	2139
75	35	5625	1225	2625
72	34	5184	1156	2448
75	35	5625	1225	2625
75	34	5625	1156	1550
80	39	6400	1521	3120
74	35	5476	1225	2590

Basketball Skills Test (X)	*Basketball Rating Scale (Y)*	$(X)^2$	$(Y)^2$	(XY)
73	34	5329	1156	2482
73	33	5329	1089	2409
76	36	5776	1296	2736
$\Sigma X = 2958$	$\Sigma Y = 1390$	$\Sigma X^2 = 220578$	$\Sigma Y^2 = 49150$	$\Sigma XY = 104024$

Therefore

$$r = \frac{40 \cdot 104024 - (2958)(1390)}{\sqrt{[40 \cdot 220578 - (2958)^2][40 \cdot 49150 - (1390)^2]}}$$

$$r = \frac{4{,}160{,}960 - 4{,}111{,}620}{\sqrt{[8{,}823{,}120 - 8{,}749{,}764][1{,}966{,}000 - 1{,}932{,}100]}}$$

$$r = \frac{49340}{\sqrt{[73356][33900]}} = \frac{= 49340}{\sqrt{2{,}486{,}768{,}400}}$$

$$r = \frac{49340}{49867.5} = .99$$

The calculations for the coefficient of correlation appear complicated. This is not the case, however. Often, the computations will result in large numbers, but the formula is quite easy to follow. The following steps can serve as an aid for computing the product-moment correlation (r).

1. Develop a column for each set of scores. Label the first set of scores X and the second set Y.
2. Develop an X^2 column. In this column, square each raw score under the X column and enter the result in the corresponding position in the X^2 column.
3. Develop a Y^2 column. In this column, square each raw score under the Y column and enter the result in the corresponding position in the Y^2 column.
4. Develop an XY column. Multiply each raw score under the X column by each raw score under the Y column and enter the result in the corresponding position in the XY column.
5. Find the sum of each column and enter the result at the bottom of each column as shown in Table 3.5.
6. Substitute the five values at the bottom of Table 3.5 into the correlation formula shown on the previous page and complete the computation.

If the means and standard deviations are available for each set of scores, another procedure might be used. This second procedure, which is somewhat easier to compute, is

$$r = \frac{\sum XY/N - (\overline{Xx})(\overline{Xy})}{(s_x) \quad (s_y)}$$

where

r = correlation coefficient

$\overline{Xx}$ = mean of the raw scores (X column)

$\overline{Xy}$ = mean of the raw scores (Y column)

s_x = standard deviation of raw scores (X column)

s_y = standard deviation of raw scores (Y column)

Therefore

$$r = \frac{104024/40 - (73.95) \quad (34.75)}{(6.86) \quad (4.66)} = .99$$

Computation of the Rank-Difference Correlation. This method of correlation is simply a way to express the degree of relationship between two sets of ranks. The relationship is basically the same as the product-moment correlation with the exception that ranks rather than raw scores are considered in the rank-difference procedures. The formula and computations from the data in Table 3.6 are shown below.

Table 3.6 Rank-Difference Correlation Between a Skills Test Score and Position in a Round Robin Tournament (N = 15)

Student	*Score on Skills Test*	*Rank on Skills Test*	*Rank in Round-Robin Tournament*	*Difference in Rank (d)*	*Difference in Rank Squared (d^2)*
A	58	9	1	8	64
B	74	1	2	−1	1
C	69	4	3	1	1
D	54	10.5	4	6.5	42.25
E	60	7.5	5	2.5	6.25
F	66	5	6	−1	1
G	71	3	7	−4	16
H	61	6	8	−2	4
I	72	2	9	−7	49
J	54	10.5	10	0.5	0.25
K	48	14	11	3	9
L	49	13	12	1	1

M	50	12	13	−1	1
N	60	7.5	14	−6.5	42.25
O	44	15	15	0	0
					$\Sigma d^2 = 238$

$$\rho = 1 - \frac{6\sum d^2}{N(N^2 - 1)}$$

where

ρ = rho

1 = constant

6 = constant

Σ = summation

d^2 = sum of d^2 column

N = number of students

Therefore

$$\rho = 1 - \frac{6(238)}{15\,(15^2 - 1)} = 1 - \frac{1428}{3360}$$

$$\rho = 1 - .425 = .575$$

The calculations for rho are very simple and are presented in step form below.

1. Place each set of scores in a column.
2. Rank students for each set of scores. In Table 3.6 the round robin tournament resulted in a natural ranking; however, the skills test had to be ranked from 1 to 15.
3. Determine the difference (d) in the ranks by subtracting the scores in the right-hand rank column from the scores in the left-hand rank column. Arrange these results in column d in their appropriate positions.
4. Square each difference in rank to obtain d^2. Again place these results in column d^2 in their appropriate locations.
5. Obtain the sum of d^2 by adding all entries in the d^2 column.
6. Apply the formula for rank-difference correlation, which was presented on the previous page.

Interpretation of Correlation. The coefficient of correlation provides a numerical representation of the relationship between two or more sets of scores. Correlations range from +1.00 for a perfect positive relationship to 0.00 for no relationship to −1.00 for a perfect negative relationship. If the correlation is a perfect positive (+1.00) relationship, it is then indicated that the higher the score on the first test, the higher the score will be on the second test. For example, if a +1.00 correlation were found between a strength test and a shot-putting performance, we may conclude that the individual in the test with the highest strength score would also have the highest shot-putting performance. It is also true that the person with the second highest strength score would have the second highest shot-putting score and so forth, until the lowest score on both tests would also belong to the same individual.

Possible relationships between two variables are shown graphically in Figure 3.6. Some of the relationships between strength and shot-putting ability are hypothetical because many of these correlations could not occur in actual testing situations between these two variables. A perfect correlation is graphically shown as a straight line, and a zero correlation appears as a circle. The shapes of the remaining correlations are between a circle and a straight line on the graph. In addition, positive correlations are linear from the lower left part of the graph to the upper right as shown in Figure 3.6. Negative correlations are represented in the opposite direction, from upper left to lower right as seen in Figure 3.6.

Correlation coefficients are used most often in measurement to establish validity, reliability, and objectivity. These procedures and how they are interpreted are discussed extensively in Chapter 5. There are, however, certain cautions that must be exercised when applying the coefficient of correlation to measurement problems. The teacher should never attempt to infer that one of the sets of scores causes the other. In other words, correlations are meant merely to describe relationships. They are not meant to determine cause and effect between two sets of scores. For example, if a group of students of various ages are measured on an intelligence test and a motor ability test battery, a high correlation may be computed. However, both variables are related to age. That is, intelligence and motor ability are related because they are both closely related to age. One variable does not have a causal relationship with the other. Another caution deals with the magnitude of the correlation. Table 3.7 includes a list of correlational ranges. In addition, judgements regarding their worth in assessing such measurement topics as validity and reliability are included.

Table 3.7 Correlations and Evaluation of Usefulness

Range of Correlation	*Usefulness*
± .90 − 1.00	Very high correlation
± .70 − .89	Good correlation
± .50 − .69	Fair correlation
± .20 − .49	Low correlation
Below ± .20	Extremely low correlation

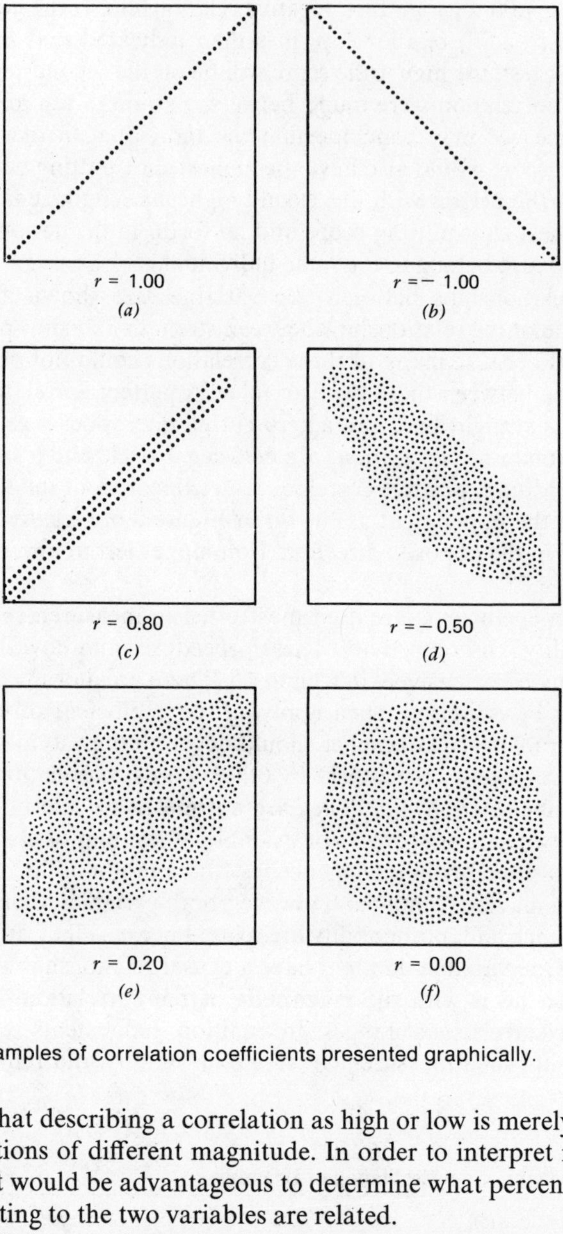

Figure 3.6. Examples of correlation coefficients presented graphically.

Notice that describing a correlation as high or low is merely an attempt to label correlations of different magnitude. In order to interpret more fully correlation (r), it would be advantageous to determine what percentage of the factors contributing to the two variables are related.

The coefficients of determination and nondetermination are used by most experts to interpret r more fully. For example, if an r of .80 were obtained between shot-putting distance and strength, the coefficient of determination would be found by squaring r and the coefficient of nondetermination would be found by computing $1 - r^2$. In the example the coefficient of determination is $.80^2$ or .64, and the coefficient of nondetermination is $1 - .64$ or .36. This means that 64 percent of the variance in shot-putting skill (Y) is related to the variance in strength (X) and that 36 percent of the variance in shot-putting skill (Y) is not related to the variance in strength (X). The use of r^2 and $1 - r^2$ provides considerably more information than the simple labeling system discussed previously. In addition, r^2 and $1 - r^2$ are not affected by the sign of r, since the value is squared. Therefore, an $r = -.80$ would be interpreted in exactly the same way as the one in the example. For the most part, correlations are concerned with predicting one set of scores if the second set is known. For example, in concurrent and predictive validity the concern is to obtain a high correlation between two sets of scores. In reliability, the interest is in obtaining a high correlation between the scores on the same test administered a second time. The teacher must be warned not to conclude usable validity or reliability unless the correlations are fairly high. The usefulness of correlations below .5 is considered questionable by many experts. In fact, many measurement experts argue that reliability coefficients should be higher than .90 and validity coefficients should be higher than .70.

UNDERSTANDING AND USING THE ELECTRONIC COMPUTER

The computer is a modern measurement and research tool that is capable of accepting and manipulating tremendous quantities of data and executing numerous mathematical calculations of extreme complexity at tremendous speed. Any of the statistical tools discussed earlier in this chapter may be carried out using any standard computer. The computer should not be seen as a secondary tool in measurement, but like statistics, as a tool that has varied and growing applications for the classroom teacher.

The combination of speed and precise accuracy enables the computer to carry out complex measurement tasks involving many students and many scores. Some understanding of the capabilities and limitations of the computer are important to the classroom teacher before attempting to use the device as a tool to facilitate data handling and score analysis.

Contrary to common belief, the computer has no independent intelligence. It must rely upon man-made instructions for each task; it does only what it is directed to do. With the rapidly advancing computer technology, the machines may in time be superior to people in following complex decision rules.

Computers can be programmed by a person called a *programmer* to manipulate data related to test scores in an unlimited number of ways. Programs may be short or long, complex or simple, depending almost entirely on the skill and resourcefulness of the programmer. Before any program can be developed, the problem must be analyzed and a logical method of solution determined. Most of the programs used by the classroom teacher in measurement have already been developed and are readily available. Examples of these programs are presented in Appendix F. However, some elementary programming skills can be helpful in providing the teacher with a better idea of how to use available programs and in communicating computer needs to specialists in the area.

Organization of the Basic Computer

The modern computer system contains an input device that reads the data into the computer (see Figure 3.7). Most sophisticated computers have a variety of input devices that are used for this purpose. Card readers, typewriter terminals, optical scanners, disk files, magnetic tapes, paper tapes, touch tone telephones, or other computers are examples of input devices that are commonly used to enter data into various computer systems. The purpose of the input devices is to translate data into electrical impulses that can be handled by the computer. The input devices vary widely in the speed with which they can move data in and out of the computer. Typically, in tests and measurements, optical scanner sheets and punch cards are used to enter the data into the basic computer system.

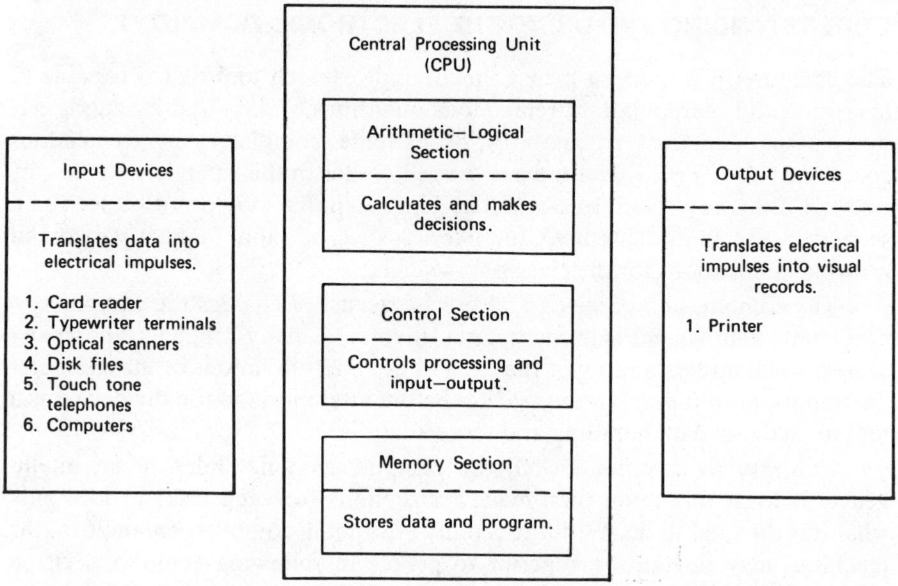

Figure 3.7. Organization of typical computer (from M. Clemens Johnson, *A Review of Research Methods in Education,* Rand McNally College Publishing Company, Chicago, copyright © 1977, p. 269; reprinted by permission.

The optical scanner input system was developed by E. F. Lindquist at the Measurement Research Center, State University of Iowa. The device is capable of handling 2000 or more answer sheets at a time and then automatically senses the marks on either side of the sheet by transmitting light through it.

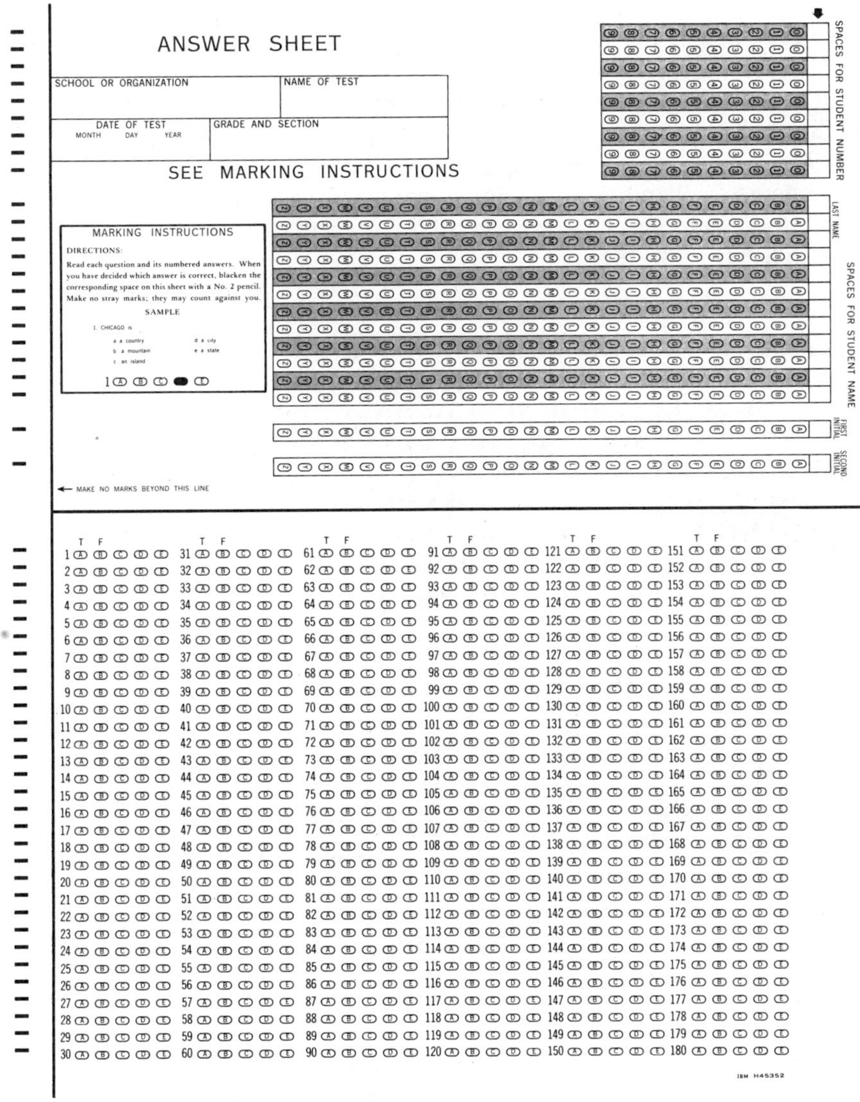

Figure 3.8. Optical scanner sheet.

This process is handled at a rate of approximately 100 sheets per minute. Simultaneously, the machine compares the mark on the sheet with an answer key stored in memory, counts the number of right answers, and corrects the final score for any weighted formula desired. The machine can convert scores to standard scores or scale scores if desired. Finally, all of the students' demographic data can be read from the sheet, and all of the information can be placed on a punch card, a tape, or be fed directly into a computer system for further analysis. A typical optical scanner sheet is shown in Figure 3.8.

Perhaps the most frequently used input device in research and measurement is the familiar punch card (see Figure 3.9). The standard punch card is 3¼ inches wide and 6⅜ inches long, and it is divided into 80 columns and 12 rows. The 80 columns correspond to 80 spaces in which 80 numbers, letters, or other measurement symbols may be recorded. Each of the 80 columns has spaces for as many as 12 punches, one in each of its 12 rows. Ten of the rows are numbers 0 — 9 and two are unnumbered. The unnumbered rows are used for recording minus and plus signs. In addition, these rows can be used for recording alphabetic information.

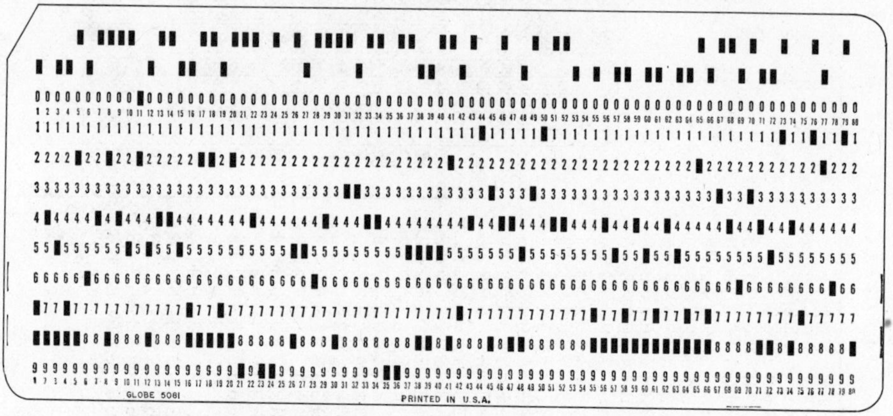

Figure 3.9. IBM punch card.

Data are entered on the punch cards by using a *card punch machine,* which resembles a common typewriter. As the card punch key is depressed, a hole is punched in the corresponding spot on the card. Numbers are recorded by punching a single hole in one of the 0-9 rows of a given column. Letters and punctuation symbols are recorded by punching two or three holes in a given column. For example the letter A consists of a punch in the top row (the twelfth row) and the first row. The letter B consists of a punch in the twelfth row and the second row.

The information from the cards is then read into a computer system by a *card reader.* This is a high-speed machine that feeds the information from the punch cards into the analysis system where it is stored, analyzed, and ultimately fed back to the operator.

The computer proper is called the *central processing unit* or *CPU.* The CPU is made up of three parts: an *arithmetic-logical section,* a *control section,* and a *memory section.*

The arithmetic-logical section contains the circuitry that enables the computer to execute both logical and arithmetic operations. It is the logical operation section that provides the computer with decision-making capabilities. It makes decisions by comparing the values of the numbers stored in its memory.

The computer can be programmed to take alternative actions depending on whether the difference between two numbers is positive, negative, or zero.

The control section monitors and initiates data processing. The programmed instructions are systematically retrieved from memory, and its meaning is decoded. A programmed instruction indicates which operation the computer is to perform and which numbers the machine is to operate on. While carrying out an instruction, the computer takes numbers out of memory and transfers them to the arithmetic-logical section for action.

The memory section provides an *electronic storage* for the program to be executed and for the data that has been entered into the machine for computation. The size of the memory is very important, and it is the limiting factor in determining how large a problem the computer is capable of handling at one time. The longest programs included in Appendix F are designed for use by computers having at least 32,000 memory locations over the number required by the control section in executing the program.

Even very large computers are incapable of storing large amounts of data from many measurement and research projects. The memory in the CPU would soon be filled with scores, grades, or reserach data and would be unable to handle additional projects. Computer system memories are often supplemented by *magnetic disk storage* or *magnetic tape storage*. Magnetic disks resemble stereo records coated on each side with iron oxide. The data are placed or stored on the disks as minute, magnetized spots. Several million numeric or alphabetical characters can be placed on a single magnetic disk.

The memory on a magnetic disk is of the random access type, which means that data can be retrieved from any position on the disk at about the same speed. The data is read in and out of the disk by "read" and "write" heads on the machine that travel rapidly across the surfaces of the disks.

Another form of storage is the magnetic tape, which is somewhat slower than the previous form of memory discussed. A reel of magnetic tape, 2200 feet long, accepts and stores the data in sequence along the length of the tape and must retrieve the data in the same manner. This form of storage is inferior to the random access type found in the magnetic disk because of the slowness of the retrieval system; however, magnetic tapes can store more data more economically than the magnetic disk.

The most commonly output device used by computers is the *line printer*. The data are printed out by the line printer at the computer center. This device translates impulses into a printed record at a very high rate of speed. The typical printer can print entire lines of output at one time at phenomenal speeds, up to 1200 lines per minute.

Printer output is not the only means of obtaining data from the typical computer. Magnetic disks, magnetic tapes, punched cards, visual display devices, or even other computers may be incorporated as output devices. These devices are the exception rather than the rule in acquiring output from any computer system.

Using the Computer

Not all teachers or students will be interested in learning to use a computer. However, some introduction to its use and programming will help every educator and student of tests and measurements. Usually, a high level of mathematics is not required for writing programs or using a typical computer, but the ability to think logically is important. The programmer must have a basic understanding of the formulas and computations that will be used in the solution of a particular problem as well as understanding the procedures and instructions in the programming *language* that will be used.

Perhaps the simplest of the many computer languages available for the teacher is BASIC. The BASIC language consists of a number of common instructions in English as well as mathematical notations. This language is extremely useful in time-sharing systems where one large computer is shared by a number of users through the use of many remote control terminals. Another relatively easy-to-learn, user-oriented language is COBOL. It is also based on English instructions and was designed for use in business settings.

The most commonly used language and the one that will be used for sample purposes in this chapter and in Appendix F is FORTRAN. The original FORTRAN language has undergone numerous revisions over the years and is based on highly sophisticated English instruction. It is particularly useful in mathematical computations such as the ones presented earlier in this chapter.

Regardless of the specific language used in finding a solution to a specific problem, the teacher must develop a procedure to follow that will reduce the time involved as well as the number of errors made while programming or running the program. A *flow chart* can often provide a level of organization that will accomplish these goals. A flow chart is a graphical presentation of the main steps that will be followed during the development of the program. It also indicates the data that must be read into the computer and the expected results that are to be printed by the output device. This is done without including too much detail, which would interfere with the graphical value of the chart. The flow chart is then connected to the instructions in the appropriate language, which are carried out by the computer.

An example of a flow chart that can lead to the computation of the mean, standard deviation, and standard *T*-scores is shown in Figure 3.10. The flow chart begins by reading in the raw scores (X). The mean and standard deviation are then computed using standard formulas and, finally, a *T*-score is computed for each raw score.

The student or teacher will find it difficult to follow the steps in the flow chart because of the symbols and unique references. Basically there are no set procedures to follow when developing a flow chart. Different geometric shapes such as circles, squares, rectangles, and diamonds are used to facilitate the reading process. In this sample flow chart a basic rectangle sectioned into

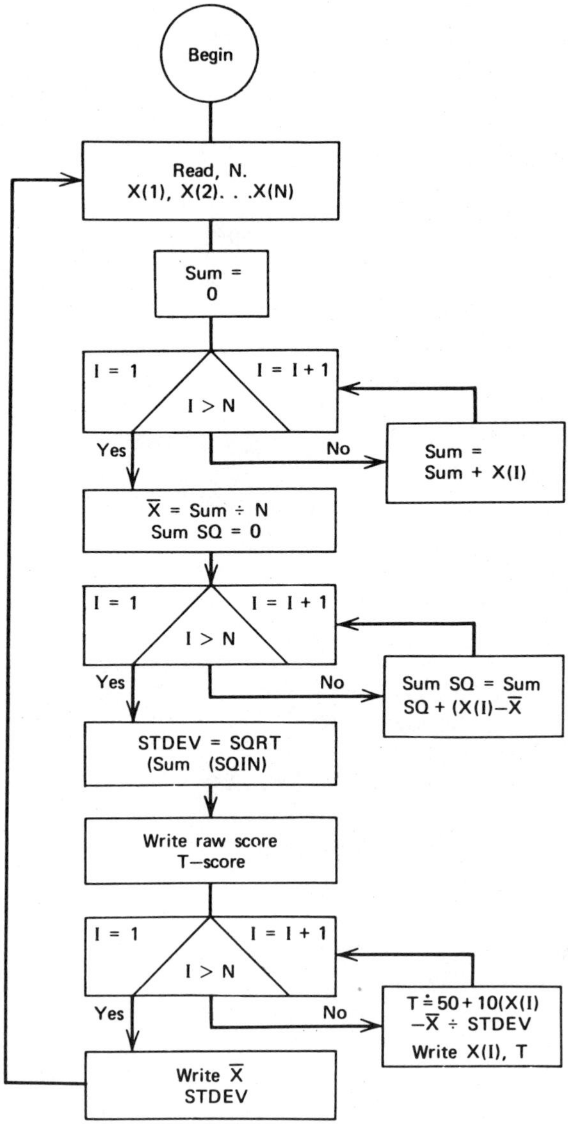

Figure 3.10. Flow chart for determining the mean and standard deviation of *T*-scores from one group.

three triangles is used to represent a *loop*. This occurs when the computer is required to execute one or several instructions repeatedly. A form of computer counter must be used to keep track of the number of times the machine works through the loop. In this example the counter is represented by I, which is increased by one each time the computer executes a loop. When I or the counter surpasses the total number of subjects (N), the loop is stopped; then the machine is instructed to go on to the next step. The program will stop or terminate when there is no more data to be analyzed.

Figure 3.11 presents a FORTRAN language program based upon the flow chart discussed above. The program is designed specifically to read in all of the raw scores, compute the corresponding mean and standard deviation, and transform each raw score into its respective *T*-score. The computer is instructed to print out the raw scores of each student, the *T*-scores, the mean, and the standard deviation.

```
      DIMENSION X(500)                                  1
1     READ(1,2)N                                        2
2     FORMAT(I3)                                        3
      READ(1,3)(X(I),I = 1,N)                           4
3     FORMAT(20F3.0)                                    5
      SUM = 0.                                          6
      DO 4 I = 1,N                                      7
4     SUM = SUM + X(I)                                  8
      XBAR = SUM/N                                      9
      SUMSQ = 0.                                        10
      DO 5 I = 1,N                                      11
5     SUMSQ = SUMSQ + (X(I) -XBAR)**2                   12
      STDEV = SQRT(SUMSQ/N)                             13
      WRITE(6,6)                                        14
6     FORMAT(I RAW SCORE T-SCORE)                       15
      DO 8 I = 1,N                                      16
      T = 50 + 10.* (X(I) -XBAR)/STDEV                  17
      WRITE(6,7)X(I), T                                 18
7     FORMAT('0',2F10.0)                                19
8     CONTINUE                                          20
      WRITE(6,9)XBAR, STDEV                             21
9     FORMAT('0MEAN =', F8.2,5X,'SIGMA =',F8.2)         22
      GO TO 1                                           23
      END                                               24
```

Figure 3.11. FORTRAN Program to Compute Mean, Standard Deviation, and *T*-Scores (from M. Clemens Johnson, *A Review of Research Methods in Education*, Rand McNally College Publishing Company, Chicago, copyright © 1977, p. 270; reprinted by permission).

A detailed explanation of programming is beyond the scope of this text. The reader is referred to any standard FORTRAN language manual for in-depth details concerning the nature and purpose of each of the steps in the program found in Figure 3.11. A brief discussion of each step will provide the student with at least a cursory understanding of the programming technicalities of a typical computer. The numbers on the right side of the figure are for identification and are not part of the instruction to the computer.

The first instruction, DIMENSION X (500), instructs the computer to allocate 500 locations in the internal memory for storing scores. Specifically the storage locations are labeled X(1), X(2) . . . X(N). The second instruction is for reading in the value of *N* or the number of scores. Instruction 3 indicates do the computer place on the data card where the value of *N* is located. The 13 following the term FORMAT indicates that the variable *N* will be an integer (no decimal places) and that the actual number will be found in the first three columns on the punch card.

Instruction 4 is the READ statement, which instructs the input device to read numerical scores for each student in the distribution. Instruction 5 is similar to number 3 in that the location of each score in the memory system is indicated as well as the decimal appearance of each score.

Instruction 6 begins the actual process of computing the intended results. This instruction designates the specific memory location where the sum of the scores is to be located. The name Sum is the location designated in this program, which is a unique feature of the FORTRAN language system. Of course, the initial value of Sum must be set equal to zero. The actual summing of the socres in the distribution is carried out by instructions 7 and 8. A DO loop is used to carry out this computation. The loop is executed *N* times and each time through, adds one more score to the location named SUM until each score is accounted for in the total.

The ninth instruction is used to compute the mean of the scores and place the result in a memory location named XBAR. The computer indentifies another location in the memory called SUMSQ in instruction 10. This result will be used in computing the standard deviation. The actual result that is stored in the location SUMSQ is carried out in a DO loop as provided in instructions 11 and 12. Finally, instruction 14 instructs the computer to divide the result in SUMSQ by *N* and also to obtain the square root. This is the standard deviation.

Instructions 14 and 15 are the first print instructions in this program. They instruct the computer to print the headings RAW SCORE and *T*-SCORE. Still another DO loop is found in instruction 16 through 20 which the computer is instructed to compute a *T*-score for each student and to print out the results under the headings printed above.

Instruction 21 instructs the computer to print the values of XBAR and STDEV calculated earlier in the program. Instruction 22 merely instructs the computer to slip two lines for printing these values. Finally, instruction 23 instructs the computer to return to step 1 to check for more data. If no more data is available to the program will end according to instruction 24.

Packaged Computer Programs

The teacher of physical education can save a great deal of time and effort by using readily accessible *packaged computer programs*. A packaged or "canned" program is a general program written so that anyone having a proper set of instructions can utilize it. For example, there are numerous packaged programs for performing item analysis on objective test scores. The teacher with access to such a program merely has to punch the scores on cards and prepare the proper set of program instruction cards. It is common practice for any computer center to keep a library of these packaged programs on file. The professional computer staff obtains the programs and makes them readily available to the users center. The staff often provides help in preparing the instruction program cards for all of the programs at their disposal. Complete programs of the statistical techniques discussed in this chapter and in Chapters 4 and 7 are found in Appendix F.

Summary

Statistics is a branch of mathematics that deals with the analysis of scores for individuals or groups. The statistics considered essential to measurement and evaluation have been presented in this chapter.

Before an analysis of scores can be made, some form of organiztion must be carried out. One method of organizing sets of test scores involves ranking the scores from high to low. The statistics that are considered essential to measurement and evaluation include measures of central tendency, measures of variability, and measures of correlation. The mode is one measure of central tendency and is the score that occurs most frequently in the distribution. The median is the middle score, and the mean is the arthmetic average of the distribution of scores.

The three measures of variability identified are the range, quartile deviation, and standard deviation. The range is the high score in the distribution minus the low score plus 1. The quartile deviation is one half of the distance between the 3rd quartile and the 1st quartile. It can also be thought of as the spread of the middle 50 percent of the score around the median. The standard deviation is defined as the average difference from the mean and is very useful in interpreting individual student scores.

The coefficient of correlation reflects the degree of relationship between two or more sets of scores. The product-moment and rank-difference methods are considered to be the most commonly used procedures computing correlation. In interpreting correlation the numerical coefficient might be labeled as very high, good, fair, low, or very low. Another procedure for interpreting correlations is to compute the coefficient of determiantion and the coefficient of nondetermination.

The computer is becoming a very important tool in the field of test and measurements. The typical computer is made up of input and output devices as well as a central processing unit (CPU). The CPU is further divided into an arthimetic-logical section, a control section, and a memory section. Supplemental memory devices such as magnetic tapes or disks are common with most computer systems.

The use of the computer involves programminq the machine by using one of the common computer languages such as BASIC, COBOL, or FORTRAN. The user will often develop a flow chart of plan to follow in developing the program to carry out the assigned task. The programs can be written in any known computer language; however, in computational fields such as tests and measurements, FORTRAN seems to work the best. Many packaged programs are available for the teacher and student, which will save vast amounts of time and effort.

Study Questions

1. Organize the following raw scores using the method presented.

48	35	30	20	23
27	36	29	17	33
15	26	20	28	20
30	20	29	25	29
37	33	23	20	44
28	32	41	30	21
25	30	18	21	32
35	24	13	24	17
16	38	20	32	18

2. From the date above compute the following.

(a) Mode
(b) Median
(c) Mean
(d) Range
(e) Interquartile range
(f) Quartile deviation
(g) Standard deviation

3. Compare and contrast the mode, median, and mean as measures of central tendency. Indicate when each might be used.

4. Compute a raw score correlation from the following data.

Student	*(X)*	*(Y)*
A	19	38
B	24	41
C	17	31
D	21	30
E	27	27
F	16	39
G	23	33
H	20	38
I	17	29
J	14	28

5. Interpret the correlation computed in Question 4.

6. Compute a rank-difference correlation for the following data.

Student	*Rank in Ladder Tournament (X)*	*Raw Scores on* Skill Test (*Y*)
A	3	97
B	7	64
C	1	106
D	4	93
E	9	61
F	2	110
G	8	71
H	5	80
I	6	74
J	10	64

7. Interpret the correlation obtained in Question 6.

8. Identify some uses of the computer in tests and measurements.

9. Why would a flow chart be useful in writing a complex computer program?

10. Diagram and discuss the characteristics of a typical computer. Include in your discussion the various options within each of the main characteristics of the computer.

11. Use one of the programs found in Appendix F and ask your computer center to help you in running the program with a set of real or hypothetical test scores.

CHAPTER **4**

Norms and Their Use in Physical Education

After you have read and studied this chapter you should be able to:

1. Define the term "norm."
2. Differentiate beween criterion-referenced and norm-referenced measures.
3. Explain the factors important in developing and interpreting norms and individual test scores.
4. Differentiate between age, grade, percentile, and standard-score norms.
5. Calculate percentiles from ungrouped data.
6. Calculate various types of standard scores given the raw scores, mean, and standard deviation of the distribution.
7. Evaluate each type of norm in terms of uses, advantages, and disadvantages.
8. Interpret a raw score in a distribution in terms of several types of norms.
9. Outline the uses of national and local norms.

David, an 11-year-old, completes the shuttle run, an item on the AAHPER Youth Fitness Test, in 10.9 seconds. Kristin, a 12-year-old, completes the same test in 10.9 seconds. What do these scores mean? How good are they? They are numerically equal but do they have the same meaning for an 11-year-old boy as for a 12-year-old girl? Obviously, once David and Kristin have completed the test, the performance has meaning to each of them. The times may be better or worse than previous performances. If others of the same ages have taken the same test, their scores could be compared. A simple ranking of times from best to worst for both boys and girls would give additional meaning to the performances because, then, David and Kristin could compare their scores with the rest of the respective classes. But the scores still have limited meaning. The test item, the shuttle run, has been given to many students, and the AAHPER has developed percentile standards of performance for various age levels. These norms provide more meaning to the scores. For example, according to the AAHPER Youth Fitness Test Manual, David's shuttle run time of 10.9 seconds has a percentile rank of 50. Fifty percent of the 11-year-old boys of a national sample have scores equal to or lower than David's. His score falls in the middle of the distribution of 11-year-old shuttle run scores. Kristin's score of 10.9 seconds, when compared with national norms for 12-year-old girls, has a percentile rank of 70. Her score, then, is better than about two thirds of the girls her age. The use of percentile norms thus gives a deeper meaning to the actual scores. David and Kristin may or may not be in the top half of their specific classes, but the norms indicate that their scores are at least as good as most students their ages.

Consider another example. Mr. Thompson, a physical education instructor at the college level, teaches a beginning racquetball class. Doran, a student in the class, takes a knowledge test constructed by Mr. Thompson and scores a 40. What does this mean? How should his score be interpreted? At face value, the score of 40 has very little meaning. Suppose there were 50 items. Therefore, Doran had 40 of 50 correct answers or 80 percent. What then? Assume that another knowledge test in racquetball is available. It is also a 50-item test, but it is normally taken by those who wish to become a qualified referee and is much more complex than the first test. Another score of 40 would have a vastly different meaning, even though 40 of 50 items is 80 percent.

The scores on the tests have very little meaning or significance unless there is some standard with which to compare them. Consider the possibility that Doran was unable to answer any question correctly on the referee test. Does this mean he has zero racquetball knowledge? Actually he may be able to answer many questions regarding racquetball. Therefore, a person who has 40 right does not demonstrate twice the knowledge of someone who has 20. In practice, a teacher assumes students have a certain amount of basic knowledge and measures from that arbitrary point. This prevents interpreting a zero score as no achievement at all. Qualified terms such as "more" or "less" can be used to describe achievement on a given characteristic but not quantified terms such as "twice" as much.

To overcome this lack of a definite frame of reference in educational measurement, a variety of methods of expressing scores has been developed. This chapter is divided into two major categories. The first deals with *interpreting test scores* while the second part discusses various *norms*, their calculation, and uses.

INTERPRETING TEST SCORES

Raw Scores

If a student answers 40 questions correctly on a 50 question test, his or her raw score will be 40. A *raw score*, then, is the actual score an individual obtains on a test, when the test has been scored according to directions. Even if some items are weighted more than others or all items are worth more than one point, the score obtained is the raw score.

Interpretation of a raw score is difficult and not meaningful without further information. Meaning can be given to a raw score by converting it into a description of specific tasks that the pupil can perform. This is called a *criterion-referenced* interpretation. Another method of enhancing meaning is by converting the raw score into some type of derived score that indicates the student's relative position in a clearly defined reference group. This second method is called a *norm-referenced* interpretation.

Criterion-Referenced Measures

A criterion-referenced interpretation allows describing an individual's test performance without reference to the performance of others. For example, student performance may be described in terms of the speed or the accuracy with which a task is performed, the percentage of items correct on some defined set of learning tasks, or the proportion learned of what he or she could have learned. A common method is the conversion of raw scores to percentage-correct scores and is widely used for competency-based tests.

This ordinarily involves writing behavioral objectives and using sufficient items for each objective to make it possible to describe test performance in terms of a student's competency or mastery of each objective. For example, in the racquetball knowledge tests described earlier, an 80 percent level of mastery may be set by the instructor. The instructor must construct representative test items within prescribed limits of the behavioral objectives.

There are two consequences of using percentage-correct scores on written tests. The first lies in the determination of the difficulty of the test. The racquetball knowledge test for beginners and the racquetball test for potential referees vary in difficulty, but no real basis is available for determining appropriate difficulty levels. A second consequence is the necessity of different standards for different groups. The racquetball knowledge test for referees, if given to both beginners and potential referees, might have different mastery levels. For example, mastery for beginners could be 50 percent of the items while mastery for prospective referees might be as high as 90 percent. For these reasons the majority of standardized tests are not criterion-referenced.

Tests of motor skills are more often criterion-referenced. When a skill test is given, usually there are a number of trials of the same specific task (i.e., sit-ups). The test often does not contain different items of various difficulty levels. Experience in testing can help determine what competency or mastery level is selected. Still, there is the problem of making direct comparisons with percentage-correct scores. Consider this example: bent-leg sit-ups are often used to measure endurance of the abdominal muscles, and are often an item in a test battery that measures physical fitness. From prior experience, a high school physical educator selects 80 as the maximum performance for boys and 60 as the maximum performance for girls. A boy who performs 60 bent-leg sit-ups has a percentage-correct score of 67. A girl who performs 40 sit-ups has the same percentage-correct score of 67. However, the scores really should not be compared.

A knowledge of percent-correct sit-ups will not help in making comparisons with other items of fitness tests nor will it be applicable for comparison of two different groups on the same test. For these reasons, norm-referenced measures are most often used. We do not discourage the use of criterion-referenced measures. They should be used and reported when possible, especially when mastery or competency levels are prescribed in behavioral objectives.

Norm-Referenced Measures

Norm-referenced measurements allow interpretation of students' achievement in terms of the performance of others who have taken the same test. One simple way to utilize a norm-referenced interpretation is to rank scores from high to low and identify where individual performances occur. This ranking is common in developing grades and is easy to interpret for both student and teacher. However, this ranking system loses significance beyond the specific class because the meaning of rank is based upon the number of group members. More sophisticated normative systems have been developed utilizing *derived* scores.

A derived score is a numerical measure of test performance on a score scale that has well-defined characteristics and gives normative meaning. Derived scores most commonly used in physical education fall into four categories: *age equivalents*, *grade equivalents*, *percentile ranks*, and *standard scores*. Age- and grade-derived scores describe test performance in terms of the group in which the students' raw score is *average*. Percentile ranks and standard scores demonstrate the student's relative standing in some particular group.

NORMS

Norms represent the achievement level of a particular group to which obtained scores can be compared. In a table of norms, raw scores and derived scores are typically presented in parallel columns for easy conversion to derived scores. Examples of such tables can be found in norms for various tests in Chapter 13.

It is obvious that a test accompanied by norms has several advantages over tests without norms. Norms enable the instructor to interpret student scores in relation to a large group in the same population. Their use enables a comparison of the performance of a student with other pupils, and gives uniform meaning to the comparison of a student's score on one test with his or her score on another. In addition, norms provide a reliable and useful basis for interpretation and evaluation of test results.

There are several important factors, all of which must be taken into consideration in the development and use of norms. These same criteria are important in evaluating the adequacy of norms already developed and in interpreting scores based on norms. These factors are:

1. *Sample.* The sample must include a large number of cases.

Generally, the larger the sample the more likely it approximates the population. Sampling procedures must be based on a wide distribution of the population. If national norms are to be developed, geographical distribution is an important factor. Even in developing or using local norms, residency (geographical distribution) must be taken into consideration. Other factors such as age, sex, race, educational level, socioeconomic status, and sampling method are also important.

2. *Administration.* The administration of the test must be standardized. Directions should be clear and concise. The test situation has to be taken seriously by the test administrator as well as the students taking the test. Scoring instructions for the test must also be clear and relatively simple.
3. *Representativeness.* Norms should be representative of the population for which the test is intended. They must not be applied to groups of students for which the norms were not originally established. For national norms the sampling procedure is especially important. In evaluating test norms, emphasis must be given to sampling procedure as well as size. The more closely students approximate those in the group used for norm development, the more it is certain that the norms are a meaningful source for comparison.
4. *Temporariness.* Norms should be currently applicable. In general, norms are temporary and can be expected to change. They must be periodically evaluated. For example, norms for the AAHPER Youth Fitness Test were first developed in 1958 and updated in 1963 and again in 1975. An example of the temporary nature of norms is shown by the 600-yard run for girls, an item of the AAHPER Youth Fitness Test. (Figure 4.1). If norms are old and have not been reevaluated, their worth as a basis for interpretation is seriously in question.
5. *Presentation.* Norms should be presented in a format that is easily understood. Typical norms used for physical education tests include various standard score scales, percentile norms, as well as age and grade norms.
6. *Comparability.* Often, it is necessary to compare scores from different tests to evaluate student performance. The norms for the separate tests should be comparable. In a battery of tests such as the AAHPER Youth Fitness Test it is important that each item uses the same sample in the development of norms. Without this, the norms may not be representative and should be questioned.

Although it will soon be demonstrated that norms are advantageous to develop and use, certain cautions must be applied to the interpretation of test scores. A test score should be interpreted in the following ways.

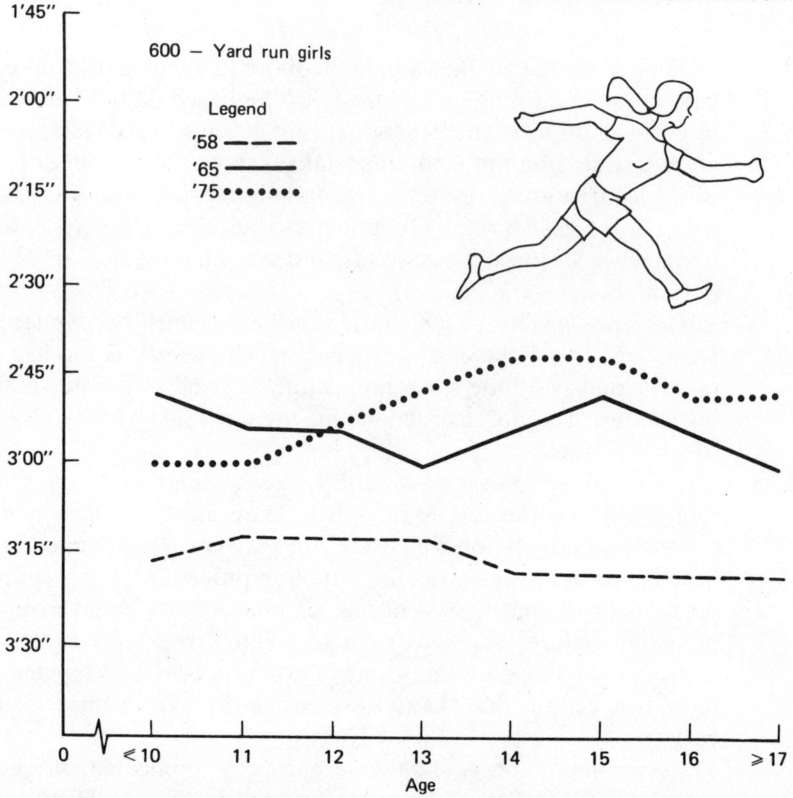

Figure 4.1. Comparisons of norms of the 600-yard run for girls of various ages (from *AAHPER Youth Fitness Manual*, Revised 1976 Edition, American Alliance for Health, Physical Education, and Recreation, Washington D.C., 1976, p. 2; reprinted by permission).

1. *As a specific test score derived from a specific test.* Various tests of motor ability and physical fitness measure different traits. With such great variation it is misleading to interpret a student's score as representing general achievement in any particular area.
2. *In terms of the relevant characteristics of the student.* Test performance is influenced by the student's aptitude, educational experiences, cultural background, emotional adjustment, health, etc. Consequently if a student performs poorly on a fitness test, it is appropriate first to consider the possibility of illness or lack of motivation that may have contributed to his or her poor performance. Such factors apply to cognitive tests in physical education as well as to tests of the psychomotor and affective domain.
3. *In terms of the type of decision to be made.* The meaning of the test score is determined to a considerable extent by the use to be made of it. For example, scores on a backboard test of tennis ability would have different meanings if the teacher or coach were selecting team members for a college tennis team, testing skill in a college activity

class, or using the scores as a criterion to determine the best of three different methods of teaching tennis. Test scores are much more useful when they are evaluated in terms of their significance to the specific decision to be made.

4. *As a band of scores rather than a specific value.* Every test score is subject to error. This error must always be considered when the test is interpreted. To allow for possible error, a student's test performance can be interpreted as being in a band of scores one standard deviation above and below his or her obtained score. Bands help prevent making interpretations more precise than the test results warrant. Percentile bands, for instance, have been developed for use with the AAHPER Cooperative Physical Education Tests.
5. *As supplementary evidence.* It is impossible to determine the extent to which the basic assumptions of testing have been met such as optimum motivation and similar background in subject area. Likewise, it is difficult to determine which conditions of testing have been precisely controlled. For instance, a skill test may be administered differently by separate testers or may be scored differently by different scorers. Thus, a test score may contain an indeterminate number of errors because of unmet assumptions and uncontrolled conditions. One protection against such errors is to place little reliance on a single test score.

A summary of the most common types of test norms is presented in Table 4.1. The remainder of this chapter will deal with the characteristics, advantages, limitations, calculation, and use of these norms.

Table 4.1 Norms Used in Physical Education

Norm	*Comparison*	*Interpretation*
Age Norms	Successive age groups	Age group in which student's score is average
Grade Norms	Successive grade groups	Grade group in which student's score is average
Percentile Norms	Age or grade group in which student is a member	Percentile of scores that fall below student's score
Standard Score Norms	Age or grade group in which student is a member	Distance in standard deviation units that student's score is above or below the mean

Age Norms

These norms can be constructed for any trait or performance that shows a progressive change with age. They are based on the average scores earned by students at different ages and are interpreted through the use of age equivalents. A student's raw score is then interpreted in terms of an age equivalent or age average. For example, if the average shuttle run for 11-year-old boys is 10.9 seconds, a score of 10.9 seconds has an age equivalent of 11 years. Age norms are sometimes subdivided into months, ranging for example from 10 years 0 months to 10 years 11 months. Table of age norms typically present parallel columns of raw scores and their age equivalents.

Notice that age equivalents indicate average or "normal" performance of students of various ages. For any particular age, 50 percent of the students in the sample group are above the norm and 50 percent are below. There should be no specific goal expected of each student. If about half of a group of students performs above and half below the age norm, we may conclude that the group essentially conforms to the norms. Whether this characteristic is positive or negative depends on a number of factors including the ability of the students, the extent to which the curriculum of the school is represented by the test, and the quality of the educational environment. In any event, the norm is representative of normal performance of average students in typical schools and should not be considered as a standard of excellence to be achieved by others. This same limitation holds true for grade norms, which will be discussed later.

The use of age norms in physical education is somewhat limited, since a student's maturational age is often more indicative of physical performance than chronological age. Clarke found in the Medford Boys Growth Study that great differences exist in the physiological maturity of students of the same chronological age. For example, at age 14, "approximately two thirds of 168 boys tested had skeletal ages between 14 and 16 years — a span of two years; yet, these same boys were tested within two months of their birthdays, so they could not vary chronologically by more than four months. The skeletal range, of course, was much greater, between 10.3 and 16.9 years."*

Age norms in physical education-related areas are used for traits that depend on normal growth. Norms for preschool and elementary school motor development, for example, would be appropriate in terms of age equivalents. The use of age norms is more popular with achievement tests in such general education areas as reading, mental ability, and mathematics, which occur fairly continuously and regularly through the elementary school years.

In addition to the limitations outlined there are other disadvantages in the use and interpretation of age norms.

H. Harrison Clarke, *The Application of Measurement to Health and Physical Education*, Fifth Edition, 1976, pp. 70-71. Reprinted by permission of Prentice-Hall Inc., Englewood Cliffs, New Jersey.

1. Units are not equal on different parts of the norm scale. One year's growth does not mean the same at one level as it does at another and, therefore, the scale lacks uniform measuring. For example, there might be much more or much less improvement in volleyball ability from age 8.00 to 9.00 years than from 11.00 to 12.00 years. Being advanced, then, often has a different meaning for different parts of the age norm scale.
2. An additional liability occurs as growth in a trait slows down as a student reaches maturity. For example, a flattening of the normal height curve for boys has an added problem in giving an age equivalent for a 6 foot-6 inch boy. At no age will a 6 foot-6 inch boy ever be average. Likewise, growth in a number of psychological traits is uneven.
3. Growth curves are substantially different for different traits and therefore not comparable. A 5-year-old performing at an age 7 equivalent in a motor skill test may have much more superiority than a five-year-old performing at an age 7 equivalent in a reading test, and any comparison between the two performances makes little sense.
4. A common misinterpretation of age norms is to assume that if a student performs on a test at a certain age equivalency, he is ready to do work at that level. Performances may be caused by rapid and accurate work. A literal interpretation of the norm should be avoided.
5. The use of age norms at the high school level is usually not very meaningful since growth in many abilities tapers off during the high school years.

In summary, age norms are based on the average performance of students at various age levels. They are relatively easy to understand. Comparisons of different traits are difficult to make because of the lack of uniformity of units. They are most meaningful at the elementary school level, where growth is relatively continuous, and lose meaning as adulthood is reached. Such physical traits as age, height, and motor development are appropriate for interpretation by age norms.

Grade Norms

Grade and age norms have similar characteristics and uses. Grade norms are based on the average scores earned by students of several grades and are interpreted through the use of grade equivalents. If grade norms are constructed for the shuttle run, for example, and the average time for fourth grade boys is 10.9 seconds, a score of 10.9 seconds has a grade equivalent of 4th grade. Grade norms are often subdivided into grade and month equivalents. A student whose raw score is indicative of a fourth grade performance at the beginning of the school year has a grade equivalent of 4th grade 0 months. A student whose score is indicative of a performance at the middle of the year has a grade equivalent of 4th grade 5 months. Thus, most grade norms have delineations of grade equivalents in tenths. This division assumes there is little change in test performance during summer vacations. In practice, a raw score that falls between the norm for two successive grades is given the grade equivalent by interpolation. Tables of grade norms typically present parallel columns of raw scores and their grade equivalents.

The uses of grade norms are similar to those mentioned earlier for age norms. Since students are usually placed into grades by chronological age, many differences in physical or skeletal development are present within each grade. Grade norms have limited use in physical education. Developing norm equivalents for each grade is difficult, especially in the performance of physical skills. They are much more popular at the elementary level in subjects such as arithmetic, reading, and language skills, which receive relatively consistent emphasis. One reason for this popularity is that norms in these areas are easy to develop since the norm equivalents are based on grades that are already present in a typical school system. The concept of performing at a certain grade level is also meaningful to teachers, students, and parents alike.

To summarize, grade norms are not often used in measures of physical performance. They are used at the elementary school level because of the relative ease of development and interpretation, especially in monitoring growth in basic subjects such as mathematics and reading. Grade equivalents are based on units that are unequal from grade to grade, and this complicates interpretation substantially. Other limitations on the use of grade norms parallel those of age norms.

Percentile Norms

One of the most commonly used methods of describing relative status of test performance is the percentile rank. Norms using percentiles are widely applicable, appropriate for many situations, and easy to interpret by the student as well as the instructor. Percentile norms have been developed for several popular tests in physical education. Examples are the AAHPER Youth Fitness Test, the AAHPER Sports Skills Tests, and the Texas Physical Fitness-Motor Ability Test, all of which include percentile norms for boys and girls of various ages. Grouping by age should not be confused with age norms. When age norms are used, the age is the norm. With percentile norms, the percentile rank is the norm. A test in the sociological area, the Cowell Social Behavior Trend Index, also gives scores using percentile rank.

A percentile score norm indicates a student's relative position in a group. It informs the student of the percentage of students who score below his or her score. Percentile norms for the 50-yard dash, an item of the AAHPER Youth Fitness Test, are presented in Table 4.2. As an example, for 10-year-old boys a score of 8.2 seconds equals a percentile rank of 50. That is, an individual who runs the 50-yard dash in 8.2 seconds scores better than 50 percent of the group on which the norms were based. A boy of the same age who is able to run the 50-yard dash in 7.3 seconds, which corresponds to the 95th percentile, surpasses 95 percent of the group on which the norms were based. In many percentile tables all percentiles are not shown. In Table 4.2, for instance, the percentiles are given by steps of five score units. Because percentile norms do not consider the distance between scores, a single score may represent different percentile values, as in the case of an 8.0 second 50-yard dash. It is even possible for different scores to represent the same percentile value. In Table 4.2 a time of 9.9 and 10.0 both have a percentile rank of 5. If the norm table were presented in greater detail, these scores would represent different percentile ranks. Practically, however, finding a student's position to the nearest 5 percentile points usually is sufficient.

Percentile norms are especially useful in physical education because many components of the psychomotor domain can be tested. Percentiles allow a comparison of the performances on different test items. For example, performances on all of the items of the AAHPER Youth Fitness Test can be compared. A teacher can compare an 8.2-second performance in the 50-yard dash with a performance of 5 feet, 8 inches in the standing long jump. The 8.2 50-yard dash corresponds to the 50th percentile while a 5 feet-8 inch standing long jump corresponds to the 85th percentile. The student's score is much better than the average score in the group used for norms in the standing long jump, but average in the 50-yard dash. With percentiles there is a reference point from which to compare the two different items.

Thus far, discussion of percentiles has centered on the interpreting and utilizing of standardized percentile norms. Perhaps a more practical use of percentile norms is possible in all teacher-made testing situations. Percentile norms can be used to interpret a student's performance in terms of any group in which he or she is a member. Usually, performance is reported in terms of the student's percentile ranking in his or her own class or age group. When the number of subjects is small, percentiles and percentile ranks are less meaningful. For example, if six students completed a 30-second rally test in racquetball and the scores were 12, 15, 17, 19, 21, and 24 respectively, little meaning would be added to the raw data by calculating percentiles. Ordinary ranking procedures are probably sufficient for interpretation of the scores. Typically, group sizes must be much larger or comparisons must be made to previously developed percentile norms.

Calculation of Percentiles. Percentiles can bc calculated from both grouped and ungrouped data. Because of the extensive use of the electronic calculator, only ungrouped procedures are presented in this chapter. See Appendix E for the grouped technique.

Table 4.2 Norms: 50-Yard Dash for Boys

	Percentile Scores Based on Age								*Test Scores in Seconds and Tenths*
Age Percentile	9-10	11	12	13	14	15	16	17+	Percentile
100th	7.0	6.3	6.3	5.8	5.9	5.5	5.5	5.4	100th
95th	7.3	7.1	6.8	6.5	6.2	6.0	6.0	5.9	95th
90th	7.5	7.2	7.0	6.7	6.4	6.2	6.2	6.0	90th
85th	7.7	7.4	7.1	6.9	6.5	6.3	6.3	6.1	85th
80th	7.8	7.5	7.3	7.0	6.6	6.4	6.4	6.3	80th
75th	7.8	7.6	7.4	7.0	6.8	6.5	6.5	6.3	75th
70th	7.9	7.7	7.5	7.1	6.9	6.6	6.5	6.4	70th
65th	8.0	7.9	7.5	7.2	7.0	6.6	6.6	6.5	65th
60th	8.0	7.9	7.6	7.3	7.0	6.8	6.6	6.5	60th
55th	8.1	8.0	7.7	7.4	7.1	6.8	6.7	6.6	55th
50th	8.2	8.0	7.8	7.5	7.2	6.9	6.7	6.6	50th
45th	8.4	8.2	7.9	7.5	7.3	6.9	6.8	6.7	45th
40th	8.6	8.3	8.0	7.6	7.4	7.0	6.8	6.8	40th
35th	8.7	8.4	8.1	7.7	7.5	7.1	6.9	6.9	35th
30th	8.8	8.5	8.2	7.9	7.6	7.2	7.0	7.0	30th
25th	8.9	8.6	8.3	8.0	7.7	7.3	7.0	7.0	25th
20th	9.0	8.7	8.5	8.1	7.9	7.4	7.1	7.1	20th
15th	9.2	9.0	8.6	8.3	8.0	7.5	7.2	7.3	15th
10th	9.5	9.1	9.0	8.7	8.2	7.6	7.4	7.5	10th
5th	9.9	9.5	9.5	9.0	8.8	8.0	7.7	7.9	5th
0	11.0	11.5	11.3	15.0	11.1	11.0	9.9	12.0	0

Source. AAHPER Youth Fitness Test Manual. Revised 1976 Edition, American Allicance for Health, Physical Education, and Recreation, 1976, p. 50. Reprinted by permission.

Although there is a distinction between a percentile point and a percentile rank, the terms have essentially the same interpretations. This distinction is aptly described in Ferguson (1976). A percentile rank is a value on a derived or transformed scale corresponding to the percentile point on an original scale. If 80 percent of the students taking a test score less than 50, 50 is the 80th percentile point. If 50 is a score below which 80 percent of the individuals fall, then 80 is the corresponding percentile rank. All values on the transformed scale (percentile rank) correspond to values on the original scale (percentile point). No matter what the distribution of the raw scores, the percentile points and ranks will range from 1 to 99. Technically, it is not possible to achieve a 100 percentile rank since a student cannot beat or be worse than his or her own score. For an illustration of the calculation of percentiles, consider the information in Table 4.3.

Table 4.3 Physical Fitness Knowledge Test Scores, Arranged in Order ($N=30$)

Student	*Score*	*Student*	*Score*
1	10	16	22
2	11	17	22
3	13	18	23
4	14	19	24
5	15	20	24
6	16	21	24
7	17	22	24
8	17	23	25
9	18	24	26
10	18	25	26
11	19	26	27
12	19	27	28
13	21	28	29
14	21	29	29
15	22	30	30

To calculate any percentile, the following formula is applicable.

$$P_x = N(x)$$

where P_x = the desired percentile score

N = number of students

x = percentile desired

For example, to determine the 20th percentile or the point below which 20 percent of the students' scores lie, the following computations must be made.

$P_x = N(x)$	$P_x = 30\,(.20)$	Substituting .20
	$P_x = 6$	for x and 30 for N

Therefore, the sixth score as shown in Table 4.3 is the 20th percentile. In reality, numerical data are considered to be continuous. Continuous data imply that a number has real and actual limits. The lower real limit of 16 is 15.5 while the upper real limit is 16.5. A further discussion of real and actual limits is found in Appendix E. The upper real limit is used in interpreting percentiles. Therefore, the actual score of 16 is included in the group of scores below which 20 percent of the scores lie. Or to put it another way, in a group of 30 scores the sixth score falls below the 20th percentile and the remaining 24 scores above comprise the remaining 80 percent of the scores.

To determine the 90th percentile,

$Px = N(x)$	$Px = 30.\,(.90)$	substituting .90 for x
	$30\,(.90) = 27$	and 30 for N

Ninety percent of the scores then lie below the upper real limit of the 27th score, which is 28.5.

Approximation and interpolation may be required to calculate some percentiles. With the data in Table 4.3, calculation of P_{40} requires some approximation. The 40th percentile is a point below which 12 and above which 18 of the scores lie. The twelfth student in the distribution has a raw score of 19, which has an upper real limit of 19.5. However, the thirteenth student has a score of 21, which has a lower real limit of 20.5. Therefore, P_{40} falls somewhere between 19.5 and 20.5. By interpolation of a value, halfway between these two values is chosen. Thus $P_{40} = 20$. This was found by determining the arithmetic average of the two upper real limits.

Ties in raw scores require interpolation in the computation of percentiles. Consider the computation of P_{70}, the point below which 21 and above which 9 of the scores lie. Students 19, 20, 21, and 22 have the same raw score of 24. The raw score 24 has a lower real limit of 23.5 and an upper real limit of 24.5. Since four students occupy this position, P_{70} by interpolation is one fourth of the way into the interval, or 23.5 + .25, or 23.75. Since percentiles are written as whole numbers, the nearest whole number, 24, is used.

The calculation of some specific percentiles has proved to be very meaningful. Such percentiles have been utilized in evaluation for classification purposes, for grading and comparing individuals and groups to each other. Several key percentiles have been identified, namely the *median*, *quartiles*, and *deciles*. The median, described in Chapter 3, is actually the 50th percentile and is a point below which 50 percent of the scores lie. Quartiles, which are often calculated, have Q_1 or the first quartile as the 25th percentile, Q_2 or the second quartile as the 50th percentile, and Q_3 or the third quartile as the 75th percentile. In addition, deciles are sometimes calculated, dividing the 100 percentiles into 10 equal parts. The 10th percentile is synonomous with the 1st decile, the 20th percentile is equal to the 2nd decile, and each of the remaining deciles are represented by percentiles in a similar manner. The relationship of percentiles and deciles to quartiles, and the median is shown in Table 4.4. The percentiles for the ungrouped data from Table 4.3 are also shown.

Table 4.4 Selected Percentiles, Deciles, Quartiles, and the Median From an Ungrouped Distribution of Physical Fitness Knowledge Test Scores (*N* = 30)

Raw Score	Percentile	Deciles	Quartiles	Median
30	P_{99}			
28	P_{90}	D_9		
26	P_{80}	D_8		
25	P_{75}		Q_3	
24	P_{70}	D_7		
23	P_{60}	D_6		
22	P_{50}	D_5	Q_2	Mdn
20	P_{40}	D_4		
18	P_{30}	D_3		
17	P_{25}		Q_1	
16	P_{20}	D_2		
13	P_{10}	D_1		
12	P_5			
	P_4			
	P_3			
	P_2			
10	P_1			

Additional information is contained in Table 4.4. For instance, 50 percent of the students scored below the score 22. By subtracting the raw score of one decile from the raw score of the next higher decile, the *interdecile difference* can be found. These interdecile differences, when calculated for the entire distribution, give information regarding the concentration of scores. Similar information is attained when the *quartile deviation* is calculated as discussed in Chapter 3. The middle 50 percent of the scores, the interquartile range, is between 17 and 25; therefore the quartile deviation, which is one half of the interquartile range, is 4.

For most practical purposes, all percentiles are not computed. A simple procedure is to calculate the deciles, D_1, D_2 . . . D_9, and then interpolate between them for other desired percentiles. Refer to Table 4.4. If only the deciles were calculated, the first quartile, Q_1, and third quartile, Q_3, as well as most of the other percentiles not shown, could be calculated by interpolation.

Percentile norms are widely used in physical education. However, they should be used with caution. The major limitation of percentile norms is the problem of inequality between units. A percentile difference of 10 near the middle of the scale represents a much smaller difference in raw scores than the same percentile difference near the ends of the distribution. For example, in Table 4.4, although the data are not normally distributed, a percentile difference of 20 near the low end of the scale ($P_{30} - P_{10}$) represents a much greater difference in raw scores than a percentile difference of 20 near the middle of the scale ($P_{70} - P_{50}$). The raw score differences are 5 and 2 respectively. This variation occurs because a large number of students tend to score near the middle, while comparatively few individuals have extremely high or low scores.

Figure 4.2 clearly demonstrates the inequality of percentile units when data are normally distributed. The distances between the shown percentiles at the lower and upper ends of the scale are much greater than those near the middle. Equal percentile differences are not representative of like differences in raw scores. This occurs because the raw score distribution is changed into a rectangular distribution with 100 equal parts representing the percentiles. For illustration purposes, only the deciles are shown in Figure 4.2. Each decile contains the same number of raw scores. Thus, a student whose raw score is near average can surpass another 10 percent of the class by increasing his or her raw score just a few points. In comparison, however, a student close to either end of the percentile scale must improve his or her score by a greater number of points, because there are so few students at the extreme levels of the distribution. In other words, the computations of percentiles are clearly not sensitive to the numerical distance between the raw scores. Because of the inequality of units, it is necessary to take special precuations when interpreting percentiles. A difference of several percentiles at the end of the scale should be given greater weight than percentile differences near the middle of the distribution. Also, because of the inequality of units, percentiles cannot be averaged arithmetically. However P_{50}, the median, which is the middle score in the distribution, is sometimes a better estimate of a distribution than the mean or arithmetic average. Certain other limitations of percentiles must be considered in their use and interpretation. The group used in the development of norms is always an important consideration. It makes no sense to evaluate 10-year-olds with norms based on the performances of 14-year-olds. The appropriate norm group in every situation is the group to which the individual belongs and must be compared.

A student has a certain percentile rank in some particular group. A raw score of 9.5 seconds in the AAHPER shuttle run may be the 60th percentile for 17-year-old boys according to the national norms, but only the 40th percentile when high school athletes are considered, and only the 20th percentile when compared with students who have received a college athletic scholarship

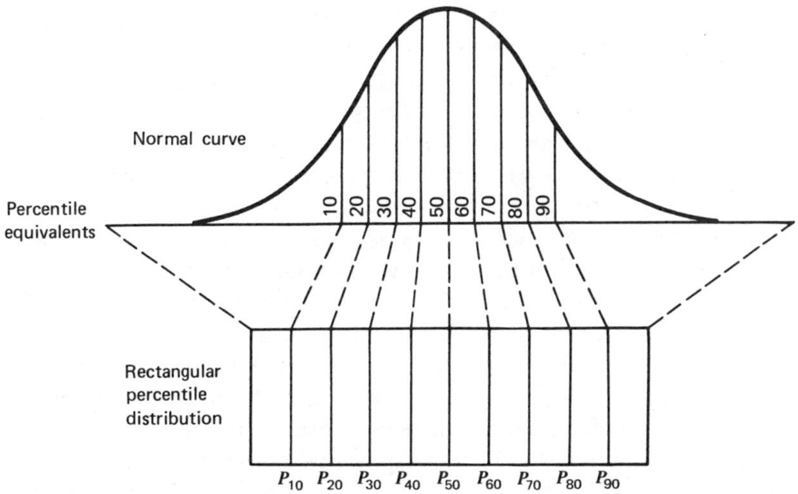

Figure 4.2. The normal curve compared with the rectangular distribution of percentiles.

offer. Relative standing within percentile ranks obviously changes when different reference groups are used for comparison. Thus, a need exists for numerous sets of norms. At the secondary school level, where various curricula are offered, there is especially a need for different sets of norms based upon courses completed and educational and vocational choices. However, there is often difficulty in developing numerous sets of norms. Although many standardized tests have norms for various age and grade levels, it is obvious that local norms are often more valuable than nationally standardized norms. For instance, national norms have been developed for each item of the AAHPER Youth Fitness Test. Great value could be obtained from developing local norms, which will then permit interpretation of individual scores in terms of the local group.

In summary, percentile norms are widely used, easily calculated, and relatively well understood. They provide a basis for interpreting an individual's score in terms of his or her standing in some specified group. Numerous sets of norms are needed for meaningful interpretations, but local norms are often more important than published norms. The major drawback of percentile norms is inequality of units. In the middle of the normal distribution a rather small change in the raw score gives a rather large percentile change. At the ends of the distribution the reverse is true. With careful interpretation, the limitations of percentiles can be overcome.

Standard Score Norms

Because of the limitations of a norm system based on percentiles, attempts have been made to find scales that have units with the same meaning throughout the entire range of scores. Several sophisticated standard-score scales have been developed to serve this purpose. Figure 4.3 presents a normal curve together with commonly used standard-score scales. They are *z*-scores, *T*-scores, stanine scores, six-sigma scale, and the Hull scale. Standard-score norms have been developed for many physical education tests. The *z*-score serves as a basis for the other standard scores but is not used in reporting norms for reasons that will be discussed later. The *T*-scale is very popular as a tool to present norms for physical education traits. A few examples of some tests that use the *T*-score as a norm are the Iowa-Brace Test of Motor Ability, the Scott Motor Ability Test, the Harrison Basketball Test for Boys, the Borleske Touch Football Test, the Fox Swimming Power Test, and Wear Attitude Inventory. Other standard score systems have been used less frequently in the presentation of norms. Stanine scores, for example, have been used in the AAHPER Cooperative Physical Education Tests. The six-sigma scale is currently utilized in the National Section of Women Athletics (now the NAGWS) Physical Performance Test, the Dyer Backboard Test in tennis, and the Russell-Lange Volleyball Test, while the Hull-scale has been utilized with the Oregon Cable Tension Strength Tests.

As stated earlier, standard scores have a distinct advantage over the percentile rank. With standard scores, the relative performance of an individual can be expressed in units that are equal over the entire scale so that a small difference at one point on the scale has the same meaning as an equal difference at some other point.

***z*-Score.** A measure of central tendency, the mean, and a measure of variability, the standard deviation, are used in determining a *z*-score, which is the basic standard score. The meaning and computation of the mean and standard deviation as well as the normal curve were discussed in Chapter 3. A *z*-score represents the number of standard deviations by which a particular raw score deviates from the mean of the distribution. Further more, a *z*-score occurs in a modified distribution having a mean of zero and a standard deviation of 1.0. This meaning can be interpreted in the formula for calculating *z*, which is

$$z = \frac{X - \overline{X}}{s}$$

where

X = raw score

X = arithmetic mean of raw scores

s = standard deviation of raw scores

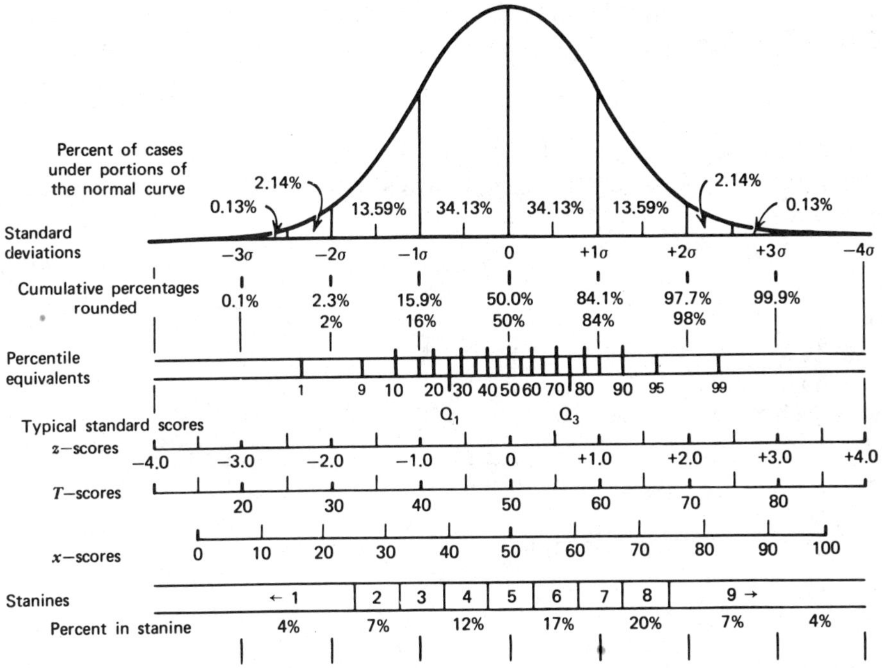

Figure 4.3. The normal curve and various scales (from H. Harrison Clarke, *Application of Measurement to Health and Physical Education*, Fifth Edition, 1976, p. 358; reprinted by permission of Prentice-Hall, Inc., Englewood Cliffs, New Jersey).

By subtracting the mean from each score in a typical distribution of scores, a new distribution is obtained with a mean equal to zero. Then if we divide each of the above by the standard deviations of the raw scores, a standard deviation of 1.0 results for the new distribution. This can easily be seen by inspecting Figure 4.3. The *z*-scores can be positive or negative and will generally vary between ± 3.00.

Consider an example. The data in Table 4.5 has been found for two members of a group of 13-year-old boys on several standardized tests. The Cooper 12-minute run is a popular cardiorespiratory endurance test. The Iowa-Brace Test of Motor Educability measures inherent motor skills by testing performance on 10 separate stunts. In the rebounding item of the Harrison Basketball Test, the subject tosses the ball against the backboard and returns it as often as possible for 30 seconds. Finally, a teacher-made test of bowling knowledge is provided as an example in this table.

To compute a *z*-score, the group mean is subtracted from each raw score and the difference is divided by the standard deviation. For example, we will compute Paul's *z*-score for the Cooper 12-minute run.

$$z = \frac{1.9 - 1.5}{.2} = \frac{.4}{.2} = 2.00$$

How is the z interpreted? It indicates that Paul obtained a raw score that was 2.00 standard score units above the mean of the group within the new z distribution.

Table 4.5 A Comparison of Two Students' Raw Scores (X) and Standard Scores (z) on Four Tests

			Paul		Mark	
Test	$\bar{X}$	s	X	z	X	z
12-Minute Run	1.5 mi	.2	1.9	2.00	1.4	−.50
Iowa Brace	14	3	11	−1.00	17	1.00
Harrison Basketball	23	4	17	−1.50	25	.50
Bowling Knowledge	30	2	36	3.00	30	0.00
				2.50		1.00

Mark's z-score for the 12-minute run is computed below.

$$z = \frac{1.4 - 1.5}{.2} = \frac{-.1}{.2} = -.50$$

A z-score of $-.50$ indicates that Mark is one-half standard score unit below the mean. Remember that the new distribution has a mean of 0.0 and a standard deviation of 1.0. Obviously, then Mark's score is below average in distance covered in the 12-minute run.

It can be seen from the z-scores in Table 4.5 that Paul performed much better on the bowling test and 12-minute run than on the remaining two tests. Mark, on the other hand, had no extreme standard scores. Comparisons can certainly be made between students by utilizing relative standing as determined by standard scores. Paul performed much better than Mark on the 12-minute run and bowling test, but somewhat lower on the Iowa-Brace Test and rebounding test. In addition, z-scores can be used to average student scores on different tests, a procedure that cannot be done using percentiles. This averaging of standard scores is possible because all of the transformed scores (standard scores) have the same mean (0.0) and the same standard deviation (1.0). Averaging standard scores is often a great advantage. It generally makes no sense to average the raw scores on individual tests such as the Cooper 12-minute run with the scores from other tests. However, once the data is transformed into z-scores, averages may be computed and comparisons can readily be made.

In the tests illustrated, Mark actually would have a higher raw score mean score, but Paul has a much higher z-score mean as shown in Table 4.5 This disparity is caused by the relatively small numerical contribution of the Cooper 12-minute run in determining the mean for the raw scores. In reality there is no meaning derived from averaging raw scores from different types of tests. Thus, the use of the standard score yields a much more meaningful picture of individual performances and allows valid comparisons to be made.

Notice that when percentile ranks are converted to z-scores, the percentiles can then be averaged. Two assumptions must be made to obtain this average. First, the raw score distribution is assumed to be normal. Second, all percentiles are taken from the same norm group. The procedure that is necessary to compute average percentiles is as follows.

1. Convert percentiles to z-scores by using a table frequently found in most statistics books, areas and ordinates of the normal curve, and is shown in Appendix B. The z-scores can also be estimated from Figure 4.3 since each percentile in a normally distributed curve corresponds to a specific z-score. Thus, given any raw score one can find either the z or percentile.
2. Average the z-scores of the various tests.
3. Find the percentile of the average z-score by use of the table in Appendix B or Figure 4.3.

Since percentile norms are popular in interpreting physical education tests and since percentiles from different tests cannot be averaged, this technique provides a procedure for converting percentiles to z-scores, averaging the z-scores, and then converting them back to percentiles once again. This final percentile becomes the average percentile for all tests. Application and interpretation are necessary for tests that have several items such as the AAHPER Youth Fitness Test.

Even though the use of z-scores has many advantages, several limitations prevent them from being commonly used in norm tables. First, from the data given in the example and from Figure 4.3, it can be seen that z-scores may be either positive or negative. The sign of the z-score is sometimes overlooked or miscopied. A second related drawback is that in averaging z-scores, the sign of each score must be taken into consideration. Figuring the average of z-scores with unlike signs is often confusing. Finally, z-scores are expressed as decimals, which can be cumbersome. Several standard score variations have been developed to counteract the deficiencies of the basic standard z-score.

Z-Score. This is one specific variation of the z-score transformation. It transforms the z-score into a score in another new distribution that has a mean of 50 and a standard deviation of 10, thereby avoiding decimals and negative values.

To calculate Z, a simple transformation is necessary.

$$Z = 10_z + 50$$

Where Z is a standard score in a distribution with a mean of 50 and a standard deviation of 10.

A Z-score can also be calculated directly from raw scores. To accomplish this the formula for z is substituted into the above formula.

$$Z = \frac{10(X - \overline{X})}{s} + 50$$

where

X = any raw score

$\overline{X}$ = arithmetic mean of raw scores

s = standard deviation of raw scores

For an example, refer once again to the data in Table 4.5 Paul's z-score for the Harrison Basketball Rebounding Test is -1.50. His Z-score is then $10(-1.50) + 50$ or 35. This Z-score could also have been calculated directly given the raw score, the mean, and standard deviation for the distribution. A large number of subjects in a distribution of scores might result in a z distribution with a normal range of -3.00 to $+3.00$ standard score units. By referring again to Figure 4.3, we see that the Z-scores for the same distribution would range from about 20 to 80 standard score units. In a normal distribution this includes about 99.7 percent of the scores. In fact, between Z scores of 30 and 70, over 95 percent of the scores will be included in a similarly normal distribution of scores.

This occurrence provides a basis for some criticism of the Z-score. Although the Z may range mathematically from 0 to 100, Z-scores below 25 or above 75 are very uncommon. Thus, about one half of the Z scale is usually not used.

Although reference has been made to the normal distribution of scores, the Z transforms the raw score into a standard score but does not alter the distribution. The Z, therefore, is a *linear transformation*. If the distribution of scores is not normal, and in fact many are not, the distribution of Z-scores is also not normal. Some texts consider the Z-score to be identical with T-scores or instead of using the term Z-score use the terms linear T and normalized T. The linear T is actually a Z-score (linear transformation) while the normalized T, which is described in the next section involves an area transformation.

***T*-Score.** Occasionally, when a test is given, the data do not conform to the typical normal curve. Data that are not normally distributed can be converted into an artifically normalized distribution by an area transformation. This is accomplished by transforming the raw scores into *normalized* T *scores*. The normalized T is a score in a distribution with a mean of 50 and a standard deviation of 10 just as Z, thereby eliminating negative numbers and decimals. However, normalized T-scores are obtained by a completely different computational procedure. The steps in calculating the normalized T are as follows.

1. Convert each raw score into a percentile.
2. Determine the z-score that each percentile rank would have in a normal distribution, using the table found in Appendix B.
3. Convert each z-score to a normalized T using the formula $T = 10_z + 50$.

Similarly the procedure of going from raw scores to percentiles to the corresponding z-scores in a normal distribution provides a normalized z-score. This process results in a normal distribution of standard scores regardless of the nonnormal shape of the original distribution of raw scores. When T-scores are used to develop norms, the result is often called a T-scale. The T-scale has similar characteristics as Z-scores — the majority of T-scores also fall between 20 and 80, for instance — and about half of the scale is not used in a typical classroom testing situation. When test scores are normally distributed, Z and T are identical.

To calculate a normalized T-score, assuming a nonnormal distribution, refer to Table 4.3. The scores in this ungrouped distribution are not normally distributed. The T -score for the raw score 28, a relatively high score in the distribution, will be computed. The raw score 28 has the percentile rank of 90. The z-score for the 90th percentile according to the table of areas and ordinates of the normal curve (Appendix B) is $+1.28$. Transforming this z (multiplying by 10 and adding 50), a T-score of 63 is obtained.

If the entire distribution of scores in Table 4.3 were transformed to T-scores, the resultant set of scores would be artifically regrouped into a normal distribution. Therefore, the process of converting raw scores to T-scores distorts the shape of the original distribution unless the original scores were normally distributed.

Stanine Scores. These scores have been used in several standardized tests in physical education and education. The stanine system receives its name from the division of the distribution of raw scores into nine parts (standard nines). Stanine scores were originally used in World War II and in the Air Force Psychological Program.

The stanine scale is a normal distribution in which nine score categories are involved. The transformed raw score values are assigned the integers 1 to 9. The stanine scale has a mean of 5 and a standard deviation of approximately 2 (1.96). Stanine 5 is located in the exact center of the distribution and includes the interval from $-.25$ to $+.25$ in standard deviation units. Approximately 20 percent of the scores are expected to occur in stanine 5. The remaining stanines are evenly distributed above and below stanine 5. Each stanine, except for stanines 1 and 9, which cover the extremes of the distribution and are open-ended, includes a band of raw scores the width of one half of a standard deviation unit. The percentages of raw scores that are found in each of the stanine score categories from 1 to 9, respectively, are 4, 7, 12, 17, 20, 17, 12, 7, 4. Refer to Figure 4.3 for a comparison of stanines to the normal curve. The transformation of raw scores to stanines is a relatively simple process. Each stanine has a prescribed percentage of the distribution as shown above. Scores are then ranked from high to low with the top 4 percent of the scores assigned to stanine 9, the next 7 percent to stanine 8, the next 12 percent to stanine 7. The assignment is continued until all stanines have been considered. For any size group, the number of scores associated with each stanine can be determined by multiplying the number of cases (N) in the group by the percentage of cases for each stanine. Problems occasionally arise in assigning scores to stanines when ties in rank are present at the division points. Durost (1961) presents a procedure for transforming raw scores to stanine scores that provides a solution to this concern.

Stanine scores are often used in the development of local norms because of several advantages.

1. Stanines are easily computed; test scores can rapidly be converted to stanines.
2. The stanine scale uses a nine point scale that is readily understood by teachers, students, and parents.
3. Since stanines are normalized standard scores, comparison can be made from one test to another.
4. Stanines are computed like percentiles; but since they are expressed in standard score form, stanines can be added together.

Two limitations prevent stanines from being used more widely. The first is that growth cannot be shown from one year to the next. If a student's performance matches that of the norm group, he or she will retain the same position in the group and therefore will be assigned the same stanine. However, changes in performance can be seen by comparing the raw scores. A second limitation is that there are only nine categories in which scores may be placed, and they are, therefore, rather crude approximations of performance. Based on the practical nature of norm usage, stanines do provide enough refinement for use in physical education.

Sigma-Scale (6-Sigma Scale). In statistical terminology, the standard deviation is often represented by the Greek letter sigma (σ). The vast majority of scores in any distribution occur between $\pm$ 3 standard deviations. Out of this concept, a normal transformation, the sigma scale or six-sigma scale, developed. The sigma scale has a mean of 50, and typical scores may range from 0 to 100. Recall that Z-scores and normalized T-scores can range from 0 to 100, but usually are between 20 and 80 standard score units. The sigma scale attempts to use more of the scale to describe raw scores.

The sigma score may be calculated from z-scores or directly from raw scores. The mean and standard deviation of the distribution are required in order to calculate sigma scores. The formula for calculation is.

$$\text{Sigma Score} = 16.67z + 50$$

or substituting for z

$$\text{Sigma score} = \frac{50(X - \overline{X})}{3s} + 50$$

In very large distributions of scores, some student performances occasionally fall beyond ± 3 standard deviations from the mean. In the sigma scale this results in scores below 0 or above 100. Although this occurrence is infrequent, it does somewhat restrict the use of the sigma scale.

Hull Scale. The Hull scale alleviates some of the criticism common to the sigma scale and the z- or normalized T-scale. With the sigma scale, some raw scores may be given scaled scores below 0 or above 100. However, in the Z- or normalized T-scales, standard scores below 20 and above 80 are uncommon. The Hull scale utilizes all the numbers in its range of 0 to 100 without going beyond them. This is accomplished by developing a scale that extends ±3.5 standard deviations from the mean. By inspection of the normal curve in Figure 5.3, it is seen that virtually all scores will fall within this range.

The formulas for calculating the Hull score are similar to the others with the exception of the different standard deviation base. The formula for computing the Hull score from raw data is.

$$\text{Hull score} = \frac{50\,(X - \overline{X})}{3.5s} + 50 \quad \text{or} \quad \frac{100\,(X - \overline{X})}{7S} + 50$$

where

X = any raw score

$\overline{X}$ = arithmetic mean of raw scores

s = standard deviation of raw scores

The formula using z-scores is.

$$\text{Hull score} = \frac{50z}{3.5} + 50 \quad \text{or} \quad 14.29z + 50$$

The Hull scale thus seems to be very appropriate but has been used little in the standardized test norms in physical education.

Interchangeability of Norms. It would be convenient if one standard score were accepted by all as a common scale. However, as each was described, certain inherent similarities, differences, advantages, and disadvantages became apparent. Publishers of tests that have standardized norms have utilized the standard score most appropriate for their specific use. This is especially true in physical education. Normed tests have used every scale discussed in this chapter. The various standard scores are different ways of interpreting the same data.

It is important, then, to be able to convert a score on one standard scale to a corresponding score on any of the others. This is made relatively easy with the use of Figure 4.3, which includes the normal curve as well as percentiles, *z*-scores, *Z*-scores, *T*-scores, sigma scores, Hull scores, and stanine scores. With few exceptions standard norms are interchangeable.

Consider this example. The Dyer Backboard Test of Tennis Ability is given to a group of women physical education majors. The resulting distribution is found to be normal. Sigma-scale norms for the Dyer test have been published. As mentioned earlier, the sigma scale is not used as widely as some of the other standard scales. Thus, it seems important to be able to express individual performances on some other scales, which may be interpreted more easily. The test consists of volleying a tennis ball as many times as possible in 30 seconds against a backwall. The mean is found to be 33 volleys with a standard deviation of 11. Joan has a score of 44. Her sigma-scale is 67.

Finding other standard scores that are equivalent can be done in two ways. The simplest method, although just an approximation, is to find a presentation of the normal curve with all the standard scores represented. Figure 4.3, for instance, demonstrates that given the distribution above, Joan's raw score of 44, which has a sigma scale score of 67, can be translated to:

z-score	+1.0
percentile	84th
Z-score	60
T-score	60
Hull score	64
Stanine score	7

An alternate method of finding the above standard scores is first to calculate the basic standard score, the *z*, by using the raw score, mean, and standard deviation. Once the *z* is found, other standard scores can be found either by formula or from Figure 4.3.

By utilizing all the standard scores and percentile equivalents, we can compare a student's raw score and the most familiar scale used for interpretation. Calculating several standard scores also allows one to learn the relationships of one scale to another. To summarize, all standard scores indicate a student's relative position in terms of standard deviation units above or below the mean. In the normal distribution, the percentile scale is closely related to all the standard score scales, making the interchangeability possible. Standard scores represent the same difference in test performance throughout their scales and can be averaged arithmetically. Therefore, they have advantages over percentiles but cannot usually be interpreted as easily. Most standard scores assume a normal distribution although some standard scores normalize nonnormal distributions.

National Norms Versus Local Norms. Norms provide a basis for interpreting the performance of an individual. Norms are also used to compare the performance of a group with that of a reference group. Several factors mentioned earlier in this chapter are important in the establishment of norms. If these criteria have been met, the norms can be successfully used in interpreting individual or group performance.

Local norms are often more relevant and more useful than the norms provided in test manuals. Local norms must adhere to the same criteria in their development as national norms. But since the educational background, scholastic aptitude, and curriculum emphasis as well as other factors in the local situation may be different from the national population, it is important that local norms be developed. Local norms are also suggested when several different tests or test batteries are used in the local situation. Obviously, the same sample has not been used in the development of national norms. Developing local norms based on a common population is advantageous. In addition, local norms provide a means for a student to be evaluated in terms of other students in his school or city. In some cases, local norms and national norms for the same test are quite different. In interpreting results of the AAHPER Youth Fitness Test, for instance, a score reaching the 60th percentile nationally may reach the 80th percentile locally. Therefore, the physical education program of a particular school system can be evaluated, at least partially, by comparing local norms with national norms.

Summary

A raw score has very little meaning because there is no frame of reference with which to compare it. A *criterion-referenced interpretation* allows the description of a student's performance of a task without reference to the performance of others. The percentage-correct score is the most widely used criterion-referenced interpretation and is useful in assessing achievement of behavioral objectives. A *norm-referenced interpretation* permits evaluation of a student's achievement in terms of his or her relative position in a clearly defined reference group. Standardized tests traditionally have used the norm-referenced interpretation.

In the development and use of norms; several factors must be taken into consideration. The sample must be large and representative; norms must be relevant; they should be presented in an easily understood format; the administration of the tests must be standardized; and they must be up-to-date. In addition, when any test score is compared to norms, caution must be exhibited in putting a great deal of faith on a single test score.

There are four general types of norms. *Age norms* and *grade norms* describe a student's performance in terms of a particular age or grade in which the student's score is average. *Percentile norms* and *standard score norms* depict test performance in terms of the student's relative position in a group of test scores. A percentile rank indicates the percentage of scores falling below a specific raw score and is widely used because of ease of interpretation. Percentile units are unequal. Various standard scores have equal units and indicate by the transformations of the raw score the student's relative position in standard deviation units from the mean score.

Some of the more popular types of standard scores used in physical education are z-score, Z-score, T -score, stanine score, the sigma scale, and the Hull scale. All of these have specific advantages and disadvantages, which have been discussed.

With a normal distribution of scores, raw scores can be converted to any standard score. All standard scores are different ways of interpreting the same data. They can be interchanged for ease of interpretation. Also, when the scores are normally distributed, percentiles can be compared with any of the standard scores.

Local norms are often more relevant and more useful than norms provided with test manuals. Students can then be evaluated in terms of others in the same locality.

Study Questions

1. Distinguish between criterion-referenced and norm-referenced interpretations of raw scores. What advantage do they have over raw scores?
2. What factors should be considered in developing or using norms?
3. Why are age and grade norms rarely used with secondary school students? What are their similarities? Their differences? Advantages and disadvantages?
4. What limitations must be considered when developing and using percentile norms? Can percentiles be averaged? If so, how?
5. What effect does a nonnormal distribution have on the development and use of norms?
6. What is the major difference between a Z-score and T-score in a nonnormal distribution? Normal distribution?
7. Why is the z-score not popularly used in standard score norms?

8. Develop a table consisting of the major standard score norms that have application to physical education. What is the mean of each? Standard deviation? Range?
9. Why are local norms important for assessing physical performance of elementary students in a school system where there is no required elementary physical education? Are national norms relevant?
10. Should norms be used as standards of good performance?
11. Percentiles have unequally spaced units; standard scores have equally spaced units. Explain this statement.
12. A girl age 12 performed the 600-yard run, an item of the AAHPER Youth Fitness Test, in 3 minutes flat. What additional information would be needed to interpret this score?

Data

Below is a list of times achieved by 20 16-year-old girls on the 50-yard dash.

5.6	7.3	7.8	8.2
5.9	7.4	7.9	8.3
6.7	7.6	7.9	8.5
7.0	7.7	8.0	8.8
7.1	7.8	8.1	9.3

$s = .891 \quad \overline{X} = 7.645 \quad N = 20$

13. Calculate the quartiles and deciles for this ungrouped distribution.
14. Compare the percentiles in this sample with the national norms of the 50-yard dash for 16-year-old girls for the AAHPER Youth Fitness Test (norms are in Chapter 13).
15. Calculate the z-score for 6.7 seconds. Calculate the T-score and stanine score for the same raw score. Notice that in calculating the z-score and other standard scores attention must be given to the type of performance. In timed events, where lower scores represent better performance, the calculated z, if better than the mean, will be negative. The sign of the z-score obtained by calculation should be changed.
16. Calculate the T, sigma, and Hull scores for 8.8 seconds. Rank these standard scores from high to low. Will this relationship always hold true? Calculate other standard scores to verify your answer.

CHAPTER 5

Desired Characteristics of Measurement and Evaluation in Physical Education: Validity, Reliability, and Economy

After you have read and studied this chapter you should be able to:

1. *Define the various types of validity and distinguish between them.*
2. *Summarize the importance of validity in the evaluation of a test.*
3. *Define reliability and differentiate among methods of estimating it.*
4. *Summarize the importance of reliability in the evaluation of a test.*
5. *Calculate validity and reliability coefficients given the appropriate information.*
6. *Define objectivity and economy and understand their importance in the evaluation of a test.*

Before constructing a test or even considering selecting one from the many already completed and in print, the instructor must have the tools that will enable him to determine which instrument is best for the particular purpose.

Many decisions must be made before constructing or selecting a test, but consideration of the following three measurement and evaluation qualities will make this task easier and more logical. These topics will be discussed separately under the headings *validity, reliability*, and *economy*. Validity deals with the extent that a test measures what it was designed to measure. Reliability focuses on the consistency of the test, and economy is concerned with such practical issues as costs and time expenditures.

VALIDITY

Before using a teacher-made test or selecting any testing instrument from those in print, one must determine whether the instrument will do exactly what it is intended to do. Validity may be calculated mathematically or logically and is the *extent* that a test measures what it is supposed to measure. Often, a decision must be made between two or more testing instruments not on the exactness of each one's ability to measure a trait, but which of the possible instruments will best measure the desired trait. This decision becomes increasingly difficult when measurable traits are not clearly defined. An example is measuring strength. Strength is undoubtedly a basic performance trait, but it is also related to others such as agility, power, speed, and muscular endurance. It is very difficult to determine the extent that various instruments measure strength if there is uncertainty about what is meant by strength.

The concept of validity arises out of this dilemma. It is obvious that validity relates to the extent that an instrument measures a given trait. However, it must be realized that validity is a very broad concept. Several procedures can be utilized to determine whether the instrument measures what it was intended to measure.

Although there may be some dissent, the consensus of experts within the field of tests and measurements generally agrees with use of four validation procedures. If the teacher's concern is how well course objectives and course content are represented in the test, *content validity* is used. If the concern is whether a test indicates something meaningful about the individuals taking it, *construct validity* is determined. Should the concern be to use the test to predict some specific future performance, *predictive validity* is determined. Finally, *concurrent validity* is utilized to demonstrate the relationship between a test to be validated and another test that is known to be valid. A summary of the procedures for estimating and interpreting the different types of validity is indicated in Table 5.1.

Table 5.1 Types of Validity

Type	*Interpretation*	*Procedure*
Content validity	How well the test measures the test content and behavior under consideration.	Compare test content to the behavioral objectives.
Construct validity	How test performance can be described for behaviors that are difficult to define.	Compare the factors that influence scores on the test to the construct.
Predictive validity	How well the test performance measures a student's future performance	Compare test scores by correlation with a criterion of performance obtained at a later date.

Type	Interpretation	Procedure
Concurrent validity	How well the test performance measures a student's current performance of a trait.	Compare test scores by correlation with another measure of performance obtained at the same time.

Content Validity

Content validity is a type of logical validity that implies a close relationship between teaching and testing. The content of a course may be broadly defined to include content, subject matter, and objectives. Subject-matter refers to the topics to be covered in the instructional unit while the objectives refer to the behavioral changes expected in students as a result of the instruction. Content validity involves comparing test content with behavioral objectives and may be defined as the extent to which a test measures subject matter content and the behavioral changes under consideration. A test that has high content validity must be a product of the subject matter being taught in the instructional situation. Content validity is also used to validate instruments that are not a direct product of a teaching setting such as surveys used in descriptive research projects.

In recent years terms such as *face* validity, *logical* validity, and *representative* validity have been used to designate this same general method of validation. No attempt will be made in this text to separate those terms or their finite meanings. To appraise the content validity of any measuring device, a form of logical reasoning is incorporated. The first step is to define the characteristic or variable that is to be measured. In a classroom or gymnasium setting this is usually done by developing a thorough list of behavioral objectives. In other measurement situations, accepted definitions of the characteristic are used as bases for establishing the content validity. A separate list of the major topical areas of course content is then developed. These lists of course content and expected behavioral changes are then weighted in terms of importance. The amount of time devoted to each area during instruction, the philosophy of the school and the teacher, and the opinions of experts can be used as a rationale for developing percentage weights. Second, the items of the test must be examined to determine exactly the skills or characteristics that are being measured. The final consideration is a comparision of the definitions or objectives to the items that are included in the instrument. This comparison determines whether the test questions are representative of the content and objectives. If these correspond closely, it is generally concluded that the instrument has high content validity.

Content validity is possibly the most significant method of determining validity for the teacher of physical education. This method is necessary in any testing situation where performance or knowledge of an activity or discipline is desired. All unit or course examinations and all performance competency examinations need to be validated against the knowledges or skills presented by the teacher.

This form of validity is relatively easy to obtain by following the test construction blueprint suggestions presented in Chapter 7. In fact, it is almost impossible to construct a test low in content validity when following this procedure. However, when a standardized test is utilized or even one developed by a fellow teacher, the procedure for determining content validity must be followed since few standardized tests will have high content validity for a unit taught by a given teacher. They must often be modified or changed significantly in order to fit the subject matter taught by the teacher. Only in this way will a published instrument demonstrate high logical or content validity.

Construct Validity

Often the interest is to measure a general ability or characteristic that is difficult to observe. Attempting to determine what the test tells about an individual or about the amount of the trait that any individual possesses shows concern with construct or signifying validity. A construct is a quality that exists in order to explain some aspect of behavior.

Intelligence and critical thinking are typical examples of constructs. It is quite advantageous to be able to interpret test performance in terms of constructs. For instance, if it is known that a student is highly intelligent, certain types of behaviors can be expected of him or her in specific situations.

Construct validity may be defined as the extent to which performance can be interpreted in terms of certain constructs. Construct validity is another form of logical validity which, for the most part, has fewer specific and practical uses for the classroom teacher. However, an understanding of its development may prove useful. The first step is similar to that used in determining content validity but more complicated. A series of statements or predictions relating to the meaning of the characteristic are developed. These statements become *constructs* or traits that are to be measured and validated. The test and its individual items are then compared to the construct. This comparison may be logical or statistical in nature. If all or most of the test components are related to the list of statements that make up the construct, high construct validity is demonstrated.

This form of test validation is used most often with psychological-type traits such as motivation, personality, intelligence, anxiety, and social adjustment. This is not to say that the procedure could not measure sport skills or multiple physical traits such as general motor ability, physical fitness, or motor fitness. For example an instructor might assume that ability in the sport of racquetball is composed of such skills or constructs as serving, returning the serve, numerous offensive and defensive shots, and strategy. If a skill test battery includes items that test these skills or constructs, each individual item has construct validity, and the racquetball skill test battery is a valid measure of racquetball playing ability. This validity can be demonstrated by comparing scores of beginning and advanced players. If the individual items and total test battery have high construct validity, advanced players will achieve superior scores.

Predictive Validity

In many instances, teachers are concerned about how well a test will be able to determine a student's ability to perform a skill or task at some later date. College entrance examinations are an example. Pretests that are used for placement should often be validated using this procedure. If decisions are going to be made about a person's future abilities in an area based upon an examination, it is important to consider the predictive validity of that instrument.

Predictive validity is a form of statistical validity since this procedure is based on the extent that one characteristic of a person can be inferred from another that is related. The statistic used in this method is the coefficient of correlation, which was discussed in Chapter 3. Determining predictive validity consists of computing a correlation between scores on a *predictor test* and scores on a *criterion of success* for the trait. Generally, the *predictor test* is given before instruction and then correlated with a *criterion measure* obtained at some later period of time.

The predictor test is the instrument that has been developed by the teacher or has been selected from those in print to measure the characteristic of the students. An example might be a basketball skills test or a physical fitness test. We emphasize that the predictor test is the instrument that the teacher is attempting to validate.

Defining the criterion variable is often the most difficult task the teacher has to face in determining predictive validity. A predictive validity coefficient is only as good as the criterion that it utilized in determining the prediction. If a readiness test is given to preschoolers in an effort to predict their success in the first grade, success in the first grade must be clearly defined. Remember that the validity of the reading readiness test is only useful if it can predict success in the first grade.

The teacher or other individuals are confronted with many problems in attempting to define satisfactorily the criterion variable. For example, if a graduate school is utilizing an English writing examination for entrance into a degree program, there are often no measures of success in that program that could be related to a student's performance on the predictor examination.

We must understand that criterion measures generally account for only part of the desired success of the trait. In most instances they represent an immediate relationship and not one that might exist in time to come. If a teacher is using a predictor test to eliminate a large number of boys who have turned out for basketball, the teacher must consider whether the basketball success that is being predicted is immediate or is also indicative of basketball ability in months and years to come. For this reason it is logical not to expect perfect or even high validity coefficients between the predictor test and the criterion.

Often, one must make judgments concerning the usefulness or worth of one or more criterion measures. This task can be made much simpler by considering the following qualities desired in a criterion measure.

1. Relevance.
2. Freedom from bias.
3. Reliability.
4. Availability.

If performance on the criterion measure is related to the same factor sought in the predictor test, it is considered to be highly relevant. Many times the relevance of a criterion measure is determined by subjective judgment from an expert in the area. Freedom from bias is a very important trait to consider in evaluating a criterion measure. If everyone has an equal opportunity to score well, the instrument is considered to be free from bias. The criterion measure must also be reliable. In other words, the performance on the criterion must yield consistent results. If the criterion is not reliable, there will be no way to predict the outcomes. Finally, availability must be considered in selecting a criterion measure. Economy of time and money must be evaluated before making a final selection of the criterion measure. Specific criterion measures for establishing predictive validity of tests in physical education are similar to those used in establishing concurrent validity. Examples of such criterion measures are ratings from a panel of judges, tournament results, course grades, and another valid test of the same trait. These measures will be discussed further under concurrent validity.

Interpreting a predictive validity coefficient can be very difficult. Generally, the higher the correlation coefficient, the better the predictive ability of the test. However, decisions often must be made concerning validity with relatively low coefficients of correlation. The proper way to interpret this validity coefficient is in terms of the extent to which it indicates a possible improvement in the average performance that would be obtained by employing the instrument in question. For example, suppose a coach is in charge of a seventh-grade boys basketball team, and 400 boys turn out for the first night's practice in one gymnasium. If it is known that a certain basketball skills test correlates .96 with a thorough subjective rating of basketball playing ability, it would be better to keep only those boys who scored high on the skills test. It must be understood and accepted that some errors will occur, but there will be more success in reducing the size of the squad in this manner than trying to evaluate every boy in competition with the others.

Concurrent Validity

A fourth procedure, concurrent validity, is concerned with the relation of test scores to an accepted contemporary criterion of performance on the variable that the test is intended to measure. Concurrent validity is calculated statistically with correlation, and the higher the coefficient the higher the validity. However, unlike predictive validity, the correlation is computed between scores on a test and criterion measures available at the time the test is given.

This procedure is used primarily when a test composed of fewer items is being considered for use instead of a more time-consuming test that has already been validated. Obviously, if the correlation between the two tests in question is high, the shorter version can be effectively used. From the discussion on predictive validity, recall that the correlation is calculated between some prior test and subsequent measures of achievement. Often the most difficult task is establishing a suitable criterion measure. The task was also described with predictive validity.

One suitable criterion for establishing concurrent validity of skills tests in physical education is the use of a panel of judges. The subjective ratings of several experts are then correlated with the scores of the same individuals on the skill test to be validated. Because of the problems associated with ranking several students individually from best to worst, a numerical rating system is used. Examples of such numerical systems are evident in competitive gymnastic and springboard diving evaluations.

Another method of estimating concurrent validity, especially for skill tests in individual sports, is to compare skill test scores with some other contemporary criterion such as tournament results. A correlation coefficient is computed between the scores on the skill test to be validated and the finishing rank for each competitor in the tournament.

A third method is to correlate test scores of students with the grades teachers assign to the same students. However, there is some concern that grades are not reliable.

Each criterion mentioned to establish concurrent validity may itself not be valid. For instance, judges' ratings are indeed subjective and subject to bias; tournament ratings are not necessarily indicative of overall skill; and student grades are not based solely on skill scores. For this reason, the best criterion for establishing concurrent validity is an instrument that has already been proven valid. However, this is difficult to find, since if the criterion is highly valid, it should probably be utilized rather than the test that is being validated.

Numerous tests of basic performance traits have been determined valid because of high correlations with already validated but time-consuming tests. An example is Cooper's 12-minute Run-Walk Test, which has been validated by correlating its results with those of maximum oxygen uptake found in a laboratory research setting. Cooper (1970) found a correlation of .90 for 115 males ages 17 to 52. This test is now used as a practical method of evaluating cardiorespiratory endurance. It is often difficult to obtain extremely high validity coefficients by using this method since the test to be validated and the criterion rarely contain exactly the same content. The procedure, however, is generally thought to be excellent.

RELIABILITY

This is the second quality that is required of any measuring instrument. Reliability deals with how consistently a certain trait is measured by a particular test. It is also concerned with the repeatability of a test. Reliability is considered important because in most instances a student's ability in a certain area is measured only one time. It is important to feel confident that the score obtained is accurate.

If, for example, a student is measured two separate times using the same test and quite different results are obtained, it is difficult to determine which result is the true score. When evaluations and judgments are to be made about students based upon a test result it is absolutely crucial that the test be representative of the student's performance at that time. Once it is determined that a test is reliable, fears about a score being a consistent representation of a student's knowledge, attitude, or skill at any particular time can be alleviated.

There are four general procedures that might be utilized to express the reliability or the accuracy of a set of measures. One method demonstrates the amount of *deviation within a set of repeated scores of a single person.* A second procedure is concerned with an individual's *relative position within a group.* The third procedure included in this section deals with the items or *internal consistency* of a test. The final procedure is a nonstatistical method called *logical reliability.* A summary of the interpretations and procedures of the different types of reliability is given in Table 5.2.

Table 5.2 Types of Reliability

Type	*Interpretation*	*Procedure*
Repeated Measures of a single person	How accurate the test is when repeated on the same individual.	The standard error of measurement is computed and interpreted.
Relative position within a group:		

Type	*Interpretation*	*Procedure*
Test-retest	How accurate the test is when repeated with the same group either immediately or after a rest period.	A correlation is computed between the first and second administrations of the same test to the same group.
Parallel forms	How accurate the test is when a parallel or equal form is repeated with the same group either immediately or after a rest period.	A correlation is computed between the test and the parallel form after they are administered to the same group.
Split-half	How consistent the test is when one half is compared to the second half.	A correlation is computed between two halves of the same test. The Spearman-Brown formula is applied.
Item consistency	How consistently the items in one test measure the same general trait.	Apply one of the Kuder-Richardson formulas to the test scores.
Logical reliability	Why the test should be logically reliable.	Determine the factors that make a test reliable and demonstrate how the test contains those factors.
Objectivity	Why the test is accurate when administered by different testers.	Use any of the procedures described in the preceding areas.

Repeated Scores for a Single Person

This first method involves the amount of deviation within a set of repeated scores for a single individual. By having a single student repeat a particular test many times, a frequency distribution of all the scores can be developed. This distribution has a mean that can be considered the "true" score for the individual on the particular trait. It also has a standard deviation that represents the average difference from the mean. This standard deviation is called the *standard error of measurement*. The reliability or accuracy of the instrument is interpreted from this number. A very small standard error of measurement indicates little variation from the true score. If a comparison is being made between two tests the logical selection would be the test with the smaller standard error of measurement.

In physical education testing it is usually impossible or impractical to repeat the same test several times on the same individual. Practice, fatigue, and time limitations are but three obvious reasons for seeking other methods of determining the reliability of instruments.

Relative Position Within the Group

The second method of estimating reliability involves the concept that in a reliable test the individuals will remain in about the same relative position within the distribution of scores if the test should be repeated. It was demonstrated in Chapter 3 that the coefficient of correlation can be used to assess the relationships between two variables. By utilizing the correlation procedure with two applications of the same test a good indication of test reliability is achieved. In other words, the coefficient of correlation determines whether the individuals remain in the same relative position when the test is administered a second time.

Three procedures that can be used to measure or estimate the reliability of tests based on the above concept are *test-retest, parallel forms*, and *split-half.*

The test-retest method of determining reliability is primarily applicable to psychomotor or skills tests. In fact, many measurement experts consider it the *only* procedure that works well with skills tests because of the unique nature and number of items found in these tests.

The procedure for using this method involves administering the instrument to a group of students. Either immediately or after a variable period of rest the same instrument is again administered to the same group of students. The time between test administrations depends upon instructional objectives. If there is concern about how accurately a single measure characterizes a person at a specific point in time, the instrument should be readministered immediately. If, however, the major concern is about how precisely a given instrument characterizes students from day to day or even week to week, it is necessary to measure them on separate occasions up to two weeks apart. Once the two measures have been obtained a coefficient of correlation is computed and interpreted as described in Chapter 3.

The test-retest method of estimating reliability is not considered particularly appropriate for variables of the cognitive domain. In most instances, even after a period of rest, the student is capable of remembering items on the instrument. Memory makes taking the test easier the second time and can affect the reliability coefficient. Another problem in using the test-retest procedure is in the sample of tasks used in the instrument. It is possible for a particular student to obtain a higher score on one sample of items than the student might on a second sample of items indicating that the test-retest reliability coefficient could be much higher on the first sample than on the second.

Concern over problems that arise because of the necessity of choosing a unique sample of tasks to measure a certain characteristic of a student has led many to the *parallel-forms* method of estimating reliability. This method is an excellent procedure for use with cognitive examinations but is very time-consuming. On the other hand, because of the specific nature of most test items in psychomotor variables, the procedure is considered a poor choice for this type of test.

In using the parallel-forms method, two equivalent forms of the test must be developed. Equivalent forms of an instrument are constructed according to the same test blueprint specifications but composed of separate samples of items from the area to be examined. The types of questions and their level of difficulty should be equal. Only the specific sample might be different.

Once the two equivalent forms of the test have been developed, each student is given first one form and then the other. This may be done immediately or after a rest period by using the same decision rationale that was presented in the test-retest discussion. A coefficient of correlation is computed for the two sets of scores and is interpreted in the usual manner. Notice that this is the most rigorous procedure that can be used to estimate reliability. If a high reliability coefficient has been obtained by using this procedure, instructors can feel very confident about evaluations or judgments that might be made based on the results achieved by the students.

There are certain practical limitations in the use of this procedure. Two forms of an excellent test are often difficult to construct and are certainly time-consuming. This limitation has prompted many educators to be receptive to procedures that involve only one form and only one administration of the test such as the *split-half* method, which will be discussed next. Notice that any method that subdivides a single test is a compromise substitution at best and must be understood in this context when used.

The most widely used method of estimating reliability for cognitive and affective variables is the *split-half* method. This widespread use results primarily from the ease and practicality of the procedure and not from its soundness. The method is not recommended for psychomotor variables because of the limited number of items as well as the independent nature of most items in these tests.

The procedure is relatively simple. The test is subdivided into two equal parts after it has been administered. It is generally preferred to use an alternate number method in establishing halves, although almost any subdivision is satisfactory. A systematic effort may be made to balance the content and level of difficulty of the two corresponding half-tests. It should also be remembered that any actual division of the test is made after it has been administered. The test itself is administered one time only. After the test has been administered and the division has been carried out the result is two scores for each student similar to the parallel-forms method. A coefficient of correlation is then computed as in the other methods previously discussed.

Remember that this reliability coefficient cannot be interpreted in exactly the same manner that was used in the test-retest or parallel-forms method. The larger a sample of an individual's performance that is obtained, the more accurate or reliable that measure will be. In other words a larger sample will come closer to measuring the total variable and should therefore be more indicative of a student's true score for that variable. The computed correlation for the split-half method is applicable to the half-tests but is not directly applicable to the original full-length test. The major concern is with the reliability of the entire test.

By applying a correction formula an unbiased estimate of the total test reliability can be obtained from the correlation coefficient of the *two* half-tests. The formula is

$$r_{11} = \frac{2r^{1/2}{}^{1/2}}{1 + r^{1/2}{}^{1/2}}$$

where r_{11} is the estimated reliability of the total test and $r^{1/2}{}^{1/2}$ is the computed correlation of the two half-tests. An example of how this formula may be utilized is demonstrated. If a correlation ($r^{1/2}{}^{1/2}$) of .75 between the two half-tests is computed, the results would be

$$r_{11} = \frac{2\,(.75)}{1 + .75} = \frac{1.50}{1.75} = .86$$

This correction formula is often called the Spearman-Brown Prophecy Formula. It is indeed a functional and efficient method of estimating reliability, but care must be exercised in the interpretation of its results. The above formula is a specific case of the general Spearman-Brown formula, which may be used to predict the increase in reliability resulting from dividing or splitting a test one time only. The general formula for an unlimited number of divisions is

$$r_n = \frac{nr_s}{1 + (\mathrm{n} - 1)r_s}$$

where,

r_n = reliability of lengthened test

n = number of times the test is increased in length

r_s = reliability of shorter test

Examples of the effect of increasing test length are shown in Table 5.3 assuming an original 10-item test with a reliability of .33. If the reliability of the original test is known the effect of increased divisions or increased length on reliability can be easily found by using a calculator. Two assumptions underlie the use of the Spearman-Brown formula. The first is that added items have the same average difficulty as the original items. The second assumption is that the lengthening of the test does not alter the way the students respond to it.

Table 5.3 Relation of Test Length to Test Reliability

Items	*Reliability*
10	.33
20	.50
40	.66
80	.80
160	.89
320	.94
∞	1.00

Many measurement specialists will argue that good reliability estimates should be made on separate but parallel forms of the test after a rest period of up to two weeks. The split-half method obviously violates this principle for the luxury of time and efficiency. Another concern deals with the use of speed tests. Since some tests are concerned with rate of answering first and accuracy second, the use of split-halves in estimating reliability would be quite inappropriate.

Item Statistic Reliability

Another method of estimating reliability of cognitive and affective tests from a single test administration is the Kuder-Richardson Reliability Coefficient. This procedure is an item statistic approach and is based on the assumption that the items in one form of a test are as homogeneous as items in a parallel form of a test. In other words it is assumed that all of the items in the test are measuring the same general trait. There are several accepted forms of the Kuder-Richardson procedure in print but only those referred to as Kuder-Richardson formulas 20 and 21 will be developed in this discussion. Mathematically the Kuder-Richardson 20 is the average of all possible split-halves.

The formula is

$$r_{11} = \left(\frac{n}{n-1}\right)\left(\frac{s^2 - pq}{s^2}\right)$$

where

r_{11} = the Kuder-Richardson 20 estimate of reliability

n = the number of items in the test

s = the standard deviation of the test (s^2 is variance or square of standard deviation)

Σ = the summation

p = the percent passing a particular item

q = the percent failing the same item

The same limitations apply to this method of single application that were mentioned in the discussion of the split-half method of estimating reliability. The time involved to compute the estimate is often lengthy, since the percent passing and failing each item of the test must be figured. This is considered by many a limitation of this procedure.

In order to use Kuder-Richardson 20, information regarding correct and incorrect responses for each item must be calculated. If items do not vary in difficulty, a close approximation of Σpq can be calculated from the mean and the number of items in the test.

The resultant formula, the Kuder-Richardson 21, is quicker and easier to use. It is

$$r = \frac{n}{n-1}\left[1 - \frac{\overline{X}(n - \overline{X})}{ns^2}\right]$$

where

r = Kuder-Richardson 21 estimate of reliability

n = number of items in the test

$\overline{X}$ = mean of the test

s = standard deviation of test (s^2 is variance or square of the standard deviation)

An example utilizing formula Kuder-Richardson 21 is

$n = 100, \overline{X} = 50, s = 15$

$$r = \frac{100}{99}\left[1 - \frac{50(100-50)}{100(15)^2}\right] = \frac{100}{99}\left(1 - \frac{2500}{22500}\right) - \frac{100}{99}(.889) = .898$$

Research utilizing Kuder-Richardson formulas has found the K-R 21 to be more usable from a practical standpoint since the mean and standard deviation are calculated on most test data anyway. However, K-R 21 always gives a conservative estimate of reliability when items vary in difficulty as is often the case. When it is known that test items vary widely, — that is, when they are extremely easy or very difficult, — the more complex K-R formula 20 should be utilized.

Logical Reliability

The concept of logical reliability is not meant to be interpreted as a method of estimating reliability. Rather it is a procedure whereby the teacher who utilizes self-constructed tests can increase the chances of administering a reliable test in lieu of using one of the previously discussed methods.

It is obvious that the process of developing and insuring the reliability of teacher-made tests is very time-consuming. It may not be possible for a teacher to apply the proper procedure for estimating reliability. It is, however, possible for the teacher to apply principles that are known to enhance the reliability of most tests. Some of these principles are discussed below.

1. Detailed, clear instructions. A written list of these instructions can significantly increase the probability of having a reliable test. There are fewer chances for errors that will affect accuracy on the part of both the student and test administrator if test instructions are precise.
2. Clear, nonconfusing items. The teacher must make a sincere effort to develop items that are not confusing to the students. This will ensure a more representative response that will more accurately represent the student's true score.
3. Maintenance of a professional test attitude. The teacher must transmit to the students the importance and significance of the test's setting. The test should be used only to measure a level of ability of a certain characteristic of a student. It should never be used as a punishment or a time filler, which often gives students a bad attitude toward the testing procedure.
4. Utilization of a test blueprint. The test blueprint, as discussed in Chapter 7, is a good aid in enhancing reliability of most tests. By selecting items that were taught in class in numbers proportional to the time spent on the item, the accuracy of the students' scores will be increased.
5. Number of items. The reliability of a test can be enhanced by increasing the number of items. A longer test is always more reliable than a shorter test over the same material. This concept has been shown earlier in Table 5.3. However, good judgment must be used in the number of items selected. It is usually considered desirable for almost all students to have time to finish an examination, and it is usually considered undesirable for a test to continue for more than one class period.
6. Item analysis. Tests composed of items that are of middle difficulty, homogeneous, and require discrimination enhance reliability more than tests that have heterogeneous content or items that do not require discrimination or vary greatly in difficulty. Item analysis of

questions used in a test can determine item difficulty and the discrimination index. Item analysis will be discussed in Chapter 7.

Logical reliability is not meant to be a substitution for a sound program of establishing reliability for teacher-made tests. It is, however, a viable alternative to no program for reliability caused by lack of time and training. It is recommended that the beginning teacher use a combination of logical approaches and work slowly toward the use of established methods of estimating reliability as time and experience allow. Certainly, utilizing such logical principles as those discussed above will enhance reliability determined by statistical methods.

Objectivity

Another area of interest to the teacher when constructing or administering tests is objectivity. It is merely a specific form of reliability that is appropriate only when two or more individuals are involved in administering the test. Objectivity is the degree to which consistent results are obtained from two or more test administrators. It might be more appropriately called intertester reliability or between-tester reliability.

Most of the same principles and procedures discussed earlier in this chapter are appropriate in determining the objectivity of a test. The following is a list of the factors that enhance objectivity. We feel that by considering these elements when constructing or administering a test, high objectivity can be assured.

Objectivity is obtained by the following means

1. Accurately phrased and fully detailed instructions for measurement.
2. Simplicity of measurement procedures.
3. The use, wherever possible, of mechanical tools of measurement.
4. Reduction of results to mathematical scores.
5. Selection of trained, intelligent testers.
6. Maintenance of professional or scientific attitudes by testers.
7. Unremitting supervision of measurement procedures by test administrators.
8. Rigorous scoring procedures and standards.

It is evident that the previous list involves a logical approach to objectivity similar to the one developed for reliability. It would be possible and appropriate to use any of the other procedures for estimating reliability to determine the objectivity. Mathematically, the objectivity coefficient is calculated exactly as the test-retest reliability coefficient. By determining the reliability of the instrument and using the precautions listed above, no further considerations should have to be made.

INTERPRETATION OF VALIDITY AND RELIABILITY

A test must be reliable to be useful. A test with low reliability has little value since it has not measured the trait accurately. However, reliability alone is not sufficient for determining quality. A test could be devised that is highly reliable but measures something irrelevant. Thus indications of both validity and reliability are of importance in test selection or construction. Another important concern in the interpretation of validity and reliability is the magnitude or amount of validity or reliability necessary for the acceptance of a test.

Most experts will argue that content validity should be very high. Since the concern is with the extent that test content measures the course content and the behavioral objectives, it is important that the relationship be high. There is no reason to include any items on a test that fail to represent the course content or the behavioral objectives. The other form of logical validity, construct validity, is generally less rigid. The constructs are usually very difficult to define precisely allowing considerable variance in the interpretation and acceptance levels of this form of validity. In addition, different logical and statistical tools may be utilized to arrive at construct validity. The differences in technique also provide a basis for considerable variance in the acceptance levels of construct validity.

In the analysis of predictive and concurrent validity the only concern is the magnitude of the coefficient of correlation between the test and the criterion. The computation and interpretation of correlation coefficients are reviewed in Chapter 3. Generally, it is argued that teachers should use tests with the highest validity coefficients since they are ultimately concerned about predicting criterion performance from a teacher-made or standardized test. In terms of predictability and usefulness we suggest not to use tests unless the correlation between the test and the criterion exceeds .70. The validity coefficient is chosen somewhat arbitrarily, but it can serve as a guide in interpreting predictive and concurrent validity.

The magnitude of the reliability that teachers will accept for their tests depends on the consequence of the decision or evaluation to be made. If the evaluation will have long-range effects on the students involved, only very high coefficients of correlation would be acceptable. However, if the decisions have minor consequences for the students, tests with considerably lower reliability coefficients might be used. In the methods involving the relative position within the group as well as the item consistency and objectivity procedures, the teacher probably should not accept tests with reliability coefficients lower than .90. Again this coefficient is selected somewhat arbitrarily, but if the decisions that are based on the test results are of major consequence to the student the high correlations are essential.

Logical reliability must necessarily be interpreted differently. The procedure, of course, is logical when the teacher develops rationally the reasons that a particular test is reliable. When interpreting this form of reliability the teacher must consider the soundness of the arguments presented and make a decision based on those arguments about the potential accuracy of the test.

ECONOMY

The final characteristic desired in a test to be discussed in this chapter is economy or practicality. Economy in testing means the *costs* and *time* involved in the construction, administration, and the scoring of classroom instruments.

Costs

Every teacher should be aware of the costs of tests constructed or selected for classroom use. Often, the costs are minimal, or at least all equipment or materials are readily available. Occasionally, however, a test might be selected or constructed that involves a major expenditure for equipment. The decision depends on the use of the results of that particular test and also whether other tests might be available that would accomplish nearly the same goals. If there are no other tests available and the teacher concludes that the best results are essential for a particular measurement program, then an analysis of the intended purchase must be made. Important considerations include the frequency of use of the instrument and whether other teachers might also be able to use the instrument or at least any specific equipment in their teaching settings. Another factor that might be considered is the life of the piece of equipment. If it might last a number of years, it is easier to justify the purchase. A final consideration before one makes a major expenditure for a testing item is ease and need of maintenance.

Time

Time is another and possibly more important aspect of the economy in a measurement program. The teacher must be completely aware of the amount of time needed to construct, administer, score, and interpret any test. Of these requirements the time needed to administer the test is most crucial. Often, time available for testing is somewaht limited. Also, whenever a test is given, other important school activities cannot occur. Therefore, the time used for testing should be well planned and tests should be easily administered. Many feel that most classroom tests should not exceed one class period in length but should be long enough to be both valid and reliable. This is a formidable task especially for the beginning teacher. The time required for scoring and interpreting an examination is also important. It should not be excessive because it creates undue delays in providing feedback to the students. Also, time spent in scoring and interpreting tests might better be used elsewhere such as in preparing behavioral objectives and lesson plans.

Summary

The most important characteristic to consider when selecting or constructing a test is validity. Validity is the extent that a test measures what it purports to measure. There are four basic types of validity. Content validity refers to the extent that the test content relates to the behavioral objectives and course content. Construct validity is the extent to which factors that influence test scores relate to the construct in question. Predictive validity is concerned with the extent that a test is consistent in predicting a future performance. Finally, concurrent validity deals with the extent that a test is accurate in estimating some current performance.

Reliability is second only to validity in importance when considering a test for the measurement of a certain characteristic. Reliability refers to how accurately a test measures what it is supposed to measure. Four basic types of reliability were identified in this chapter. The repeated measures on the same individual procedure imply that the same test is repeated on a single person and a standard error of measurement is computed and interpreted. The second form of reliability deals with the relative position within a group when the same test or a similar test is repeated to the same group. The test-retest method refers to the repetition of the same test to the same group. A coefficient of correlation is computed for the two sets of scores. The parallel-forms method refers to the administration of a second but parallel form of the same test to the same group. Again a coefficient of correlation is computed between the two sets of scores. In the split-half method a single test is divided into two separate tests administered at one time. A correlation is computed between the two halves and corrected for error with the Spearman-Brown Prophecy formula. Item consistency reliability is concerned with the homogeneity of the items within a test. The Kuder-Richardson formulas 20 and 21 are computed and interpreted. Finally, logical reliability is concerned with the reasons why a test should be reliable. A logical argument is presented that demonstrates the apparent reliability of the test.

Objectivity is a specialized form of reliability that is considered when more than one person is involved in testing the same students on a single test or test item. Any of the procedures discussed for estimating reliability may be used in conjunction with objectivity.

Economy refers to the amount of time and the costs involved in the administration of a test.

Study Questions

1. Of the four types of validity discussed in this chapter, which are statistically determined?
2. What type of validity is indicated by each of the following statements?
   (a) Test items are compared with behavioral objectives.

(b) Scores on the Knox Basketball Test given to all players attempting to make a basketball squad correlate very closely with squad membership for tournament play.
(c) Scores on a skill test in gymnastics correlate .90 with opinions of a panel of judges.
(d) Scores on a skill test battery indicate superior students as determined by a class tournament achieved superior test scores.
(e) A new cardiovascular endurance test correlates .85 with the Harvard Step Test.

3. If the Educational Testing Service developed an advanced GRE test in physical education, what procedures might it use to validate the test?
4. Summarize the methods of determining reliability of a test.
5. What advantages and disadvantages do physical education course grades have as criterion measures?
6. Inspect the evidence of validity and reliability for a published test of muscular strength. A sports skill test. A test of the cognitive domain in physical education.
7. A manual for a cognitive test in golf presents reliability data based on:
   (a) Retesting with the same test form a week later.
   (b) Correlating odd with even items.
   (c) Using two forms of the same test a week apart.

   Which procedure may be expected to yield the *lowest* coefficient? Why?
   Which procedure yields the most useful estimate of reliability? Why?
8. Using the Spearman-Brown Prophecy Formula, what is the estimated reliability of the whole test if the split-half reliability is .60?
9. What is the general effect of increasing the length of a test? If a 15-item test has a reliability of .30, what is the estimated reliability of a 30-item test? A 60-item test? A 90-item test? A 150-item test?
10. What is logical reliability? How does logical reliability affect estimated reliability determined by correlation?
11. What is objectivity? How is it determined? How can the objectivity of a test be increased?
12. Should the economy be an important consideration in test selection? Why or why not?
13. Use the Kuder-Richardson formula 21 to find the estimated reliability of a 20-item test with a mean of 60 and a standard deviation of 12. For what general types of test are the Kuder-Richardson formulas applicable?

CHAPTER **6**

Behavioral Objectives in Physical Education

After you have read and studied this chapter you should be able to:

1. *Define general educational and curriculum objectives and give examples for physical education.*
2. *Define behavioral or instructional objectives and give specific examples for physical education.*
3. *Compare the various types of objectives in terms of specificity and purpose.*
4. *Identify and recognize the five elements necessary in writing behavioral objectives.*
5. *Define the domains of behavior.*
6. *Identify the level of the taxonomies that are utilized in stated behavioral objectives.*
7. *Write behavioral objectives for a prescribed unit in physical education using various levels of the taxonomies.*

One of the major purposes of measurement and evaluation in physical education is the improvement of teaching and learning. A simplified model of instruction was presented in Chapter 2 to to help demonstrate this purpose. The most important component of the model is the statement relating to instructional or behavioral objectives. As instructional objectives are clearly defined, the instruction, measurement, and evaluation procedures become increasingly meaningful. Objectives can provide insight into the selection and implementation of relevant and efficient methods of instruction. Objectives can also serve as specific guides in the selection or construction of instruments or tests used in the measurement of student knowledges, skills, and attitudes. Only after instruction and measurement have been completed can the instructor evaluate student achievement. If the behavioral objectives have been developed and utilized effectively, evaluation can be made by judging the degree to which the objectives have been attained.

Unfortunately, traditional teaching and evaluation in physical education have not made optimum use of instructional objectives. One reason is that the taxonomies of behavioral objectives specifically for physical education and the psychomotor domain have only recently been completed. Without these taxonomies, physical educators have had some difficulty in precisely defining the intended outcomes of their teaching units. In addition, it is a difficult and time-consuming task to develop tests appropriate for measuring the achievement of instructional objectives. However, the time and effort is well spent. This chapter introduces the *current terminology* used in developing and stating objectives, examines the process of *writing behavioral objectives* in physical education, and analyzes the three *domains of behavior*.

CURRENT TERMINOLOGY

The terminology associated with defining, stating, and evaluating objectives is somewhat complex and often confusing to educators. However, an understanding of this terminology is necessary in order to proceed. *General educational objectives* are broad, long-range goals used as general guides. Long-range objectives are very broad in scope. These statements are better thought of as goals rather than objectives. Such statements describe the end products of education and generally give little indication of the kinds of changes to look for in student behavior. Examples of long-range objectives are the Cardinal Principles of Secondary Education and the "general objectives" of physical education. They were identified in Chapter 2. They are usually not written in terms of student behavior. Other examples of long-range or general educational objectives are:

1. The student will develop physical skills.
2. The student will develop interest in and appreciation for physical skills.

Curriculum objectives identify the behaviors that are expected of a student as a result of completing an instructional unit, a course, or a sequence of courses. They often involve "the translation of the global goals into specific behaviors that form the terminal performance capabilities of students successfully completing an instructional unit in a course, a course in itself, and in some instance, a sequence of courses (Krathwohl and Payne, 1971). Examples of curriculum objectives are:

1. The student has sufficient strength to execute skills.
2. The student can run, throw, and jump adequately enough to execute skills.

Curriculum objectives are identified by such terms as learning outcomes, learning objectives, and course objectives. The competencies expected of a student who completes a college physical education major as identified by the physical education faculty of that institution is another example of a curriculum objective. Long-range goals and curriculum objectives, because of vagueness, are difficult to evaluate precisely. However, their major purpose is to provide direction in the methodology, materials, and evaluation used in the teaching-learning process. Also, such objectives are often developed for an entire school district and are not often within the scope of the normal duties of the physical educator.

Instructional objectives are statements that describe student accomplishment after completion of a prescribed unit of instruction. They are often stated in specific behavioral terms and are therefore called *behavioral objectives*. Instructional objectives and behavioral objectives have similar meaning in this text. Other terms that have been used for such objectives are performance objectives, measurable objectives, evaluative objectives, and mastery objectives.

Instructional or behavioral objectives should reflect the philosophy of the long-range and curriculum objectives. They should be precise enough to provide the physical educator with information that can be used in the selection of specific instructional methods, measurement procedures, and evaluative techniques. An effective procedure to assure that all learning outcomes are evaluated properly is to develop the behavioral objectives comprehensively so that the long-range and curriculum objectives will also be achieved. Physical educators usually have the responsibility of writing their own behavioral objectives for specific units of instruction. The following are examples of behavioral objectives.

1. The student will be able to run 1½ miles in 12 minutes or less after a six-week cardiovascular fitness program.
2. The student can define 100 percent of the three levels of objectives as discussed in the text, without the use of class notes or other references.

The use of instructional objectives is justified for numerous reasons. The most compelling reason is that their use is consistent with the concept of accountability. To achieve the balance between spending and student learning that current accountability laws often demand, the physical educator or school system must be able to demonstrate the end results of their instructional programs. Instructional objectives provide such a vehicle for the evaluation of student progress. Another reason for using instructional objectives is that students are clearly informed of the learning that is to take place and how they are expected to demonstrate that learning. Kibler and his colleagues (1974) have identified eight logical reasons for utilizing instructional objectives. The reader is encouraged to consult their discussion.

WRITING BEHAVIORAL OBJECTIVES

The responsibility of developing and writing behavioral objectives rests primarily with the instructor of physical education. The objectives must be clearly stated in order to provide direction for teaching and to reduce wasted time and effort in the classroom. Of particular importance in this text is that behavioral objectives should also provide detailed specifications for the selection, construction, and use of measurement and evaluation instruments and techniques. Objectives have been stated in the past with a variety of terminology and have not been universally understood or accepted. In fact, objectives have usually been written in terms of the content of the course being taught or in terms of teacher behavior expectancies. A more realistic and fair approach is to state objectives in terms of observable and measurable student behavior.

General Procedures for Writing Behavioral Objectives

A number of general suggestions will enable the instructor to develop needed insights in the task of writing behavioral objectives. Behavioral objectives should be indicative of the expected behavioral changes in students after instruction has been completed. The concern of the written objective is primarily with the product or outcome of instruction and not the process or methodology. To maintain the focus on behavior change, it is advisable for the teacher when writing behavioral objectives to ask, "What should students be able to do after a unit of instruction that they could not do before?" As this question is asked repeatedly, objectives become much easier to identify and write.

Behavioral objectives must be written in measurable terms. In order for the objectives to be useful to the students, parents, and teachers, the expected outcomes from the teaching units must be observable and measurable. Nothing should be left to guesswork. The outcomes should be clear and evaluations relatively easy as a result of the behavioral objectives being measurable.

Each unit of instruction within physical education has its own unique set of instructional objectives that should reflect the general aim or goals of the profession as well as the curriculum objectives of the unit. Published lists of objectives are available for many instructional units in physical education and related areas in most curriculum texts in the profession, but should be used only as checks in evaluating the completeness and validity of the objectives developed by the instructor. Generally, published objectives will not fit exactly into the local situations, and teachers are constantly urged to write their own.

Behavioral objectives are more specific than curriculum objectives and should be written in behavioral terms. This is often done by utilizing an action verb in the statement of the objective. Such terminology should indicate specific, measurable behavior of the student. The format for writing objectives is relatively uncomplicated. First, the goals of the teaching are identified. Examples of these goals are the general objectives of physical education. Next, the curriculum objectives of the specific courses being taught are identified. These objectives should be written in terms of expected learning outcomes. The taxonomies, which will be fully explained later in the chapter, are excellent references for developing objectives. Finally, behavioral objectives are identified and written in terms of measurable student outcomes.

Necessary Elements in Writing Behavioral Objectives

In addition to the general suggestions that guide the writing of behavioral objectives, there are five specific elements developed by Kibler *et al.* (1974) that all instructional objectives should contain.

1. Who is to perform the desired behavior.
2. The actual behavior to be employed demonstrating mastery of the objective.
3. The result (i.e., the product or performance) of the behavior, which will be evaluated to determine whether the objective is mastered.
4. The relevant conditions under which the behavior is to be performed.
5. The standard that will be used to evaluate the success of the product or performance.*

Each of these elements should be readily recognized and identified if a behavioral objective is properly written. An example of developing a behavioral objective utilizing the identified elements is presented below. In each example, the element of the objective under consideration will be underlined.

Who Is to Perform the Desired Behavior? Behavioral objectives are written in terms of *student* behavior. Sometimes, such terms as "the student," "the pupil," "the performer" are not specifically mentioned in the objective.

Examples:

The student will be able . . .
The performer will be able . . .

The Actual Behavior to Be Performed. Behavioral objectives should identify specific terminal behaviors that the student must accomplish. All behavioral objectives must include the concept of "doing." This is accomplished through the use of action verbs. Examples of verbs that illustrate this "action" terminology are listed for each domain of learning.

Cognitive	*Affective*	*Psychomotor*
Describes	Replies	Moves
Defines	Listens	Performs
Generalizes	Designs	Throws
Differentiates	Questions	Runs
Interprets	Develops	Swims

*From Robert J. Kibler, Donald J. Cegala, David T. Miles, and Larry L. Barker, *Objectives for Instruction and Evaluation*, Copyright 1974 by Allyn and Bacon, Inc., Boston, p. 35. Reprinted by permission.

Several of these terms are not exclusively related to a single domain but serve to identify specific terminal behaviors that are expected of the student as a result of the instructional process. An even more comprehensive list of such action verbs for each major domain of behavior can be found in Gronlund (1976). Verbs that do not identify observable terminal behavior should not be used in writing behavioral objectives. Such words as "know," "understand," and "think" do not identify actions that are observable or measurable, which can be seen, heard, or felt.

Examples:

The student *will be able to define* . . .
The student *will be able to run* . . .

The Result of the Behavior. The third element necessary in writing behavioral objectives is the product, the performance, or *what* the student is expected to accomplish as a result of instruction. This can be determined in general ways such as perusuing old tests, reviewing notes from previous similar teaching experiences, or interviewing students who have attained the desired behavior.

Examples:

The student will be able to define *the basic performance traits in physical fitness* . . .
The performer will be able to run *1½ miles* . . .

The Relevant Conditions Under Which the Behavior Is to Be Performed. The conditions under which the behavior is expected to occur need to be identified in a behavioral objective. They include any restrictions or limitations that are imposed on students when they are performing the expected behavior. Any equipment, materials, or information that may or may not be utilized in the terminal performance must be specified.

Examples:

The student will be able to define the basic performance traits in physical fitness *without the use of class notes or other references*. . .
The performer will be able to run 1½ miles *after a six-week cardiovascular fitness program*. . .

The Standard That Will Be Used to Evaluate the Success of the Product or Performance. The criterion or standard of acceptable performance is the final element that must be included in a behavioral objective. The minimum level of acceptable performance needs to be clearly specified. This requirement may be stated in various terms including such standards as the minimum number of acceptable performances or a minimum percentage of correct responses.

Statements from behavioral objectives — the student must list five components, or the student must identify 75 percent of the items — exemplify these two types of acceptable performance standards. In addition to the minimum acceptable performance, objectives should state how accuracy will be determined. An example is the student will be able to identify four types of validity as presented in the textbook. It is important that the instructor selects the performance standard carefully. A criterion that everyone is able to achieve or no student is capable of achieving certainly would not serve the purpose.

Examples:

The student will be able to define *three of the four* basic performance traits in physical fitness as presented in lecture without the use of class notes or other references.

The performer will be able to run 1½ miles *in 12 minutes* or less after a six-week fitness program.

As experience is gained in writing behavioral objectives the task becomes much easier. In writing the objective one will be able to identify each necessary element without making reference to the list of elements.

DOMAINS OF BEHAVIOR

The remainder of this chapter describes the domains of learning and states behavioral objectives for each of these areas in behavioral terms. Bloom and his associates (1956) published a taxonomy of educational objectives that developed a detailed system for classifying objectives. The *Taxonomy of Educational Objectives* has achieved widespread acceptance. This taxonomy, which is based on systems used by biologists to classify plants and animals, has as its major purpose the facilitation of communication among teachers and all those involved with educational research and curriculum development. Also, the taxonomy attempts to be comprehensive in its classification of the goals of the educational system. It achieves these purposes by developing a set of classifications that are ordered and arranged on the bases of a single principle or on the bases of a consistent set of principles. Bloom separated objectives into three major domains: cognitive, affective, and psychomotor. The domains are defined as follows.

Cognitive Objectives which emphasize remembering or reproducing something which has presumably been learned, as well as objectives which involve the solving of some intellective task for which the individual has to determine the essential problem and then reorder given material or combine it with ideas, methods or procedures previously learned. Cognitive objectives vary from simple recall of material learned to highly original and creative ways of combining and synthesizing new ideas and materials.

Affective. Objectives which emphasize a feeling tone, an emotion, or a degree of acceptance or rejection. Affective objectives vary from simple attention to selected phenomena to complex but internally consistent qualities or character and conscience . . . such objectives as interests, attitudes, appreciations, values, and emotional sets or biases.

Psychomotor. Objectives which emphasize some muscular or motor skill, some manipulation of materials and objects, or some act which requires a neuromuscular coordination.*

It is obvious that although much of the behavior in physical education is psychomotor, knowing the how and why of physical performance is also very important. All three domains have significant effects. An actual performance depends on such factors as knowledge of the task, emotional set, and psychomotor skill. Although cognitive, affective, and psychomotor domains will be discussed separately, remember that a student performs as a whole, and each domain may affect performance in the other areas.

Cognitive Domain

Bloom and his associates organized the *Taxonomy of Educational Objectives, Handbook I: Cognitive Domain* in a hierarchy from simple to complex and included six major categories. These categories include knowledge, comprehension, application, analysis, synthesis and evaluation. Each category depends on the mastery of the prior categories. For example, before an analysis of a cognitive skill can be made, mastery of knowledge, comprehension, and application objectives must be achieved. The taxonomy was originally concerned with student behaviors in a classroom setting, but application can certainly be made to the gymnasium setting more typical of physical education. A skeleton model of the taxonomy of the cognitive domain is given in Table 6.1.

Table 6.1 Skeleton Model of the Taxonomy of Educational Objectives: Cognitive Domain

Knowledge

1.00 Knowledge. Recall of appropriate information.
  1.10 Knowledge of specifics. Recall of specific and isolated information.
    1.11 Knowledge of terminology.
    1.12 Knowledge of specific facts.
  1.20 Knowledge of ways and means of dealing with specifics. Knowledge of the

*From *Taxonomy of Educational Objectives: The Classification of Educational Goals, Handbook II: Affective Domain*, by David R. Krathwohl, et al. Copyright © 1964, Copyright © 1977 by Longman Inc, pp. 6-7. Reprinted by permission of Longman.

Knowledge
ways of organizing, studying, judging, and criticizing.
1.21 Knowledge of conventions. Ways of treating and presenting ideas.
1.22 Knowledge of trends and sequences. Processes, directions and movements of phenomena with respect to time.
1.23 Knowledge of classifications and categories.
1.24 Knowledge of criteria.
1.25 Knowledge of methodology.
1.30 Knowledge of the universals and abstractions in a field. Major schemes and patterns by which phenomena and ideas are organized.
1.31 Knowledge of principles and generalizations.
1.32 Knowledge of theories and structures (body or principles, generalizations, and interrelations).
Intellectual Skills and Abilities
2.00 Comprehension. Understanding of material being communicated, without necessarily relating it to other material.
2.10 Translation. From one form of communication to another.
2.20 Interpretation. Explanation or summarization of a communication.
2.30 Extrapolation. Extension of trends beyond the given data.
3.00 Application. The use of abstractions in particular and concrete situations.
4.00 Analysis. Breakdown of a communication into its constituent parts so that hierarchy of ideas is clear.
4.10 Analysis of elements. Identification of elements included in a communication.
4.20 Analysis of relationships. Connections and interactions between elements of communication.
4.30 Analysis of organizational principles. Systematic arrangement.
5.00 Synthesis. Putting elements into a whole.
5.10 Production of a unique communication. Conveying ideas, feelings, experiences to others.
5.20 Production of a plan or proposed set of operations.
5.30 Derivation of a set of abstract relations. Development of a set of abstract relations to explain data or phenomena.
6.00 Evaluation. Judgments about value of material and methods for given purposes.
6.10 Judgments in terms of internal evidence. Evaluation from such evidence as logical accuracy, consistency, etc.
6.20 Judgments in terms of external criteria. Evaluation with reference to selected or remembered material.

Source. Taxonomy of Educational Objectives: The Classification of Educational Goals, Handbook I: Cognitive Domain, credited by Benjamin S. Bloom et al. Copyright © 1956 by David McKay Company, Inc., pp. 201-207, Copyright © 1977 by Longman Inc. Reprinted by permission of Longman.

A study of major components in the hierarchy is necessary for writing and classifying behavioral objectives in physical education. The domain is subdivided into two categories: knowledge and intellectual skills and abilities. The majority of the taxonomy deals with the second category.

Once any taxonomy is understood, it can be used as a guide for writing behavioral objectives. Instructors must make decisions relative to the levels in the cognitive taxonomy that are desired of their students and then must write objectives reflecting those levels. Physical educators often limit behavioral objectives to the lower levels of the taxonomy. This is done generally because of the difficulty of writing good objectives at the higher levels. Most teacher-developed instructional units include behavioral objectives that relate to recall information (Knowledge 1.00) such as terminology, specific facts, and rules. Fewer units have examined the ability to make application (3.00 Application) or evaluations (6.00 Evaluation). Although the behavioral objectives should include the lower knowledge levels, certainly upper levels of the taxonomy should also be included in the final list of behavioral objectives developed in the cognitive domain by the teacher.

Included in Table 6.2 are examples of behavioral objectives that comply with Bloom's cognitive taxonomy and that also relate to a college class in measurement and evaluation in physical education. The objectives have been shortened and do not include all of the elements necessary in properly stated objectives as presented earlier in this chapter.

Table 6.2 Illustrative Behavioral Objectives for the Cognitive Domain

1.12	Knowledge of terminology. Identify the major periods of emphasis in the history of measurement and evaluation of physical education.
2.10	Translation. Convert raw scores from a physical fitness test administered to local high school students into a graphical representation.
3.00	Application. Administer a psychomotor test to a group of friends, employing the proper techniques and procedures as presented in class.
4.20	Analysis of relationship. Differentiate between predictive, content, concurrent, and construct validity of a test.
5.20	Production of a plan. Design an innovative test for a unit of instruction in physical education.
6.20	Judgments in terms of external criteria. Appraise the quality and usefulness of two tests, both of which supposedly measure physical fitness.

Each of the objectives in Table 6.2 have been written in behavioral terms that are directly measurable. Such objectives are typically written in "action" terms signifying specific and directly observable behavior. The behavioral objective should also be written with the broader educational or curricular objectives in mind.

The Affective Domain

Objectives of this domain include statements of interest, attitudes, motivation, and character development. The affective domain includes feeling or emotions. Much of a student's psychomotor behavior has an emotional or affective source. Thus, it is important that an instructor understand the component of the affective domain.

The taxonomy of the affective domain was completed by Krathwohl *et al.* and published in *Taxonomy of Educational Objectives, Handbook II: Affective Domain* (1964). The taxonomy is divided into five major categories: receiving, responding, valuing, organization, and characterization and is presented in a hierarchy similar to that of the cognitive domain.

A skeleton model of the affective domain is presented in Table 6.3.

Table 6.3 Skeleton Model of the Taxonomy of Educational Objectives: Affective Domain

1.00	Receiving (Attending). Willingness to receive or attend to certain phenomena or stimuli.	
	1.10	Awareness. Consciousness of phenomena
	1.20	Willingness to receive. Tolerating a stimulus or phenomena.
	1.30	Controlled or selected attention. Differentiation of stimulus.
2.00	Responding. Active attention to stimuli or phenomena	
	2.10	Acquiescence in responding. Compliance.
	2.20	Willingness to respond. Voluntary response.
	2.30	Satisfaction in response. Enjoyment or pleasure from response.
3.00	Valuing. Behavior motivated by individual's commitment to underlying values of behavior.	
	3.10	Acceptance of a value. Beliefs.
	3.20	Preference for a value.
	3.30	Commitment. Conviction.
4.00	Organization. Organizing, interrelating, and analyzing dominant relevant values.	
	4.10	Conceptualizing of a value. Comparison with those already held.
	4.20	Organization of a value system.
5.00	Characterization by a value or value concept. Acts according to held values.	
	5.10	Generalized set. Internal consistency.
	5.20	Characterization. Generalization of values into consistent philosophy.

- 5.30 Production of a unique communication. Convey ideas, experiences to others.
- 5.40 Production of a plan or proposed set of operations.
- 5.50 Derivation of a set of abstract relations.

6.00 Evaluation. Judgments about the value of material and methods for a given purpose.

- 6.10 Judgments in terms of internal evidence. Logical consistency.
- 6.20 Judgments in terms of external criteria. Consistency with reference to selected or remembered criteria.

Source. Taxonomy of Educational Objectives: The Classification of Educational Goals Handbook II: Affective Domain, by David R. Krathwohl et al. Copyright © 1964 by David McKay Company, Inc. pp. 176-185. Copyright © 1977 by Longman Inc. Reprinted by permission of Longman.

The affective taxonomy is based on the process of internalization, which can be aptly described by summarizing the hierarchy at successive levels as they appear in the *Taxonomy of Educational Objectives, Handbook II: Affective Domain.*

"The process" begins when the attention of the student is captured by some phenomenon, characteristic, or value. As he/she begins receiving or attending to the phenomenon, characteristic, or value, it is differentiated from others present in the student's perceptual field. With differentiation of the value comes a seeking out of the phenomenon as emotional significance is gradually attached to it. The student eventually assigns a value to the attitude. As the process unfolds he or she relates this phenomenon to other phenomena which also have value. This responding becomes sufficiently frequent so the student comes to react regularly, almost automatically, to it and to other things like it. Finally the values are interrelated in a structure or view of the world, which he/she brings as a "set" to new problems.*

Writing behavioral objectives for the affective domain is a difficult task. Indeed, the volume dealing with the affective domain was not completed until 1964 because of several problems relating to the development of terminology and the evaluation of affective behavior. Relatively little published material was found by Krathwohl and his co-workers relating to such affective behavior as desirable interests, attitudes, and character development. Most instructors should be and are concerned with affective behavior of students. However, because of the difficulty in defining and evaluating adjustment, interests, atti-

*From *Taxonomy of Educational Objectives: The Classification of Educational Goals Handbook II: Affective Domain,* by David R. Krathwohl et al. Copyright © 1964 by David McKay Company, Inc. New York, p. 33. Copyright © 1977 by Longman Inc. Reprinted by permission of Longman.

tudes, values, and appreciations, or because instructors feel it is not appropriate to grade behavior, students have rarely been evaluated on affective traits. These instructors generally agree that it is vitally important to present a desirable role model relative to the affective domain, but they find the evaluation procedures to be unreliable for everyday classroom use.

An additional problem is that behaviors are slow to change relative to the other domains. Knowledge in the game of tennis (cognitive) or skill in the game of tennis (psychomotor) can be learned in a relatively short period of time, but a student's attitude (affective), in contrast, seems to change more slowly over longer periods of time.

If affective objectives and goals are to be realized, they must be defined clearly; curricula and methods must be provided that help students develop affectively, and there must be some systematic method for appraisal of affective behavior. Figure 6.1 attempts to clarify the meaning of the terminology typically used in the affective domain of behavior. For instance, the term "adjustment" ranges from 2.2, willingness to respond, to the upper end of the continuum. Notice that all the terms overlap in the middle of the taxonomy continuum. By writing objectives with proper terminology and the taxonomy as a guide, methods can be developed and measurements utilized that will more effectively evaluate changes in affective behavior of students.

The importance of the affective domain cannot be underestimated. Teachers of physical education should especially be aware of the effects of interest, motivation, and attitude upon skill performance.

Statements of general objectives have almost always included reference to improvement of attitude, interest, or emotion. Thus, an instructor should be able to write behavioral objectives in the affective domain that reflect the broader objectives. Some examples of behavioral objectives using the taxonomy, which are indicative of the affective domain in a secondary level physical education class, are given in Table 6.4.

Table 6.4 Illustrative Behavioral Objectives for the Affective Domain

1.20	Willingness to receive. Listens with respect when classmates are explaining and demonstrating a psychomotor skill.
2.20	Willingness to respond. Practices the rules of safety in the gymnasium or on the playground.
3.10	Acceptance of beliefs. Desires to attain physical fitness.
4.20	Organization of value system. Develops proper techniques for controlling aggressive behavior in competitive situations.
5.20	Characterization of a value into philosophy. Develops a generally consistent code of ethics that guides behavior.

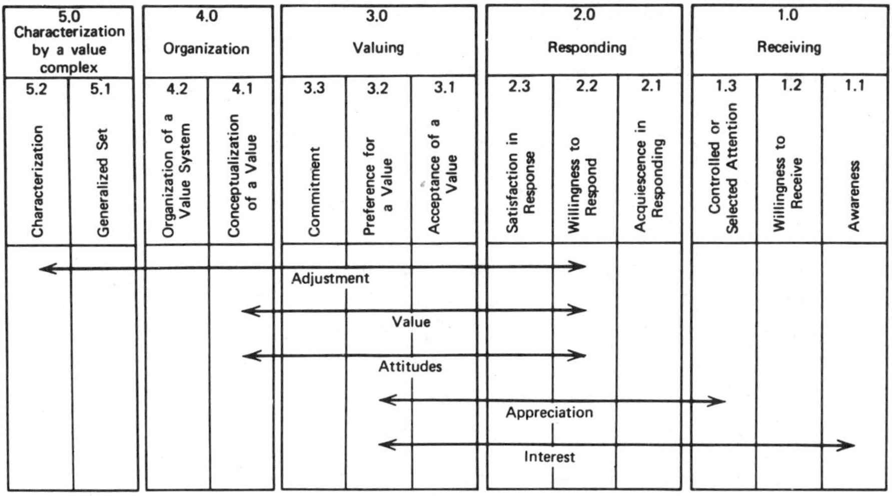

Figure 6.1. The range of meaning typical of commonly used affective terms measured against the *Taxonomy* continuum – affective domain of behavior (from *Taxonomy of Educational Objectives: The Classification of Educational Goals: Handbook II: Affective Domain*, by David R. Krathwohl et al., copyright © 1964 by David McKay Company, Inc., New York, p. 37, copyright © 1977 by Longman, Inc.; reprinted by permission of Longman Inc., New York).

Psychomotor Domain

This domain includes all movement behavior. Objectives that emphasize the ability to demonstrate motor skill requiring neuromuscular coordination, manipulative skill, and movement are considered goals of the psychomotor domain. The psychomotor domain is of major concern to the physical educator since most of the subject matter taught in the physical education curriculum deals specifically with motor skills. Obviously then, it is the job of the physical educator through the physical education curriculum to provide experiences that will enhance the development of these skills. Lists of general objectives in physical education have always included neuromuscular skill development. However, as with the cognitive and nontaxonomic affective domains, various classification schemes have used differing terminology. Recently, however, several taxonomy systems have been developed for the psychomotor domain. Simpson (1966), Harrow (1972), and Jewett (1971) have developed such taxonomies using the general format of the previously published volumes on the cognitive and affective domains. Each of these taxonomies provides insights into important concepts unique to the psychomotor domain. However, each describes psychomotor behavior using different terminology.

Jewett's *Taxonomy of Educational Objectives: Motor Domain* (1971) has been chosen for illustration purposes because of its simplicity. As with the cognitive and affective taxonomies, this motor domain taxonomy is organized in a hierarchy along a continuum from the lowest level of motor behavior to the highest level. Jewett's taxonomy includes three major levels: 1.00 generic movement; 3.00 ordinative movement; and 2.00 creative movement. Each succeeding level depends on the mastery of prior levels. Jewett's *Taxonomy of Educational Objectives: Motor Domain* is presented in Table 6.5.

Table 6.5 Jewett's Proposed Taxonomy of Educational Objectives: Motor Domain

- 1.00 Generic movement. Movement operations or processes which facilitate the development of human movement patterns.
  - 1.10 Perceiving. Recognition of movement positions, postures, patterns, and skills by means of the sense organs.
  - 1.20 Imitating. Duplication of a movement pattern of skill as a result of perceiving.
  - 1.30 Patterning. Arrangement and use of body parts in successive and harmonious ways to achieve a movement pattern of skill.
- 2.00 Ordinative movement. Meeting the requirements of specific movement tasks through processes of organizing, performing, and refining movement patterns and skills.
  - 2.10 Adapting. Modification of a patterned movement or skill to meet specific task demands.
  - 2.20 Refining. Acquisition of smooth, efficient control in performing a movement pattern or skill as a result of an improvement process, e.g.,
    - (a) Elimination of extraneous movements.
    - (b) Mastery of spatial and temporal relations.
    - (c) Habitual performance under more complex conditions.
- 3.00 Creative movement. Processes of inventing or creating skillful movements which will serve the unique purposes of the learner.
  - 3.10 Varying. Invention or construction of unique or novel options in performing a movement pattern or skill.
  - 3.20 Improvising. Extemporaneous origination or initiation of novel movements or combinations of movements.
  - 3.30 Composing. Creation of unique movement designs or patterns.

Source. Ann Jewett *et al.*, "Educational Change Through a Taxonomy for Writing Physical Education Objectives," *Quest, 16*: 35, 1971. Reprinted by permission.

The taxonomies of Jewett and Harrow are undoubtedly the most sophisticated attempts to date to develop, explain, and categorize the components of the psychomotor domain.

Behavioral objectives for the psychomotor domain can be written quite easily through the use of the taxonomy. As when writing objectives for the cognitive and affective domains, the instructor must make decisions relative to levels of the psychomotor taxonomy desired. The objective should then be written with this level specifically in mind. Educators have stated that the psychomotor domain is by far the easiest of the three domains for which to write educational objectives. Most psychomotor behaviors are observable, and most psychomotor behaviors can be objectively measured.

Some examples of behavioral objectives in physical education based on Jewett's taxonomy are given in Table 6.6.

Table 6.6 Illustrative Behavioral Objectives for the Motor Domain

1.10	Perceiving. Identify various strokes in the game of badminton.
1.20	Imitating. Hit an effective forehand stroke in tennis as a result of perceiving a demonstration by the instructor.
1.30	Patterning. Shoot a successful lay-up in a basketball unit.
2.10	Adapting. Run 1½ miles in 12 minutes or less.
2.20	Refining. Hit a successful passing shot in racquetball from various court positions.
3.10	Varying. Ride a skateboard while doing a handstand.
3.20	Improvising. Originate a novel skill during a routine on the parallel bars.
3.30	Composing. Create a movement sequence and perform it to music.

CRITICISMS OF BEHAVIORAL OBJECTIVES

The cognitive, affective, and psychomotor taxonomies have allowed consistent accepted terminology to be utilized in the development of objectives. They have caused a re-evaluation of what is being taught and what behaviors are expected of students as a result of instruction. Therefore, the time necessary in writing and evaluating the behavioral objectives seems justified. Behavioral objectives have not gone without challenge. Opponents criticize behavioral objectives on several premises. First, since behavioral objectives are usually detailed statements of educational outcomes and also guide teaching, they might unnecessarily restrict the instructor. A second criticism is related. Opponents feel that education should result in innovative and creative behavior on the part of students and claim that statements of intended outcomes discourage such behavior. A third objection is that behavior stated by the upper ends of the taxonomies is very complex, and therefore, cannot be measured objectively or evaluated in behavioral terms. A related objection is that the lower levels of the taxonomies are easily described in behavioral terms, but the most important behaviors, those outcomes associated with upper levels of the taxonomy, are more difficult specifically to identify behaviorally.

In any event, the mere fact that objections are raised indicates that behavioral objectives have caused teachers, curriculum designers, and others to concentrate on the outcomes of teaching. Behavioral objectives represent a viable method of providing a synchronization of process and product.

Summary

Objectives serve a valuable function in the educational process. Properly stated, educational objectives give specific insight into the development and use of instructional methods, and measurement and evaluation procedures.

Objectives may be defined according to their specificity. General educational objectives are long-range goals. Curriculum objectives identify behaviors expected of students as a result of completing a unit, course, or series of courses. Instructional or behavioral objectives are specific statements that describe what students will be able to do after a prescribed unit of instruction. The responsibility of writing behavioral objectives usually lies with the physical educator while the other types of objectives, which are more general, are most often developed for an entire school district.

Writing behavioral objectives becomes easier by understanding the elements of a behavioral objective. They are:

1. Who is to perform the desired behavior.
2. The actual behavior to be performed.
3. The result of the behavior.
4. The conditions under which the behavior is to be performed.
5. The standard used to evaluate success.

Objectives are usually written in three domains of behavior. The cognitive domain is concerned with intellectual abilities, skills, and knowledge; the affective domain includes attitudes, interests, and appreciations; and the psychomotor domain includes behaviors that emphasize some motor skill or neuromuscular coordination.

Taxonomies have been developed for each domain. These orderly presentations give much insight in the development of behavioral objectives. Although there has been some criticism of the use of behavioral objectives, there is little doubt that their use has precipitated a re-evaluation of what is taught, measured, and evaluated.

Study Questions

1. Distinguish between general educational objectives, curriculum objectives, and behavioral objectives.
2. Identify the elements necessary to state properly a behavioral objective.

3. Give 10 examples of action words used in expressing behavioral objectives.
4. Identify the major components of each of the three domains of behavior.
5. Compare and contrast the 1.00, 2.00, and uppermost levels of each taxonomic domain. In your experience, what levels of each domain were tested in your high school physical education class? In college?
6. Using the skeleton taxonomies for each domain as presented in this chapter, write a behavioral objective for the 3.00 level.
7. Make a list of curriculum objectives for a unit of instruction in physical education. Next, for each curriculum objective list three specific behavioral objectives.
8. Select a unit of your choice. Write three behavioral objectives for each domain of behavior.
9. What criticisms have been made against the use of behavioral objectives? Do the values outweigh the liabilities?

CHAPTER 7

Test Construction

After you have read and studied this chapter you should be able to:

1. *Determine the purpose of a test.*
2. *Plan a test using a test blueprint.*
3. *Develop a test blueprint by utilizing objectives and content outline.*
4. *Identify the different types of cognitive test items.*
5. *Correctly construct different types of objective tests including true-false, matching, completing, identification, and multiple-choice items.*
6. *Correctly construct different types of subjective tests including essay and short essay items.*
7. *Identify the different types of psychomotor test items.*
8. *Correctly construct different types of psychomotor or performance tests including simulated conditions, game performance items, and rating scales.*

Throughout this textbook the emphasis has been on the evaluation and development of the teacher's own tests. Additional emphasis of these goals will be provided in this chapter with the development and construction of teacher-made tests as the primary concern. In order to prepare valid, reliable, and useful tests, physical education teachers should utilize a specific set of procedures that include *determining the purpose of the test, planning it with a test blueprint, and constructing the test items.*

DETERMINING THE PURPOSE OF THE TEST

Classroom tests in physical education can be used for a variety of purposes. These purposes were listed and discussed in Chapter 1 and only a brief review will be included in this section. From the purposes reviewed below the teacher can determine the type of examination that might be most appropriate for the instructional unit as well as the types of items that might be included in the test.

It was indicated in Chapter 1 that measurement and evaluation serve many purposes in physical education. Students may be evaluated and placed in appropriate groups to enhance learning. Another purpose of measurement is to diagnose learning problems. Progress during the unit of instruction and achievement after the unit can be evaluated by using formative and summative evaluation procedures respectively. The improvement of students can be measured and evaluated by using proper procedures. We also feel that the students can be motivated with a measurement and evaluation program by providing them with immediate feedback. Other purposes are to provide a sound basis for evaluation of teachers and the curriculum. Teachers can use evaluation to develop norms as well as to help predict future success of their students in specific skills. Finally, measurement and evaluation is important in the process of research. It is probably true that teachers are often interested in having a particular test serve more than one purpose. However, it is likely that each test has a primary purpose. It is this primary purpose that should be most important in the physical education teacher's mind as the test is planned.

PLANNING THE TEST WITH A TEST BLUEPRINT

Too often, tests in education are constructed as a last minute task. Teachers, upon realizing that a test is needed, often develop it the day before it is to be administered without the assistance of proper pretest planning. These last-minute tests usually result in too much or too little emphasis on certain instructional objectives. Teachers may have only the number of items or number of possible points in mind when beginning to write items and fail to cover all of the concepts developed during the teaching unit. Occasionally, concepts not taught during the unit will be tested.

To plan for any test adequately the teacher must clearly state the purpose of the test and its impact and importance to the unit evaluation. The teacher must also define in behavioral terms the *objectives* that are to be measured by the test and identify the actual *content* to be covered by the test. The behavioral objectives, of course, determine the basis for what should be taught in the instructional unit whereas the content outline is the vehicle through which the objectives are achieved. This implies that the development of a test is started long before the first lesson is taught. In addition the relative importance of each of the objectives and each content area must be reviewed and determined.

The teacher or test planner must realize that a given test is a sample of all possible questions that could be developed for the teaching unit. Pretest planning will provide assurance that the sample of questions constructed reflect the objectives, content, and actual teaching emphasis. No attempt will be made in this chapter to discuss objectives or content area since they have already been discussed in other chapters. However, the following sections will explain their roles in planning a test.

Objectives

The first procedure in planning any test is to define carefully the objectives of the unit of instruction. They should be completed and presented to all students during the first class meeting. That the use of objectives is incorporated in the test-planning procedure indicates that test construction must begin long before a single lesson is taught.

Various aids in the development of objectives are available — curriculum guides, district guides, or professional association guides, for instance — but ultimately the responsibility of developing behavioral objectives for any group of students lies with the classroom teacher.

The teacher should develop a comprehensive list of behavioral objectives, following the suggestions and guidelines presented in Chapter 6. The objectives are condensed or shortened so that they can be used in the development of the test blueprint, which will be discussed later in this section.

Content

The second preparatory step in test construction is to specify the content to be covered. This task is also completed prior to development or presentation of any lesson. The content outline is very important because it is the vehicle through which the behavioral objectives are accomplished. The content outline is actually a list of major topics that are to be covered during the course of instruction. The detail of the content outline will vary depending on the personal preference of the instructor as well as the purpose of the test, the length of the unit, and the type of test that will be developed. For example, when criterion-referenced tests are used the teacher should develop the content outline in more detail than when norm-referenced tests are administered.

The development of a content outline is beyond the intended scope of this text; however, almost any introductory methods test will provide the student with sufficient information to understand and complete this section. It should be understood that the content outline is prepared from the teacher's experience, textbooks in the area, or perhaps from school or district curriculum guides. Upon completion of the unit outline, the teacher is ready to begin the process of instruction through the development and use of daily lesson plans. In addition the teacher is now ready to begin the process of test construction through the development of test blueprints.

Test Blueprint

The content outline and the list of behavioral objectives represent the two dimensions from which a test should be planned. These two dimensions need to be placed together to determine the objectives that relate to each content topic. This combination of the content outline and behavioral objectives is called a *test blueprint*. It is an outline or framework for the construction of a test. By following the test blueprint the teacher will be certain that all materials taught will be tested and that the correct weight will be given to the topics.

Figure 7.1 shows an example of a test blueprint for a unit examination in volleyball. As prepared, the test blueprint requires the construction of two separate tests since both psychomotor and cognitive performances are included. Notice that the behavioral objectives list in the blueprint is not a comprehensive list of all objectives. By combining similar behavioral-objective topics the test blueprint is more manageable and considerably easier to use. The student should keep in mind that a complete list of behavioral objectives is important to develop and use during the instruction of the unit. The condensed list is used only to aid in the development of a workable test blueprint.

The test blueprint is best developed on a large piece of construction cardboard approximately 18 by 30 inches. The work on the board should be done with a soft lead pencil to enable the teacher to make additions or changes as the unit progresses. In the sample blueprint the condensed list of behavioral objectives for the volleyball unit is shown in the left-hand column. The objectives are subdivided into the cognitive and psychomotor domains with the cognitive area further divided into the objectives concerning rules, strategy, terminology, and techniques. The psychomotor domain is listed simply as skills.

Also found in the left-hand column with the objectives are percentages with the approximate amount of time the teacher shall spend in each category during the instruction of the unit. For example, the teacher would be expected to spend about 2 percent of the total instructional time teaching rules as they relate to the serve. Similarly, 4 percent of the teacher's time would be utilized teaching strategy as it relates to the pass. Finally, 12 percent of the teacher's effort would be spent teaching skills of the serve, the set, and the spike, and approximately 24 percent of the total instructional time would be spent teaching skills of the pass.

The percentage and time allotted to each content area may seem cumbersome and somewhat confusing at first. However, if they are used as guides in the development of the daily lesson plans the confusion will be minimal. The teacher should be prepared to alter the blueprint and the specific percentages as the unit progresses. If, for example, less time is spent on the serve and more time is spent on the pass the changes are noted on the test blueprint so that they can be referred to later during the construction of the test.

One additional consideration must be made about the test blueprint in Figure 7.1. Within each cell or box the teacher should number and briefly write a summary of each concept that was taught during the unit. This recording task should be carried out on a daily basis to insure accuracy. In the sample test blueprint, only the cells corresponding to the objectives concerned with terminology are filled in. For example, under the content area of setting the teacher recorded six different terms that were taught during the unit. They are quick center set, high center set, short shoot set, and so forth. The teacher must develop an efficient procedure of recording the topics, which is a primary

Figure 7.1 Example of partially completed test blueprint.

Behavioral Objectives		*Content Outline* *Serve*	 *Set*	 *Spike*	 *Pass*	*No. of Items*
Cognitive		Concept 2%	2%	2%	4%	
Rules	10%	1.____ 4.____ 2.____ 5.____ 3.____ 6.____	1.____ 5.____ 2.____ 6.____ 3.____ 7.____ 4.____ 8.____	1.____ 5.____ 2.____ 6.____ 3.____ 4.____	1.____ 4.____ 2.____ 5.____ 3.____	10
		2%	2%	2%	4%	
Strategy	10%	1.____ 4.____ 2.____ 3.____	1.____ 4.____ 2.____ 5.____ 3.____ 6.____	1.____ 4.____ 2.____ 3.____	1.____ 4.____ 2.____ 5.____ 3.____	10
		2%	2%	2%	4%	
Terminology	10%	1. cross court serve 2. down the line serve 3. short serve 4. long serve 5. floater serve 6. top spin serve 7. round house serve	1. quick center set 2. high center set 3. short shoot set 4. shoot set 5. short back set 6. high outside set	1. down the line spike 2. cross court spike 3. soft spike 4. dink or tip 5. off speed spike 6. cut shot spike	1. dig pass 2. dive 3. roll 4. defensive pass 5. collapsed dig 6. bump	10
		2%	2%	2%	4%	
Techniques	10%	1.____ 2.____ 3.____	1.____ 4.____ 2.____ 5.____ 3.____ 6.____	1.____ 4.____ 2.____ 5.____ 3.____ 6.____ 7.____	1.____ 4.____ 2.____ 5.____ 3.____	10
		12%	12%	12%	24%	
Psychomotor						60
Skills	60%	1.____ 6.____ 2.____ 7.____ 3.____ 8.____ 4.____ 9.____ 5.____ 10.____	1.____ 5.____ 2.____ 6.____ 3.____ 7.____ 4.____ 8.____	1.____ 5.____ 2.____ 6.____ 3.____ 7.____ 4.____	1.____ 6.____ 2.____ 7.____ 3.____ 8.____ 4.____ 9.____ 5.____ 10.____	
Number of Test Items						
Cognitive items		8	8	8	16	100
Psychomotor points		12	12	12	24	

reason for using the large piece of cardboard in the development of the test blueprint.

The preparation of a two-dimensional test blueprint is a time-consuming and difficult task. The busy physical educator might rationalize that the time is perhaps better spent elsewhere. However, the construction of a test blueprint will not only clarify the objectives of a specific unit, but will also aid the teacher in developing sound tests for measuring student progress in the unit. Once a blueprint has been developed it can be used repeatedly with only minor adjustments to the percentages or concepts taught during subsequent years.

The specific use of the test blueprint is for the construction of the unit test and in the selection of the specific topics for the test items. The proportion of test questions from each content and objective area should correspond to the emphasis given to the topic during instruction. For example, the teacher may choose to construct a 100-point summative examination to measure student progress at the end of the instructional unit. By referring to the test blueprint (Figure 7.1), the teacher would divide the examination into a cognitive test consisting of 40 percent of the total or 40 points and a psychomotor test consisting of 60 percent of the total or 60 points.

Also, the teacher would develop 10 percent or 10 questions from the rules objectives with 2 percent or 2 questions each coming from the content areas of serving, setting, and spiking and 4 percent or 4 questions coming from the content area of passing. Similarly, 10 percent of the total test points would come from each of the three remaining cognitive behavioral objective categories with the same content area percentages as discussed for the rules section. The psychomotor part of the examination would be developed following the same procedures. Twelve percent of the total test points or 12 points would come from each of the content areas except passing, which would consist of 24 percent of the total or 24 points.

The items for the test would be constructed from the written notes that the teacher has made in each of the individual cells. From the test blueprint we see that the final test should consist of two questions from the cell represented by serving terminology. The teacher would review the concepts taught during the instructional unit and select two of them from which to develop the actual test items. Similarly, two items would be constructed from the concepts noted under setting terminology. For example, the teacher might choose to construct a test item about the quick center set and another about the shoot set. It might be possible to combine two or more of the concepts into a single question. This procedure would be repeated until the entire test has been constructed.

By adhering to the percentages in the test blueprint and to the planning of the test according to the suggestions in this section the teacher should develop a test with high content validity. For the busy teacher the time saved in determining the content validity for each of the unit examinations during test construction may be reason enough for using the test blueprint for all instructional units.

Even after the teacher has developed a test blueprint and made definite the specific concepts that are to be measured in the unit examination, a formidable task remains. The items to be included in the test must be constructed by selecting from numerous types of items that may be included in any measuring instrument. The following sections will provide the teacher with insights and expertise in the selection and construction of the specific test items.

CONSTRUCTING THE TEST ITEMS

In the previous section, two general types of tests were mentioned. The *cognitive test* may consist of either subjective or objective items. The *psychomotor test* may involve the measuring of individual skills or the performance in a game situation. Often, a *rating scale* is developed to measure psychomotor performance and will be discussed in this section.

Types of Cognitive Test Items — Objective

Cognitive or knowledge tests can consist of either *objective* or *subjective* items. Objective test items are questions that have responses or answers that are brief and specific. The objective item or question should provide a limited, specific set of choices from which the student must select. The correct answer is determined as the test is constructed. The problem presented by the teacher and the students' choice of answers are completely structured. There is little freedom on the part of the student either to define the problem or to organize an answer. The structured nature of the objective question allows each student to deal with the same problem and also, the instructor to break complex problems into their component parts and obtain measures that are quite specific. Objective items provide comparable measures for all students, and test results can provide significant diagnostic information about the student. The common types of objective test items are the *true-false item*, the *matching item*, the *completion item*, the *identification item*, and the *multiple-choice item*.

True-False Item. This item consists of a statement that the student is asked to answer true or false, yes or no, right or wrong, agree or disagree, or correct or incorrect. The most commonly used response form is true-false; thus the common reference to the true-false item. This type of objective test item is used most often in measuring the correctness of facts, terminology, rules, court dimensions, and the like.

The advantages of using true-false items are somewhat limited. The ease of test construction for the teacher is often considered an advantage. This advantage generally reflects the construction of poor true-false items rather than well thought out and developed questions. Another advantage for using true-false items is the large number of questions and wide range of course material that may be covered in a single testing period.

The disadvantages of the true-false item are numerous. Perhaps the most serious disadvantage is the type of material that can be measured. The teacher is limited to test fairly simple and factual learning outcomes that can be expressed as true or false without qualification. A second limitation of this type of item is its susceptibility to guessing. Students have a 50 percent opportunity to select correct answers based on chance alone. Because of clues and other problems in constructing items the guess factor is often considerably above 50 percent. Finally, the reliability of each item is fairly low so that a true-false section would require a large number of items to achieve an accurate representation of each student's knowledge.

Writing True-False Items. Most of the suggestions for writing true-false items are in the form of pitfalls to avoid. It is important to write items that are clear and free from ambiguity and irrelevant clues.

1. *Each item must be totally true or false.* Each statement should be written so that experts would unanimously agree on the answer. Statements that can be qualified cause most informed students to be confused or unsure.
2. *Avoid the use of specific determiners in the construction of the item.* Words such as all, never, no, always, or impossible should not be used in false statements, whereas words like sometimes, usually, often, or occasionally should be avoided in true statements.
3. *Try to avoid the use of negatives or double negatives in the statements.* The inclusion of such words as no, not, or none contributes to confusion and ambiguity and certainly not to understanding on the part of the student.
4. *Do not include trivia.* Attempt to construct items that are meaningful and significant to the learning process of the student.
5. *True and false statements should be of the same approximate length.* The tendency of many teachers is to make true statements longer than false statements. This can become a clue to many perceptive students. The problem can be corrected by adding qualifying phrases where necessary to false statements.
6. *The number of true and false statements should be equal.* Students have a tendency to respond in favor of either true or false when the answer is in doubt. By having an equal number of true and false items the individual student scores will not be unduly inflated or deflated.
7. *Limit statements to a single concept.* Items that include more than one concept are often misleading and confusing to the students.
8. *Underline the key phrase or words in the statement.* Underscoring the

part of the statement that is to be considered by the student reduces ambiguity and confusion.

9. *Correct false statements.* If students are asked to correct any statements that are false, more depth of understanding can be measured.
10. *Use a guessing correction formula.* Most experts will agree that true-false scores should be corrected for the guessing factor. One procedure that works very well is to subtract incorrect responses from correct responses. Statements that are left blank are not counted as correct or incorrect.

Examples of True-False Items.

1. T. F. The median is a measure of variability.
2. T. F. The player may not touch the net with the free hand in the volleyball spike.
3. T. F. There are two types of serves in volleyball.
4. T. F. The arms and legs produce force simultaneously in the breast stroke.
5. T. F. The arms recover out of the water in the elementary backstroke.

Matching Items. Usually, the matching item consists of two columns. A word, number, or symbol in one of the columns is matched with a word, sentence, or phrase in the second column. Generally, the items in the first column from which a match is sought are called *premises* whereas the items in the second column from which the selection is made are called *responses*.

The matching examination is limited to the measurement of factual information based on simple associations. If the emphasis is on the ability to identify the relationship between two things and there are sufficient premises and responses available, a matching test would be appropriate. The matching item can also be used for identifying various parts of sports equipment from pictures or diagrams.

An advantage of the matching item is the ease of construction. Relative to other types of objective items the matching item is considerably easier to develop, and much less time is required in the construction phase. Another advantage of the matching test is its compact form, which allows the teacher to measure large amounts of factual material in a comparatively short time.

The main disadvantage of the matching item is its restriction to the measurement of factual information, which leads to an emphasis of rote memorization. The nature of the matching items with the two corresponding columns makes them highly susceptible to the presence of irrelevant clues. These irrelevant clues often interfere with the reliability of the test. Another disadvantage is the difficulty of obtaining enough similar or homogeneous material that related to the objectives or the learning outcomes. Frequently, many of the items on the matching list are trivial in nature and often not emphasized during the teacher's unit in an effort to develop an examination that is long enough to be useful.

Writing Matching Items.

1. *The set of items in a single matching list should be homogeneous.* Only if the items in the set are similar or homogeneous will the student be forced to make relatively fine discriminations to arrive at a correct response. If the incorrect responses are to serve as plausible choices for students who are in doubt, the items in the list must be homogeneous.
2. *The sets of items should be relatively short.* It is much easier to develop homogeneous items if the sets are restricted to approximately 5 or 10 items. In addition the shorter lists enable the student to read and respond more rapidly and with less confusion than long lists of 20 to 50 items.
3. *The responses are generally shorter than the premises.* Placing the shorter items on the right and designating them as responses will help the student. Generally the response column will be read each time the student moves to another premise. By having short statements as responses the time spent by the student on the items will be reduced.
4. *Provide in the directions the basis for matching the responses and premises.* In many instances the direction for the matching is obvious; however, for the sake of clarity for all students this direction should be stated. For younger students it is perhaps advisable to direct them to draw lines between the items to reduce further confusion.
5. *Develop a heading for each column of items.* To aid the student further in understanding the task, clear and definitive headings should be developed and placed at the top of each list of items.
6. *Develop more responses or answers than premises.* Guessing will be reduced by having approximately three more responses than premises for each set of items. It will also eliminate the automatic selection of the last item in the list.
7. *Arrange responses in a logical order.* Perhaps the best order for the responses is an alphabetical listing. This will reduce the time required of the student to find the correct answer. It will also prevent any unnecessary clues to the appropriate responses by the student seeing the order in which they are presented in the list.

Examples of Matching Items.

Indicate in the space at the left the letter of the muscle action that is associated with each muscle.

Muscles	*Actions*
_____1. Semitendinosus	(a) Flexion of the trunk
_____2. Sartorius	(b) Extension of the forearm
_____3. Triceps brachii	(c) Outward rotation of the hip
_____4. Adductor magnus	(d) Flexion of the hip
_____5. Rectus abdominous	(e) Flexion of the shoulder
	(f) Flexion of the wrist
	(g) Extension of the hip

Completion Items. The completion item may include questions, statements, or incomplete statements that can be answered by a word, phrase, symbol, or number. Basically the forms are similar and can be used interchangeably to measure such things as knowledge of vocabulary, terms, names, dates, simple concepts, or some quantitative problems.

An advantage of the completion item is that the student must supply the entire response. This, of course, reduces the possibility that the pupil can obtain the correct answer simply be guessing. Generally, partial knowledge of a topic or concept is insufficient for responding successfully to this type of item. Another advantage of the completion examination is the ease of construction. The items usually require response to relatively simple factual concepts and are usually very easily and rapidly developed.

The major disadvantage of this type of item lies in its unsuitability for measuring more complex concepts. The highly specific nature of the answer required of a question seriously limits the types of objectives or learning outcomes that can effectively be measured. A second shortcoming of the completion item is in the difficulties confronted in the scoring procedures. Unless extreme care is taken in the development of each item, a number of answers with varying degrees of correctness might be possible. The student must be able to determine which response the teacher is requesting, and often the teacher will have to spend extra time approving and correcting responses that are also adequate. Spelling also presents another problem in the scoring procedure. Many teachers are currently demanding that students be able to spell responses correctly to be given full credit for the question. These spelling decisions also take extra time and consideration.

Writing Completion Items.

1. *Omit only significant words in incomplete statement items.* Omitting insignificant words or phrases in completion items will only contribute to the confusion and frustration of students and will certainly not contribute effectively to the measurement experience.
2. *Construct items so that the required response is brief and precise.* This type of item is objective, which implies the use of questions having definite answers. The only reason a student should fail to respond

with the correct response is a lack of knowledge. This requirement is more easily met by including items with only one precise answer.

3. *Avoid lifting statements directly from textbooks.* Items taken directly from textbooks promote memorization by the student. In addition these items are often vague and unclear as they represent only one sentence of several that are presented by the author in developing a concept.
4. *Avoid overmutilated statements in incomplete items.* When too many blanks are provided in a single statement the item usually has little or no meaning. It is usually better to write several more items with only one or two incomplete words or phrases in each.
5. *Blanks for responses should be equal in length.* Unequal lengths for the blanks often provide unnecessary clues to the correct answer. It is suggested that a column of blanks be included at the left-hand edge of the test paper to eliminate the problem as well as to facilitate ease of scoring.

Examples of Completion Items.

Complete each item by writing the correct response in the blank on the left.

_____1. A takedown in wrestling counts_____points.
_____2. A wrestler's team receives_____points when he wins a first round tournament match with a fall.
_____3. A_____occurs when the wrestler obtains the advantage over his opponents from the neutral position.
_____4. A major decision is awarded when a wrestler beats his opponent by at least_____points.
_____5. In a single leg takedown the wrestler must place his head_____his opponent's leg.

Identification. The identification test emphasizes knowledge of the implements and products that students use in sports-skill situations. In this type of examination the student is required to identify the *nature* and *function* of the various parts of a typical piece of sports equipment. For example, the student might be asked to identify the various parts of a golf club and to explain the function of each part.

The primary advantage of such an item is that students must demonstrate knowledge of the basic equipment that they are expected to learn to use. Another advantage of the identification test is that the students become aware of the important relationship between the content being taught in a unit and the functions of the various parts of the implements being utilized.

One disadvantage of the identification item is that the relationship between knowing the parts and functions of a sports implement and being able to adequately use the implement in a game situation is not known. If the teacher understands this possible limitation of the identification item, there should be few problems in its use. A second disadvantage is the amount of time necessary to measure all students with this type of item. Each student must be examined by the teacher independently, and the time required may prohibit the use of the identification item in large classes. This time problem can be overcome by using diagrams and drawings instead of the actual implement. The students would then be required to write their responses, and all students could be tested simultaneously.

Writing Identification Items.

1. *Provide sufficiently clear directions so that students understand desired response.* If the teacher is concerned only with identification, it should be made clear to the students. If both identification and function of an implement part is desired, again the student should be made totally aware and be given adequate time to respond accordingly.
2. *Students should be required to explain the function as well as identify the implement.* The teacher is measuring recall by requiring the student to identify the implement parts; however, by also requiring the student to explain the function the teacher can also measure the level of understanding that the student has about the implement.
3. *Drawings, when used, should be carefully reproduced and correctly labeled.* It was stated earlier in this section that drawings could be used to reduce the time necessary for identification testing. When they are utilized every effort should be made to insure accuracy and clearness of the reproduction.
4. *Students should be required to identify only the significant aspects of the implement.* Emphasizing trim or unimportant parts of the implement can only cause students to do poorly on the test or encourage them to memorize unnecessary details strictly for the sake of the test.
5. *Scoring should be simple.* One point should be allowed for each correct response to save time and facilitate ease of scoring. It probably makes no sense to weigh the different parts of the test.

Examples of Identification Items.

Golf Identification Test

Direction: Identify and give the function of each part of the golf club (Figure 7.2). Write your answers in the blank on the left.

Multiple-Choice Items. The most commonly used form of multiple-choice items consists of a problem and a list of possible solutions. The problem is written either as a question or incomplete statement called the *stem*. The list of

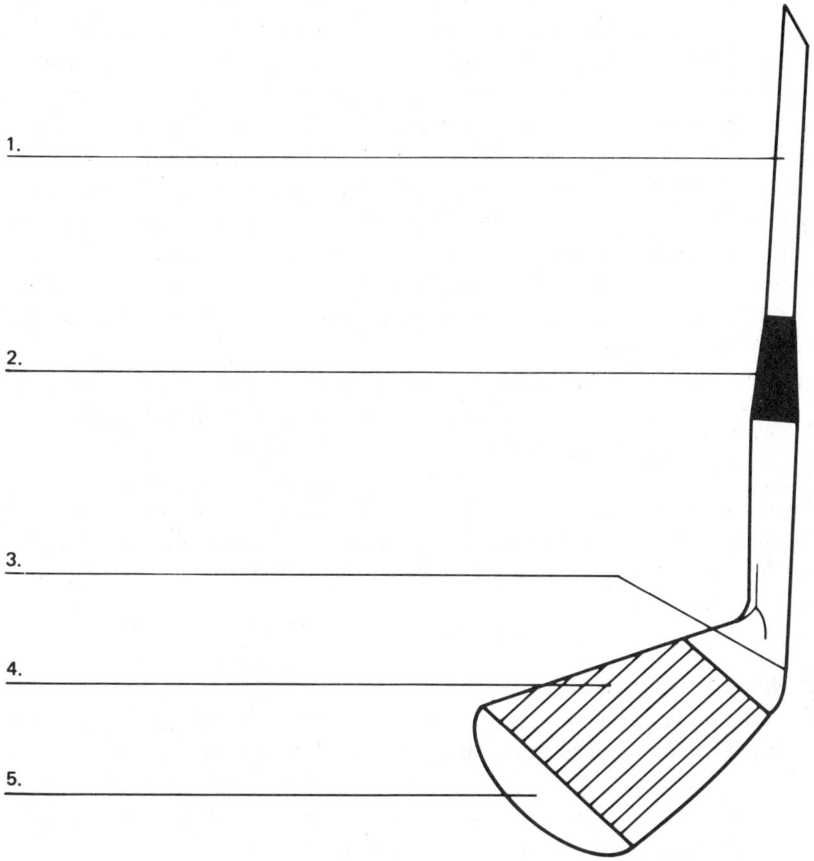

Figure 7.2. Golf club.

solutions are typically single words, numbers, symbols, or phrases and are called *responses*. The student is asked to read the problem or stem and select the best solution or response. The remaining solutions are *distractors*, which develop their name from their intended purpose of distracting students who do not know the correct response.

The multiple-choice item is considered by most experts to be the best and most versatile type of objective test question. The teacher can measure a wide variety of objectives and learning outcomes with multiple-choice items ranging from very simple, knowledge-level concepts to complex synthesis- or evaluation-level items. Such learning outcomes as rules, terminology, specific facts, principles, methods, procedures, and applications are easily measured with well-written multiple-choice items.

The most important advantage of using the multiple-choice item — a reason mentioned in the preceding paragraph — is this item's versatility and adaptability in measuring different levels of knowledges and concepts effectively. The ambiguous nature of other objective items is often not present in multiple-choice items because the multiple responses provide more clarity for the student. Another advantage is that the need for similar or homogeneous material is eliminated because each item represents a single concept and does not have to be like the one preceding or following. The problem of guessing is minimized in this type of item, which indeed makes it a more reliable item than other objective test types. Finally, with regard to advantages the multiple-choice test is relatively free from response sets, which means that students do not usually have tendencies to favor particular solutions when they do not know the correct answers.

The multiple-choice item, despite its many positive attributes, does have certain disadvantages. First, since this type of item does require the selection of a correct response, it is not particularly useful for the measurement of problem-solving skills or for the measurement of the ability to organize or present ideas. Perhaps a more significant limitation of the multiple-choice item is the difficulty in obtaining a sufficient number of incorrect but truly plausible distractors. Teachers will often fill in with distractors that are nonsensical or at least clearly not plausible.

Writing Multiple-Choice Items.

1. *The problem should be stated in the stem.* A properly developed multiple-choice item should contain a complete problem in the stem that actually has meaning without the responses. This procedure will cut down on each student's reading time as well as decrease the chances of the students misunderstanding the item.
2. *All responses for each item should be grammatically consistent.* This suggestion is presented to prevent unnecessary clues from appearing in the items. It seems that grammatical clues occur most frequently in the correct response and are most often disregarded in the distractors. This, of course, provides the students with unneeded assistance on the questions.
3. *Avoid the use of negatives in the stem.* The use of negatives such as no, not, least, and except contribute little to the value of a multiple-choice item. Negatives often present problems in understanding to students and provide the teacher with little information concerning positive student knowledges.
4. *Each item should contain only one correct response.* Items that have more than one correct response indicate more than one problem in the stem. The process of answering the question requires a mental response of true or false to each alternative rather than the comparison and selection of one response.

5. *All distractors should be plausible.* Each distractor should function to distract students who do not know the correct response. The distractors should appear similar to the correct response, and some students should select each distractor. If the distractors are not similar to the correct response or are not chosen by any of the students, they are making no contribution to the student's discrimination of the item and should be eliminated.
6. *The length of the alternatives should not provide a clue to the correct answer.* Often, a correct response needs to be qualified and, as a result, is written in a longer form than the distractors. The teacher should make a special effort to control the length of all responses in order not to provide unnecessary clues to students who do not know the correct response.
7. *Avoid patterns in the positions of the responses.* Placing the correct response in a certain place more often than others provides another irrelevant clue for students who do not know the correct response. In addition to placing the correct response in each position approximately an equal number of times, the teacher should avoid any pattern to the order of the responses.
8. *Avoid using the response "none of the above" too frequently.* None of the above is often used as a last resort distractor, and students soon learn that it is not a plausible response. Infrequent use of the response is suggested and, in addition, the response should be correct on certain occasions.
9. *Avoid using the response "all of the above."* This response is considered poor because the student will be able to determine that it is correct if they can determine that any two of the remaining responses are correct. Since it was previously advised that each item have only one correct response it is inconsistent to have all of the responses on an item correct.

Examples of Multiple Choice Items.

Choose the *one* correct answer for each of the items. Write the letter of the response in the blank at the left.

_____1. In volleyball what is the appropriate referee's decision when a member from team A serves to a member of team B, and as the ball is returned to team A the ball touches the net.

(a) Point
(b) Net serve
(c) Legal play
(d) Side out
(e) None of the above

_____2. In badminton singles play which basic stroke should the player use when in doubt which to use?

(a) Lob
(b) Smash
(c) Drive
(d) Drop
(e) None of the above

_____**3.** The most commonly used measure of physical fitness is obtained through
(a) Tests of balance
(b) Tests of agility
(c) Blood analysis
(d) Tests of cardio-respiratory endurance
(e) Tests of muscular strength

_____**4.** In the second period a wrestler from team A has the choice and chooses the up or advantage position. What will occur in the third period?
(a) Determined by a coin toss
(b) A's choice
(c) B's choice
(d) B in up position
(e) A in up position

_____**5.** In an overhand volleyball serve, the hand should make contact with the ball
(a) At the first joint of the fingers
(b) Just behind the head
(c) In front of the shoulders, but over the head
(d) Directly up from the shoulder
(e) None of the above

Item analysis of the Objective Test Items. Once the objective test has been administered to a group of students, a thorough *item analysis* should be completed to provide the physical education instructor with information concerning the effectiveness of the test. The analysis can be used to make decisions about individual items within the test as well as the worthiness of the test as a whole.

Item analysis can be carried out with modern hand calculators or through the use of the electronic computer. Programs for item analysis using the computer are included in Appendix F. Procedures and formulas for item analysis using the hand calculator will be included in this section.

It is generally agreed that item analysis should be done with sample sizes in excess of one hundred students because of the number of errors associated with this type of analysis. Often, the teacher must combine two or three classes to obtain the desired number of student tests for analysis purposes.

The *difficulty rating, index of discrimination,* and *point biserial correlation* are three different item analysis procedures. Each of these methods provides information about the test items and will be discussed in this section.

Item Difficulty. The difficulty rating (*DR*) is determined by the percentage of students who choose the correct response for a particular test item. The formula for computing the difficulty rating is:

$$DR = \frac{P}{N}$$

where DR = difficulty rating
P = number of students answering an item correctly
N = number of students

For example, if 35 students from a class of 100 answer a question correctly the difficulty rating would be

$$DR = \frac{35}{100} = .35$$

The difficulty rating does not provide information about the extent that the item discriminates between good and poor scores on any test. The difficulty rating can help the classroom teacher considerably when concern for the relative levels of student achievement is important. Most experts agree that a difficulty rating range of 30 to 70 percent works adequately for student achievement discrimination. Remember that this range is used only in norm-referenced tests and that difficulty ratings of 90 percent or higher are required when utilizing criterion-referenced tests.

Index of Discrimination. The index of discrimination (ID) provides information to the teacher about the number of high and low performers on a specific test who answer each item correctly. It is basically a coefficient of correlation between the responses on a test item and the scores on the total test. The index of discrimination is usually computed with a hand or desk calculator and uses scores from the top and bottom 27 percent of the students taking the test.

The formula for computing the index of discrimination is

$$ID = \frac{Cu - C_l}{Nu}$$

where ID = index of discrimination
Cu = number of correct responses in upper 27 percent
Cl = number of correct responses in lower 27 percent
Nu = total number of students in upper group.

For example, if the class size was 100, the upper and lower 27 percent would be 27 students. If the Cu is 21 and Cl is 7, the ID would be

$$ID = \frac{21 - 7}{27} = \frac{14}{27} = .52$$

The index of discrimination indicates the extent that each test question discriminates between the students who scored high on the test and those who scored low. It is desirable for each item to be correctly answered by more students in the high group than by those in the low group. When this occurs the item is considered as a positive discriminator by the teacher. If the opposite occurs the item is said to discriminate negatively. It is important for the teacher to remove any items from the test that are negative discriminators.

The index of discrimination has a range of +1.00 through 0.00 to −1.00. In actuality the index of discrimination never reaches the plus or minus 1.00 levels. Most measurement experts agree that items having an index of discrimination of .30 or above are considered good, whereas items with discrimination indexes below .30 need improvement or should be eliminated from the test.

Individual Item Comparison. The *point biserial* correlation is similar to the index of discrimination. It provides a measure of the relationship between the scores on a specific test and the correct or incorrect reponse on each item. Point biserial correlation is a form of product-moment correlation and is interpreted in the same way as the Pearson product-moment correlation described in Chapter 3.

The formula for the point biserial correlation is

$$r_{pbi} = \frac{\overline{X}_p - \overline{X}_q}{s_x} \sqrt{pq}$$

where r_{pbi} = point biserial correlation
Xp = mean score of those students who answer a certain item correctly
Xq = mean score of those students who answer a certain item incorrectly
s_x = standard deviation of all scores
p = percentage of students who answer a specific item correctly
q = percentage of students who answer a specific item incorrectly

The calculation of the point biserial correlation without a computer is somewhat time-consuming but is not considered difficult. An example of the computation of a point biserial for one item on an objective test item is shown below.

Total mean score for students answering item correctly: $Xp = 49.31$

Total mean score for students answering item incorrectly: $Xq = 21.78$

Standard deviation for all scores: $s_x = 11.93$

Percentage of students who answer the item correctly: p 74/88 = .84

Percentage of students who answer the item incorrectly: q 14/88 = .16

Therefore,

$$r_{pbi} = \frac{49.31 - 21.78}{11.93} \sqrt{.84 \times .16} = .85$$

Any test item that correlates near zero with the test scores is carefully analyzed. It is still possible for the item that correlates near zero with the total test score to be valid but it is not likely. Usually these items are excessively easy or difficult, ambiguous, or actually have very little to do with the trait being tested. They usually should be discarded from the test or reconstructed by following the procedures discussed earlier in this chapter. Items that have higher correlations with the total test score are generally considered better items. The item difficulty cannot be too extreme in either direction when high point biserial correlations are obtained, and this type of item will contribute greatly to increasing the reliability of the final test.

Types of Cognitive Test Items — Subjective

It was stated earlier in this chapter that cognitive tests can consist of either objective or subjective items. Only objective tests have been discussed so far. Subjective examinations are designed to measure a student's ability to interpret, integrate, organize, or synthesize basic and complex information. They also test the student's ability to identify and solve problems. The subjective test can measure the students' abilities to express themselves in writing and to supply information rather than merely identifying or recalling factual concepts. Generally, subjective tests can be divided into two types of items: the *short essay* item and the *essay item.* Because of the similarities of these items, they will be presented together.

Short Essay and Essay Items. The short essay item consists of a statement or question developed by the teacher that elicits a fairly precise response from the student. The short essay examination has two limiting factors — the nature of the content of the item and the nature of the student's response. The depth and breadth of the content is limited by the scope of the topic to be discussed. The wording of the short essay question usually limits the form of student response.

The short essay test is very useful in obtaining measures of learning that require the interpretation and application of data in one specific area. In many ways this type of item is similar to many of the objective items discussed earlier in this chapter. The primary difference is that the objective items are concerned with the recognition and recall of the information whereas in the short essay the information must be totally provided by the student. The limitations placed on the scope of the content and the student's responses to the short essay items make them very valuable as testing tools that are quite specific in nature. However, the restrictions limit both the teacher and the student in measuring the student's ability to organize, integrate, and synthesize important information. This must be generally measured by the regular essay examination, which allows greater freedom in these areas.

The essay item consists of a question or statement developed by the teacher that elicits a more general response from the student. The student is generally free to select and present in any logical manner factual information that is considered pertinent. The student is also free to organize the response in any way that will appropriately fulfill the task. It is this freedom of response that allows the pupil to demonstrate and the teacher to measure the ability to select, organize, integrate, synthesize, and evaluate complex ideas.

The essay test provides a necessary ingredient in current educational practices; it fulfills the need to be able to measure a student's total approach to the solving of fairly complex problems. The student must present multiple skills in answering an essay question. Students must not only be able to present an answer, but they must be able to communicate, spell, use correct grammar and paragraph structure, as well as certain basic principles of logic and reasoning. In summary most experts agree that the standard essay examination is an extremely useful and valuable form of measurement and should be included in practically all educational settings where obtaining information about complex concepts is desired.

Advantages and Disadvantages of Essay and Short Essay Items. The advantages of the short essay and essay items are many. The essay item can measure complex learning outcomes. There are certain times when this form of examination is the only way to obtain information about complex concepts. Another important advantage of the essay item is the manner in which it can measure thinking ability and problem-solving skills. Finally, the ease of construction is another advantage of the essay item. In a relatively short time the teacher can develop a number of adequate essay questions.

The disadvantages of the essay item are quite serious and must be considered carefully by the teacher before including it in an examination. The lack of reliability in scoring is one concern. It has been shown that different teachers often score the same questions very differently and, in fact, the same teachers often score the tests totally differently on a second reading. The problem of reliability of scoring can be minimized by following the procedures suggested later in this chapter.

Another disadvantage of the essay item is the amount of time required to read it properly. A great deal of time must be allocated by the teacher to score the essay test. This is often difficult in the typical physical education class, where large numbers are the rule rather than the exception. A final limitation of the essay examination is the restricted nature of the sample of questions. When a teacher chooses to ask three or four questions on an examination, it is difficult to cover all of the major concepts. In fact, the essay examination, because of this limited sampling of concepts, is generally not considered adequate for measuring factual material. This function, of course, is reserved for objective type tests.

Writing Essay and Short Essay Items.

1. *Include the appropriate number of essay items.* It is important for the teacher to know how many questions the students can answer in the time allowed. Of course, the actual number of questions to be included on the test is determined by the complexity of the required answer. However many experts agree that an essay examination should be limited to 2 to 5 regular essay questions and 8 to 15 short essay questions in a specific testing period.
2. *State each question clearly so that students are sure of the required outcome.* Vague and ambiguous phrasing of essay questions can confuse students and cause a wide variation in the responses received. It is unfortunate if students write incorrect answers because they misinterpret the question rather than because they did not know the correct response.
3. *State a point value and an approximate time limit for each question.* In most essay tests, teachers will have questions of varying importance and complexity with the more complex items requiring more time on the part of the student in responding. In addition the more complex items should count more in the final point total. The teacher should indicate on each question the approximate amount of time that the student should spend on each question and the total points that will be given for the appropriate response.
4. *Require all students to answer the same set of questions.* When students are allowed to select a given number of questions from a fairly long list, they are, in practice, taking different tests. Each student then demonstrates ability to different learning outcomes, and any comparison between students is very difficult. In addition students will select only questions that they are quite sure of, and no measures are obtained of the information that the students avoid.
5. *Limit the essay test to measuring concepts that cannot be measured by using objective items.* There is no reason to use an essay test to measure learning outcomes that can be measured more satisfactorily by some form of objective item. For most factual materials the objective examination is considered superior to the subjective item. It is when the learning outcome is very complex that the subjective item is valuable, and it should be used despite the limitations described in the previous section.

Examples of Essay and Short Essay Items.

Read each question carefully and answer each one as completely as possible.

1. Compare and contrast the hip joint to the shoulder joint.
2. Identify the mechanical principles that are involved in the sprint start.
3. Compare the zone press to the person-to-person press.

4. Develop a joint and muscle analysis of the high hurdler approaching and crossing the hurdle.
5. Discuss the strengths and weaknesses of the 4-2 defense in volleyball.

Scoring Essay Items. The most serious limitation in the use of the essay test is in the scoring of the individual items. It is important for the teacher to plan the scoring procedure and to have firmly in mind what will be accepted as an appropriate response before the scoring procedure begins. The following suggestions have been prepared to aid the teacher in scoring the essay examination.

1. *Prepare a model response to each question.* The teacher should outline all of the major topics that should be included in the response. In addition the points that the student can achieve for each major topic should be determined. For example if a question requires the student to respond to five topics, the teacher may assign 3 points to each topic making the total response have a value of 15 points. The teacher can then read the question and award from 0 through 3 points for each of the required topics in the response. The points are then totaled and recorded as the score on the question.
2. *Include comments and corrections for each question.* A test is more useful to students if they can see their errors. It is important for the teacher to include the comments for each topic within the question. This can also aid the teacher in determining the effectiveness of instruction in the various areas of the unit.
3. *Read and score all answers to one question before going on to the next.* By reading the same question on all tests before proceeding to the next one the teacher can reduce the chance of being biased by a poor response. Often if teachers find a bad response on the first question, this will negatively influence their grading on the remaining questions of that test. In addition, reading each question on all papers can help standardize the scoring. The teacher can concentrate on only one question and response, which will certainly provide more uniformity and fairness on the final evaluation.
4. *Avoid knowing students' names while reading responses.* In fact the less the teacher knows about the student the more fair and objective he or she can be relative to the final evaluation.
5. *Determine procedures for handling considerations such as spelling, handwriting, grammar, and irrelevant information.* Factors such as handwriting, spelling, and grammar should not unduly influence the evaluation of the learning outcomes that are being measured. It is suggested that the teacher determine a separate score for these considerations rather than let them alter the evaluation of the student's

response. Irrelevant information is another important consideration. Students should be required to answer only the specific question asked and should be penalized for adding unnecessary and irrelevant material. The amount of penalty should be decided in advance by the teacher.

Types of Psychomotor Skills Tests.

It is very important for the teacher of physical education to develop an understanding of the construction of skills tests. There is a definite trend in physical education away from the extensive use of preconstructed or standardized skills tests. This is due primarily to the discrepancies between the teacher-developed objectives and the objectives actually measured by the standardised tests. The remainder of this chapter identifies and explains procedures that might be used by the physical education teacher to evaluate skills presented during the instructional unit.

Psychomotor or performance items can be categorized into three types: (1) simulated conditions, (2) game performance items, and (3) rating scales. Each of these items will be discussed in the following sections and can be evaluated in several ways including (1) accuracy measures, (2) timed measures, (3) distance measures, and (4) combinations thereof. Each of these methods of evaluation will be discussed in detail in Chapter 14.

Simulated Condition Items. In this item the individual skills are isolated and measured as carefully as possible. The skills are identified and tested independently of a competitive game or situation. The students are asked to simulate the conditions of the game by executing each skill just as they might when playing a game.

Skills tests of this type require that the instructor create an environment similar to the game situation during the administration of the test. It is possible to judge the content validity of the simulated condition item by comparing the testing environment with the performing environment. If, for example, the teacher requires students to execute a skill differently for test purposes than it would be performed in a game situation, content validity would be considered very low. On the other hand, content validity would be high if the individual skills evaluated on the test were being executed as in an actual game.

The simulated conditions test is perhaps the most commonly used instrument for measuring psychomotor skills. Generally the physical educator can select from two different scoring approaches. The first is objective and involves the assignment of predetermined point values to each level of performance. For example the teacher may ask each student to shoot 10 jump shots from the free throw line — giving one point for each successful attempt. In another example the teacher would place targets on the floor of the opposite court during a badminton serving test. Each area in the court would be assigned a numerical value from 1 to 5 with the student receiving the points corresponding to the landing position of each serve.

The second scoring approach for the simulated conditions test is subjective and involves the use of a rating scale to evaluate the overall performance of the student on each skill. For example, if the teacher wanted to evaulate the student's ability to execute the jump shot by the subjective scoring approach, he would have to develop a rating scale following the procedures presented later in this chapter. Students would then be rated subjectively by the teacher on their ability to execute the shot. Such factors as correct form, timing, arch and speed of the ball would be more important than accuracy on this type of test. In the previous scoring procedure, accuracy was the only trait considered in the evaluation.

The advantages of the simulated conditions test are many. Possibly the most important advantage is the amount of time required for testing. Usually a simulated conditions skill test can be administered in one well-planned class period. A second advantage is the ease in scoring. The students are awarded points based on their performance. A final advantage is in the administration of the simulated conditions test. The teacher can easily use assistants to help with the scoring and recording of scores which, of course, can greatly increase the number of students that can be tested in one class period.

One disadvantage of the simulated conditions test is the amount of time required to prepare the test and the test area. Often the teacher must prepare floor areas by taping targets on the floors or walls. This kind of advanced preparation indeed takes time. A second disadvantage is the possibility that the simulated condition test might not be totally realistic when compared to the skills performed in the actual situation.

Writing Simulated Condition Items.

1. *Select only important skills, which are fundamental to the activity being taught in the instructional unit.* Remember that only skills that are taught in the unit should be selected as skills to be measured on the examination.
2. *Develop test conditions that simulate the game situation as closely as possible.* A very good way to enhance the validity and reliability of a simulated conditions skill test item is to develop a game-like testing environment.
3. *Try to involve only one performer at a time in the testing procedure.* Even though more time is involved when testing students one at a time, the results justify the effort because of the improvement in the reliability of the test.
4. *Use only the most accurate measurement technique that is available.* Again the reliability of the test is greatly reduced when the teacher incorporates measurement techniques of questionable accuracy.

5. *The teacher should require that students utilize the same skill, form, and technique that is used in the game situation.* For example, the testing of the volleyball serve should not sacrifice form, speed, or accuracy since all three are of paramount importance during game situations.
6. *The simulated condition item should provide a degree of discrimination.* The purpose of the examination is to provide the student and teacher adequate information about the performance of a skill to make sound interpretations and evaluations. Unsophisticated items often will not provide this information.
7. *It is imperative that the items be suitable for the age and grade levels that are being examined.* A good rule of thumb is to test at the same level that the instruction is being presented. Attempting to use the same test for several grade or age levels usually results in the test being too easy for some and too difficult for others.
8. *Eliminate or minimize extraneous variables during the development of the simulated condition item.* For example, when measuring basketball dribbling ability, use obstacles that are high enough to force students to dribble around them. This prevents students from bouncing the ball over the obstacle for a faster time.
9. *Simulated condition items should be kept simple.* Many teachers have a tendency to make skills tests too complicated by attempting to measure several aspects of a specific skill simultaneously. The end result is a meaningless distribution of scores since all of the traits are interrelated and make varying contributions to the final score. The item should measure one aspect of the skill as simply as possible while minimizing the effects of the remaining parts of the performance.
10. *The teacher should develop and follow a set of clearly defined instructions and administrative procedures.* The result of well thought out examinations will become quite useless if directions and administrative procedures are not followed. In addition any claims of validity and reliability are significantly reduced unless these practices are followed.
11. *All simulated condition items must be valid and reliable.* The procedures for determining the validity and reliability of any test item were discussed in Chapter 5.

Example of Simulated Conditions Item.

Volleyball Serving Test using predetermined points as scoring procedure.

Required Equipment and Time. Volleyballs, net, standards, court marked and numbered as shown in Figure 7.3. Length of test is approximately one class period.

Directions. Server stands opposite the marked court in the properly

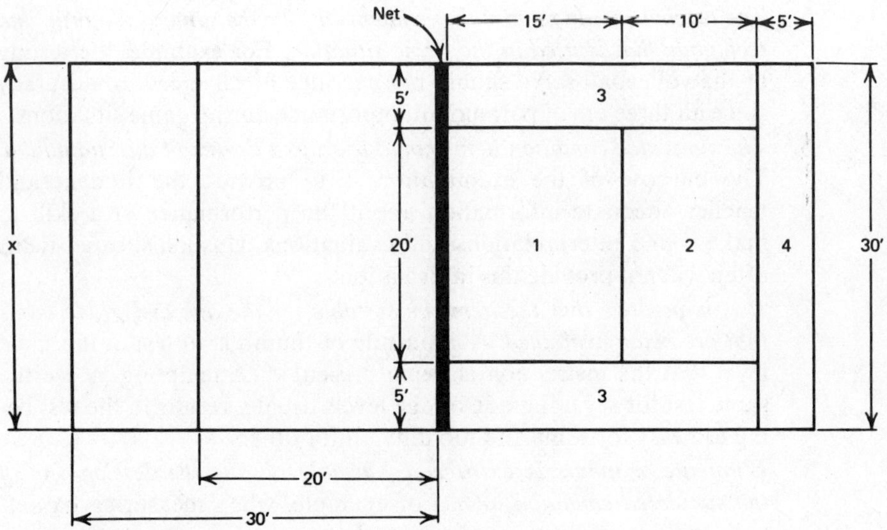

Figure 7.3. Volleyball court diagram.

marked serving position. Only the serves taught during the unit utilizing proper speed, form, and techniques will be allowed. Each student will be given 10 trials. Any ball hitting the net counts as a trial but no points are awarded.

Scoring. The score that each student achieves is determined by where the ball lands in the opposite court. No score will be awarded for any serve that is not acceptable in form, speed, and technique. Any ball that lands on a line will be awarded the higher number of points.*

Game Performance Items. This item is the most comprehensive of the psychomotor tests. Both the process and the product can be measured by using this technique. The game performance item is used to measure the end product of the instructional unit, which is the ability of the student to utilize the various skills presented in the unit in a game situation. In physical education, game performance can be evaluated in two different ways. In the first the teacher uses a rating scale of the individual skills that are used in an actual game or competitive situation.

In this type of measuring procedure the teacher must first identify the specific skills to be measured and then develop a rating scale form for each of these. A game situation is developed, with competition equalized, and the teacher rates each student for each skill as it is performed in the game.

*Adapted from *AAHPER Skills Test Manual,* Washington D.C., American Association for Health, Physical Education and Recreation, 1969, p. 20. Reprinted by permission.

In the second type of game performance examination, the student is evaluated through the result of the performance of the game. For example, the bowling average achieved after 10 complete games could be used as an objective measure of a student's bowling skill.

One advantage of the game performance item is that students are measured while performing the skills in a realistic environment. Second the game performance test includes only skills that are used in playing the game. No similar or predictive skills are used in this form of testing.

The primary disadvantage of the game performance test is the time required to measure all students fairly. The teacher must observe a student performing a skill several times before a decision can be made on the rating. This process takes a great deal of effort and time and is usually carried out over several days of testing. A second disadvantage is the difficulty in equalizing competition and the accompanying problems that occur when the two teams or individuals are not approximately equal in ability.

Writing Game Performance Items. The game performance test involves more organizational and procedural concerns than other forms of items that have been discussed. These concerns as well as suggestions for the test are presented below.

1. *Identify only skills that are commonly used in the actual game.* In order for the test to be valid and reliable the student should have the opportunity to perform all of the skills required during the course of the game situation.
2. *Develop a rating scale to measure each skill.* Following the procedures discussed in this chapter the teacher must develop a rating scale that includes each skill that the student is required to perform. The number of rating points in the scale must be decided, and a list of the desired observable characteristics must be developed.
3. *Not all students can perform all skills.* The teacher must be aware of the physically limiting factors in performing each skill in a game situation. For example, if students are too small to spike in volleyball, no attempt should be made to rate them on that particular skill.
4. *Equalize competition and do not hesitate to change the competition during the course of the game.* The fairness and success of the game performance test lies in the equality of the competition between the two teams or individuals being measured. If one group is allowed to dominate the game, the level of skill often decreases. Similarly the number of different skills that might be performed by the students in more equal competition is often reduced.
5. *Observe the skill being performed several times before evaluating the students.* As with any instrument, the reliability of this test can be in-

creased by observing each student performing each skill a number of times before making a decision on the final evaluation.

Example of Game Performance Tests

Badminton Game Performance Test

Directions. The four areas in the test will be rated during equal competition. Each rating area is scored on a 3-2-1 basis using the following guidelines:

3 points — above average ability, considerably more skillful than the performance typical for the student's sex and age.

2 points — average ability, typical performance for sex and age.

1 point — below average ability, far inferior to typical performance.

For each sub-area, circle the appropriate score.

I. Serve

A. Position of shuttlecock upon contact — racket head strikes shuttlecock below waist level. 3 2 1

B. Position of racket at end of serve — if short serve, racket head does not rise above chest; if long serve, racket head stops between shoulders and top of head at end of serve. 3 2 1

C. Placement of serve — well-placed relative to type of serve and position of opponent. 3 2 1

D. Height of serve relative to type of serve — short serve is low over net; drive serve is low over net and deep; clear serve is high and deep. 3 2 1

II. Strokes — consider placement and quality of each stroke.

A. Clear — high and deep.

B. Smash — hit from position above head and in front of body. 3 2 1

C. Drive — sharp and low over net; hit from position about shoulder height; can be deep or midcourt, but not short. 3 2 1

D. Drop — hit from position waist-to-shoulder-height; low over net; a hairpin-type shot. 3 2 1

III. Strategy

A. Places shots all over court. 3 2 1

B. Executes a variety of shots at the most opportune moments. 3 2 1

C. Takes advantage of opponent's weaknesses (for example, poor backhand, strength problem in back court, poor net play). 3 2 1

D. Uses own best shots. 3 2 1

IV. Footwork and Position

A. Near center court position so flexible that one can play any type of shot.	3 2 1
B. Control of body demonstrated at all times during play.	3 2 1
C. Body is in correct position (usually determined by the feet) for each shot.	3 2 1
D. Racket is shoulder-to-head-height and ready for use (wrist cocked) at all times; eyes are on the shuttlecock at all times.*	3 2 1
Total Score	____

Rating Scales. These scales provide the teacher with a systematic and fair procedure for reporting the judgments of expert observers. A rating scale usually consists of a set of traits to be judged by the expert and some type of scale for indicating the extent to which each trait is present. Usually, rating scales serve three significant functions in evaluation: (1) they direct the observations of the teacher or expert toward specific and clearly defined aspects of behavior; (2) they provide a common frame of reference for comparing all pupils on the same set of traits; and (3) they provide an excellent method for recording the judgments of teachers or experts.

Rating scales are one of the best methods for teachers to use in observations of individual student performances. They allow the teacher to focus on the more important aspects of the traits being measured. The rating scale itself is actually a tool or aid to be used by the teacher in evaluating the performance of students; this scale helps the instructor to identify the degree or amount of the trait that the student possesses. Rating scales are, in fact, a means of objectifying subjective evaluations. In other words, with a rating scale, the teacher can assign a numerical value to qualitative judgments.

Constructing Rating Scales. The appropriate use of rating technique requires very careful attention to the selection of the traits to be rated, the development of the rating scale form, and the testing situation under which the ratings are obtained. The following suggestions of rating scale development will prove most helpful to the teacher selecting this method of measurement.

1. *The traits or skills selected should be educationally significant.* It is extremely important that the traits or skills to be measured are in agreement with the behavioral objectives presented by the teacher and with the skills taught during the instructional unit.
2. *The traits or skills selected should be observable forms of behavior.* The traits measured with a rating scale must clearly be observable forms of behavior that the teacher can evaluate.

*From Ted A. Baumgartner and Andrew S. Jackson, *Measurement for Evaluation in Physical Education*, copyright © 1975 by Houghton Mifflin Co., Boston, p. 241. Reprinted by permission. (Suggested by Bill Landin, Indiana University.)

3. *Select between 3 and 7 rating positions on the scale.* Only the teacher can select the exact number of rating points that will be used on each rating scale. This will usually be determined by the nature of the evaluations that are to be made. In measures where differences in performance are difficult to discriminate, as few as 3 rating points might be used. In finer measures, however, as many as 5 or 7 points might be used to differentiate in performances. Most experts agree that no more than seven rating points are necessary in typical classroom evaluations.

4. *Specific characteristics and points on the rating scale should be clearly defined.* Most of the poor reliability often associated with rating scales is attributed to the lack of proper identification of the specific characteristics that will be measured by the rating scale. The teacher must prepare in writing a list of all of the characteristics for each point within the rating scale. These written characteristics must be specific and contain sufficient detail for the rater to discriminate accurately between the different levels of skills. Terms such as excellent, good, average, and below average are not usually considered specific enough for the evaluations to be made.

5. *When possible, use more than one rater for each skill.* It is generally accepted that combining the rating from more than one teacher will provide a more reliable measure of the observed skill than a rating obtained from one teacher. Such factors as personal bias, overrating, and underrating will average or cancel each other out when using more than one rater.

Example of Rating Scale

Volleyball Rating Scale

Directions. Each of the three components of volleyball-playing ability has a point value of 15, and is scored on a 5-4-3-2-1 basis:

5 points — Exceptional ability, near perfect for the age and sex of the participant.

4 points — Above average ability, not perfect, but quite skillful for the age and sex of the participant.

3 points — Average ability, typical for the age and sex of the participant.

2 points — Below average ability, characterized by more mistakes than is typical for the age and sex of the participant.

1 point — Inferior ability, far below typical performance for the age and sex of the participant.

For each subheading, circle the appropriate score.

I. Serve	
A. Height above net	5 4 3 2 1
B. Accuracy of placement	5 4 3 2 1
C. Difficulty of return	5 4 3 2 1
II. Setting or Spiking — choose one	
A. Setting	
1. Height above net	5 4 3 2 1
2. Accuracy of placement	5 4 3 2 1
3. Coordination with spiker	5 4 3 2 1
B. Spiking	
1. Accuracy of placement	5 4 3 2 1
2. Difficulty of return	5 4 3 2 1
3. Coordination with setter	5 4 3 2 1
III. General team play	
A. Hustle	5 4 3 2 1
B. Alertness — saves and play of difficult shots	5 4 3 2 1
C. Teamwork*	5 4 3 2 1
	Team Score____

Summary

Before beginning to develop tests in physical education the teacher must review the purpose of the test to be adminstered. Only after the purpose has been ascertained does the teacher begin planning the test by incorporating a test blueprint. The test blueprint is a tool developed by the teacher that can be used to construct highly valid and reliable tests. The test blueprint consists of an abbreviated list of behavioral objectives and a content outline. The objectives constitute the subject matter to be taught and the content outline is the vehicle through which the objectives will be presented. Finally the test blueprint is made up of cells that include the actual concepts demonstrated in class and the approximate amount of time for the presentation of each concept.

In developing the test the teacher refers to the blueprint and selects concepts from the cells in proportion to the time spent in teaching them. It has been suggested that a test developed from a test blueprint has the most representative sample of concepts presented in class that is possible to achieve.

Cognitive tests are categorized into two types. Objective tests contain items that are precise and have brief and specific responses. The true-false, matching, completion, identification, and multiple-choice items are objective

*From Ted A. Baumgartner and Andrew S. Jackson, *Measurement for Evaluation in Physical Education*, copyright © 1975 by Houghton Mifflin Co., Boston, p. 237. Reprinted by permission.

items. Each of these types has unique characteristics and should be used by the teacher when the appropriate situation exists. Subjective items measure a student's ability to interpret, integrate, organize, synthesize, or solve problems. The short essay and essay items are examples of subjective items. Again, both of the subjective items serve unique testing purposes and should be used in the appropriate testing situation.

Psychomotor tests can be categorized into three types: (1) simulated conditions, (2) game performance, and (3) rating scales. In the simulated conditions test, the individual skills are isolated and measured by either quantifying the student's performance for accuracy, speed, and distance, for example, or by observing the student's performance and then rating the abilities in that skill with a rating scale. The game performance test involves the measurement of skills taught in class as they are performed in a game situation. The students are placed in units of equal competition and are rated by the teacher as they perform the skills in the actual game. A rating scale is a set of charactertistics to be judged by experts. Rating scales are used in both simulated conditions and game performance evaluations and are very useful in helping the teacher determine the amount of the trait that students possess.

Study Questions

1. Identify the purposes of measurement in physical education.
2. Develop a test blueprint for a unit in basketball for high school students. Be sure to develop categories for your behavioral objectives. Defend your time percentages throughout the entire blueprint.
3. When is it most appropriate to use true-false items? What are some suggestions for improving the typical true false question?
4. Select a topic of your choice and construct a matching item in which all of the responses are plausible choices for the premises and in which there are more responses than premises.
5. Why do many experts consider the multiple choice question to be the best objective item?
6. Describe the procedures that a teacher should follow in conducting an item analysis. Define all of the necessary terms and explain how each would be used.
7. Compare and contrast the short essay and the essay items.
8. Construct one short essay question and one essay question relating to defensive strategy in basketball.
9. What are some reasons for using the identification test?
10. Construct an identification test for a unit in badminton.
11. What are the advantages for using a simulated conditions test?
12. Compare the two types of simulated condition items.
13. Construct a rating scale for measuring the set in volleyball.
14. Construct an individual skills test to measure the set in volleyball.
15. Discuss the advantages and disadvantages for using the game performance test for a unit in soccer.

CHAPTER 8

The Organization, Administration, and Interpretation of Tests in Physical Education

After you have read and studied this chapter you should be able to:

1. *Identify the organizational procedures required in planning a test.*
2. *Summarize the procedure of administering a test.*
3. *Outline the interpretation procedures required following the administration of a test.*

In the preceding chapters the emphasis has been on test content and how the development of instructional objectives leads to the selection or construction of an instrument that is valid and reliable. A major limitation, however, exists because many teachers lack adequate understanding and preparation in the knowledges and methods related to the organization, administration, or the interpretation of tests within a measurement and evaluation program.

These three areas of weakness on the part of many classroom teachers will be the main topics discussed in this chapter. The *organization* of tests will deal with those problems related to selecting a test and the preparations necessary before administering it to a group of students. The second topic, *administration* of tests, will identify the problems that teachers face while administering the test. Finally the *interpretation* of tests will be concerned with the responsibilities of the teacher after the students complete the examination.

THE ORGANIZATION OF TESTS

The organization of tests involves a thorough job of pre-planning. The teacher who selects or constructs good tests but fails to organize the testing situation has completed only half of the procedure. The organization that is necessary before the students actually take the test include *selecting the test according to purpose, selecting the test according to quality, selecting and preparing equipment and facilities, selecting and preparing scoring procedures, preparing instructions, selecting test administration procedures, orienting the students,* and *selecting and training testing assistants.*

Selecting Tests According to Purpose

In Chapter 1 the purposes and functions of measurement and evaluation were listed and discussed in detail. As a review and for reference in this section they will again be listed.

1. Placement.
2. Diagnosis of learning problems.
3. Progress during instruction.
4. Achievement after instruction.
5. Determination of improvement.
6. Motivation of students through feedback.
7. Assessment of teaching.
8. Assessment of the curriculum.
9. Prediction of future success.
10. Development of norms.
11. Research tool.

The first consideration by the teacher in selecting a test is the purpose of the test to be administered. Obviously, different types of tests will be used for placement and for performance after instruction. Similarly, different tests must be used for developing norms and for measuring a student's progress during instruction. Without an understanding of the purposes of measurement and a decision by the teacher as to the one purpose most appropriate for the immediate testing situation, the entire process has little meaning or value.

Selecting the Test According to Desired Qualities

It is incumbent upon the physical educator to select good instruments to be used in measurement. The purposes of testing must be kept in mind since the purposes dictate test selection. Often such factors as the instructor's philosophy of education, methodology of teaching, and behavioral objectives will dictate the extent to which testing is done. Tests should never be given just for the sake of obtaining measurements.

Once the philosophy, objectives, and purposes dictate what testing is to be done, specific qualities of a test instrument should be taken into consideration. Whether a teacher-made or standardized test is considered, it is crucial that the instrument has the desired qualities of validity, reliability, objectivity, and economy or practicality. Validity is very important because it measures the degree to which a test actually measures what it purports to measure. Reliability is a measure of accuracy; that is, if tests were repeated using the same students, reliable tests would produce similar scores. Objectivity is the degree to which consistent results are obtained from the use of the test by different examiners. Recent texts include objectivity as a part of reliability. Administrative economy or the feasibility and practicality of using the test are also important. A good test must be economical in terms of both time needed for administration and cost if the test must be purchased. These desired characteristics of measurement were discussed in detail in Chapter 5.

Related to the validity and reliability of a test, teachers should have a thorough working knowledge of the test and should know precisely what it will measure. They should also fully understand the various administrative techniques required to give the test to the students. The working knowledge and administrative techniques should be studied and analyzed completely before making a decision concerning the selection of any testing instrument.

Another practical consideration that is important in the selection of a test instrument is the availability of norms. If standardized tests are under consideration, the existence of usable norms may lead to one test being selected over another. Test norms represent typical performance of students in groups on which the test was standardized and provide a means for evaluating raw scores of students.

The presence of norms for a standardized test can be a valuable aid in interpreting performance, and therefore an instrument with representative norms is certainly one that should be given serious consideration. Norms can also be developed for teacher-made tests. Norms and their uses have been discussed in detail in Chapter 4.

A final consideration in the selection or construction of a test is the specific information relating to the group taking the test. For example, the age and size of the group would be important as well as its general level of ability.

Selecting and Preparing Equipment and Facilities

Because most of the testing in physical education involves human movement, unique facilities and equipment are often necessary. In the selection or construction of a test, the equipment needed and facility space requirements are a high priority. For example, the AAHPER Youth Fitness Test items were intentionally developed with simple facility and equipment requirements in mind.

Once a test or test item has been selected or developed, a complete list of supplies, equipment, and facility requirements should be developed. As the administration time nears, all equipment such as parallel bars, or high jump areas, and supplies such as stop watches, measuring tapes, paper and pencils must be available. Special markings need to be clearly designated. For instance, the French-Stalter Clear Test in Badminton required the badminton court to be marked into specific zones, each with a different scoring designation.

Test directions often give indications of the pieces of equipment, supplies, and the size of the facility needed for the administration of the test. In the use of test batteries, such as the AAHPER Youth Fitness Test, much thought is necessary in developing a usable test item rotation. The facility and equipment should be organized in an efficient manner. Inherent in this organization is the possible influence of one item on the performance of another. In consideration of this, the strenuousness of each item dictates how many items of a particular battery are administered in one session. In the case of psychomotor testing, alternative muscle groups should be tested in consecutive items.

A definite aid in the administration of test batteries is the development and use of a diagram of the test area including the specific location of each test item. Each item should be clearly designated by name or number.

An underlying consideration inherent in motor performance testing is safety. Certainly the equipment and facility used in testing must be checked for safety. Sufficient space must be available for each test item in order to prevent injury.

Selecting and Preparing Scoring Procedures

Forms for scoring test performances must be available well in advance of the test. Standardized tests ususally include answer sheets or directions for preparing them. Teacher-made tests usually need to have answer sheets or score cards developed. There are several types. Answer sheets can be devised in the classroom for cognitive or affective tests or perhaps purchased from a commercial testing company.

1. Grade Book (Class Roll Sheet). The instructor's grade book already contains the data necessary for developing score cards and recording scores. This form of scoring is most usable when one examiner administers the entire test, one item at a time, or when a class roll sheet is made available at each station of a test battery. Each item score or total score can be recorded in an appropriate place in the grade book.
2. Squad Cards. If a class is organized into squads, a score card can be developed for each squad with spaces for scores of each test item provided for every member of the squad. In a test battery, as a squad moves from station-to-station, the score card can be carried by the squad leader.
3. Individual Score Cards. A card for each student has several advantages. First, an individual score card is a flexible method since a student can move individually from one test item to another without affecting others. Second, since each student carries a score card to each test item, he or she is more involved in the testing situation. Third, individual score cards give the opportunity for the development of a profile since improvement on scores from several tests may appear on an individual score card.
4. Answer Sheet. Many paper-pencil tests constructed by teachers use the test itself as an answer sheet and provide spaces for answers. For ease in correcting objective tests, separate answer sheets can be developed.

An individual score card can serve as a motivational technique. The first three types of score cards are typically used with physical performance tests of the psychomotor domain. However, the cognitive and affective domains are important facets of physical education that should be tested. Therefore a fourth score card or answer sheet is applicable when tests of the cognitive or affective domain are given. In recent years, standardized answer sheets have been developed by many manufacturers. Most of these may be used with published cognitive and affective tests in physical education or with teacher-made tests. Other supplies necessary for scoring such as pencils, or clip boards must be gathered well in advance of testing.

Preparing Standardized Instructions

Most standardized tests also contain instructions for administration. Consistent administrative procedures increase the reliability and objectivity of the measurements. Tests with standard instructions that are easily understood should be given high priority. It is also equally important in teacher-made tests for standard directions to be developed to enhance reliability and objectivity.

Standardized instructions are necessary, not only for the students being tested but also for the test examiner. Often in physical education testing situations, more than one item in a test battery is administered at one time. Obviously, then, it is imperative that each examiner administers each test item in exactly the same manner. Examiners should be thoroughly familiar with the test items they administer. Instructions for the examiner as well as for those being tested should be clearly written and well understood. The person responsible for the testing must be thoroughly aware of the purposes and all administrative procedures including instructions. The following list gives important techniques for standardizing test instructions.

1. Directions should be fully understood by the test examiner. They can be written on index cards or, in the case of standardized tests, read directly from the test manual.
2. Directions should be as brief and concise as possible.
3. A demonstration of the correct execution of each test item is especially important in the case of tests of the psychomotor domain.
4. Directions should focus on the correct performance of the test item rather than variances from correctness.
5. Most psychomotor tests require the use of specialized footwear and uniform. Students must be advised of special clothing requirements well in advance of test time.
6. Students should be advised of the purpose of the test or test item as well as the precise date and time of administration. A clear description of the test and its purposes can serve as a motivational technique for creating interest, effecting maximum performance.
7. The method of scoring and the interpretation of scores must be well understood by the students.

Selecting Test Administration Procedures

Nothing should be left to doubt when determining the procedures that will be used by the teacher during the administration of the test. The type of test, the purpose of the test, and the characteristics of the group to be tested will contribute greatly to the selection of test administration procedures. There are, however, different ways or methods that might be used in organizing a class for testing.

Depending on the group organization selected, time and space requirements for testing can be altered significantly. Most standardized tests describe how the students are to be organized for testing purposes. Teacher-made tests may use these typical class organizational groups or other alternatives. Obviously, no one method of organizing groups fits all testing situations in physical education. The way students are organized for testing depends on the type of test, the domain of learning to be tested, and the size of the group. The most applicable methods of grouping students for the administration of tests in physical education are briefly described below.

1. Mass Testing. The majority of cognitive and affective tests and many psychomotor tests utilize the method that is used in the typical classroom situation, that of testing all the students at once. Mass testing has inherent advantages of efficient time and faculty utilization. A variation of this method is to use partners and test half the students while the other half serves as helpers, scorers, or recorders.
2. Station-to-Station. In testing the psychomotor domain, many items are often necessary to ascertain levels of skill or fitness. Test items can be organized into stations. A large group of students can be tested individually or in small groups by moving from station-to-station as each item is completed. Items that take considerable time often require several stations to make the total time at each station equitable.
3. Squads. For administrative efficiency many physical education classes are organized into squads for instruction. This grouping is also a feasible unit for testing, especially when a test battery is being administered. A squad may be assigned to a particular item with a rotation system utilized so that a squad moves from item to item until the battery is completed. Two considerations help this method to be usable; squads should have an equal number of members, and test items should use comparable amounts of time. The second requirement can be accomplished by using multiple stations for items that take a relatively long time to administer.
4. Combinations. Some items of tests lend themselves to mass testing while others are better tested with an alternate method. Therefore, it is often feasible to use a combination of the previously mentioned methods to administer a test efficiently.

Orienting the Students

The process of the evaluation should be very open and well understood by all students. They should know in advance the purpose of the test as well as the uses of the results by the teacher. The students should be told precisely what the test attempts to accomplish. They should be notified well in advance of the testing date. Unannounced tests are somewhat questionable and their results contribute little to the evaluation of a student.

Specific instructions about proper dress, location of test, time of test, and any needed materials should be made before the examination time. Instructions at this time might also include specific procedures that the student will follow on the day of testing. The teacher might also discuss with the students in advance the significance of the test and the importance of performing to the best of their ability. These instructions involving proper attire, procedures, and the importance of performing may very well motivate students to perform to the best of their ability or at least to near maximum effort.

Selecting and Training Testing Assistants

Testing often requires more than one examiner because of the length of the test or the number of different items on the test. Each examiner must be totally aware of the purpose of the test item he or she is to administer. The directions for the execution of each item must be clearly written and available to each tester. All testers must be capable of transmitting the directions clearly and correctly to the students. In the many psychomotor tests used in physical education, scoring is a necessary duty of the examiners. They must be trained to differentiate accurately between levels of correct and incorrect performance and to operate any special testing equipment. They must also be carefully trained in all of the administrative procedures necessary to carry out the entire testing procedure. It is important that the training sessions be completed prior to the testing session.

Several different personnel may administer or assist in the administration of physical education tests. Among these are:

1. The Physical Educator. The instructor of the group to be tested is most often the main test administrator. It is her or his responsibility for the overall success or failure of testing.
2. Partners. Testing in physical education gives ample opportunity for development of responsibility. Especially in mass testing situations, one student can serve as a scorer for his or her partner.
3. Squad Leaders. If tests are administered by squads, each squad leader can serve as an assistant to the test administrator. The squad leader can score and record test data for each member of the squad.
4. Assistants. Trained assistants are often necessary to supervise and

score efficiently a test or test battery. Assistants may be older students, other educators, student teachers, or interested parents.

5. Special Testing Personnel. Some school systems utilize a school psychologist to administer various tests. Some of these tests may involve tests of physical performance. School psychologists are trained in testing procedures but may be unfamiliar with equipment and facilities used in physical education. Therefore, the physical educator should cooperate with other administrative testing personnel.

It is often advisable to train the testing personnel in a special session a day or so prior to actual testing. When directions or techniques become complicated, the importance of trained personnel cannot be overemphasized. Student leaders and other assisting personnel should go through the items as though being tested and must be thoroughly acquainted with the test items and duties of test administration.

THE ADMINISTRATION OF TESTS

Once a meaningful instrument has been developed or selected and all pretest duties completed, the task of actually administering the instrument still remains. Efficient test administration is necessary to assure reliable test scores. Usually the actual administration of the test takes less time than the preparation necessary before the test; but the pretest planning is indispensable.

The duties of the examiner and the assistants, if needed, are relatively simple and straightforward during the actual test administration. The underlying principle in administering a test is that all students must be given an equal chance to demonstrate their achievements of the learning outcomes being measured. This means that a physical and psychological environment must be established that is conducive to the student's best efforts. Also, factors that might interfere with valid measurement must be controlled by the teacher. Responsibilities during testing are varied and include *evaluation of organizational preparation, explanation of testing procedures, demonstration and warm-up, test administration, motivation of students,* and *safety*.

Evaluation of Organizational Preparation

All of the duties associated with preparing for administering the test must be checked well ahead of test time so that all time allocated for testing is used efficiently for that purpose. The physical conditions such as equipment, facilities, and supplies need to be evaluated for suitability of use. The test stations should have adequate space, and the test area, if indoors, should be well lighted, ventilated, and at a comfortable temperature. Obviously, equipment and supplies necessary for testing must be available and accessible. The organizational grouping of students for testing should be analyzed and developed so students can be tested efficiently. For example, if any special uniform requirements are needed for physical performance, arrangements should be made ahead of time so that students will come to the test properly equipped for performance. Instructions, which are crucial for valid and reliable results, should be checked for clearness and conciseness. All test personnel must be aware of their specific duties during testing. In summary, all the physical arrangements should be checked so that students have the optimum conditions for responding to the test. The psychological climate in preparing the testing environment is as important as the physical arrangements. Students will not perform properly if they are unduly tense or anxious during testing. The physical educator must attempt to create a psychological climate that encourages optimum performance. Since an underlying purpose of measurement and evaluation is the improvement of learning, students should be made aware that testing is being done to help accomplish that purpose and that the test is an extension of the classroom teaching. Any technique to reduce anxiety or to establish rapport prior to the test administration should improve the psychological climate.

Explanation of Testing Procedures

One way to increase the chances for an optimal performance on a test is to make certain that directions are understood by all students. This is espcially important in psychomotor tests but should also be considered in tests that measure the cognitive or affective domains in physical education. The instructions, as mentioned earlier, should be concise enough so that the students know exactly what is expected, but short enough for them to avoid unnecessary time involvements. It is also important that if students are tested individually, in squads, or other groupings, instructions should be written and read. Another technique that is becoming popular and provides consistent instructions is the use of a cassette tape and tape player.

Demonstration and Warm-Up

Since many tests in physical education require physical performance, a demonstration of the test should be included. If a skill is demonstrated, the examiner or demonstrator must use the correct fundamentals and must be visible so that all those to be tested can easily see the demonstration. The demonstration can also be accomplished in cognitive and affective tests by including a sample question or item with the appropriate response marked. The students should be given the opportunity to ask questions for clarification of procedures at the conclusion of the demonstration.

Most students feel they can perform better on a psychomotor test after a sufficient warm-up. Therefore the warm-up should be planned and adequate time allotted for the activity. A form of warm-up might also be included on cognitive tests. The teacher should construct the test in such a manner that the first one or two items would be easy enough for almost every student to be able to answer correctly. This mental warm-up might encourage many students and ultimately improve their performance on the test.

Test Administration

If proper organizational and administrative arrangements have been considered, the actual test administration is a relatively simple procedure. Most cognitive and affective tests are practically self-administering if instructions are included on the test. However, because of equipment and supplies needed in many physical performance tests, more constant monitoring of the test items is required. In all test situations the following suggestions by Gronlund (1974) facilitate a fair testing situation.

1. The teacher should not talk unnecessarily before the test. Students are mentally set for the test and will often ignore anything not pertaining to the test for fear it will hinder recall of information.
2. The teacher should keep interruptions during the test to a minimum. Occasionally, students will ask to have ambiguous items clarified, and it will be desirable to explain the items to the entire group at the same time. Such interruptions are necessary but should be minimized. Other interruptions, both from within and without the classroom, should be eliminated where possible.
3. The teacher should avoid providing hints to pupils who ask about individual items. An ambiguous item should be clarified for the entire class. Otherwise, a student should be told to answer or perform the item as well as possible.
4. The teacher should discourage cheating at all times. Cheating can be reduced by using alternative forms of a test, separating students, or close supervision by the teacher. Any attempt to enhance the reliability or validity of the test is impaired if cheating is allowed to occur.

Motivation of Students

A conscientious effort should be made by the teacher and all testing assistants to motivate students and to encourage them in all testing situations. Students should be provided with a clear explanation of the purpose of the test. They should be told of previous levels of achievement and of the importance of each individual test upon the total measurement and evaluation.

Motivation during the administration of psychomotor tests should remain consistent from student to student. Above all, no student should be criticized or embarrassed about his or her performance during the test. Generally a positive and enthusiastic attitude on the part of the teacher and all testing assistants will contribute greatly toward the needed motivation of students before and during the testing session.

Safety

Safety must be made a very high priority in the minds of teachers and testers during the testing session. Often the test situation creates a good deal of excitement, enthusiasm, and competition among the students. Occasionally they may attempt skills in an unsafe manner, or they may try activities for which they are not totally prepared or skilled. It is the responsibility of the teacher to anticipate safety problems and develop safeguards to prevent any unnecessary injuries or unfortunate accidents. If a test cannot be conducted in a safe facility in a safe manner, it should not be administered. Especially in test batteries such as the AAHPER Youth Fitness Test, care must be taken so that all test items are administered safely and precautions are taken for any possible safety problem.

Other Administrative Considerations

All testing should be done in the same facility with identical equipment. Some testing may be conducted indoors or outdoors with similar results but because of the unpredictability of the weather, arrangements should be made, if possible, for a testing site indoors if for some reason an outdoor facility is unusable. For instance, a backboard test of tennis ability may be administered indoors or outdoors, but specific differences in backboard surfaces or other variables may alter the results.

Some physical test items are strenuous. Items should be arranged from least strenuous to those that require the most effort. For example, the 600-yard run, an item of the AAHPER Youth Fitness Test, should not be an initial item of the test battery. An alternative, when a test battery is given, is to test on alternating days with an equal number of strenuous and nonstrenuous items each day. Another similar example occurs when muscle groups are being tested. Succeeding test items should test different muscle groups.

INTERPRETATION OF TESTS

The interpretation of tests is much too broad a topic to discuss in this section. It includes the areas of objectives, statistics, norms, and grading, each of which is the subject of a chapter in this text. This discussion will be limited to the more immediate responsibilities of the teacher following the administration of the test. Such areas of concern as *gathering test materials, test scoring, interpreting test scores,* and *utilizing results* will be developed.

The examiner has a number of tasks after the test that are relevant in the evaluation process. Depending on whether the test has measured cognitive, affective, or psychomotor abilities, differing posttest duties are required.

Gathering Test Materials

Whatever type of test is given, test materials should be received from each student before the student has left the testing area. In the case of classroom paper-pencil tests, the test and answer sheet must be collected. In psychomotor tests, the completed individual score card, the squad card, or the class roll sheet needs to be gathered. The task of gathering such answer sheets can be given to assistants or responsible students such as squad leaders. Often in the case of motor performance testing, equipment has been utilized. All of the equipment should be checked for damage and returned to its proper storage place.

Scoring Tests

The test must be scored as quickly as possible. It is important to provide feedback to the students rapidly, and this can only be accomplished after the tests are scored. Depending on whether the test was constructed by the teacher or some related group and whether the test is cognitive, affective, or psychomotor in nature, the scoring task may be very simple or relatively difficult. The details for the scoring of specific tests are found in the instructions or manuals for each test and will not be discussed in detail in this chapter.

Interpreting Test Scores

Following the collection and scoring of the test the teacher might transform the raw scores to one of the norms discussed in Chapter 4. In many instances, the raw scores do not have enough meaning so that the transformation to a norm needs to be computed. The teacher should develop a system on the score cards or on the grade sheet to record the norm conversions. After the routine of gathering the tests, scoring them, and making necessary norm conversions the teacher must interpret the results to the student.

Students should be notified of their scores as quickly as possible accompanied by a thorough explanation of their meaning. The teacher also needs to review the entire test including correct responses to all students. The students should be given the opportunity to ask questions about the test. Only if these last two procedures are carried out by the teacher will the test serve as a complete learning device.

Using Results

What occurs after evaluation of students may be the most important aspect of the measurement program in physical education. Test results must be used to improve a student's performance. Test results, in fact, imply that a follow-up must occur. However, the follow-up may lead to redefining the goals, curricular objectives, or behavioral objectives. It may also lead to a replanning of the various teaching methods used in the teaching unit. This evaluation process is ongoing and continuous. The performances of the students are in turn utilized to evaluate both the appropriateness of the behavioral objectives and the specific methodology.

Summary

The process of giving a test to a group of students involves the organization of the testing procedure, the administration of the test, and the interpretation of the results. In organizing the test, teachers must first consider the purposes of the test and its qualities. This involves analyzing the reason for evaluating the student and ultimately selecting or constructing the correct instrument. The teacher must also select and prepare the equipment needed during the test. Both facilities and testing equipment must be checked and made ready for use at the time of testing.

Determining scoring procedures and the proper standardized instructions are two additional reponsibilities of the teacher in organizing a test. This may involve developing score cards, grade sheets, or other forms of scoring. The methods or procedures to be used during the time of testing must be developed. The type of test, its purpose, and the characteristics of the group being tested contribute to the selection of the proper test administration procedures. Finally the teacher must provide an orientation for the students to be examined and train any assistants who will help with the testing.

Once the meaningful instrument has been developed and all organizational duties completed, the task of administering the instrument becomes most significant. The responsibilities during testing are relatively simple and include an evaluation of the organizational procedures. This evaluation is a last minute check of procedures and equipment to assure an uninterrupted test. In addition, proper test administration provides an explanation of the testing procedures to the students and also provides for a demonstration of the items being tested. A warm-up is also considered important and necessary by most measurement experts. Finally the teacher must attempt to motivate all students equally and provide a safe environment during the actual time of testing.

The interpretation of tests is a complex issue involving objectives, statistics, norms, and grading. These topics are discussed fully in other chapters. Issues of immediate concern to the teacher relative to the interpretations of test scores are the gathering of test materials, scoring the tests, interpreting the test scores, and developing an efficient program of continued use of the evaluation results.

Study Questions

1. Review the purposes of measurement and evaluation in physical education.
2. What are the important considerations in the standardizing of test instructions?
3. Why is the demonstration and warm-up considered essential before the administration of a test of the psychomotor domain?
4. Class organization is important in terms of time and space conservation. How might a class be grouped to be tested efficiently in a psychomotor skill?
5. Identify suggestions that enhance the probability of a fair testing situation.
6. Why is it often important to interpret test data to a student as soon as possible after the test is given?
7. Select a test of the psychomotor domain. Evaluate the test in terms of pretest organization, test administration, and posttest interpretations. Does the test have sufficient positive qualities to be considered for use?

CHAPTER 9

Assignment of Grades

After you have read and studied this chapter you should be able to:

1. *Identify the philosophical considerations in grading including improvement, performance, effort, contracts, pass-fail, distribution of grades, and weighting of grading components.*
2. *Distinguish between criterion-referenced and norm-referenced grading systems.*
3. *Calculate grades using such mechanical systems as:*
   (a) absolute percentage grading
   (b) relative absolute percentage grading
   (c) normal curve grading
   (d) natural break grading

Grading may be one of the most difficult yet most important tasks with which teachers are presently confronted. Grades are evaluations of a students' performance, which become integral parts of their permanent records. The importance of such an evaluation should be evident to every teacher in the profession. This, unfortunately, is not the case. Many teachers assign grades with little or no *philosophical* basis for their decisions. Many never develop a sound *mechanical* grading system that is valid and, above all, impeccably fair to every student involved. This chapter will attempt to deal with these two common deficiencies in grade assignment.

The primary rationale for utilizing grades to report to students and parents is to facilitate learning and development of the students by stimulating, directing, and rewarding their efforts. Many educators currently argue that most of the functions of grades are best served by the formative evaluation and feedback received during instruction. However, we feel there is a unique need for a periodic summative statement of progress in the form of grades. Most students seemingly find it difficult to integrate cognitive test scores, rating scale scores, and other evaluation results into an overall appraisal of their success in attaining unit objectives. Of course, the periodic grade report provides this summary appraisal.

The use of grades as a motivational device is at best questionable. If grades are used solely to stimulate student performance, the outcome is apt to be disasterous. However, if the grades can be viewed as opportunities to monitor learning progress, they may serve to motivate students in the form of short-term goals. The delay in the feedback may hinder the motivational aspect somewhat, but a carefully prepared grade report has the advantage of providing a comprehensive and systematic overview of each student's strengths and weaknesses in the teaching unit.

Grade reports to parents should be comprehensive enough to inform them of the objectives of the grading period and the progress that their child is making toward those objectives. This allows parents to aid and cooperate with school personnel in promoting a learning environment for the child. It also allows them to assess their child's successes, failures, and problems in each teaching unit. These reports provide parents with information that can serve as an aid to help the child make future educational and employment decisions.

Grades are also used by other teachers and counselors. Grades provide essential information to these professionals, which contribute significantly to the instructional and guidance programs of the school. The grade report becomes a very substantial part of each student's cumulative record. By knowing and understanding a student's past achievement, teachers and counselors can better predict areas in which the student is likely to be successful in the future. This information may be used by teachers in grouping students for instructional purposes and also by counselors in diagnosing and working with students who have personal-social or emotional problems.

The final function of grades to be discussed in this chapter is their use by administrators. Grade reports serve a number of useful functions for administrators such as determining promotion, graduation, honors, and athletic eligibility; and grades can be reported to other schools and prospective employers. There is some argument that the administrative functions of grades, in fact, hinder some newer, innovative grade report practices. Administrators traditionally have held fast to the utilization of a single symbol for grading purposes because of the enormous paper-work problem that the multiple reporting procedures create. This should not, of course, deter teachers from attempting to develop new and better grade report systems that can be used more effectively by students, parents, teachers, counselors as well as administrators.

PHILOSOPHICAL CONSIDERATIONS IN THE ASSIGNMENT OF GRADES

Every teacher in the field of education needs to develop a philosophy to use as a basis for the assignment of course or examination grades. This discussion will identify some of the topics to consider in the development of one's own personal grading philosophy. A considerable part of this text has concentrated on the philosophical basis for measurement and behavioral objectives in physical education, both of which are important in the present discussion.

Improvement Grading

The assignment of a grade based upon a student's improvement has been a point of contention for many years in the field of tests and measurements in physical education. The procedure implies that the most important consideration in the interpretation of the grade is the improvement of the students after they have experienced the teaching unit. The concept allows for students of various initial skill levels to achieve the highest possible mark. It provides a good deal of motivation for students who generally achieve low to average grades in more traditional or performance oriented grade assignment systems.

The use of improvement as a primary consideration in the assignment of grades is not totally positive. This procedure demands the utilization of a pretest to determine a student's initial position in the unit. This is sometimes unwise because of the time involved. In addition some physical performance tests may be dangerous if conducted without instruction and training. Improvement scores have also been shown to be unreliable. Also an inherent weakness in improvement grading is that students who score lower initially have much more room for improvement than those scoring high on the pretest. For example a student scoring 5 out of 25 attempts in a basketball free throw test is more likely to make a significant improvement than the student scoring 20 out of 25 on the same pretest. This very problem often leads some students intentionally to score poorly on pretests in order to obtain high improvement ratings on the later test without actually learning or improving during the teaching unit.

Some measurement experts argue that improvement grading is not congruous to actual situations. These individuals argue that although improvement in real-life occupations (i.e., salesperson) is important, it is the actual performance that receives the rewards in the form of higher commissions and promotions. It is similarly argued that using improvement as a grading base is out of step with other subject areas in education such as mathematics and history. The grading in these areas is generally based on performance on examinations and written assignments with the students who obtain the highest point totals or percentages on tests receiving the highest marks on grade reports.

Performance Grading

It is probably safe to assume that most physical educators utilize performance measures as the basis for their course grades. Many teachers will argue that physical education grading must be compatible with the grading procedures of the other subject areas within the curriculum. Mathematics teachers, for example, seldom consider anything except performance in assigning grades. This is presumed true in most other areas within the traditional school curriculum.

It can also be argued that the consideration of performance in grading is reflective of actual life situations. In business or professional careers, performance is almost the only factor considered for rewards such as commissions or promotions. It may appear harsh but in the real world improvement and effort are regarded as expectations and performance, a primary source of evaluation.

Opponents of the performance-referenced grading criterion argue that students unable to achieve high marks will become discouraged and turned off by physical education. Class participation and attitude as well as attendance in elective classes will suffer.

Effort Grading

Another philosophical consideration concerns the use of effort as a basis for assigning course grades. Many teachers feel quite strongly about rewarding with high marks students who participate regularly and demonstrate a high degree of effort in the teaching units. The primary problem of educators using this consideration in grade assignment is the difficulty in obtaining a procedure that is valid, reliable, and fair to all students. It is quite easy to depict the students at both ends of the effort scale; however, it is very difficult to determine effort fairly for the approximately 80 percent of the students in the middle.

Eclectic Approach to Grading

An eclectic approach or one that combines parts of many grading philosophies often provides a viable solution to the grading dilemma. If it is felt that performance is the most important consideration in assigning grades but that improvement and effort do contribute to the quality of a class and should be incorporated into the final marking decision, it is possible to develop a grading program with this in mind. A form of weighting system for each of the considerations might be used or simply a point system that allows the teacher the flexibility to assign points to each of the areas. Such considerations as skill performance, including improvement, knowledge, attitude, leadership, sportsmanship, and attendance often comprise the majority of components in such a system.

Contract Grading

Contract grading involves a written agreement between the student and teacher that clearly defines the various requirements for the individual grades. A decision must be made in advance regarding the minimal amount of performance that is acceptable in the unit or course. This minimum is assigned the lowest passing grade (a D is considered passing in most traditional grading programs). Options for the minimum acceptable level for each of the other grades (C, B, and A) are formulated. The teacher must be very explicit about the requirements for each grade level with the higher grades requiring more rigorous levels of performance and mastery on the part of the student. It is quite important that the grading considerations involve additional and often different requirements for the various grades. Merely requiring more of the same characteristic is not considered ideal. Most proponents of contract grading feel that individual student initiative, effort, and skill development are essential in achieving the higher grades of A and B. Student leadership and creativity on independent projects are additional considerations when developing a system of contract grading.

The teacher must be flexible and willing to modify the contracts if a majority of the students are unable to achieve satisfactory grades. It is unwise, however, to make a change in the system during a grading period, even if students find the contracts too easy. This can be disrupting and demoralizing, and contracts should only be changed after the grading period is completed.

The teacher should not be overly concerned if the grades under this system are quite high. The contracts should be achievable and fair — often, students become highly motivated to achieve the higher grades, and their efforts should not be thwarted.

Pass-Fail Grading

Pass-fail grading or satisfactory-unsatisfactory grading is in many ways similar to contract grading. The teacher must predetermine and present to the student the minimum requirements for successfully passing the course. The D grade is again considered the criterion for passing in most traditional educational systems. Many educators feel this system of grading provides a relaxed non-pressure atmosphere conducive to learning. Others, however, feel that students are difficult to motivate without the traditional discriminating grades.

Behavioral Objective Checklist

Some teachers and schools have supplemented or totally replaced the traditional grading system with a list of behavioral objectives to be checked or rated. These grade reports usually include check ratings of progress toward the major objectives in each teaching unit. Often symbols such as O or + (outstanding), S or − (satisfactory), and N or U (needs improvement) are utilized.

The behavioral objective checklist has the obvious advantage of providing a detailed analysis of each student's specific strengths and weaknesses. It also serves to acquaint or remind students and parents of the objectives of the teaching unit. Drawbacks of this procedure include the large amount of book work required to carry it out satisfactorily and the difficulty encountered in paring the large list of behavioral objectives down to a list usable on a grade report card. Sometimes it is difficult to state these objectives briefly since they must fit on a grade report card and yet be understood by everyone who will receive them. An illustration of such a checklist is shown in Figure 9.1.

Figure 9.I
Checklist for Attitude and Effort

University High School

Year 19____

Student's name

Symbol Explanation

+ Outstanding

S Satisfactory

U Unsatisfactory

↑ Improving

↓ Regressing

ATTITUDE AND EFFORT

	Grading Period			
	1	2	3	4
Is Considerate of Others				
Practices Self-Control				
Is Careful with Property				
Assumes Responsibility				
Uses Time to Advantage				
Contributes to Class				
Follows Directions				
Completes Assignments on Time				
Thinks and Works Independently				

Parent-Teacher Conferences

Many teachers and schools have incorporated the parent-teacher conference to supplement the traditional grade report system and to help establish better cooperation and lines of communication between teachers and parents. This vital grade report aid provides for two-way communication between parents and the school personnel. The conference permits parents the opportunity to ask questions, to discuss their son or daughter in detail, and to develop with the teacher plans for improving the student's learning environment. Quite often, misunderstanding by either the parents or teacher can be avoided through the use of these conferences. No form of grade report is totally positive, and the parent-teacher conference is no exception. A great deal of time and skill is required in planning and effectively carrying out parent-teacher conferences. Also because of the informality of the conference procedure, they should never be considered a substitute for more traditional grade report forms; instead they should supplement the time-tested report procedures currently in practice.

Distribution of Grades

Traditionally, grades in physical education have been extremely inflated. Many teachers assign only A's and B's to their classes with varying justification. Some feel low grades turn off students and interfere with participation in elective classes. Still others feel the typically large physical education classes are too difficult and time-consuming to evaluate fairly with letter grades A through F. It is a matter of professional responsibility to develop and implement a system of grading.

A recent trend in the profession has been to evaluate physical education classes with the same guidelines used in other classes in the school district. This provides the long needed uniformity between the various classes within the total curriculum. In other words an A in physical education might be interpreted as excellent performance, just as an A in mathematics.

In terms of distribution of final grades in physical education several other philosophical considerations arise. Elective classes often contain students who enjoy or excel in physical education. It seems reasonable that elective classes be graded somewhat differently than required classes. Several of the mechanical grading systems to be discussed later in this chapter identify a certain percentage or number of each of the traditional grades to be assigned. When students in a class are all of high ability, it might follow that the majority of grades are in the A-B range. However, the intent of this philosophical argument does not imply that students in low-ability classes of physical education can achieve only grades of C, D, or F.

Similar rationale is given for classes that include primarily juniors or seniors. Upper-level students are usually more proficient in skills and physical maturity. Therefore, the summative evaluation may have a substantial percentage of high grades.

Weighting the Grading Components

Weighting of the various parts or components that figure in the final compilation of a letter grade can be very confusing and certainly complicated. Questions arise such as how much weight should be given to the skill aspect and how much to the knowledge areas. If one chooses an eclectic approach, the problem of how much weight performance, effort, and improvement should have in the final grade can present much concern to the beginning as well as the experienced teacher.

Probably the easiest solution to this problem is the utilization of *raw scores* for all of the components that will make up the final grade. The teacher first determines the percentages of the total raw score points that will be allowed for each area. For example, a typical teaching unit might consist of a possible 300 points. The percentages might be as follows: skill performance 50 percent or 150 points; knowledge performance 25 percent or 75 points; improvement 10 percent or 30 points; effort 5 percent or 15 points; and physical fitness 10 percent or 30 points. These percentages are presented as an example and might not be appropriate for teachers' particular needs.

Once the percentages are determined, instruments are selected or constructed in such a manner to allow each student the opportunity to score the maximum number of points alloted each area. The points are totaled at the end of the unit, and one of the grading systems presented later in this chapter is then applied.

It is important to note some limitations to this particular weighting system. We cannot assume that the means and standard deviations between the various tests will be equal. Vast differences in the standard deviations may hinder the assignment of grades. The difficulty of the different tests often varies making the weighting system questionable. If, for example, 75 points was set as the upper limit or total possible on the knowledge tests and in reality the top score was 60 points, the weighting percentage would be considerably out of balance.

Another procedure in weighting is to convert all raw scores to standard score norms such as *z*- and *T*-scores. Refer to Chapter 4 for methods of evaluating and interpreting standard scores. The standard score is then multiplied by the decided weighting to arrive at a single, weighted standard score, which is used in computing the final grade. An example of this procedure using the same weighting as in the raw score method is shown in Table 9.1. The final, weighted standard score can then be used in computing the grade according to one of the procedures discussed later in the chapter.

Table 9.1 Weighting of *T*-Scores in a Typical Grading Situation

Area To Be Evaluated		*Skill*		*Knowledge*	*Improvement*	*Effort*	*Fitness*
Percent of grade contribution or weighting		50%		25%	10%	5%	10%
Test results converted *T*-scores	Test 1	55	Test 1	44	60	60	42
	Test 2	60	Test 2	50			
	Test 3	50	Test 3	47			
Average *T*-score		55		47	60	60	42
Average *T*-score multiplied by weighting		27.5		11.75	6.0	3.0	4.2
Final weighted *T*-score		27.5 + 11.75 + 6.0 + 3.0 + 4.2 = 52.45					

MECHANICAL GRADING SYSTEMS

Over the years, teachers of physical education have developed numerous systems for the assignment of test or unit grades as shown in Table 9.2. Several of these methods will be discussed here. This section is not meant to include all grading systems but rather to be representative of the many systems that are most commonly used by current physical education teachers.

Table 9.2 Norm-Referenced and Criterion-Referenced Grading Systems

Norm-Referenced Grading Systems	*Criterion-Referenced Grading Systems*
Normal curve grading	Absolute percentage grading
Natural break grading	Relative absolute percentage grading
Rank order grading	Contract grading
Norm grading	Objective checklist grading
	Teacher standard grading
	Pass-fail grading
	Mastery grading

Before developing the actual systems, the frame of reference must be considered, which will enable instructors to choose the proper grading procedure for their particular needs. Letter grades are usually assigned on the basis of performance in relation to other group members or to predetermined standards. The astute reader will recall from the discussion in Chapter 4 that we refer to *norm-referenced* grading in the first case and *criterion-referenced* grading in the second.

Assigning grades on a norm-referenced basis involves comparing a student's performance with that of a group, usually his or her own. The grade is therefore determined by the student's relative ranking within that group. If the performance places high in the group, a high grade will be awarded; however, if the performance ranks low in the group, a low grade will be given. Assignment of grades on a criterion-referenced basis involves comparing the student's performance to a predetermined absolute standard usually established by the teacher. An example is the student who attempts to achieve a certain percentage of correct responses on a cognitive examination or a certain time in the 600-yard run as specified by statements of behavioral objectives or other predetermined standards. A specific grade for a student is not affected by the performance of others in the group. All students meeting the standards set by the teachers will receive appropriate evaluations.

This brief review of norm-referenced and criterion-referenced interpretations is to help the reader better understand the four mechanical grading systems that are presented next. The first two procedures, *absolute percentage method* and *relative absolute percentage method*, are criterion-referenced and the last two, *normal curve method* and *natural break method*, are norm-referenced.

Absolute Percentage Grading

In the absolute percentage grading method, predetermined standards for each grade to be assigned are established by the teacher or school. Raw scores converted to percentages of the total possible responses are used in the grading procedure. For example the percentage score for a raw score of 25 when 30 points were possible would be 83 percent. All scores for all tests must be similarly converted to a percentage of the total possible points. At the end of the grading period an average percentage score must be computed for each student, which would represent his or her work for the unit. Another way to find the absolute percentage is to total all raw scores and divide by the total possible points. This results in the same composite score with somewhat less computation and less rounding error.

Percentages such as the following are used in this grading procedure.

90 - 100 = A	95 - 100 = A	88 - 100 = A
80 - 89 = B	85 - 94 = B	76 - 87 = B
70 - 79 = C	75 - 84 = C	64 - 75 = C
60 - 69 = D	65 - 74 = D	52 - 63 = D
Below 60 = F	Below 65 = F	Below 52 = F

The actual percentages are determined by the teacher using such considerations as test difficulty, prior experience, or personal preference for making the decision. Advantages of this system are that students are always aware of their grades throughout the grading period and the grade is not dependent on performance of others in the class. The computations are also rather simple when compared to some of the other grading systems.

An example of the absolute percentage method of grading is shown in Table 9.3. Some disadvantages of this system include the following: 1) tests that are very easy or very difficult require numerous adjustments for the high or low scores; 2) consideration needs to be given to borderline percentages; and 3) the percentages utilized are sometimes unrealistic.

Table 9.3 Absolute Percentage Procedure (N = 19)

Raw Scores	*Percentage completed for each student*	*Grade*
50 Points Possible		
49	49/50 (100) = 98%	A
48	48/50 (100) = 96%	A
48	48/50 (100) = 96%	A
47	47/50 (100) = 94%	A
46	46/50 (100) = 92%	A
44	44/50 (100) = 88%	B
43	43/50 (100) = 86%	B
42	42/50 (100) = 84%	B
40	40/50 (100) = 80%	B
39	39/50 (100) = 78%	C
37	37/50 (100) = 74%	C
36	36/50 (100) = 72%	C
36	36/50 (100) = 72%	C
35	35/50 (100) = 70%	C
35	35/50 (100) = 70%	C
32	32/50 (100) = 64%	D
31	31/50 (100) = 62%	D
29	29/50 (100) = 58%	F
21	21/50 (100) = 42%	F

Absolute Percentage Standard	*Frequency*
90 - 100 = A	5
80 - 89 = B	4
70 - 79 = C	6
60 - 69 = D	2
Below 60 = F	2

Relative Absolute Percentage Grading

The relative absolute percentage method of grading is similar in many ways to the absolute percentage method. The specific standards for each letter grade are determined in the same manner for both procedures.

Either raw scores or raw scores converted to standard scores may be used in the final computations. For this discussion, raw scores converted to *T*-scores will be used. Each test score during the unit is converted to a *T*-score, and the proper weighting procedure is applied as discussed earlier in this chapter. *T*-scores for each test are added, and finally an average *T*-score is computed, which is used in the grading procedure. Recall from the discussion on standard scores in Chapter 4 that the *T*-score has a mean of 50 and a standard deviation of 10.

The highest student average in the class is selected rather than the total number of possible points and is utilized in computing the percentages. Each of the other *T*-scores in the class are then divided by the top *T*-score, resulting in a percentage. This percentage is applied to the predetermined standards as described in the previous section. An example of this method is shown in Table 9.4.

Table 9.4 Relative Absolute Percentage Grading Procedure (N = 23)

Average Student T-Scores Listed in Rank Order for Each Student	*Percentages Computed*	*Grade*
70*	70/70 (100) = 100%	A
68	68/70 (100) = 97%	A
66	66/70 (100) = 94%	A
63	63/70 (100) = 90%	A
60	60/70 (100) = 85%	B
58	58/70 (100) = 83%	B
57	57/70 (100) = 81%	B
57*	57/70 (100) = 81%	B
54	54/70 (100) = 77%	C
53	53/70 (100) = 76%	C
52	52/70 (100) = 74%	C
52	52/70 (100) = 74%	C
50	50/70 (100) = 71%	C
50	50/70 (100) = 71%	C
50	50/70 (100) = 71%	C
47	47/70 (100) = 67%	D
45	45/70 (100) = 64%	D

44		44/70 (100) =	63%	D
43		43/70 (100) =	61%	D
40		40/70 (100) =	57%	F
38		38/70 (100) =	54%	F
36		36/70 (100) =	51%	F
35		35/70 (100) =	50%	F
	Grade Standards	*Frequency*		
	90–100 = A	4		
	80– 89 = B	4		
	70– 79 = C	7		
	60– 69 = D	4		
	Below 60 = F	4		

70 is the top *T*-score average in the class.

The advantages of this system are similar to the absolute percentage system; students are always aware of their grading position in the class. The procedure is also similar although there are some additional computations necessary. By using a member of the class as the criterion for the percentage standard rather than the total possible points during the unit, the tests are not required to comply to a traditional set of grades. Because the highest average score is used in computing percentages rather than the total number of points, the relative difficulty of the tests is less important than in the absolute percentage grading method. Some disadvantages include the number of computational steps needed in the procedures and the lack of sensitivity near the breaking points of the grading standards.

Normal Curve Grading

Normal curve grading is a norm-referenced system as opposed to the criterion-referenced systems discussed earlier. This method is based on the assumption that raw scores from a test are normally distributed. The normal curve is utilized to determine cutoff points between grades. A discussion of the normal curve and its interpretation may be found in Chapter 3. To demonstrate normal curve grading, *z*-scores will be used. However, it is equally appropriate to utilize any standard score scale or raw scores.

The first part of this discussion will be limited to explaining how to arrive at grades in the normal curve procedure.

1. Divide the number of grades used in the system (normally 5) into the number of standard deviations necessary to represent data found in the typical classroom situation (normally 5). Notice that almost all the scores will be included in the area of the curve ± 2.5 standard deviations from the mean for a total of 5. In the normal curve, 98.76

percent of the scores are contained within this area. For the typical A, B, C, D, F grading system, 1.0 is obtained when the 5 standard deviations are divided by the number of grades. The 1.0 is the number of standard deviations necessary to represent each letter grade.

2. Beginning with the C range, the 1.0 is located ±.5 standard deviations on either side of the mean. The remainder of the grade distribution is then developed. The B range is .5s to 1.5s above the mean and the A range is 1.5s and above. Likewise the D range is .5s to 1.5s below the mean and the F range includes any score more than 1.5s lower than the mean. The percentage of grades as determined by the cutoff points are as follows (a normal distribution is assumed).

A	7%	1.5s and above	$z = +1.5$ and above
B	24%	.5 to 1.5s above mean	$z = +\ .5$ to $+1.5$
C	38%	± .5 from mean	$z = -\ .5$ to $+\ .5$
D	24%	.5 to 1.5s below mean	$z = -\ .5$ to -1.5
F	7%	1.5s and below	$z = -\ 1.5$ and below

This 7-24-38-24-7 grading system is well-known as a sound method to evaluate students and is shown in graphic form in Figure 9.2.

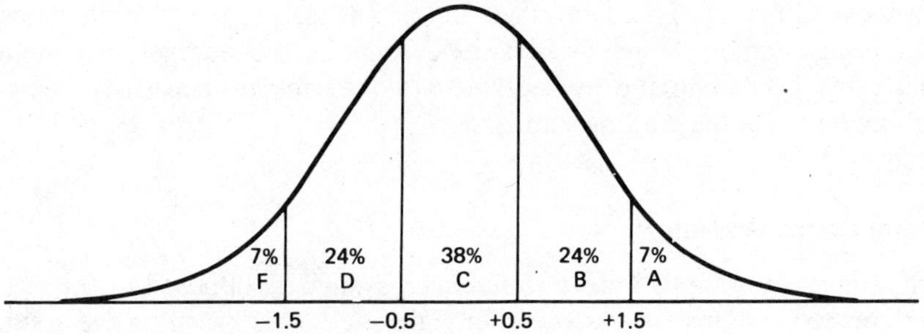

Figure 9.2. An example of normal curve grading.

If raw scores are utilized, another step is required.

3. Cutoff points in raw score values for specific grades must be calculated. Some standard score is often preferable since various test or unit grades can be equitably compared. This is not the case with raw scores where different tests usually have different means and standard deviations. To find raw score value cutoff points, the standard deviation value for each grade (determined in Step 2) is multiplied by the standard deviation of the specific distribution and then added to or subtracted from the mean depending on whether the grade is above or below the mean. In effect this is a specific application of the formula for z-scores, as discussed in Chapter 4.

An example of the normal curve grading procedure is found in Table 9.5 using z-scores as the basis for determining grades. An example of determining raw score values as cutoff points will be given later in this chapter.

Table 9.5 Normal Curve Grading Procedure Utilizing z-Scores (N = 30)

Student	*Raw Scores*	*z-Score*	*Letter Grade*
1	176	−1.35	D
2	239	1.58	A
3	213	.37	C
4	200	−.23	C
5	191	−.65	D
6	168	−1.72	F
7	180	−1.16	D
8	230	1.16	B
9	220	.70	B
10	212	.33	C
11	246	1.86	A
12	162	−2.00	F
13	201	−.19	C
14	214	.42	C
15	210	.23	C
16	229	1.12	B
17	198	−.32	C
18	213	.37	C
19	230	1.16	B
20	203	−.09	C
21	179	−1.21	D
22	212	.33	C
23	220	.70	B
24	192	−.60	D
25	176	−1.35	D
26	225	.93	B
27	205	.00	C
28	219	.65	B
29	179	−1.21	D
30	208	.14	C
$N = 30$	$\overline{X} = 205$	$s = 21.5$	$z = \dfrac{X - \overline{X}}{s}$

Total possible points = 260

Grade Standards		*Frequency*
1.5 and above	= A	2
.5 to 1.5	= B	7
−.5 to .5	= C	12
−1.5 to −.5	= D	7
−1.5 and below	= F	2

A more generalized method of determining grades by using the normal curve involves: selecting percentages of each grade to award or selecting z-score values, which also dictate certain percentages of each grade to be awarded.

The steps of this more generalized approach are:

1. Select the percentage of students to receive each letter grade or the z-score cutoff points between each grade. For instance the teacher may decide to utilize the 7-24-38- 24-7 system described earlier or if using z-scores may decide to use the cutoff points where $z = -1.5$, $-.5$, $+.5$, $+1.5$. Any other values could also be arbitrarily chosen.
2. Determine the cutoff points between each grade by using the normal curve. A statistical table indicating percentage of the total area under the normal curve between the mean and ordinate point should be consulted (Appendix B). For instance, if 10 percent of the grades to be given are A's, 40 percent of the area under the curve lies between the unknown z-score and zero. (Recall that z-scores have a mean of 0 and a standard deviation of 1). In Appendix B we see that 39.97 is the closest to 40 percent and is in the row where $z = 1.2$ and the column where $z = 1.28$. If z-scores are originally chosen as cutoff points, this step is unnecessary since its purpose is to convert percentage values to z-score values.
3. Determine raw score cutoff values for each letter grade by multiplying each of the z-score values from Step 2 by the standard deviation of the distribution and adding the mean. In effect the formula for z-scores,

$$z = \frac{X - \overline{X}}{s}$$

is used, and we solve for X so that $X = sz + \overline{X}$. Cutoff values should be rounded to the nearest unit of measurement.
4. Grade are then assigned using the raw score cutoff points.

An example of such a system can be given using the data in Table 9.5.

Step 1. Assume the teacher decided to assign grades as follows: A 15 percent, B 40 percent, C 35 percent, D 5 percent, F 5 percent. Appendix B is then consulted to find z values that correspond to the percentages.

Step 2. If 15 percent of the grades are A's, then 35 percent of the grades must fall between the mean and the cut off point for A's. The z value for the cutoff point is approximately $+1.05$ (since excellent scores are obviously above the mean). Similarly the cutoff value for B's is $--.13$; C's and D's are found in the table, -1.38 and -1.65 respectively.

Step 3. Using the formula

$X = sz + \bar{X}$, raw score cutoff values are computed:

A $(1.04)\ (21.5) + 205 = 227$ and above
B $(-.13)\ (21.5) + 205 = 202$
C $(-1.38)(21.5) + 205 = 177$
D $(-1.65)(21.5) + 205 = 170$
F 169 and below

Step 4. Therefore,

		Frequency
A	= 227 and above	5
B	= 202-226	13
C	= 177-201	8
D	= 170-176	2
F	= 169 and below	2

The normal curve grading is based on the assumption that the student scores will distribute themselves according to the normal curve discussed earlier. This may not be the case, however, in small groups. For this reason the normal group grading procedure is not recommended for groups less than 30 or so in size and should be used with certain precautions even with moderately sized groups.

This approach to determining grades is quite objective and allows the teacher to distribute grades based on the ability of the individual group. In this procedure as well as in other norm-referenced grading methods the tests may be very difficult or very easy, and the top students will still receive excellent grades. For the teacher who chooses to discriminate in ability through the use of exceptionally difficult examinations this grading method is more desirable than criterion-referenced methods. That grades are somewhat balanced (similar numbers of A's and F's, B's and D's) on the curve is a problem with normal curve grading that can be overcome by applying common sense. Rather than predetermining the number of grades to be awarded in each category, one may use percentages only as a guide. Perhaps no one deserves to receive a failing grade and probably more than 7 percent deserve A grades. An instructor should not hesitate to award the grades according to personal considerations using the normal curve as an aid in making these decisions. The same common sense decisions should be made when a grade falls on or is very near a cutoff point.

Natural Break Grading

The second form of norm-referenced grading to be discussed is the natural break method. This procedure is exceedingly simple because raw scores can be used without additional computations. The teacher should be cautioned against using raw scores when extreme differences in the variances in the different sets of scores occur. *T*-scores, *z*-scores, percentages, or even percentiles might better be used if extreme variances do occur. A consideration of the weighting techniques presented earlier in this chapter is particularly important when applying natural break grading.

The scores are listed in order from high to low. The teacher then uses the percentages listed under the discussion of normal curve grading or any percentages selected by personal preference to determine the approximate number of grades desired in each area. For example from a class of 40 students the teacher might desire to have 7 percent A's, 24 percent B's, 38 percent C's, 24 percent D's, and 7 percent F's. The percentages and numbers in each letter grade are illustrated in Table 9.6.

Table 9.6 Natural Break Grading Procedure ($N = 40$)

Grade	*Number of Students*	*Percentage of Each Grade*	*Number in Each Grade*
A	40	7%	2 or 3
B	40	24%	9 or 10
C	40	38%	16
D	40	24%	9 or 10
F	40	7%	2 or 3

Using the number of each grade desired as a guideline and by carefully searching the distribution of scores for natural breaks, the teacher can make some rather quick but fair decisions about the awarding of the grades. An example of this system and the grades awarded is shown in Table 9.7.

Table 9.7 Distribution of Grades Using the Natural Break Method ($N = 40$)

Raw Score	*Points*
295	
290	A
289	
277	
277	
274	

Raw Score	*Points*
270	
268	
266	B
263	
263	
260	
258	
250	
249	
249	
247	
246	
245	C
245	
245	
242	
240	
237	
237	
235	
234	
232	
231	
231	
228	
219	
217	
216	
210	
208	D
200	
199	
197	
171	F

Grade	*Frequency*
A	3
B	10
C	18
D	8
F	1

Total points on test = 300

The natural break system can also be used in conjunction with the criterion-referenced absolute percentage system — this procedure is a combination of the two original methods. For example, using the typical percentage system discussed earlier where A = 90–100 percent, B = 80–89 percent, C = 70–79 percent, D = 60–69 percent, F = below 60 percent, the instructor can look for natural breaks in the actual test scores with the absolute percentage system as a guideline. Table 9.8 demonstrates this method. Notice that the natural breaks in the test scores together with the absolute percentage method yields a system that is simply to use and is somewhat flexible. Another alternative is to look for the natural breaks and then determine the percentages at each break.

Table 9.8 Natural Break Grading Using Absolute Percentages as a Guideline ($N = 19$)

Raw Scores Rank Order	*Percentages*	*Grade*
50 points possible		
49	98	
48	96	
48	96	A
47	94	
46	92	
44	88	
43	86	
42	84	B
40	80	
39	78	
37	74	
36	72	
36	72	C
35	70	
35	70	
32	64	
31	62	
29	58	D
21	42	F

The natural break grading procedure has certain drawbacks. Natural break grading lacks consistency from one semester to the next. Grades are based on the performance of others in the same class, and scores on tests may vary significantly. Also, when raw scores are utilized to determine natural breaks, standards of performance are somewhat arbitrary. When the mean and standard deviation are calculated and some standard score is used, this problem is somewhat alleviated.

Assigning grades using the natural break method allows a teacher to use a student's performance in relation to a group without the rigidness of other norm-referenced grading methods. This procedure allows the teacher needed flexibility in this delicate area of grade assignment especially in situations where point totals or standard scores are found very near grade borderlines.

Summary

Students of physical education as well as parents and teachers find the assignment of grades useful. Grades summarize the learning progress and keep the student and parents aware of that progress.

Many philosophical considerations provide the basis for teachers to develop personal grading systems. Teachers must decide whether to consider performance, effort, improvement, or a combination of the three in their final grading procedures. Other considerations such as contracts, pass-fail grading, distribution of grades, and the weighting of grading components are essential methods to understand for teachers who are developing or modifying their grading philosophy.

Criterion-referenced grading involves comparing the student's performance to a predetermined absolute standard. Absolute percentage grading and relative absolute percentage grading are two examples of criterion-referenced grading. Both procedures involve converting the student's score to a percentage and comparing that percentage to the standard that has been predetermined by the teacher. In the absolute percentage method the percentage is a ratio of the items correct divided by the items possible, and in the relative absolute percentage procedure the ratio consists of the items correct divided by the highest score achieved on the test.

Norm-referenced grading involves comparing the student's performance with that of a group, usually his or her own. Curve grading and natural break grading are two examples of norm-referenced grading. Both procedures are based on the assumption that the scores from a test are somewhat normally distributed. Grades assigned from the normal curve method are distributed according to the standard deviation units along the normal curve base line. Using the percentage of scores that will occur under the normal curve, the standard deviation units can be converted to the percentage of students or scores within each grade range. Grades can then be assigned from those percentages. Grades assigned from the natural break method are distributed according to natural separations along a frequency distribution. The percentage of expected scores for each grade that is developed in the normal curve procedure may be used as a guide when assigning grades by the natural break method.

Study Questions

1. Identify three functions of grades and defend each one.
2. Defend improvement as a basis for a final grade in physical education.
3. Many teachers argue that performance should be considered the most important factor in determining course grades. Develop an argument for or against this position.
4. How does effort have a place in physical education grading?
5. Compare and contrast pass-fail grading with contract grading.

6. Some physical educators feel grade distribution is uniquely different in their physical education classes. Others argue that grades assigned in physical education classes should be distributed similarly to other subjects. Select one of these positions and defend it in writing.
7. For a unit that you plan to teach, list the factors you would consider in arriving at a course grade. Indicate and defend the weight given to each.
8. Define norm-referenced grading and criterion-referenced grading. Compare and contrast these two grading schemes.
9. When might you choose to use the absolute percentage method of grading? Using 10 students and hypothetical data, develop a grading scale using this method.
10. Compare the relative absolute percentage method to the procedure outlined in Question 9. Discuss its strengths and weaknesses as a grading method.
11. When is it appropriate to use normal curve grading? When is it not appropriate? How are the grades determined using this method?
12. List several reasons for and against using the natural break method of assigning grades.
13. From raw data in Table 9.5, calculate grades using any of the three absolute percentage scales presented in the chapter. Determine the frequency of each letter grade.
14. From raw data in Table 9.5, calculate grades using the relative absolute percentage grading system. Use the same percentages as in Question 13 and determine the frequency of each letter grade.
15. From raw data in Table 9.5, calculate grades using natural break grading. Determine the frequency of each letter grade.
16. Compare and contrast the results of the criterion-referenced systems (Questions 13 and 14) with the results of norm-referenced systems (Question 15 and normal curve example in text from Table 9.5). Which method gives the greatest number of high grades? The most failing grades?

CHAPTER 10

Locating Tests in Physical Education

After you have read and studied this chapter you should be able to:

1. *Distinguish between such resources as the Mental Measurements Yearbooks, Educational Resource Information Center, Dissertation Abstracts International, Psychological Abstracts, Completed Research in Health, Physical Education, and Recreation, and various periodicals in terms of their value in locating and evaluating tests.*
2. *Utilize several kinds of resources in locating a test.*
3. *Locate reviews of the specific tests under consideration.*
4. *Find research that has utilizied a specific test under consideration.*
5. *Evaluate the quality of a test with evidence obtained from resources.*

The majority of published tests in physical education, and educational and psychological tests related to physical education are products of the twentieth century. Indeed, most of the tests in physical education have publication dates later than 1930. As the profession has developed, so too have specific areas of testing within the profession. As mentioned in earlier chapters, measurement can be broadly divided into three categories; the cognitive, the affective, and the psychomotor domains.

The major problems involve locating, selecting, and then obtaining the published test. Published tests vary widely in content, procedures, and the group for which they are designated. There are cognitive knowledge tests, affective rating scales, and a wide range of psychomotor tests measuring structural or functional traits. The majority of tests published in physical education are of the psychomotor domain and were constructed to measure basic or multiple performance traits. In contrast, very few instruments for measuring traits of the affective domain have been published. Many attempts have been made to develop cognitive tests in various content areas of physical education, but they often become outdated soon after publication and serve mainly as guides in developing teacher-made tests. There are tests in each domain designated for infants, preschool children, elementary students, secondary students, college-age students and adults, with the majority of tests intended for secondary and college-age students.

It is not the intent of this text to introduce the student to all of the tests used in physical education. Chapters 11, 12, 13 and 14 include examples of the various test types, concentrating on those tests that are most functional for school situations. This chapter attempts to describe the various sources available for locating such tests. The knowledge of where to locate tests for a particular purpose and how to evaluate a test when found is probably more important than a great deal of information regarding a specific test. Some tests become outdated, and test items change. In fact the purposes of measurement and evaluation often change. More important then, is knowing where to find current tests available for a desired purpose and how to evaluate their strengths and weaknesses. Chapter 5 and Chapter 8 have provided some insight into the selection of a test once it has been located.

Several resources are available to help locate and evaluate tests in physical education and related areas. Among these are: (1) *Mental Measurements Yearbooks*; (2) *Educational Resource Information Center*; (3) various *abstracts* and *indexes*; (4) *journals* and other *periodicals*; (5) *tests* and *test manuals*; and (6) general or specific *texts* in physical education that include published tests.

MENTAL MEASUREMENT YEARBOOKS

The major resource in terms of a comprehensive listing of all tests is the *Mental Measurements Yearbook (MMY)* series edited by Buros. The series is designed to assist test users in education, psychology, and industry in making more intelligent use of the standardized tests of various purposes and descriptions. The objectives of the *Mental Measurement Yearbooks*, according to Buros, are:

1. To provide information about tests published as separates throughout the English-speaking world.
2. To present frankly critical test reviews written by testing and subject specialists representing various viewpoints.
3. To provide extensive bibliographies of verified references on the construction, use, and validity of specific tests.
4. To make readily available the critical portions of test reviews appearing in professional journals; and
5. To present fairly exhaustive listings of new and revised books on testing, along with evaluative excerpts from representative reviews which these books receive in professional journals.*

The yearbooks were initiated in 1938 with the publication of the *Nineteen Thirty Eight Mental Measurements Yearbook*. Since each succeeding edition supplements the preceding yearbook, it is necessary to consult all volumes for complete coverage of tests, test reviews, and bibliographies for specific tests. The latest editions are of more value, and the most current is the *Eighth Mental Measurements Yearbook* published in 1978. The yearbooks are usually available in the reference section of most college and university libraries.

*Oscar Krisen Buros, *The Eighth Mental Measurements Yearbook*, The Gryphon Press, Highland Park, N.Y., 1978, xxxi. Reprinted by permission.

The *Mental Measurements Yearbooks* include information about tests such as author, publisher, publication date, cost, time to administer, grades for which tests are suitable, validity and reliability data, and number of forms available. This information is obviously important for new standardized tests but can also be gained from most of the sources described later in this chapter. In addition the *MMY* includes test reviews, a bibliography of books and articles that have utilized the test, listing of significant books on measurement for the period covered by the specific *Mental Measurements Yearbook* as well as reviews of these books, and finally a comprehensive index and directory section.

Other information in the *Mental Measurements Yearbooks* is not obtained as easily from other sources. Each new test is reviewed by one or more experts. The reviews are comprehensive, indicating strengths and weaknesses of the test, comparing it with others in the same area, and indicating the purposes for which the reviewer considers it useful.

One guideline regarding the quality of a test, although not the only one, is the use it receives. The *Mental Measurements Yearbooks* present a bibliography of published studies that have utilized each classified test. In some cases, books and periodicals that discuss the construction, use, and validity of specific tests are included in the bibliography. As an example of the 15 major test classifications listed by Buros in the *Seventh Mental Measurements Yearbook*, specific physical education-related tests are included under the title "Health and Physical Education." One specific test listed under this title, the AAHPER Youth Fitness Test, has 67 bibliographic references listed for the years 1965 to 1969 or an average of about 13 a year. Thus the *Mental Measurements Yearbooks* can be useful sources for locating studies dealing with specific tests in physical education.

Another feature that is very useful to the teacher who wishes to locate tests is a section of the *MMY* that lists significant books in measurement and evaluation. In addition this section contains reviews of each listed book that has appeared in the various professional journals. Thus the book bibliography and reviews provide a guide to and an evaluation of measurement publications in physical education.

A final important facet of the *MMY* series is a comprehensive index and directory section. Included in this section are: (1) a directory and index of the 99 periodicals that have given the *MMY* permission to reprint reviews of tests or books on testing; (2) a directory and index of the 440 publishers of the tests and books on testing reviewed in the volume; (3) an index of titles of books (4) an index of titles of tests; (5) an index of names associated with tests; and (6) a classified index of tests organized by content or type. This index and directory section provides the means for locating tests, test types, test reviews, and publishers of various tests and books related to measurement.

Several other publications have developed as a result of the *MMY* series.

Among these are *Tests in Print (TIP)* published in 1961 and *Tests in Print, Volume 2* published in 1973, which include comprehensive bibliographies of standardized tests and valuable information necessary for the evaluation and selection of such tests. The *Tests in Print* volumes also provide a much needed master index to the *Mental Measurements Yearbooks*. In addition, *Personality Tests and Reviews (PTR)*, a monograph published in 1970 as a result of the *MMY*, makes readily available vast information about personality-related tests found in the first six *Mental Measurement Yearbooks*. To summarize, the *Mental Measurements Yearbooks* and related publications are viable sources in locating and evaluating published tests in physical education and related areas. Few tests of basic performance traits have been classified to date. Most tests included are test batteries of multiple performance traits such as the previously mentioned AAHPER Youth Fitness Test.

In addition to psychomotor tests, numerous general tests that measure affective traits can be adapted for use in physical education. The *MMY* provides comprehensive information for instruments that measure such traits as attitude, self-concept, and character.

The value of the *Mental Measurements Yearbooks* goes beyond the location of a specific test. Such information as test reviews, bibliographies, and indexes make the *MMY* series a valuable resource for any type of test-related information.

EDUCATIONAL RESOURCE INFORMATION CENTER

Another reference source usually available in major libraries is the Education Resources Information Center, (ERIC) a national information system that disseminates educational research results, research-related materials, and other resource information. Through a network of 16 specialized clearing houses, each responsible for a particular education area, information is acquired, evaluated, abstracted, indexed, and listed in a monthly catalog entitled *Research in Education (RIE)*. This reference publication provides access to government documents, technical reports, presentations, project descriptions, book descriptions, and curriculum materials that are generally out of print within a few months after the date of publication. In addition, a second publication has been devoted exclusively to periodical literature. The *Current Index to Journals in Education (CIJE)* was created to serve the information needs of the practicing educator, reference librarian, or education researcher. Over 700 publications are currently indexed in *CIJE*, several of which have direct application to physical education. These two publications are available at over 5000 libraries world-wide.

Information contained in the ERIC publication is also available on magnetic tapes. ERIC computer searches can be obtained at over 200 locations while ERIC microfiche is available at more than 600 locations. Also both major national vendors of on-line bibliographic search services, Lockheed and Systems Development Corporation, provide access to the ERIC data.

One of the 16 major clearing houses of ERIC, The Educational Testing Service, Princeton, New Jersey 08540, concentrates specifically on tests, measurements, and evaluation. Through data gathered by the Education Testing Service or any of the other 15 clearing houses and published in *RIE* or *CIJE*, valuable information can be found about tests in physical education and related areas. The clearing houses also produce various publications of their own, which might provide helpful information.

ABSTRACTS AND INDEXES

In addition to the two resources mentioned above, other sources may be used for gathering information about tests in physical education. The major purpose in consulting abstracts and indexes is to locate current literature in a particular test area. The indexes and abstracts provide references to published and unpublished research that utilizes specific test instruments. Such research generally uses valid and reliable tests. One viable source is the publication *Completed Research in Health, Physical Education, and Recreation.* This volume, published yearly since 1959 and preceded by the *Annual Bibliography of Research in HPER*, includes a compilation of research completed in the year preceding the publication date. Generally an abstract of the nature of each report and the findings is included. In a separate bibliography section a listing of published research articles citing 180 periodicals that pertain to physical education and related areas is included.

A number of other sources may be valuable for locating research that has utilized various tests in physical education. The *Dissertation Abstracts International* contains listings of doctoral dissertations in all fields and includes essentially every dissertation accepted since 1861. The relevance of *Dissertation Abstracts International* as a source is that many tests have developed or improved during the completion of dissertation requirements. Also, published tests are often utilized in dissertations, and usually such qualities as validity and reliability are discussed in these works. While *Completed Research in Health, Physical Education, and Recreation* specifically includes abstracts of research in this field, the *Dissertation Abstracts International* has been published for a much longer time and covers many areas considered peripheral to physical education. *Dissertation Abstracts International,* formerly called *Dissertation Abstracts,* is a monthly compilation of abstracts submitted by 270 cooperating institutions in the United States and Canada. The abstracts are indexed according to subject and author and are published in two volumes. The dissertations in physical education are included in the *Humanities and Social Science* Volume. The *Sciences and Engineering* Volume includes dissertations from some related areas such as physiology and health sciences.

Another source, the *Psychological Abstracts*, includes a listing of current publications of a scientific and technical nature in psychology. Each publication is represented by author, title, and an abstract, indicating the problem and major findings of each study. In *Psychological Abstracts*, new tests are listed at the beginning of each monthly issue. The reference also reports published research using tests and presents findings and conclusions with respect to the tests. Many areas of psychology relate closely to physical education and therefore offer valuable information about the obtaining and selecting of tests in physical education. Additional information can be obtained from *Biological Abstracts* and the *Bio Research Index*, which cover the full spectrum of life science in periodical literature, conference proceedings, and reports; and *Index Medicus*, which covers journals associated with the medical professions. The data from several of these published compilations of current periodical literature and dissertations are available through computer searches. Over 1000 schools, universities, companies, and other organizations have access to data through on-line computer searches. Information from at least 43 different data bases, including most sources mentioned in this chapter, are available through two major vendors, System Development Corporation and Lockheed.

A more familiar source of information, which gives direct bibliographic information about physical education as well as other education areas, is the *Education Index*. This source provides no information about the nature and content of the publication but does include a specific bibliography indicating where such information may be located. Material is topically organized, and information can be found by consulting such topics as "physical education tests" or "tests and scales."

Through the use of various abstracts and indexes people interested in quality measurement can find information that will identify, describe, and evaluate tests on any specific physical education topic.

JOURNALS AND OTHER PERIODICALS

The majority of sources described heretofore in this chapter are secondary sources in the sense that they provide direction in finding test information but do not give access to the test. Periodicals such as the *Research Quarterly*, the *Journal of Physical Education and Recreation, Perceptual and Motor Skills*, and numerous others have included tests in physical education. Bibliographic information for articles in these periodicals may be located through the *Current Index to Journals in Education, Completed Research in HPER*, or the *Education Index*. Often, in addition to the publication of tests, publications such as the *Research Quarterly* include reviews on specific tests.

A list of the periodicals that will help in obtaining, selecting, and evaluating tests in physical education can be found in any volume of *Completed Research in HPER*.

TEST MANUALS

Once initial information about a test is obtained, valuable aids in the selection and evaluation process include a copy of the test manual, information from the test publisher or equipment manufacturer, and the actual test itself. Many tests in physical education involve the measurement of structural or functional traits and require explicit directions. For example the AAHPER publishes a *Test Manual* for the Youth Fitness Test, which includes background information regarding the development of the test items, national norms, and directions for administration of the test battery. Such a manual gives data that will aid in the selection or rejection of such a test or test battery.

However, since test publishers are in the business of marketing tests, information published by them is sometimes biased. Also, many tests utilized in physical education are physical performance tests that do not have manuals or have been published in journals but are not copyrighted. A perusal of test reviews and studies that have utilized the test under consideration will help one to make an objective decision.

TEXTS

A final source for locating tests in physical education is textbooks of both a general and specific nature. The traditional tests and measurements books in physical education have devoted a substantial number of pages to the publication of tests that encompass anthropometric traits, basic and multiple performance traits, and the domains of behavior. The texts given below include an extensive listing of tests.

1. *Application of Measurement to Health and Physical Education* by H. Harrison Clarke.
2. *A Practical Approach to Measurement in Physical Education* by Harold M. Barrow and Rosemary McGee.
3. *Evaluation in Physical Education* by Mary Jane Haskins.
4. *Measurement in Physical Education* by Donald K. Mathews.
5. *Measurement and Statistics in Physical Education* by N. P. Neilson and Clayne R. Jensen
6. *Practical Measurements for Evaluation in Physical Education* by Barry L. Johnson and Jack K. Nelson.

One limitation of the inclusion of such tests in the textbooks above, for example, is apparent from an examination of publication dates. All of the book copyright dates are relatively recent, but an examination of publication dates for tests included demonstrates that many of the tests are somewhat outdated. We have already mentioned that tests often undergo revision or are found under rigid investigation to lack validity or reliability.

Well-established tests can be safely published, but a text obviously cannot keep abreast of the current changes, interests, specific test items, equipment, advances, or techniques in administration. In addition, there is often a significant time lag between the gathering of material to write such a text and the actual publication date. Another factor is that texts cannot be comprehensive in terms of the inclusion of tests. Each one must be selective in the presentation and discussion of specific tests. Thus, students or teachers of physical education cannot expect a test and measurement text to lead them to all available tests in a given area. For a comprehensive listing of currently used tests, other previously mentioned sources such as periodicals or reference publications are possible alternatives.

Measurement in the physical education profession has developed substantially since the 1860s when the first anthropometric testing was done. Professional preparation in physical education has included many varied areas of emphasis such as elementary and secondary physical education, adapted physical education, specific sports and recreation skills, anatomy, physiology, kinesiology, motor learning, and the like. Perhaps a better alternative than relying on a text in measurement and evaluation to obtain information about specific tests, equipment, and administrative procedures is to consult current texts or periodicals in each specific content area.

Summary

The knowledge of where to locate tests and test reviews is very important. Many tests have been developed and published in physical education in each of the cognitive, affective, and psychomotor domains, although tests that measure structured and functional traits of the psychomotor domain far outnumber those of the congitive and affective domains.

A variety of resources are available for locating and evaluating tests in physical education. Buros' *Mental Measurements Yearbooks* series is undoubtedly the major resource in terms of a comprehensive listing and reviewing of tests. A second major reference source is the Education Resource Information Center (ERIC), which publishes research results, research-related materials and resource information in two monthly catalogs, *Research in Education (RIE)* and the *Current Index to Journals in Education (CIJE).*

A number of publications contain abstracts of published research or dissertations. Included in this group are *Completed Research in HPER, Dissertation Abstracts International, Psychological Abstracts,* and other published compilations of current periodical literature and dissertations of a specific nature. A common index that includes only bibliographic information of published literature is the *Education Index*. The journals referred to in the *Education Index* are usually the primary sources for locating and evaluating tests in physical education. Although many periodicals have published tests that are utilized in physical education, the most common source is the *Research Quarterly*.

Another direct source for tests in physical education that have usually been copyrighted, is the test manual, which includes a description of the test and instructions and is made available by the publisher. However many tests in physical education are psychomotor tests, which typically are not copyrighted.

A final source for locating tests in physical education is textbooks. Traditional textbooks in measurement and evaluation of physical education contain tests in each of the cognitive, affective, or psychomotor domains. Another alternative is to consult texts in specific content areas such as motor learning or kinesiology.

Thus a number of resources are available to help locate and evaluate tests. Most important is the knowledge of where current information can be obtained about tests in physical education.

Study Questions

1. Locate the AAHPER Youth Fitness Test in the current *Mental Measurements Yearbook*. How much research has been done utilizing the test? Have the reviews of the test battery been good?
2. What is the difference between ERIC publications *Research in Education* and *Current Index to Journals in Education*?
3. Locate a volume of the *Completed Research in Health, Physical Education, and Recreation*. Select a test area such as physical fitness or a specific skill. How many references from published journals are there in the bibliography section regarding the selected topic? How much graduate research is reported in the *Theses Abstract* section? Is there a test that is utilized more than others? Which one?
4. *Dissertation Abstracts International* includes abstracts of dissertations in all fields while *Completed Research in HPER* includes only those in HPER areas. Select a study in *Completed Research* that utilizes a specific test and find the same study in *DAI*. What are the differences in reporting style of the two resources?
5. Using the *Education Index*, find reference to a test in physical education. Is the article in the *Current Index to Journals in Education* and *Completed Research in HPER*? Is it also included in *Psychological Abstracts*? What are the differences in the types of information given?

CHAPTER 11

Anthropometric Traits and Measurements

After you have read and studied this chapter you should be able to:

1. *Identify various anthropometric traits and measurements.*
2. *Utilize various anthropometric measurements to monitor physical growth.*
3. *Understand the meaning of the terms: endomorphy, mesomorphy, ectomorphy, and somatotype.*
4. *Calculate or estimate somatotype.*
5. *Identify methods of assessing body composition.*
6. *Calculate or estimate body composition.*

Anthropometric traits and measurements have been utilized in numerous classification schemes. As early as 1861, when the scientific era of measurement began in America, age, height, weight, and anthropometric measurements were taken. Since Hitchcock's initial interest, it has been demonstrated in several studies that students who differ in these factors also differ in their ability to perform psychomotor skills. More recently, anthropometric measurements have been used to assess body type and body composition. *Growth measures, body type, and body composition* will be discussed in this chapter.

GROWTH MEASURES

Numerous studies have determined that motor performance is related to chronological age. The school system in the United States is based on chronological age. That is, most students begin formal schooling when they are about 5 and if satisfactory progress is made, students in the same grade are typically the same chronological age. However, Clarke (1971) has shown that great differences exist in the physiological maturity of boys and girls of the same chronological age. An excellent method of determining maturity of growing children is to assess skeletal age through the use of an X-ray of the wrist or hand. This method, unfortunately, is not practical for school situations.

Growth is a complex process that is affected by genetic and environmental factors. Growing body mass is reflected by increased weight and longer length or taller height. Numerous growth standards or norms have been derived. Some norms have been developed from small or biased samples, and this has tended to limit their application and usefulness. Recently, in 1976, the National Center for Health Statistics (NCHS) has prepared percentiles for assessing growth based on large nationally representative samples. These norms are available from the National Center for Health Statistics, Hyattsville, Maryland 20782.

Several other attempts have been made regarding the assessment of growth. One of these, the Wetzel Grid (1948), has received much use. The child is assessed over his or her school career with measures of height and weight taken at various prescribed ages. Nine general body types are designated on the grid, and the child's physique is recorded for each age. He or she is then placed into a developmental level for each age, and the developmental levels are used as criteria for identifying normal and abnormal growth patterns. Although the grid is very complicated, once its component parts are understood, it can serve as a useful tool for evaluating growth.

Another system using age, height, and weight is Meredith's Height-Weight Chart (1949). Its purpose is to provide useful information about the status and physical growth of students. Norms have been developed for heights and weights at various ages. Height is categorized into five zones (i.e., tall, moderately tall, average, moderately short, and short). Weight is categorized similarly (heavy, moderately heavy, average, moderately light, and light). When height and weight are plotted for an age, a check can be made to determine if height and weight are in similar zones. With the use of successive plottings, growth patterns can be developed. A complete discussion accompanied by physical growth records for interpreting height and weight can be found in Barrow and McGee (1971).

Thus, most measures of growth are utilized to monitor or predict physical growth of students of various ages. Classification systems using age, height, and weight were developed in the 1930s and were utilized quite extensively to classify students into homogeneous groups. The most popular indexes have been those of Cozens (1929), Neilson and Cozens (1934), and McCloy (1954). Research by Espenshade (1963) demonstrated that chronological age is an adequate criterion for classification purposes, and age-height-weight indexes give little additional information. Such classification indexes have been used sparingly in the past 15 years.

BODY TYPE

There has always been much interest in describing and assessing body types. In ancient Greece, Hippocrates designated two fundamental physical types. Later, Rostan, Reynolds, and Kretschmer each developed descriptions of various body types. However, Sheldon, Stevens, and Tucker (1940) introduced the concept of somatotyping. Their classification included the three major components: endomorphy, mesomorphy, and ectomorphy.

Endomorphy refers to the relative fatness of the physique and also, to relative leanness. It is characterized by a predominance of soft roundness throughout various regions of the body. Mesomorphy refers to relative musculoskeletal development. It is characterized by the dominance of muscle, bone, and connective tissue. Ectomorphy refers to the relative linearity of the physique. It is characterized by a frail, delicate body structure, with thin body segments. Sheldon and his colleagues developed a 7-point continuum to describe the presence of each component in each individual physique. A rating of 1 in any component signified the least presence of that component, 4 was average and 7 the most.

The somatotype is given in a three-number sequence: the endomorphic rating is given first, followed in order by the ratings for mesomorphy and ectomorphy. Somatotyping according to Sheldon's method involves a great amount of training and practice. Photographs from three perspectives, front, side, and rear are taken according to precise specifications, as published in the *Atlas of Man* (1954). The photographs are then analyzed for the presence of each component.

Sheldon found the most common male somatotype to be ratings in the middle of each component scale (i.e., 3—4—4, 4—4—3) and also found in another study that women were more endomorphic and less mesomorphic with 5—3—3 as the most common female somatotype. The process of somatotyping according to Sheldon's method is quite complex, and although it has been used extensively in research, it is not practical for use by physical educators.

Research has shown that there is a positive relationship between certain somatotypes and personality traits, health of the individual, success in psychomotor skills, and longevity. Somatotypes are also used as a classification device, to predict success, and to gain a better assessment of the capabilities of students. Somatotype data on students, therefore, has the potential of being very useful.

Several less precise methods of assessing body type have arisen from Sheldon's system. An example is Cureton's Simplified Physique Rating (1947) in which subjective ratings are made regarding the presence of three gross aspects of physique: external fat, muscular development and condition, and skeletal development. Each aspect is rated using a 1-7 scale with the criteria presented in Table 11.1.

Another method of estimating somatotype is relatively simple and very useful. This process involves subjectively rating the primary components according to Sheldon's 1-7 scale. The second component is then rated and finally the third component is rated in a similar matter. Next, the ponderal index (height-weight ratio) as developed by Sheldon is calculated: height in inches or centimeters is divided by the cube root of weight in pounds or kilograms. The computation can be accomplished by using a hand calculator or a nomograph, or calculating as found in Figure 11.1.

Table 11.1 Cureton's Simplified Physique Rating

A. Scale for Rating External Fat

3	4	5	6	7
Extremely low in adipose tissue and relatively small anteroposterior dimensions of the lower trunk			Average in tissue and physical build of lower trunk	Extremely obese with large quantities of adipose tissue and unproportionately thick abdominal region

B. Scale for Rating Muscular Development and Condition

3	4	5	6	7
Extremely underdeveloped and poorly conditioned muscles squeezed or pushed in the contracted state (biceps, abdominals, thighs, calves)			Average in skeletal muscular development and condition	Extremely developed with large and hard muscles in the contracted state firm under forceful squeezing

C. Scale for Rating Skeletal Development

1	2	3	4	5	6	7
Extremely thick and heavy bones; short and ponderous skeleton with relatively great cross-section of ankle, knee, and elbow joints			Average size bones and joints in cross-section and length	Extremely thin, frail bones, tall linear skeleton with relatively small scorr-section of ankle, knee, and elbow joints		

To use the nomograph, a straightedge should be placed so that the subject's height and weight are connected. The ponderal index is then read according to the scale in the center of the figure. This index can be calculated according to British or Metric Units. After the ponderal index is calculated, as in Table 11.2, an updated table of distribution of somatotypes, should be consulted to determine which somatotypes are possible for the calculated ponderal index. Usually several of the alternative somatotypes can be disregarded. For example, if a ratio of 13.20 was calculated and it was estimated that the subject was highly mesomorphic, only 163, 253, and 354 would be plausible alternatives. These should be compared with the subjectively determined somatotype and the adjustments made.

The Heath-Carter Somatotype Method has modified Sheldon's original system in several ways: (1) the 7- point scale has been extended — the new scale begins theoretically at 0 (in practice at ½) and has no upper limit; (2) the table of possible somatotypes of $HT/\sqrt[3]{WT}$ ratios has been revised (Table 11.2);

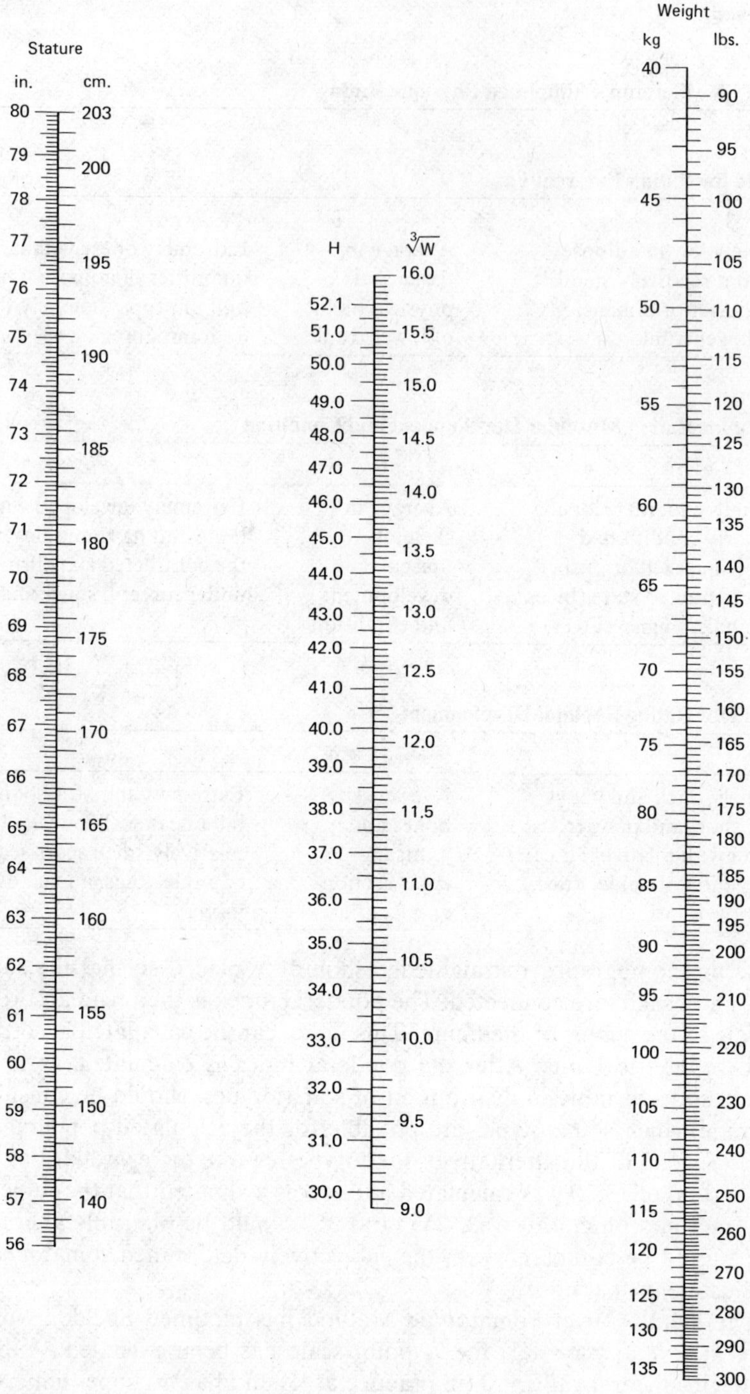

Figure 11.1. A nomograph for determining height over the cube root of weight in British and metric units (from J. E. Carter, *The Health-Carter Samatotype Method*, Revised Edition, San Diego State University, San Diego, California, 1975, Appendix D; reprinted by permission).

(3) since the permanence of somatotypes has been questioned, the same $HT/\sqrt[3]{WT}$ ratio table is used for both sexes and all ages; (4) an anthropometric method of assessing somatotype has been developed. Justification for this method is given in *The Heath-Carter Somatotype Method*, Chapter II (1975).

Ten anthropometric measurements are taken and used separately or along with photographs to estimate somatotype. The measurements are:

1. Height
2. Weight

Subcutaneous Fat

3. Triceps
4. Subscapular
5. Suprailiac
6. Calf

Bone diameters

7. Humerus
8. Femur

Muscle Girths

9. Biceps
10. Calf

Table 11.2 Distribution of Somatotypes According to

	½-1	1	2	3	4	5	6	7	8	9	
15.40										119	50.91
15.20									118	129, 219	50.25
15.00								117	128, 218		49.59
14.80								127, 217	138, 318		48.93
14.60							126, 216	137, 317			48.27
14.40							136, 316	237, 327			47.61
							226				47.61
							227			48.27	
14.20						135, 315	146, 416				46.95
						225	236, 326				
14.00					134, 314	145, 415	246, 426				46.28
					224	235, 325	336				
13.80					144, 414	245, 425					45.62
					234, 324	335					
13.60				233	154, 514	255, 525					44.96
					244, 424	345, 435					
					334						
13.40				153, 513	254, 524						44.30
				333	344, 434						
13.20			242, 422	163, 613	354, 534						43.64
				253, 523	444						
				343, 433							
13.00			162, 612	263, 623							42.98
			252, 522	353, 533							
				443							
12.80		341, 431	172, 712	363, 633							42.32
			262, 622	453, 543							
			352, 532								
			442								
12.60		171, 711	182, 812								41.66
		261, 621	272, 722								
		351, 531	362, 632								
		441	452, 542								

12.40		181, 811 271, 721 361, 631 451, 541	282, 822 372, 732 462, 642 552	40.99
12.20		191, 911 281, 821 371, 731 461, 641 551		40.33
12.00		291, 921 381, 831 471, 741 561, 651		39.67
11.70	5-6½-½, 6-6-1 10-2-1, 2-10-1	391, 931 481, 841 571, 751		38.68
11.40	10-3-1, 3-10-1 10½-2½-½, 11-2-1	491, 941 581, 851 671, 761		37.69
11.00	6½-7½-½, 7-7-1 10½-3½-½, 11-3-1	4-10-1, 10-4-1 5-9-1, 9-5-1 6-8-1, 8-6-1		36.37
10.50	7-8-1, 8-7-1 11½-3½-½, 12-3-1	4-11-1, 11-4-1 5-10-1, 10-5-1 6-9-1, 9-6-1		34.71
10.00	7½-8½-½, 8-8-1 11½-4½-½, 12-4-1, 13-3-1	5-11-1, 11-5-1 6-10-1, 10-6-1 7-9-1, 9-7-1		33.06
9.50	12-5-1 13-4-1	7-10-1, 10-7-1 8-9-1, 9-8-1 11-6-1		31.41
9.00	12-6-1 13-5-1 14-4-1	8-10-1, 10-8-1 9-9-1 11-7-1		29.75

Source: Carter, J. E., *The Heath-Carter Somatotype Method*, San Diego: San Diego State University, 1975, Table 3-1. Reprinted by permission.

The fat tissue measurements are essentially the same as those used in body composition studies. Directions for taking the measurements must be strictly adhered to and are illustrated in Appendix A of *The Heath-Carter Somatotype Method.*

BODY COMPOSITION

Body weight is composed of two factors: fat tissue and lean body weight or mass. Age-height-weight tables have traditionally been used to determine whether an individual is underweight or overweight. However, research has shown that individuals of the same height, weight, and age can vary significantly in body shape and body composition. For example, most football players are overweight according to typical age-height-weight tables, but most are not obese. If trained football players are compared with less developed individuals of the same age, height, and weight, differences in body shape and composition are obvious. Because of the emphasis of physical fitness in today's society, various methods of assessing body composition have been popularized.

A more appropriate evaluation of a person's weight can be made if measurements of body composition are used. Various methods of evaluating body composition can be very useful in assessing obesity and physical fitness, in classifying students into homogenous groups, and for prediction of success in motor activities especially those that require strength and endurance.

An accurate way to determine the level of obesity is to measure the percentage of body weight that is fat tissue. Several laboratory methods have been developed to accurately measure the fat tissue. Behnke and Wilmore (1974) identify such methods as underwater weighing, radiographic analysis, a biochemical approach, and ultrasound.

A commonly used formula derived by Siri (1956) for determining the percent of body fat is

$$\text{Percent body fat} = \left(\frac{4.95}{\text{density}} - 4.50\right) 100$$

The most popular research method to determine body density involves weighing an individual in the air and then again when the individual is completely submerged in water. When using the underwater weighing technique the density of the body can be determined by the following formula.

$$\text{Density} = \frac{Wa}{(Wa - Ww)/Dw - (RV + 100)}$$

where Wa = Individual's body weight in air
Ww = Individual's body weight in water (maximal expiratory condition)
Dw = Density of water at time of weighing
RV = Residual lung volume
100 = Constant approximating air volume in milliliters in gastrointestinal tract

This formula is based on Archimedes' principle that a body immersed in a fluid is acted on by a buoyancy force that is evidenced by a loss of weight equal to the weight of the displaced fluid. When an individual is weighed underwater, the total body volume is equal to his or her loss of weight in water. Since Density = Weight/Volume, the above formula for body density was derived, and corrections were made for the density of water at the time of underwater weighing and the air remaining in the lungs and gastrointestinal tract. Constants are sometimes used for the residual lung volume (RV) and air volume in the gastrointestinal tract. Research has found little difference in assumed and actual volumes. Because this method is complicated and requires special equipment, other, more practical methods of assessing body fat have been popularized.

The most common method is to measure skinfold thickness with the use of skinfold calipers. Three quality instruments are the Lange, Harpenden, and Vernier Skinfold Calipers. This method is considered quite accurate since 50 percent of fat tissue is localized immediately under the skin. Directions for testing skinfolds are relatively simple, but considerable practice is required to achieve reliability of readings. General directions state that a double layer of skin and subcutaneous tissue be grasped with the thumb and forefinger. The caliper is applied about 1.0 centimeter from the skinfold with measurements taken to the nearest .1 millimeter, after full spring pressure of the caliper is applied. The procedure for measuring skinfold is shown in Figure 11.2. The most common sites for measuring skinfold are:

1. Triceps. Skinfold is taken parallel to long axis of arm with arm at side of body midway between acromion and the elbow. (Subject should lock elbow to exclude muscle fibers.)
2. Subscapular. Skinfold is taken at the inferior angle of the scapula running downward and outward in the direction of the ribs.
3. Abdominal. Horizontal skinfold is taken adjacent to the umbilicus.
4. Suprailiac. Skinfold is taken 1 to 2 inches above anterior superior iliac spine running forward and slightly downward.

Other skinfold measures sometimes utilized are the chest, the waist, the knee, the calf, the thigh, and the midaxillary skinfolds. Specific directions for taking skinfolds must be followed closely to assure reliable measurements. To interpret skinfold measurements, various regression formulas have been devel-

Figure 11.2. Procedure for taking skinfold measurements.

oped to calculate body density. Wilmore and Behnke have utilized the following formulas for calculating body density for men (1969) and women (1970).

$$(\text{Men})\ D = 1.08543 - .00086\ (\text{abdominal skinfold}) - .00040\ (\text{thigh skinfold})$$

$$(\text{Women})\ D = 1.06234 - .00068\ (\text{subscapular skinfold}) - .00039\ (\text{triceps skinfold}) - .00025\ (\text{thigh skinfold})$$

Others have used different skinfolds and have developed similar formulas for determining body density. Once body density has been found, it can be substituted in the formula for determining percent of body fat. A computer or programmable calculator should be utilized in the mathematical calculations.

Since the reading on the skinfold calipers is in millimeters, several researchers have published tables that relate obesity directly to measurement in millimeters. An example is Figure 11.3, where lower limits of obesity are indicated for Caucasian Americans. Even though skinfold measures are more feasible to administer than underwater weighing, the calipers are relatively expensive and the measurements are time-consuming. Therefore, skinfold measures have had limited use in public schools. Inexpensive plastic spring calipers have recently been marketed, making skinfold measurements more usable in schools. Mayer (1968) has suggested several methods of assessing fatness that are not based on scientific measurement, but have practical use in physical education. These are:

The mirror test: Looking at yourself naked in the mirror is often a more reliable guide for estimating obesity than body weight. If you look fat, you probably are fat.

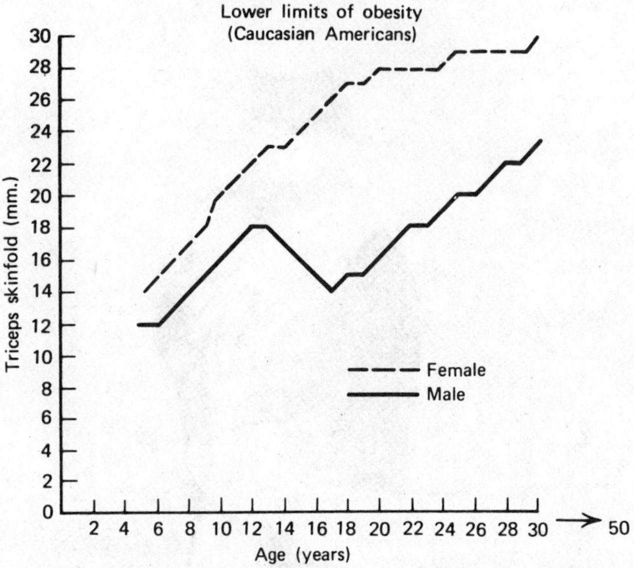

Figure 11.3. Lower limits of obesity in Caucasian Americans (from Jean Mayer, *Overweight: Causes, Cost, and Control*, 1968, p. 33; reprinted by permission of Prentice-Hall, Inc., Englewood Cliffs, New Jersey).

The pinch test: If appearance does not give a clear answer, the pinch test usually will. It has been estimated that in persons under 50, at least half of the body fat is found directly under the skin. At many locations on the body — such as the back of the upper arm, the side of the lower chest, the back just below the shoulder blade, the back of the calf, or the abdomen — a fold of skin and subcutaneous fat may be lifted free, between the thumb and the forefinger, from the underlying soft tissue and bone. In general, the layer beneath the skin should be between one-fourth and one-half inch; the skinfold is a double thickness and should therefore be one-half to one inch. A fold markedly greater than one inch — for example in the back of the arm — indicates excessive body fatness; one markedly thinner than one-half inch, abnormal thinness.

The ruler test: This test has to do with the slope of the abdomen when an individual is lying on his back. If he or she is not too fat, the surface of the abdomen between the flare of the ribs and the front of the pelvis is normally flat or slightly concave, and a ruler placed on the abdomen along the midline of the body should touch both the ribs and the pelvic area. It goes without saying that pregnancy and certain pathological conditions can interfere with this test.

The belt-line test: In men the circumference of the chest at the level of the nipples should exceed that of the abdomen at the level of the navel. If the latter is greater, it usually means that abdominal fat is excessive.*

Jean Mayer, *Overweight: Causes, Cost, and Control*, 1968, pp 29-30. Reprinted by permission of Prentice-Hall, Inc., Englewood Cliffs, New Jersey.

Detailed information on body composition can be found in Behnke and Wilmore (1974), and Katch and McArdle (1977).

Summary

Anthropometic measurements were central concerns of the first phase of the scientific era of measurement, which began in the 1860s. Current interest in anthropometric measurements focuses on three areas: growth measures, body type, and body composition. The uses of such measures include classification, predictions of growth patterns, and prediction of success in motor activities as well as assessment of obesity.

Stringent measures, some of which are not economically or logistically feasible for the physical educator, have been developed to assess anthropometric traits. However, in most instances more useful measures have been developed and are widely used.

Study Questions

1. Locate an age-height-weight table or growth index. Evaluate its usefulness.
2. Why have the classification indexes (McCloy, Neilson and Cozens) lost the popularity they once had?
3. Identify and describe the components of a somatotype.
4. Using Figure 11.1, calculate your height-weight ratio. Using Table 11.2, identify the most plausible somatotypes associated with your height-weight ratio. Are you primarily endomorphic, mesomorphic, ectomorphic?
5. Identify the most common methods of assessing body composition. Which of these are useful to the physical educator?

CHAPTER **12**

Basic Performance Traits

After you have read and studied this chapter you should be able to:

1. *Identify the basic performance traits.*
2. *Understand the uses of tests designed to measure each basic performance trait.*
3. *Identify the various types of testing for each basic performance trait.*
4. *Recognize commonly used tests for each basic performance trait.*
5. *Use a practical test for measuring each basic performance trait.*

Numerous performance traits provide a basis for motor ability, physical fitness, motor fitness, and psychomotor skill. These qualities, called basic performance traits, include *strength, muscular endurance, cardiorespiratory endurance, flexibility, agility, balance, coordination, power, kinesthetic sense,* and *speed of reaction and movement*. Each of these traits will be discussed separately in this chapter.

STRENGTH

Strength is considered a primary component in the performance of physical skills, in physical fitness as well as in general motor ability and motor fitness. Strength may be defined as the contractive power of muscles attained by a single maximum effort. This definition reinforces the importance of strength in physical activities. The world's strongest man is determined by the cumulative best single lifts in two separate kinds of weightlifting. In almost all competitive activities, the performer with the most strength has the advantage. Athletes often perform movements against greater resistance than normal. Examples are sprinting and most of the field events in track, competitive swimming, and various gymnastics events where the entire body or specific muscle groups exert a maximum force.

Since strength is such a basic performance trait it is easy to understand its role in such multiple traits as physical fitness and motor ability. Strength, however, also plays an important role in other basic traits such as muscular power, muscular endurance, speed of movement, and agility. This relationship with other traits has caused some misunderstanding about what some physical tests really measure. For instance, power involves force and speed. The speed at which the force is moved depends on strength; therefore, strength contributes to power. This concept will be expanded later in this chapter, when power is discussed. Strength also contributes to the ability to continue work, or muscular endurance, and in the ability to move and change direction rapidly and accurately, or agilely.

Three major methods of strength training are currently in use, and instruments and methods for measuring strength have been developed for each. *Isotonic* exercises take place when muscular force moves a fixed weight throughout the full range of motion, even though the strength of the muscle varies considerably throughout the range. The concentric and eccentric contractions that occur in and through the range motion suggest the name *dynamic* contraction. *Isometric* exercise occurs when maximum muscular force is exerted over a short period of time against a fixed resistance. There is little joint movement in isometric exercising and, therefore, the term *static* strength is used. Isotonic and isometric strength are easily measured in the typical physical education situation. More recently a new type of strength training, that of *isokinetic* exercising has developed. The isokinetic method involves moving a variable force, allowing the development of maximum tension throughout the full range of motion. Some limited research has shown that isokinetic high-intensity training throughout the range of motion increases strength, power, and resistance to fatigue more than isotonic exercise. Although this method of training seems to have advantages over other methods, instrumentation is currently expensive and research is relatively limited. For an excellent discussion of each of the training methods, read Clarke's (1974) review article.

Many instruments have been developed to measure strength. Among the more common instruments for measuring static or isometric strength are the hand dynamometer, the back and leg dynamometer, the cable tensiometer and iso-scale. These instruments, used correctly, provide accurate measurement of isometric strength. Few instruments have been developed for measuring dynamic strength. Isotonic strength, however, can be measured through various calisthenic activities that need little or no equipment and through numerous weight-lifting events. Isokinetic training is a method to improve strength. The Cybex machine manufactured by Lumex, Inc., a popular isokinetic strength training apparatus, can be utilized to measure either isometric or isotonic strength.

Strength test items have been used as components of physical fitness, general motor ability, and motor fitness. They also can be used to predict success in specific sport activities, as a means of demonstrating the accomplishment of behavioral objectives relating to improvement of strength, and as a factor in grading in the conditioning and weight training phases of physical education.

Many tests of static strength have been developed by using the instruments mentioned above. Measurements are usually very precise and easy to administer. The Grip Strength Test will be illustrated because it can be administered most easily in a physical education class. The back and leg dynamometer is somewhat expensive for the limited use it receives. The cable tensiometer tests likewise are not feasible as practical tests of isometric strength. They have, however, been used for research purposes, and at least 38 accurate tests of strength have been utilized with the tensiometer and testing table.

Although dynamic strength is used more often in athletic activities, it is somewhat difficult to measure. By definition, strength involves a one-time maximal exertion.

Many tests classified as dynamic strength tests involve repetitions of the skill (i.e., push-ups) and, thus, muscular endurance becomes a factor. To be consistent with the definition of strength, any test developed should measure a one-time exertion. To effectively do this, some type of overload must be introduced. The most typical overload with calisthenic activities is a weight plate from a barbell set. The weight is either held in the hands (i.e., sit-ups) or strapped to the body (pull-ups, dips or parallel bars). The performer attempts to execute the calisthenics with the maximum amount of extra weight possible.

Weight lifting also can measure dynamic strength. Single exertions of the bench press, military press, arm curl, and the like are often used with maximum weight. Unfortunately, it usually takes some experimentation for a performer to determine the maximum weight that can be lifted at once.

For illustration purposes one isometric strength test, the Grip Strength Test, and one isotonic strength test, the Bent Knee Sit-Up Test, are given below.

Grip Strength Test

Measurement Objective To measure grip strength (isometric) of each hand.

Test Qualities Content validity is accepted. Reliability coefficients are consistently in the .90's.

Test Application Male and female, all ages

Equipment and Materials Hand dynamometer, equipped with adjustable handle (Figure 12.1).

Procedure Performer places the hand dynamometer in the palm of the right hand, with dial toward the palm. The grip is adjusted so that the bottom of the dynamometer is resting against the base of the palm and the fingers grasp the adjustable portion of the handle. The hand should then be stretched so that the grip is taken between the first and second joint of the fingers. The performer should bend the elbow slightly and raise the arm. He or she then moves the arm forward and downward gripping with maximum strength. Two trials should be given for each hand with a 30-second rest between trials. Thirty students can be measured in 40 minutes with one dynamometer.

Scoring The score is the best of two trials for each hand. The dynamometer scale is read in kilograms (1 kilogram = 2.2 pounds). Any trial in which performers touch part of his or her body or any object should be discarded.

Norms Norms for boys and girls 6 to 18 based on 2788 boys and 3471

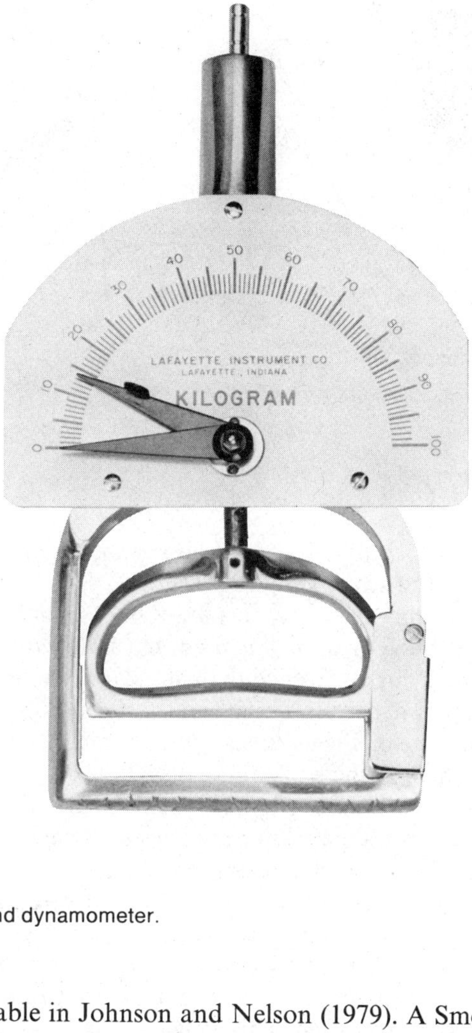

Figure 12.1. Hand dynamometer.

girls are available in Johnson and Nelson (1979). A Smedley dynamometer was used. Norms for a slightly different instrument, the manuometer, are available for men and women in Melograno and Klinzing (1974).

Flexed-Leg Sit-Up (Dynamic Strength)

Measurement Objective To measure the strength of abdominal muscles.
Test Qualities Content validity is accepted. Reliability was .91 when scores recorded on separate days were correlated.
Test Application Male and female, junior high through college.

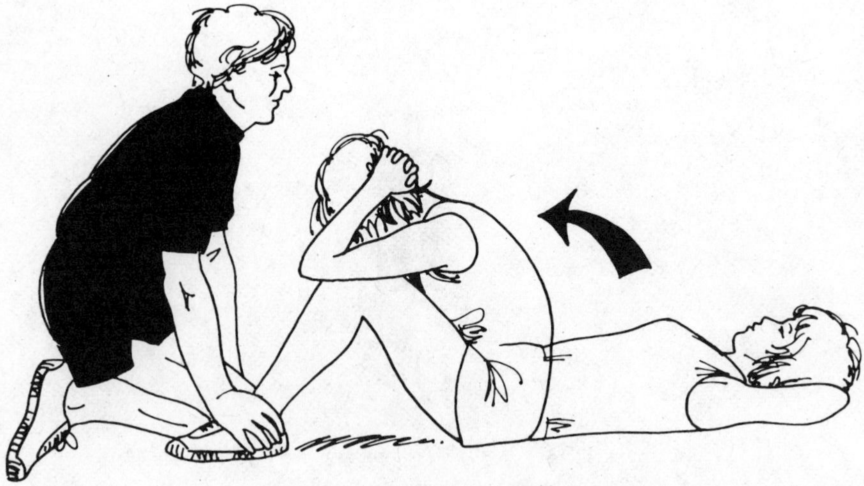

Figure 12.2. Bent-leg sit-up.

Equipment and Materials Standard floor mat, dumbbell bar, an assortment of weights, and scales (Figure 12.2).

Procedure Performer may choose a dumbbell, weight plate, or possibly a barbell. If a dumbbell or barbell is used, the attached weight plate should not have a greater circumference than standard 5 pound plates. After selecting the desired maximum weight, the performer should place it on the mat so that when he or she assumes supine position, the weight can easily be grasped and held to the back of the neck.

Legs should be bent to an angle that is slightly less than 90 degrees at the knees. Performer should be allowed two trials. If performer can do the sit-up with the weight, he or she adds more weight for second trial. If he or she cannot do the sit-up, the weight to be lifted is reduced. If the second trial is also unsuccessful, the performer should take a short rest and then be retested with a further reduced load.

Scoring The greatest amount of weight held on either trial when performing the sit-up is recorded. This weight is then divided by the performer's body weight for the test score. A performer who cannot do a sit-up with any extra weight receives a score of zero.

Norms Norms based on scores of 100 college men and 100 college women are published in Johnson and Nelson (1979).

More tests of dynamic and static strength can be found in Baumgartner and Jackson (1975), Clarke (1976), and various issues of the *Physical Fitness Research Digest*.

MUSCULAR ENDURANCE

Muscular endurance may be defined as the ability of the muscles to sustain work by holding a maximal contraction for a given length of time or by continuing to move a submaximal load. This ability of the muscles to continue to perform isometric or isotonic work is of obvious importance in many everyday life activities as well as in the majority of competitive sports and physical activities. In such tasks as holding heavy objects, the fingers sustain isometric contraction, while sweeping with a broom requires both isotonic and isometric muscular endurance. In the sport activities of weight training, the principle of lifting a certain number of times through the full range of motion implies isotonic muscular endurance. The old saying "football games are won or lost in the fourth quarter" suggests that those competitors with the greatest muscular endurance are the ones who can continue performing the necessary skills with efficiency and effectiveness and are also the ones who will win the game. Everyone has had the sensation of tired muscles. Muscular endurance implies the resistance to muscular fatigue. Many tests of muscular endurance have been used in batteries of tests measuring traits of physical fitness, motor fitness, and motor ability. Tests of muscular endurance have several other functions. These tests can be used to predict success in activities that require muscular endurance; to demonstrate the accomplishment of behavioral objectives relating to improvement of muscular endurance; to demonstrate the positive results of exercise; for research purposes; and as a means of grading when muscular endurance is a factor.

Muscular endurance is closely related to strength. Strength involves the maximum power that can be attained in a one-time effort while muscular endurance implies the ability to persist to submaximal work. The relationship is somewhat circular. Strength is needed to perform work and therefore influences muscular endurance; yet, as work is continued, strength of contraction is usually lessened as muscle groups are unable to respond. Thus, tests of endurance are usually characterized by repetitive actions of the same exercise or movement. Muscular endurance is also related to other basic performance traits such as muscular power, speed of reaction and movement, and agility.

Tests of muscular endurance are of two basic types: isometric or isotonic. Each type may test either absolute or relative muscular endurance. An absolute muscular endurance test involves the use of a fixed load for all performers without a relationship to the maximum strength of the individual or to his or her body weight. In contrast, a relative muscular endurance test is one in which the muscles work with a load, proportional to the maximum strength of a specific muscle group.

Isometric muscular endurance tests are further subdivided into two distinct categories. In repetitive tests the performer executes repetitions of force against a static measuring instrument such as a hand dynamometer. The test is then scored in terms of the number of times the performer is able to exert a force maximum equal to a certain percentage of strength or body weight. The second category of isometric endurance test involves the performer sustaining one muscular contraction for as long as possible. The score is simply the amount of time the contraction is held. An example would be the amount of time a hand dynamometer could be depressed to 30 kilograms.

The second basic type, the isotonic or dynamic muscular endurance tests, are quite common. All of us have attempted to do more push-ups or pull-ups or to lift a certain amount of weight more times than others. In other words, we have attempted to demonstrate muscular endurance. Numerous tests have been developed to test specific muscle groups, most notably the arms and shoulder girdle, and the abdominal muscles.

Examples of muscular endurance tests are evident in the AAHPER Youth Fitness Test. The flexed-arm hang for girls is a timed isometric test. The pull-up test for boys is a dynamic test of muscular endurance. The sit up test for boys and girls is also a dynamic test of muscular endurance. All of these muscular endurance tests will be presented with norms later in the section on physical fitness/motor fitness. The Squat Thrust or Four-Count Burpee Test is an example of an agility test that could also be used as a dynamic muscular endurance test if exercise is continued as long as possible. Another popular test of dynamic muscular endurance, the push-up, will be given as an illustration, with variations for males and females.

Push Up

Measurement Objective To measure the dynamic muscular endurance of the arms and shoulder girdle.

Test Qualities Content validity is accepted. No reliability coefficient for floor push-ups was found but reliability is undoubtedly high if no endurance training occurs between the test and retest. Reliability of modified push ups is .93.

Test Application Male, junior high through college (floor push-ups). Female, junior high through college (modified push-ups).

Equipment and Materials A floor mat.

Procedure Floor push-up — Performer takes a front-leaning ready position with arms and legs straight. He then lowers the body until the chest touches the mat and pushes up to the straight arm position. The exercise is continued as many times as possible without a rest (Figure 12.3a).

Modified push-up — Performer takes a front-leaning ready position with body weight supported by fully extended arms and knees bent at right angle. Performer lowers her body to the mat and pushes back to straight arm position. The exercise is continued as many times as possible without a rest. (Figure 12.3b).

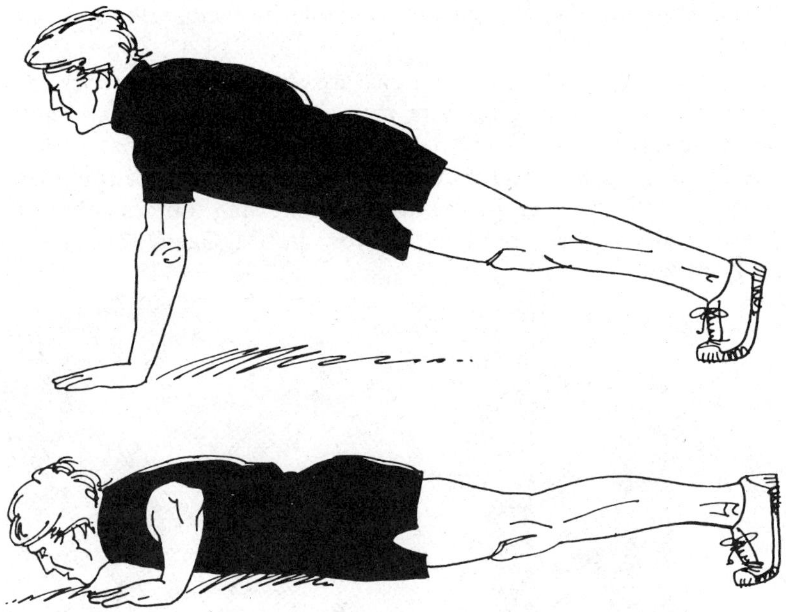

Figure 12.3a. Floor push-ups.

Note: There are several variations in terms of administrative procedures, fingertip push-ups and modified bench push-ups, for instance. Consistency must prevail when testing.

Scoring Floor push-ups — Score is the number of correct push-ups continuously executed. When body pikes or sags, chest does not touch mat, or arms do not fully extend, that trial does not count. If performer stops to rest, the test should be considered completed. As a helpful technique in determining correctness of the push-up, the tester or partner can place his hand on the mat under the performer's chest. If the chest is lowered enough, it will touch the hand of the tester.

Modified Push-up — Score is the number of correct push-ups continuously executed. If performer stops to rest, the test should be considered terminated. If the body sags, chest does not touch mat, or arms are not fully extended, the trial does not count.

Norms Norms for junior high boys are available in Johnson and Nelson (1979).

Norms for girls age 6 to 18 are available in Johnson and Nelson (1979).

Norms for high school boys are available in Nelson and Jensen (1972).

Norms for men and women are available in Melograno and Klinzing (1974).

Tests of dynamic muscular endurance are often used in batteries of physical fitness or general motor ability or motor fitness. Tests of static muscular endurance are less popular as test items, primarily because dynamic muscular endurance is a more common requisite for successful physical performance. More tests of both types can be found in the following sources either as individual tests or items in test batteries: Barrow and McGee (1971), Johnson et al. (1975) and Willgoose (1961).

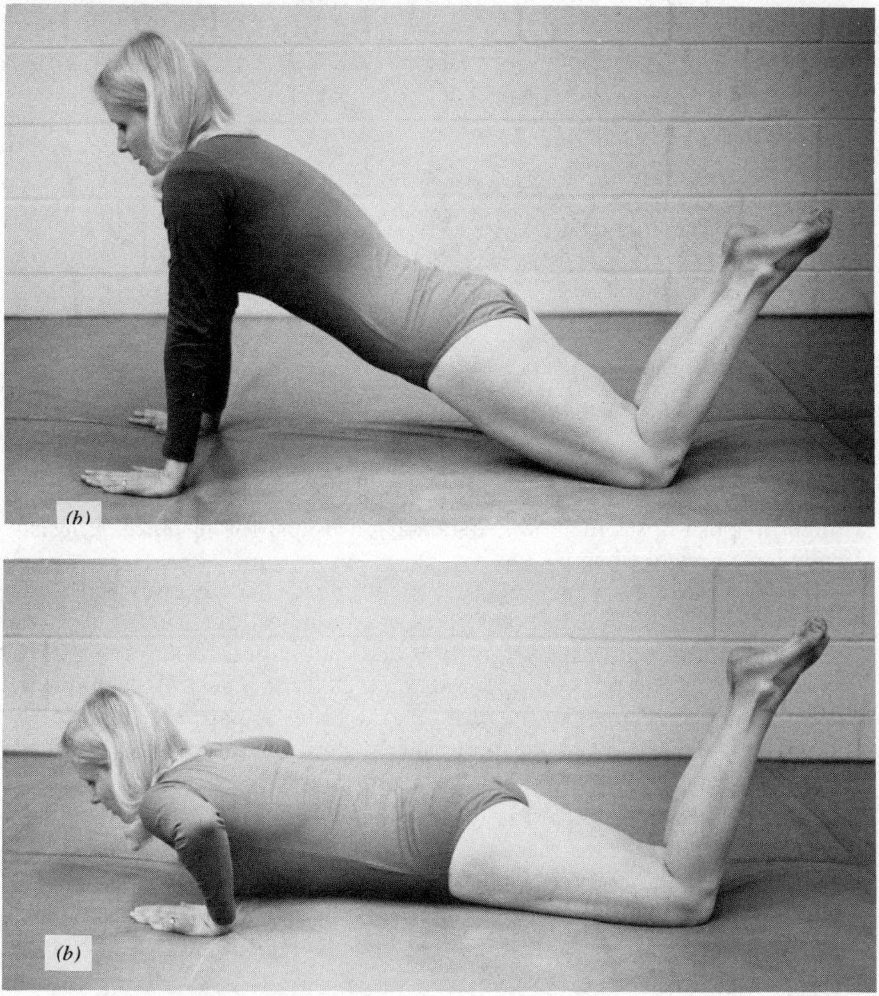

Figure 12.3b. Modified push-ups.

CARDIORESPIRATORY ENDURANCE

Cardiorespiratory (CR) endurance is the most basic component of physical condition. Most of us have had the feeling of being in relatively good shape and understand that vigorous exercise on a regular basis will allow us to perform skills or work without becoming tired. However, the concept of cardiorespiratory endurance is much more complicated than just being in shape. It can be defined as the ability of the circulatory and respiratory systems to adjust to vigorous exercise and to recover from the effect of that exercise. Cardiorespiratory endurance is very complex and involves the functioning of the heart, the lungs, the blood and its capacity to carry oxygen, the blood vessels and capillaries supplying blood to all parts of the body, and ultimately the muscle cells, which use the oxygen to provide the energy necessary for continuing exercise.

Many sport activities require CR endurance. Jogging and distance running, distance swimming, bicycling, cross-country skiing, and soccer all demand high levels of CR endurance. Performance in activities such as basketball, football, and the majority of court games (i.e., tennis, racquetball, badminton) is usually enhanced with a high level of CR endurance. The lack of such endurance causes decrements in several other basic performance traits such as strength, coordination, speed of reaction and movement, and power mainly because of fatigue.

Since CR endurance is such a significant component of physical fitness, almost all such tests involve the measurement of CR endurance, usually through the use of distance running or some other test of aerobic capacity. CR endurance tests are also used in batteries of motor ability and motor fitness. Other obvious uses are classifying students, assessing their present physical condition, and predicting success in certain activities on the basis of that result. Since the development of CR endurance should be an objective of classes in physical education, such tests can be used to demonstrate the benefits of regular exercise. Additionally, CR endurance tests have been used by exercise physiologists and physical educators for research purposes.

Tests measuring CR endurance have ranged from simply timing a distance run, to measuring pulse rate or pressure before and after a bout of exercise, to very regimented, precise tests in which expired gas is collected and analyzed, and heart function during exercise is monitored. The majority of practical tests of CR endurance used as measures of physical fitness or as parts of test involves batteries an endurance run. Since the time required to cover the prescribed distance is usually the criterion, this type of test is administratively possible for large classes in physical education.

Other tests that are somewhat practical for use in physical education classes involve measuring heart rate before and after a bout of exercise. Research has demonstrated that a conditioned performer typically has a much lower heart rate than an unconditioned performer before, during, and after exercises. In addition, recovery to normal heart rate after exercise is much faster for conditioned individuals. The famous Harvard Step Test is an example of a CR endurance test utilizing heart rate as the criterion.

The final of these three types of CR endurance tests utilizes such laboratory equipment as a treadmill, physiograph, and gas analysis equipment and although the most precise, has little practical application in terms of actual use in physical education classes. However, these laboratory tests of maximum oxygen uptake (Max Vo_2) are the most valid measures of aerobic capacity.

The 600-yard run with optional runs of 1 mile or 9 minutes for ages 10 to 12, or 1½ miles or 12 minutes for ages 13 and older — items of the AAHPER Youth Fitness Test — are typical of the distance run tests of cardiorespiratory endurance. They will be explained later in this chapter when the AAHPER Youth Fitness Test is presented in its entirety. As an example of this type of cardiorespiratory endurance test, Cooper's 12-minute Run-Walk is given below.

Twelve Minute Run-Walk Test (Cooper, 1977)

Measurement Objective To measure cardiorespiratory endurance.

Test Qualities Validity is .90 when correlated with treadmill measurements of oxygen consumption and aerobic capacity. Reliability is .94 with test-retest method.

Test Application Male and female, junior high through college. Also applicable for adult men and women.

Equipment and Materials Stopwatch or clock with sweep second hand, whistle or starter's pistol, track, football field, or some running area marked so that distance traveled in 12 minutes can be calculated easily.

Procedure Performers assemble behind starting line. At the starting signal, they run or walk as far as possible within the 12 minute time limit. An experienced pacer should accompany performers around the running area during the actual test. Performers should have experienced some practice in pacing. At the signal to stop, performers should remain where they finished long enough for test administrators to record the distance covered. Ample time should be given for stretching and warm-up as well as post-test cool down.

Scoring Score is distance in miles covered in 12 minutes. Distance in yards is converted to miles (1,760 yards = 1 mile).

Norms Norms for males and females aged 13 to 19 and 20 to 29 are presented in Table 12.1. Norms for additional ages are available in Cooper (1977). Norms for fifth-through eighth-grade boys and girls are available in Clarke (1976).

Table 12.1 Norms for Cooper 12-Minute Run-Walk

Males		*Fitness*	*Females*	
13-19	*20-29*	*Class*	*13-19*	*20-29*
0-1.29 miles	0-1.22 miles	Very poor	0-.99 miles	0-.95 miles
1.3-1.37	1.22-1.31	Poor	1.0-1.18	.96-1.11
1.38-1.56	1.32-1.49	Fair	1.19-1.29	1.12-1.22
1.57-1.72	1.50-1.64	Good	1.30-1.43	1.23-1.34
1.73-1.86	1.65-1.76	Excellent	1.44-1.51	1.35-1.45
1.87 and above	1.77 and above	Superior	1.52 and above	1.46 and above

Source. The Aerobics Way by Kenneth H. Cooper, M.D., M.P.H. Copyright ©1977 Kenneth H. Cooper, Inc., New York, New York 10017. Reprinted by permission.

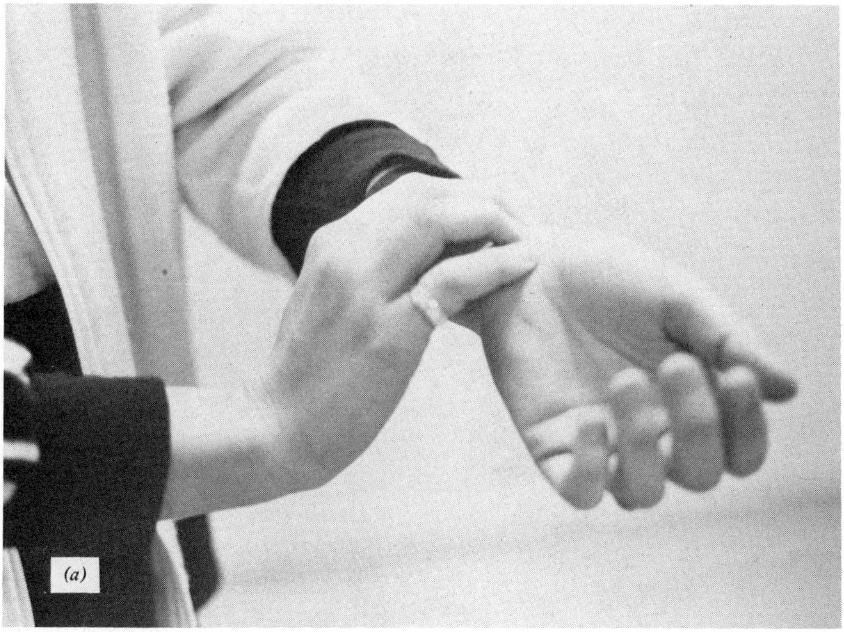

Figure 12.4a. Pulse rate taken at wrist (radial artery).

Another general indicator of cardiorespiratory endurance is the pulse rate. This is used extensively in numerous adult fitness programs. Research has shown that children have faster resting pulse rates than adults, although senior citizens usually have faster resting pulse rates than younger adults. Individuals with a high level of cardiorespiratory endurance have a lower resting pulse rate and return faster to the resting rate than physically unfit individuals. Pulse rate is easily measured by lightly pressing the fingertips against the radial artery in the wrist (Figure 12.4a) or against the carotid artery in the neck (Figure 12.4b).

The beat should be counted for at least 10 seconds and preferably for 15 or 30 seconds. Average adult's resting heart rate is about 72 beats per minute. However, pulse rate varies with amount of rest, body position, exercise, time of day, emotional changes, and food intake. Also, resting heart rate should be used as an index of a person's CR endurance changes rather than as a comparison with others. Pulse rates have been used in a number of CR endurance tests including the Ohio State University Step Test, the Tuttle Pulse Ratio Test, the Harvard Step Test. The long and short forms of the Harvard Step Test are given as examples of this type of CR endurance test.

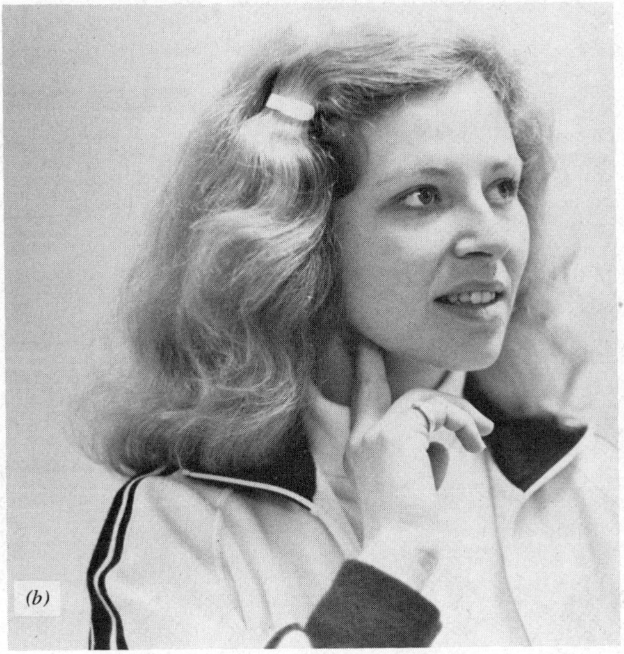

Figure 12.4b. Pulse rate taken at neck (carotid artery)

Harvard Step Test (Long and Short Forms) (Brouha, 1943)

Measurement Objective To measure cardiorespiratory endurance; ability to perform and recover from muscular work.

Test Qualities Validity — Brouha (1943) using 2200 Harvard male students in validating the tests found the following means: 75 for all students, 93 for all athletes. Correlation of 0.63 between short form and finish of cross country race. Reliability is .82 with test retest method.

Test Application Male college students; variations for girls and women, for college women, for secondary school boys, and elementary school children. These variations are well described in Clarke (1976).

Equipment and Materials Bench 20 inches high, stopwatch, and metronome (Figure 12.5).

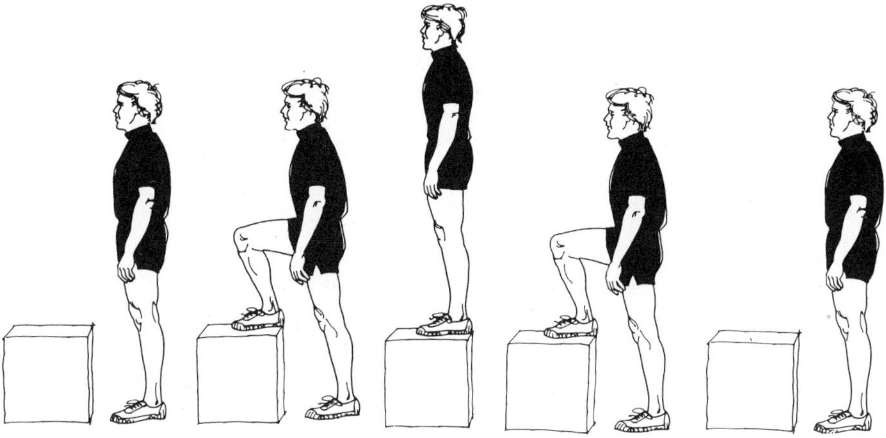

Figure 12.5. Harvard Step Test.

Procedure Performer steps up and down 30 times a minute on the bench. Each time the subject should step all the way up on the bench with the body erect. The stepping process is performed in four counts, as follows: (1) one foot is placed on bench; (2) other foot is placed on bench; (3) one foot is placed on floor; (4) other foot is placed on floor. Performer may lead with either foot and can change as long as four count cadence is maintained. Stepping exercise continues for exactly 5 minutes, unless performer is forced to stop sooner because of exhaustion. As soon as he stops exercising, performer sits on a chair quietly while pulse rates are counted 1 to 1½, 2 to 2½, 3 to 3½ minutes after exercise.

Scoring *Long Form* — Score, called the Physical Efficiency Index (PEI), is computed utilizing the following formula

$$\text{PEI} = \frac{\text{duration of exercise in seconds} \times 100}{2 \times \text{sum of pulse counts in recovery}}$$

$$\textit{Short Form}\ \text{PEI} = \frac{\text{duration of exercise in seconds} \times 100}{5.5 \times \text{pulse count for 1 to } 1\tfrac{1}{2} \text{ minutes after exercise}}$$

The short form correlates highly with long form. A table for scoring the short form of the test is available in Consolazio et al. (1963).

Norms Based on 8000 college men, these standards were developed:

Physical Condition	*PEI*	*Physical Condition*	*PEI*
Short Form		Long Form	
Good	Above 80	Excellent	Above 90
Average	50 - 80	Good	80 - 89
Poor	Below 50	High Average	65 - 79
		Low Average	55 - 64
		Poor	Below 55

Many resources are available for practical testing of CR endurance. Some sources thus identify a number of tests are: Clarke (1976), Consolazio et al. (1963), Cooper (1977), Johnson et al. (1975), and Mathews (1978).

FLEXIBILITY

This trait may be defined as the range of movement about a joint or a sequence of joints. It is limited by extensibility of the muscles and the ligaments surrounding a particular joint or sequence of joints. Individual differences in flexibility are common and depend on heredity and numerous environmental factors such as training, warm-up, temperature, and tension.

A "normal" amount of flexibility is necessary for everyday living. Researchers have found that various activities require differing amounts of flexibility for successful performance. For example, a high degree of joint flexibility is necessary in gymnastic activities, modern dance, numerous track and field events, swimming and diving, and wrestling. The most popular team sports for males on the high school and college level — football, basketball, and baseball — only require flexibility that is considered normal.

Flexibility is now considered a specific quality. Harris (1969) collected data from more than 50 flexibility measures in a study using college women. She discovered by factor analysis 13 different factors of flexibility and found no evidence that flexibility is a general factor. Flexibility is, however, considered by many measurement experts to be one of the factors of motor ability, motor fitness, and physical fitness. Although flexibility can be improved through practice, ballistic and static stretching tests have been used to predict success in various sports activities. Other uses of these tests as a means for evaluating whether behavioral objectives involving improvement of flexibility have been achieved or as one of the measures of general motor ability or motor fitness. Flexibility tests have been used medically, to diagnose injury or to evaluate posture defects. Because flexibility is not a general factor, various tests are necessary to measure joint flexibility. In addition to individual differences, there are usually differences in joint flexibility within the individual, giving more support to the view that flexibility is specific.

Much interest in flexibility arose when the now famous Kraus-Weber tests of minimum muscular fitness, which included a trunk flexibility or floor touch test, found that 57.9 percent of American youth failed at least one of the six tests, while only 8.7 percent of a similar sample of Europeans failed one or more tests (Kraus and Hirschland, 1954). Further research using the tests found that the flexibility test item had the greatest number of failures. In a sample of Oregon children, 59 percent of the boys and 33 percent of the girls failed the item (Kirchner and Glines, 1957). Most research has shown that girls are more flexible than boys.

Numerous instruments have been developed to test flexion and extension or range of motion of specific joints. Two of the most popular instruments for measuring joint flexibility are the goniometer (Figure 12.6) and the Leighton Flexometer (Figure 12.7). The goniometer consists of a 180 degree protractor with one stationary and one movable arm. The operation of the goniometer is simple. If the range of motion of the elbow is desired, the arms of the goniometer are placed with the upper and lower arms of the body with the center of the protractor at the elbow joint. Readings are taken with as full an extension and flexion as possible. The difference between the two movements identifies the range of motion.

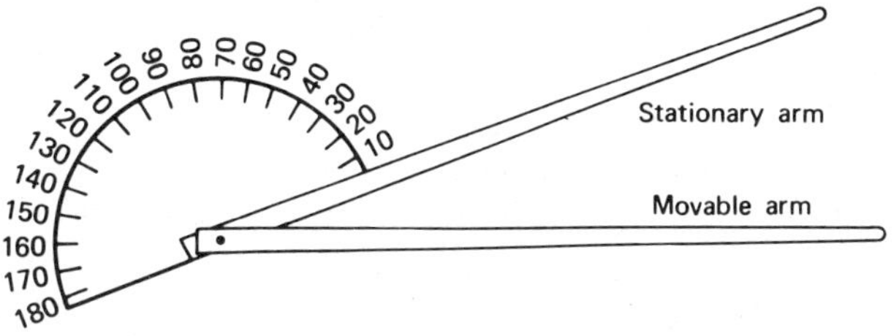

Figure 12.6. Goniometer.

Another ingenious device for measuring joint flexibility is the Leighton flexometer. It consists of a full circular dial with a weighted pointer, which both move freely as affected by gravity. To be used, the instrument is strapped on the joint to be tested. The dial is locked at one position, such as full elbow flexion; then the movement is made and the pointer is locked at another position, such as full elbow extension. The reading of the pointer on the dial indicates the range of motion. The instrument of the pointer on the dial indicates the range of motion. The instrument reliability for the Leighton flexometer has been found to be very high, ranging from .89 to a near perfect 1.00.

A more complicated instrument used in human performance laboratories is the electrogoniometer, usually referred to as an elgon, which can record joint angulation in stationary positions and also changes of a joint angle during motion.

Almost every motor fitness test battery or test of general motor ability in-

Figure 12.7. Leighton flexometer.

cludes one or more flexibility items. Numerous flexibility tests and test batteries have been developed utilizing little or no equipment. A typical example of a flexibility test item is given below. Remember that since flexibility is specific and varies from joint to joint within a person, as well as between individuals, a test battery is necessary fully to evaluate flexibility.

Sit and Reach

Measurement Objective To measure trunk flexion (hip and back flexion) and ability to stretch back thigh muscles (hamstrings).
Test Qualities Validity — Content validity is accepted for this test.
Reliability — .84-.98.
Test Application Male and female, elementary through college.
Equipment and Materials Bench, or sit and reach box or lowest row of set of bleachers, yardstick.
Procedure Performer assumes a sitting position on floor with knees fully extended and soles of feet against bench, box or lowest row of bleachers. Performer flexes trunk four times with arms fully extended and hands on top of each other. Last attempt is held for one second so measurement can be taken (Figure 12.8). This test can be administered using a partner system and with other flexibility tests; can be administered to forty students within a typical class period. The best of three trials should be used. Several test administration variations have been utilized.

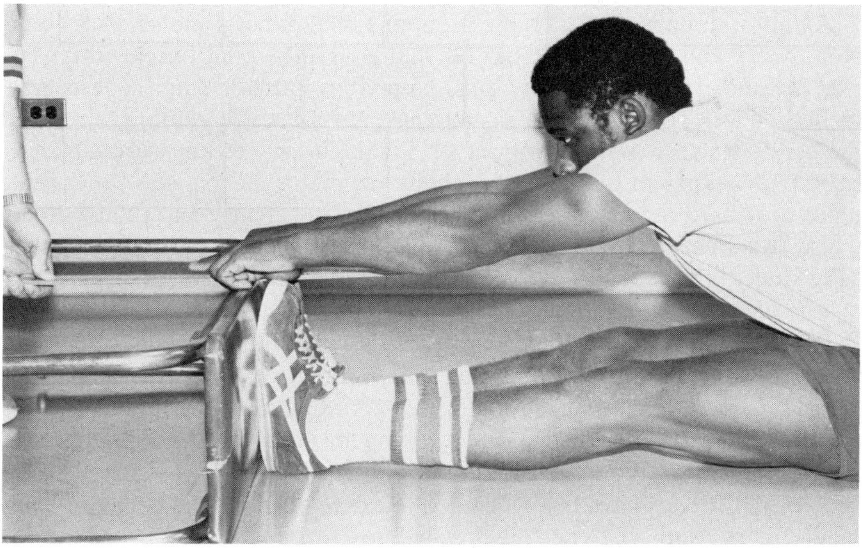

Figure 12.8. Sit and reach.

Scoring Tester places yardstick with 15 inch mark at near edge of bench, box or bleachers. Measurements approaching mark (not being able to reach toes) are scored negative while those beyond 15 inch mark are scored positive. Measure to nearest ¼ inch.

Norms Norms for a modified test are available in Getchell (1979) Johnson and Nelson (1979). Norms will be available from AAPHER in late 1979. This item is one of four in a 1979 revision of the AAPHER Fitness Test.

Tests and test batteries of flexibility can be found in the following sources: Leighton (1955), Melograno and Klinzing (1974), and Scott and French (1959).

AGILITY

Agility may be defined as the ability to change directions rapidly and accurately. It depends essentially on strength, speed of reaction and movement, and big muscle coordination.

Agility is a very important ability in most performances — in dual activities such as tennis, badminton, paddleball, racquetball, and handball; and in team sports such as basketball, baseball, football, and soccer. Quick starts and stops, rapid change of direction, and efficient footwork are essential for successful performance. In activities such as skiing, gymnastics, diving, and dance the ability to make quick adjustments of the body or some of its parts is a high priority.

Agility is usually considered a component of general motor ability and motor fitness and, therefore, most test batteries measuring motor ability or fitness include at least one agility item. Numerous individual agility tests have also been developed. The majority of these tests involve running, although some agility tests such as the Burpee or Squat Thrust Test measure how rapidly body position can be changed without locomotor movement. Agility tests are not only used as a component of general motor ability and motor fitness but also, as a predictor of success in various sport activities, as a means of classifying students for activity, or to evaluate whether or not certain units of instruction meet behavioral objectives involving improvement of agility.

Research has demonstrated that even though agility depends somewhat on heredity, it can be improved by practice, training, and instruction. Since reaction time, movement time, strength, and coordination of the large muscles are important aspects, practice and training in activities that will improve these factors will also improve agility.

Two agility tests have been included to exemplify the most common types of agility tests. Both of these tests involve little or no equipment and can be conducted in a relatively short amount of time.

Squat Thrust or Four-Count Burpee Test.

Measurement Objective To measure how rapidly body position can be accurately changed in a calisthenic activity.

Test Qualities Validity is .55 for boys and .34 for girls. Reliability is .92.

Test Application Males and females, middle school through college.

Equipment and Materials Watch or other timing device.

Procedure Student takes a standing position. On the signal "go," he or she completes as many four-count squat thrusts or parts thereof in 10 seconds, until the command "stop" is given. From a standing position the movement involved in the calisthenics is: (1) bend at the knees and waist and move to a squatting position with the hands on the floor (2) thrust the legs backward and take a front leaning rest position ("up" position in a push-up) (3) return to a squatting position (4) return to beginning standing position (Figure 12.9). This test is easily administered by using the partner system. Generally the best three totals is used as the performance score.

Scoring Each completed part of a squat thrust receives 1 point. An entire squat thrust, then receives 4 points. A performer who completes 6½ squat thrusts in the 10 second time period would achieve a score of 26. One point is subtracted for each of the following faults: (1) if the legs are thrust back before the hands touch the floor; (2) if the body is not straight

Figure 12.9. Squat thrust or four-count burpee.

in the front leaning position; (3) if the hands leave the floor before the squatting position in the third part of the movement is assumed; and (4) if at the beginning of each exercise the body is not erect.

Norms Norms for the Squat Thrust Test are available in McCloy and Young (1954) and more recently in Johnson and Nelson (1979).

Boomerang Run (Gates and Sheffield, 1940)

Measurement Objective To measure running agility.

Test Qualities Validity is for .82 boys and .72 for girls. Reliability is .93 for boys and .92 for girls.

Test Application Male and female, middle school and through college.

Equipment and Materials Five markers or chairs, stopwatch, measuring tape.

Procedure Course is set up according to Figure 12.10 with each peripheral marker or chair 15 feet from the center. On the signal "go" the performer runs from the starting line to the center point, makes a 90° right turn, and continues through the course always turning right at center until the course is completed. Course may be run with right or left turns.

Scoring The score is determined by timing the run with a stopwatch. A penalty of one-tenth of a second is deducted from the score for each marker or chair touched.

Norms Norms for the Boomerang Run are available in McCloy and Young (1954) and more recently in Johnson and Nelson (1979).

The AAHPER Youth Fitness Test has as one of its items an agility test, the shuttle run. A complete description including procedures and norms will be presented with the other items of the AAHPER Youth Fitness Test in Chapter 13.

A number of other agility tests have been used separately or as an item of

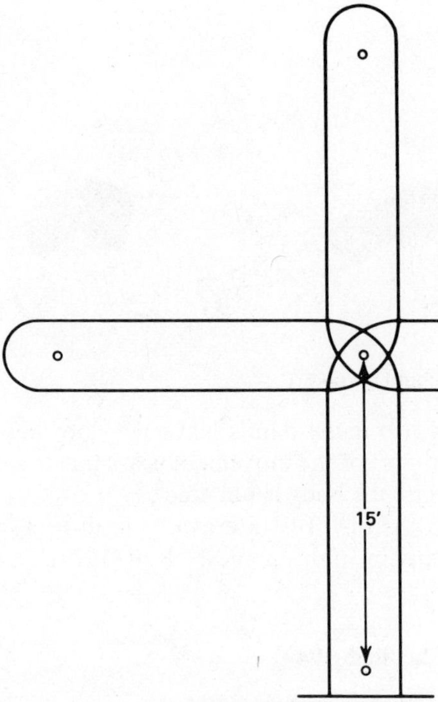

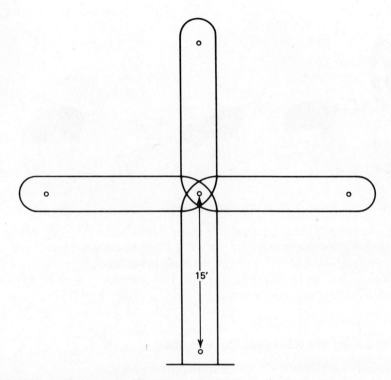

Figure 12.10. Course for boomerang run.

a battery of tests. Sources for many of the popular agility tests are Johnson et al. (1975), Johnson and Nelson (1979), and McCloy and Young (1954).

BALANCE

This trait may be defined as the ability to maintain body position. Balance tests are of two general types. Tests of static balance measure the ability to maintain stationary body positions. Tests of dynamic balance measure the ability to maintain balance while in motion. Each type of balance is highly specific, and tests of static and dynamic balance do not correlate highly with each other. Balance is an important prerequisite for a gamut of physical activities. Sage (1977) presents an excellent discussion of the neurophysiological structures, senses, and pathways involved in balancing ability.

The relatively simple activities of walking and running involve balancing ability as does participation in every sport and athletic activity. Water skiing, for instance, requires a high degree of balance, as do various gymnastic events. In sports and activities where competitive teams are involved, stability or firmness of balance is a high priority. Sports such as football, basketball, wrestling, and soccer often require the performer to resist or apply force while maintaining balance. Research has shown that balance can be improved and also that there is no general balancing ability that allows a performer to balance well in all situations.

Tests of balance are often included as items in tests assessing general motor ability. Balance tests are also useful in determining achievement of students when balance improvement is a behavioral objective of instruction. These tests are not as useful for purposes of placement, diagnosis, or prediction since significant improvement in balance can be made in a relatively short period of practice.

A number of tests of static and dynamic balance have been developed. Several of these tests are simple and utilize little or no equipment while others involve intricate instrumentation.

Stork Stand (Static Balance)

Measurement Objective To measure the static balance while student is supported on the ball of the foot (dominant leg).
Test Qualities Content validity is accepted. Reliability is .87.
Test Application Male and female, elementary school through college.
Equipment and Materials Stopwatch.
Procedure From a standing position on the foot of the dominant leg, student places the other foot on the inside of the supporting knee and places the hands on the hips (Figure 12.11). On the signal "begin" the heel is raised from the floor and balance is maintained as long as possible without moving the ball of the foot from its original position or allowing the heel to touch the floor. Each student is allowed three trials.
A large group of students can be tested within a class period if the students are paired; one recording while the other is tested.
Scoring Score is length in seconds between the time the heel is raised and balance is lost. The best of three trials is recorded.
Norms T-scores for college men and women are available in Johnson and Nelson (1979).

Bass Stick Tests (Lengthwise and Crosswise) (Bass, 1939)

Measurement Objective To measure the stick balance of the student while supported lengthwise and crosswise on a stick 1 inch high, 1 inch wide, and 12 inches long.
Test Qualities Content validity is accepted. Reliability is .90.
Test Application Male and female, elementary through college.
Equipment and Materials Several sticks 1 inch wide, 1 inch high, and 12 inches long; tape to stabilize sticks to floor surface; stopwatch.

Figure 12.11. Stork stand.

Procedure Place several sticks far enough away from each other to avoid interference. Each student being tested should place the ball of the dominant foot lengthwise (Figure 12.12*a*) on the stick. On the signal "go" the opposite foot is lifted from the floor and balance is maintained as long as possible. Tester calls out time up to a maximum of 60 seconds. Each student is tested three times on the dominant leg and three times on the nondominant leg. Testing should be done in pairs with the partner recording balance time. Repeat test with foot on stick crosswise (Figure 12.12*b*).

Scoring The score for each test is the sum of the times for all six trials.

Norms Norms for college men and women on both tests are available in Johnson and Nelson (1979).

In addition to the above three tests — all static balance tests with the student in the upright position — a series of tests have been developed to measure balance while the performer is in the inverted position. Among these are the tripod test, the tip-up test, the head on hand balance, the head and forearm balance, the two-hand balance, and the one-hand balance. These tests are aptly described in Neilson and Jensen (1972).

Figure 12.12a. Bass stick test (lengthwise).

Modified Bass Test of Dynamic Balance

Measurement Objective To measure the ability to jump accurately and maintain balance during and after movement.
Test Qualities Content validity is accepted. Reliability is .75.
Test Application Male and female, high school and college.
Equipment and Materials Masking tape, yardstick, stopwatch.
Procedure Course is set up according to Figure 12.13 with 1 inch by (3/4) inch strips of masking tape marking the proper pattern.

Figure 12.12b. Bass stick test (crosswise).

The student, with the right foot on the starting mark, begins the test by leaping to the first tape marker with the left foot and tries to hold a steady position on the ball of the left foot for up to 5 seconds. Student then leaps to the second tape with the right foot; he alternates feet for each successive tape mark to the end of the test.

Scoring The score for each mark the student successfully lands on is 5 points, plus 1 point for each second the balance is held up to 5 seconds. (10 marks at 5 points per mark + 10 5-second periods at 1 point per second = a total of 100 possible points). Penalties for this test are classified into landing errors and balance errors. Five points are deducted for each occurrence of any of the following landing errors.

(1) Failure to stop upon landing.

(2) Touching the heel or any part of the body other than the ball of the supporting foot to the floor.

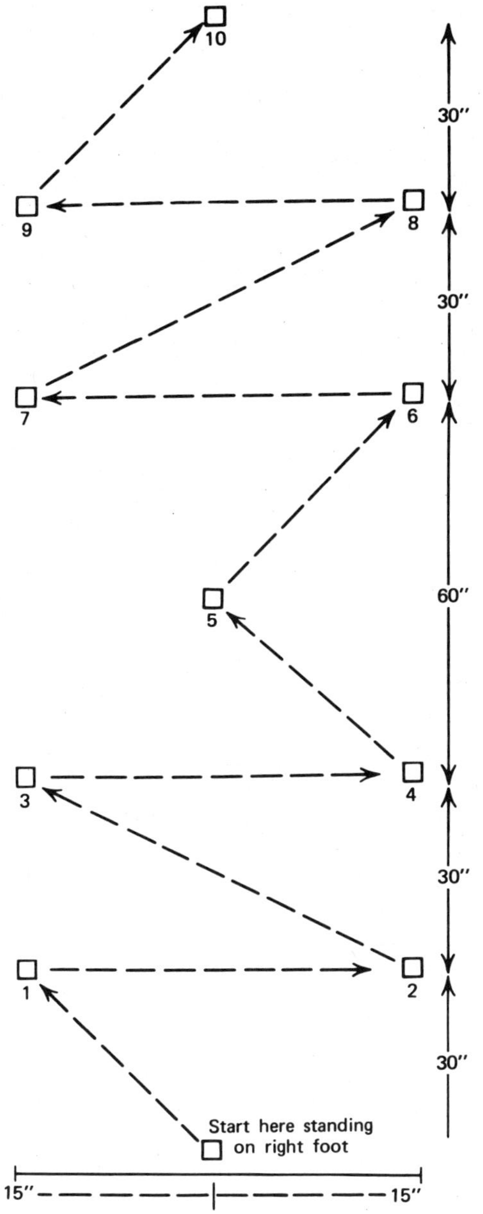

Figure 12.13. Course for Modified Bass Test of Dynamic Balance.

(3) Failure to cover the mark completely with the ball of the foot.

If a student commits a landing error he or she is allowed to reposition the foot to begin the 5-second balance. Points are also deducted for each occurrence of either of the following balance errors prior to the completion of the 5-second balance.

(1) Touching the heel or any part of the body to the floor other than the ball of the supporting foot.
(2) Moving the foot while in the balance position. If a student loses balance, he or she must step back on the appropriate mark and leap to the next mark.

The tester should count aloud the balance time on each marker and should record both landing and balance points for each mark.

Norms Limited norms for college females are available in Johnson and Nelson (1979).

A test involving a complex apparatus is the Stability platform Test. A Stability platform is shown in Figure 12.14.

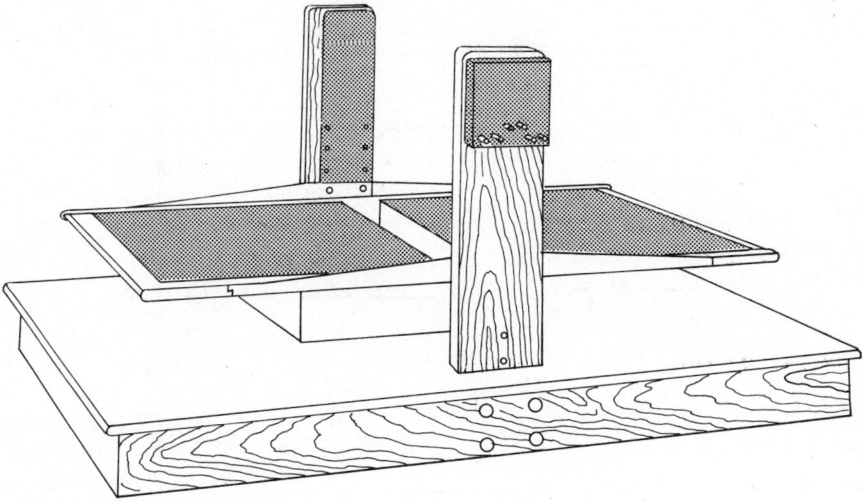

Figure 12.14. Stability platform.

Stability Platform Test

Measurement Objective To measure the ability to balance on an unstable platform.

Test Qualities Content validity is accepted. No data is available for reliability.

Equipment and Materials Stability platform with attached timing device.

Procedure Each student stands on the stability platform and signals the tester when he or she is ready to begin a trial. The student then attempts to maintain balance (platform horizontal position) for as much of a 20-

second trial as possible. A typical bout would include twenty 20-second trials with 20 seconds rest between each trial.

Scoring Score is the time for each trial in which stability platform was within tolerance of horizontal. Time is recorded for each of the 20 trials.

Norms Many investigations have been completed using the stability platform, but norms for various groups are not available.

Balance tests are often used as an item in a test battery, but separate tests of static and dynamic balance are also popular. Other, practical balance tests not discussed here can be found in Scott and French (1959), Johnson and Nelson (1979), and Johnson et al. (1975).

COORDINATION

This basic performance trait is interrelated with several other traits. Coordination may be defined as the ability to perform a skilled movement pattern. This trait is essential in every movement and as the movement becomes more complex the importance of coordination is intensified.

Various types of coordination may be required. Skills such as typewriting or throwing a ball involve hand-eye coordination. Many soccer skills and kicking a football are examples of actions that require foot-eye coordination. Still other skills necessitate total body coordination. Examples of this overall coordination are evident in dribbling a basketball or swinging a golf club. Several factors are involved in coordination — agility, balance, kinesthetic sense, power, movement precision, and speed, for instance. Coordination is an integral part of motor ability; in fact the term coordination has been used synonymously with motor ability and skill.

Tests of coordination have similar purposes to tests of agility. That is, they can be used to predict success in various sport activities, to classify students for activity, or to evaluate behavioral objectives involving coordination.

Although genetics probably dictates limitations in terms of coordination, it is obvious that coordination can be improved through practice and experience. As skill is improved, concomitant increases in coordination usually occur. However, the coordination developed is often specific to the task. Therefore it is recommended that a wide range of motor skills be offered in school curricula.

Practical tests of coordination are somewhat difficult to construct. Since there are so many closely related factors coordination cannot easily be isolated. For instance all agility tests require good coordination for superior performance. Thus an agility test measures at least to some extent total body coordination.

There are numerous laboratory instruments and tests designed to measure fine motor coordination. Two examples of tests intended to measure eye-hand coordination are the Minnesota Rate of Manipulation Test and the Crawford

Small Parts Dexterity Test. Other instruments such as the rotary pursuit apparatus have been utilized for similar purposes. Few tests have been developed for foot-eye coordination, and most athletic skills require total body coordination. Because of the difficulty in delineating practical coordination tests, no test will be given as an example.

Many popular games and puzzles are essentially coordination tasks. An example is shown in Figure 12.15.

Figure 12.15. Coordination puzzle – Drueke Model 1960 Space Maze.

Sources for the tests mentioned earlier are American Guidance Service, Inc., Minneapolis, for the Minnesota Rate of Manipulation Test; and Psychological Corporation, New York, for the Crawford Small Parts Dexterity Test.

KINESTHETIC SENSE

Kinesthetic sense is the ability to percieve the body's position in space and the relationship of its parts. The organs of kinesthetic sense are the proprioceptors, which include specialized sensory receptors in muscles, tendons, joints, and the vestibular apparatus of the inner ear. The kinesthetic or proprioceptor sense is sometimes called muscle sense because of the traditional belief that stretch receptors in muscles are the primary source responsible for kinesthesis.

Kinesthetic sense is used by both beginners and skilled performers. It is a consciousness of muscular movement, effort, and joint angulation, which is easily evident in skilled performances. Research has shown that the proprioceptors provide feedback that aids future performances of a similar nature. Also, it has been argued that in order to develop skill, the performer must "get the feel" of what it is like to execute the skill correctly. Kinesthetic sense is important in virtually every skill. A typical example of kinesthesis is the ability of a basketball player continually to make free throws or to adjust after having missed one. Another example of this sense is the baseball player's use of a weighted bat while in the on-deck circle. The weighted bat is used to give a kinesthetic after-effect. The batter feels he or she can perform better because of overload practice.

Tests of kinesthetic sense are used for various purposes. First, a test of this sense requires the performer to execute a movement without the use of typical visual or augmented feedback. Therefore such tests are used to make the performer concentrate on what it feels like to perform a task. Another use involves demonstrating the specificity of kinesthesis through a battery of tests. Third, such tests can help diagnose learning or performance problems. Kinesthetic tests are often used in research and can function as evaluative criteria when improvement of a specific movement is a behavioral objective of physical education classes.

Two separate research studies by Scott (1955) and Wiebe (1954) instigated a series of investigations relating to kinesthesis. The research led to several significant conclusions regarding kinesthesis. First, there is no general kinesthetic sense. Scott's study included 28 separate tests while Wiebe used 21 tests. The low intercorrelations between tests shed light on the specificity of kinethesis. Second, skilled performers usually perform better on selected tests of kinesthetic tests than do average or poorly skilled individuals. Therefore, it seems that kinethesis can be developed and is a function of amount of practice. Finally, skilled performers depend more on internal kinesthetic information than do beginners.

All tests of kinesthetic sense should have similar administrative components. Each performer is blindfolded and executes a series of trials on the specific test without any feedback between trials. Limited initial practice on the movement should be allowed before the kinesthetic trials are taken. Either the sum of deviations from the criterion or the mean absolute deviation is used as the score. Such a scoring system yields scores with low variability, and reliability coefficients tend to be small unless measurement errors are very small.

Instrumentation for such tests is often simple or innovative although some manufactured instruments such as a Lafayette kinesthesiometer have been utilized. Because of the specificity of kinesthesis, the use of such tests in physical education classes is not recommended. If tests of kinesthetic ability are utilized, they should be used in test batteries and devised to simulate movements necessary for successful performance in specific activity.

Examples of kinesthetic tests that have been used extensively in laboratory research are arm and leg raising, weight shifting, jumping or stepping a specific distance, and weight discrimination. An example of a typical test item is given below. Remember, however, that kinesthetic tests should be administered in batteries.

Arm Raising

Measurement Objectives To measure kinesthetic sense of arm in executing various movements.
Test Qualities Content validity is accepted when performer is blindfolded. No reliability coefficients are available.
Test Application Male and female, all ages.
Equipment and Materials Arm angle chart (Figure 12.16).

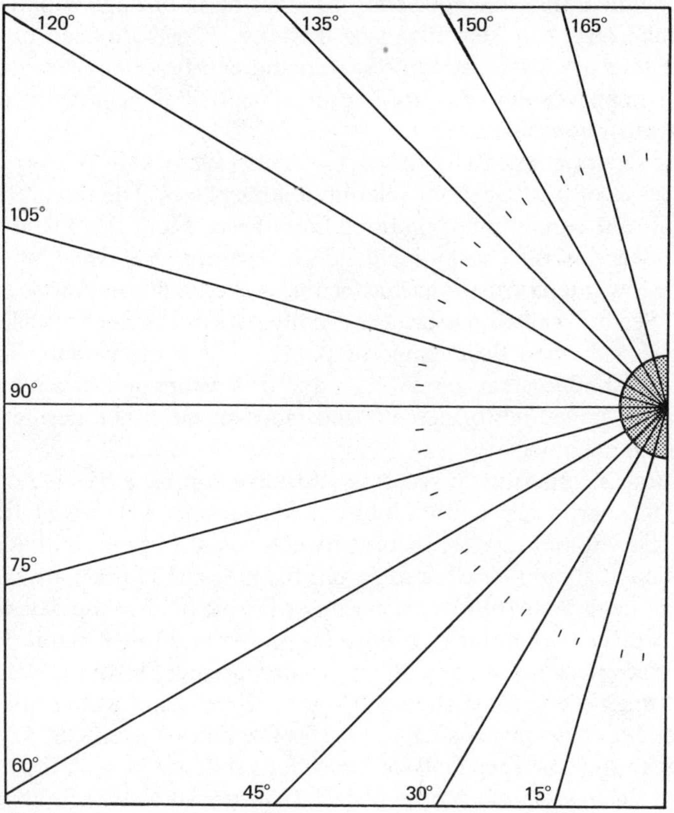

Figure 12.16. Arm angle chart.

Procedure Performer stands facing away from arm angle chart, which has been positioned on wall. The chart is adjusted to shoulder height. Performer becomes acquainted with arm raising movement (i.e., 45° from arm-at-side position). He or she is then blindfolded and given three trials to attempt to repeat the 45° movement by raising fully extended arm that is pronated so chart may be easily read. Positive or negative deviations in degrees are recorded. Additional tests at other angles (i.e., 60°, 90°, 135°) are often administered during the same test time.

Scoring Test score is total deviations in degrees regardless of sign for each angle divided by number of trials. Absolute deviations are used because deviation scores of −2°, −2°, +4° do not indicate perfect performance (i.e., 2 + 2 + 4 = 8/3 = 2.67°). Deviation signs are used because research has shown that performers are usually more conservative when blindfolded.

Norms Norms are not available.

For a detailed discussion of kinesthesis, Sage (1977) should be consulted. Numerous kinesthetic tests are available in the following sources: Sage (1977), Scott (1955), and Wiebe (1954).

POWER

This trait is a combination of strength and speed and is basic to motor performance. Power may be defined as the ability to release maximum force in the shortest possible time. For this reason, muscular power is sometimes called explosive strength. Power, then, is the ability to combine strength of muscular contraction with speed of muscular contraction.

Muscular power is a prerequisite for success in many sports and physical activities. Some performers are extremely strong but cannot execute movements quickly; others are able to move quickly but lack the strength to move quickly against resistance. Performers who are able to combine strength with speed of movement are said to be powerful. The necessity of explosive power is easily seen in a variety of activities. The long jump and shot put are track events that need powerful movement; place kicking, punting, and passing are examples of skills in football that require power; hitting and throwing for distance are baseball activities that require power. Generally, most ballistic skills demand a high level of power.

Practical tests of power include the vertical jump, the standing long jump, which is an item of AAHPER Youth Fitness Test, or any ballistic movement that requires the performer to jump or project his or her body or some object for distance. These practical tests are called tests of athletic power.

Power can also be determined mechanically, by utilizing measures of work, force, distance, and time. A few simple formulas will make this conception of power clear.

$$\mathrm{W} = F x\, D$$

where

W = work

F = force, usually weight of object or weight of person

D = distance force moves

Power, then, is the rate at which work is performed. It can be calculated by using the following formulas.

$$P = W/T \quad P = \frac{F \times D}{T} \qquad \text{or, since} \qquad V = D/T \quad P = F \times V$$

where

P = power
W = work
T = time necessary to perform work
V = velocity of person or projectile

An example of the computation of mechanical power using the above formulas will be given when the Margaria-Kalamen leg power test is described. Research to date has shown that practical tests of athletic power are not highly correlated with mechanical power tests.

Power is generally considered a component of general motor ability, motor fitness, and often, a factor in physical fitness. Thus, tests of power are often used in test batteries. Power tests are also used as motivating devices and predictors of athletic success, as well as for research purposes. Finally, power tests can be used in determining grades when improvement in muscular power is a behavioral objective of a physical education class. It is generally agreed that since skill has a significant effect on tests of power, instruction should be given in the skill used and practice should be allowed. For example in the vertical jump test, the jump should be taught and practiced before actual testing is done. Power can be improved or increased by increasing strength without losing speed of movement or vice versa. By analyzing the components of the formulas that determine power, training programs can be developed to increase this trait.

Many practical tests of athletic power have been developed. The standing long jump, a test of muscular power, will be included in the description of the AAHPER Youth Fitness Test in Chapter 13. Another practical test of muscular power that has been used extensively is the Sargent Jump. The Margaria-Kalamen Leg Power Test is a test of mechanical power and is used more often for research purposes. Both of these tests are presented below.

Vertical Jump (Sargent Jump)

Measurement Objective To measure explosive power of the legs in a vertical jump.
Test Qualities Validity is .78 when correlated with sum of four power events in track. Reliability is .93.
Equipment and Materials Vertical jump chalkboard or chalk and a smooth wall surface with adequate ceiling height.
Test Application Male and female elementary through college.
Procedure Performer stands with side towards wall, reaches as high as possible with heels on the floor, and makes a mark on the wall or chalk-

board with a piece of chalk or chalked finger. Performer then swings arms downward and backward, taking a crouched position with the knees bent at about a right angle. He or she then leaps as high as possible, swinging the arms upward. As the highest point of the jump is reached, another mark should be made above the initial one (Figure 12.17). Approximately 40 students can be tested at each station during a 40 minute class period. Some alternative methods of measuring the distance of the vertical jump are described in Clarke (1976).

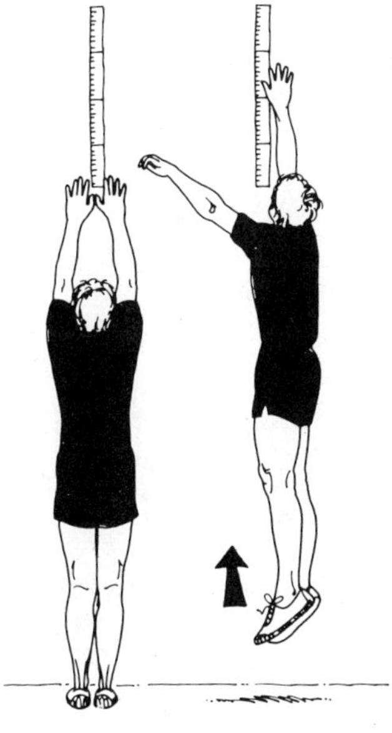

Figure 12.17. Vertical jump.

Scoring The score is the number of inches to the nearest ½ inch between the reach and jump marks (test is sometimes called Jump and Reach Test). The best of three trials should be recorded.
Norms Norms for all ages are available in Johnson and Nelson (1979) and also in Neilson and Jensen (1972). Norms for elementary ages are available as part of the Johnson Fundamental Skill Test in Barrow and McGee (1971).

Margaria-Kalamen Leg Power Test (Mathews and Fox, 1976)

Measurement Objective To measure mechanical leg power generated when moving the body.
Test Qualities Validity is .974 when correlated with 50-yard dash (with 15 yards running start).

Equipment and Materials Switch mats and Dekan Performance Analyzer or other timing device, flight of at least nine stairs.

Procedure Performer begins 6 meters from the bottom stair and runs up the stairs as rapidly as possible, taking three steps at a time. Switch mats or some devices to start and stop timing device are placed on the third and ninth steps. As the performer steps on the third stair the clock is activated; when the subject steps on the ninth stair the clock is stopped. The time recorded by the clock represents the time required to move the body a height of 1.05 meters (Figure 12.18).

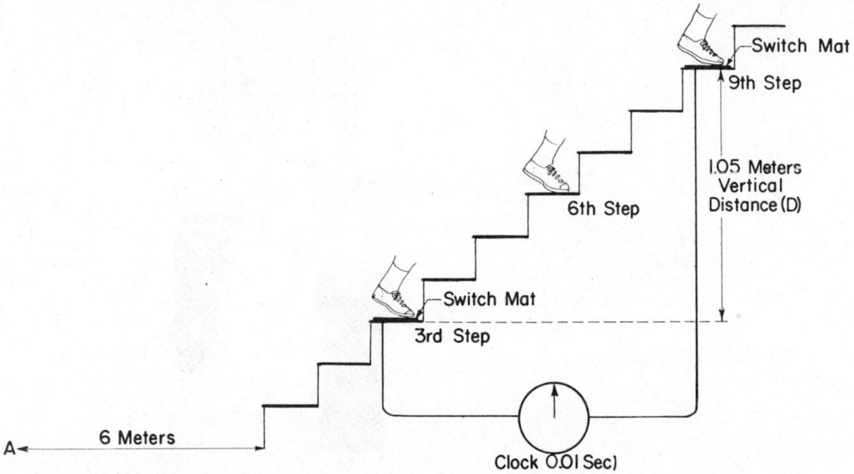

Figure 12.18. Margaria-Kalamen power test. Subject commences at point *A* and runs as rapidly as he can up the flight of stairs, taking them three at a time. The time it takes him to traverse between stair 3 and stair 9 is recorded in 0.01 seconds. The power generated is a product of the subject's weight and the vertical distance (*D*), divided by the time (from Donald K. Mathews and Edward L. Fox, *The Physiological Basis of Physical Education and Athletics*, 2 ed., 1976, W. B. Saunders Company, Philadelphia; reprinted by permission).

Scoring Since $P = \frac{F \times D}{T}$, power is calculated by the following formula:

$$P = \frac{\text{Body weight (Kg)} \times 1.05\ \text{M}}{\text{Elapsed time}}$$

Norms Norms are not available.

Although both examples involved leg power, many power tests utilize the arms. Power tests involving the arms are different in that the weight load or force (i.e., shot or medicine ball) remains constant for all performers while leg tests usually involve moving one's weight. Since each performer usually weighs a different amount, the force becomes variable for each person. Examples of arm power tests as well as other leg power tests can be found in Clarke (1976), and Johnson and Nelson (1979).

SPEED OF REACTION AND MOVEMENT

Reaction time (*RT*) is the delay in time between the presentation of a stimulus and the initiation of a volitational response. Movement time (*MT*) is the time taken to complete a task after it has been initiated. Response time or performance time is the sum of reaction and movement time. This relationship is represented in Figure 12.19. In the 100-yard dash a time of 9.4 seconds indicates the response time or performance time but is actually composed *RT* and *MT*.

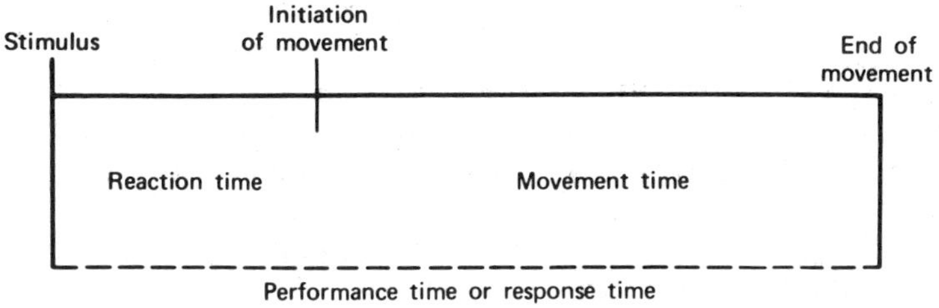

Figure 12.19. Relationship of reaction time (*RT*) and movement time (*MT*) to response time or performance time.

Performance time is the sole criterion in some sports and is one of the most important factors in others. It is quite obvious that the performer who can move the fastest has a definite advantage. However, when the time of the event or task is relatively short, reaction time becomes a major factor. For instance, the sprinter who leaves the starting block at the most appropriate time, the baserunner who can react to the pitcher's motion, the offensive lineman who can initiate movement at the exact time all have clear advantages. Reaction time is affected by a number of stimulus variables and individual variables.

Stimulus variables include mode of stimulus, stimulus intensity, the presence or absence of forewarning cues, and the complexity of the stimulus or response. Individual variables include motivation, fitness, amount of practice, as well as the sex and age of the person, and the limbs used. For a comprehensive discussion of these variables, the reader should refer to Sage (1977).

Movement time is affected by the same individual variables as reaction time. However, the major components of movement time are muscular efficiency, strength, and endurance. Research has shown that significant gains can be made in movement time through practice. As skill is developed, the time necessary to perform the task will decrease. Research has also shown there is little correlation between RT and MT. Most studies have found that the ability to react quickly and the ability to move quickly are almost entirely unrelated.

Practically speaking, the total performance time is most important. Even though each performance can be broken down into reaction time and movement time, it is the combination of RT and MT in each physical performance that is the indicator of success or failure.

Reaction time has traditionally been evaluated in a laboratory setting by using some mode of stimulus to activate an electric timer. The initiation of the performer's response stops the timer. More recently some mechanical devices have been developed utilizing the known rate of descent of an object caused by gravity. Tests of speed or performance time have included short dashes of less than 100 yards.

Speed or response time, which includes movement time and reaction time is usually considered a component of motor ability or motor fitness tests, as well as many tests of sport skills. Therefore, some sort of short sprint is included in most test batteries. Tests of response time or its components can be used for diagnosis, classification, motivation, and for research purposes. Finally, such tests can be used in determining achievement when improvement of performance speed is a behavioral objective of physical education.

Two electric instruments for measuring speed are shown below in Figure 12.20 *a* and *b*. The Lafayette Choice Reaction Timer is able to record reaction time for simple or complex stimuli and is primarily a laboratory instrument. A practical instrument, the Dekan Performance Analyzer, can record reaction or movement time and is usable on the athletic field or in the classroom as well as in the laboratory.

Research has demonstrated that the fastest reaction time is achieved when an auditory stimulus is used; that males usually have faster reaction time than females; and that reaction time improves from birth to about 20 where it peaks for about 10 years. A considerable amount of research has been done involving reaction time and movement time. The results are summarized in Sage (1977). Most tests of finger reaction involve reacting to a stimulus by pressing or releasing a button that stops a timer that has begun as the stimulus was given. The Dekan Performance Analyzer can also be used for foot and total body reaction time with the use of switch mats.

Fred Nelson has recently developed a measuring device that is practical for use in physical education classes. The Nelson Reaction Timer is based on the law of constant acceleration of free-falling bodies. It consists of a stick that is scaled to read in time units as calculated from the following formula.

$$\text{Time in milliseconds} = \frac{2 \times \text{distance stick falls}}{\text{acceleration due to gravity}}$$

Several tests of reaction and movement time have been developed that use this instrument. Two of these tests are given below:

Nelson Hand Reaction Test

Measurement Objective To measure the speed of reaction in response to a visual stimulus.

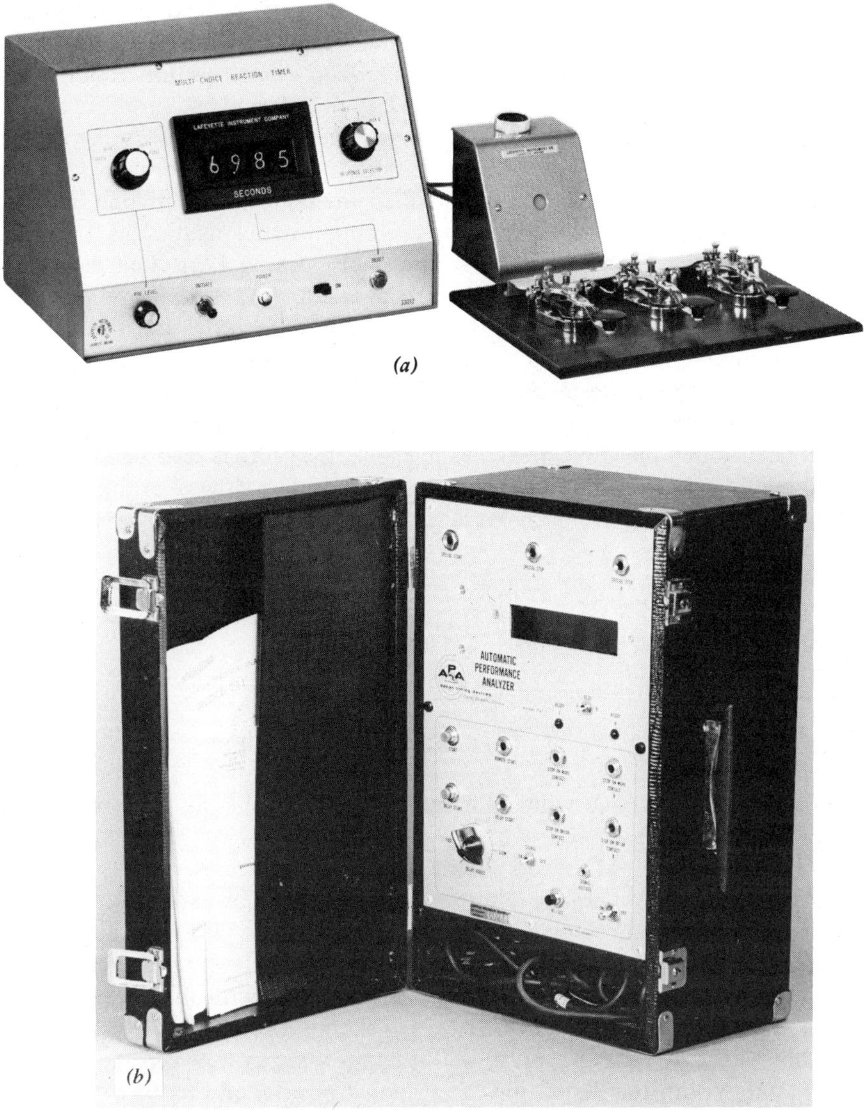

Figure 12.20. Lafayette Choice Reaction Timer and Dekan Performance Analyzer.

Test Qualities Content validity accepted, since earth's gravitational pull is consistent. Reliability is .89 using test-retest method.

Test Application Male and female, all ages.

Equipment and Materials Nelson Reaction Timer Model RT-2 or yardstick, table and chair, or desk chair. Quiet room for testing.

Procedure Performer sits with his forearm and hand resting comfortably on a table or writing area of a desk chair (Figure 12.21*a*) The tips of the thumb and index finger are held in a *ready-to-punch* position about 3 or 4 inches beyond the edge of the table. The thumb and index finger should be in a horizontal position, and the base line of the reaction timer should be even with the upper surface of the thumb. The performer is told to concentrate on a black shaded area (called the concentration zone between .120 and .130 lines) and to react by grasping the stick as soon as it is dropped, with the thumb and index finger (Figure 12.12*b*). The performer should not look at the tester's hands and is not allowed to move his or her hand up or down in grasping the falling stick. Each drop of the stick by the tester is preceded by a "ready" signal. Twenty trials are given. About 15 students can be tested in 40 minutes.
Scoring The time between "ready" and the drop should vary from trial to trial. When the subject catches the stick, the score is read just above the upper edge of the thumb (Figure 12.21*c*). The five slowest and five fastest trials are discarded and an average of the middle ten trials is recorded as the score.
Norms Norms are not available. College men average about .16 with a range of .13 to .22. With the first graders, the average is about .26.

Nelson Speed of Movement Test

Measurement Objectives To measure response time of the hands and arms.
Test Qualities Face validity is accepted. Reliability is .75 with college men.
Test Application Male and female, all ages.
Equipment and Materials Nelson Reaction Timer or yardstick, table and chair, or desk chair. Quiet room for testing, chalk or tape and ruler.
Procedure Performer sits facing table with hands resting on the edge of the table. Palms face each other (Figure 12.21*d*) with the inside edge of the little fingers 12 inches apart (lines are used on the table). The tester holds the stick near the top so that it hangs midway between the performers palms with the "base line" of the stick positioned evenly with the upper edges of the performer's index fingers. After a preparatory command "ready" is given, the stick is dropped and the performer attempts, with a horizontal movement, to stop it as quickly as possible by clapping the hands together (Figure 12.21*e*). Twenty trials are given. About 14 students can be tested in a 40 minute period with one timer.

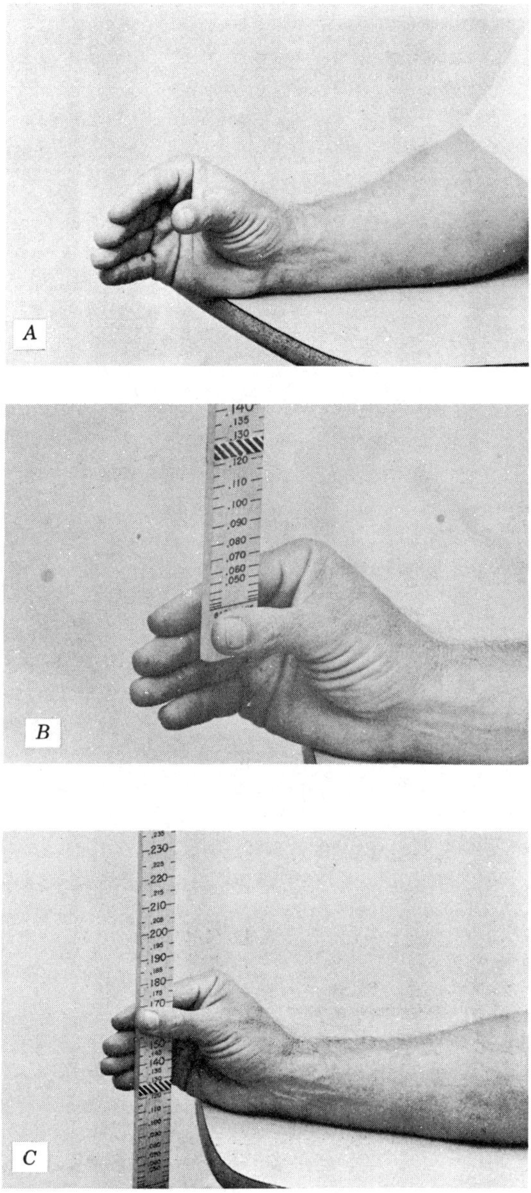

Figure 12.21. Nelson Hand Reaction Test.

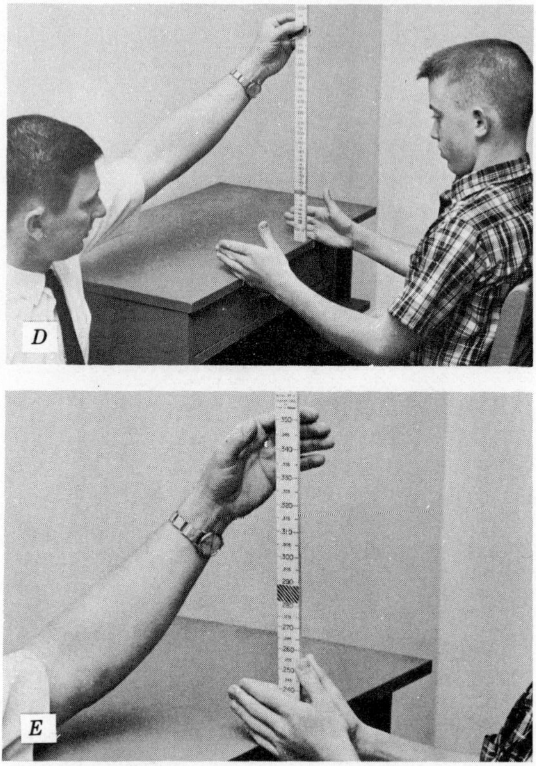

Figure 12.21. Nelson Speed of Movement Test.

Scoring The score for the response time is read from the timer at the point just above the upper edge of the hand after the catch is made. The five slowest and fastest trials are discarded and an average of the middle ten trials is recorded as the score.

Norms Although no norms are available, average time for college men has been found to be about .24.

Sprints for Speed

The most widely accepted measure of total body response is a short sprint. Sprints of varying distances and times have been utilized. Notice the following test times: 4-second dash and 6 second-dash, for instance. The 40-yard dash, often used by those associated with football, is another of many response time or speed tests that have been developed. No example of such a test is given here since the 50-yard dash is included as an item of the AAHPER Youth Fitness Test presented in Chapter 13. Other tests of reaction time, movement time, and response time can be found in Barrow and McGee (1971), Hodgkins (1963), Neilson and Jensen (1972), Sage (1977), and Singer (1975).

Summary

The basic performance traits include strength, muscular endurance, cardiorespiratory endurance, flexibility, agility, balance, coordination, power, kinesthetic sense, and speed of reaction and movement. Many tests have been devised in each of the performance trait areas and have been used for several reasons: to predict success in specific sport areas; to ascertain accomplishment of behavioral objectives; in grading; in research; as motivational techniques; and to demonstrate positive effects of exercise. In addition, tests in several of the basic performance traits have been used in test batteries designed to measure physical fitness, motor fitness, and motor ability.

Study Questions

1. Identify the basic performance traits.
2. Distinguish between isotonic, isometric and isokinetic training.
3. Distinguish between static and dynamic balance. How is each measured?
4. Identify research and practical instruments used to measure reaction time and response time.
5. Identify various research and practical instruments for measuring cardiorespiratory endurance.
6. Select a basic performance trait. Find as many tests as possible that purport to measure this trait. Evaluate each test in terms of validity, reliability, and economy.
7. Develop an innovative test to measure a basic performance trait.

CHAPTER 13

Multiple Performance Traits

After you have read and studied this chapter, you should be able to:

1. *Define the multiple performance traits.*
2. *Identify the basic performance traits that comprise each multiple performance trait.*
3. *Differentiate between tests purporting to measure physical fitness, motor fitness, and motor ability.*
4. *Utilize tests of multiple performance traits, especially the AAHPER Youth Fitness Test.*

Historically, there were two distinct waves of the measurement of multiple performance traits. At about 1900, interest in testing motor and athletic ability began and remained until about 1960.

The second movement — testing physical fitness and motor fitness — has received much emphasis since World War II, although a few instruments designed to measure these multiple performance traits were developed before 1940. These areas of emphasis were described more fully in Chapter 2. *Motor ability*, *motor fitness*, *physical fitness* will be discussed in this chapter.

DEFINITIONS

Selected basic performance traits described in the previous chapters have been combined in various test batteries designed to measure general motor ability, motor fitness, and physical fitness as well as related areas such as athletic ability, motor capacity, and motor educability. Clarke (1976) has identified the relationships between these three multiple performance traits. According to him, motor fitness is a limited phase of general motor ability but is a more encompassing term than physical fitness. The relationships among the three multiple performance traits are shown in Figure 13.1

There is no universal agreement on which basic performance traits should be included in the measurement of the multiple performance traits, as can be seen by examination of the test items of various test batteries. For instance, the AAHPER Youth Fitness Test includes items that measure motor fitness rather than physical fitness. Other terms have been used to identify similar motor performance traits. A brief description of terms associated with motor performance measurement is found in Table 13.1.

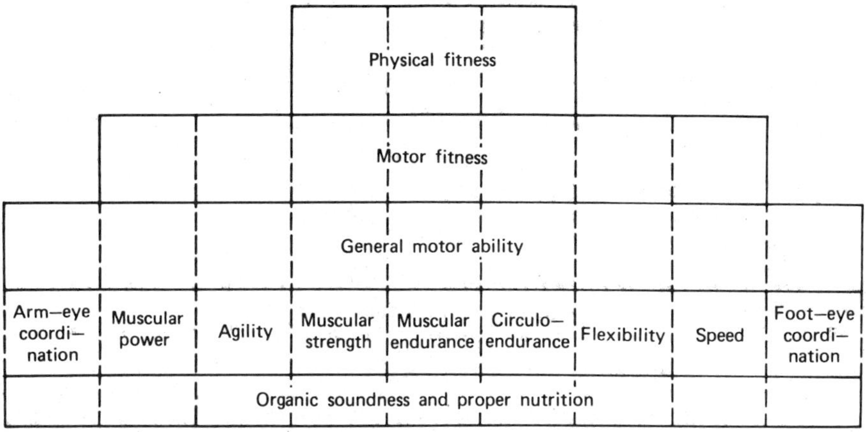

Figure 13.1. Clarke's representation of the basic performance traits included in general motor ability, motor fitness, and physical fitness (from H. Harrison Clarke, *Application of Measurement to Health and Physical Education*, Fifth Edition, 1976, p. 174; reprinted by permission of Prentice-Hall, Inc., Englewood Cliffs, New Jersey).

Table 13.1 Motor Performance Terminology

Term	*Description*
Physical fitness	Ability to carry out reasonably vigorous physical activities involving muscularstrength, muscular endurance, cardiorespiratory endurance, and flexibility.
Motor Fitness	Ability to perform fundamental motor skills involving physical fitness traits and other basic traits such as power, agility, speed, and balance.
General motor ability	Ability to perform fundamental motor skills involving all basic performance traits including coordination.
General athletic ability	Ability to perform various sports skills involving all basic performance traits including coordination.
Motor capacity	Ability to learn complex motor performance.
Motor educability	Ability to quickly learn unfamiliar motor skills.

GENERAL MOTOR ABILITY

This ability may be defined as present acquired and innate ability to perform motor skills of a fundamental nature, exclusive of highly specialized sports or gymnastic skills. This definition implies that general motor ability depends on heredity and practice, but must be measured by assessment of basic performance traits rather than by specific sports skills. The concept of general motor ability, historically a very dominant theme in physical education, has lost much popularity, primarily because of research first performed by Franklin Henry (1958, 1960) and replicated by others. Henry developed the memory drum theory, which likens human motor performance to the functioning of a computer. According to Henry, skills are efficiently performed because of specific stored, organized information. Only specific acts are stored, and even generally similar motor patterns will not correspond to the same program. The results of this research have concluded that although past experience is crucial to present performance, success in more than one skill is explained by reasons other than general motor ability, and performance in one skill has little value in predicting performance on a different motor skill. The research, in effect, has negated the concept of general motor ability. A student who does well on a general motor ability test battery does not have hiqh general motor ability, but has many *specific* motor abilities in which he or she is proficient. An excellent discussion regarding the specificity of skill can be found in Sage (1977).

Nevertheless, the term general motor ability has not disappeared. Clarke, for instance, in Figure 13.1 presented earlier in the discussion of multiple performance traits, considers general motor ability to be composed of several basic performance traits.

Whether or not the concept of general motor ability is accepted, the test batteries actually are composed of several items that attempt to measure specific traits. Just as there is discussion about whether general motor ability exists, so there traditionally have been questions regarding what traits should be measured in such a test battery. Cozens (1929) identified seven components: (1) arm and shoulder coordination with implements; (2) arm and shoulder girdle strength; (3) hand-eye, foot-eye, and arm-eye coordination; (4) jumping or leg strength and flexibility; (5) endurance or sustained effort; (6) body coordination, agility, and control; and (7) speed of legs with coordination of the body. Barrow (1971) identified: (1) arm and shoulder coordination, (2) flexibility; (3) power; (4) hand-eye and foot-eye coordination; (5) speed; (6) strength; (7) balance; and (8) agility. A recent text by Johnson and others (1975) considers only the traits of coordination, agility, balance, power, and speed (movement time and reaction time) to be the components of motor ability.

Although there is now some questions about using tests of general motor ability, such tests have traditionally been utilized for classification of students into ability groups, to diagnose weaknesses in motor performance, to measure achievement of behavioral objectives relating to physical skills, and for motivational purposes.

Brace published the first test designed to measure motor ability in 1927. Most tests of general motor ability were developed during the 30 year period from 1930 to 1960. Few attempts to measure general motor ability have been published since 1958 when Henry questioned its presence. The majority of general motor ability tests were designed for college men. Examples are tests by Brace (1929), Larson (1941), Barrow (1971), and Seymour (1953). The batteries designed by Barrow and Larson have been used with high school boys. Several general motor ability test batteries have also been designed for college women, including those by Humiston (1931) and Scott (1939). The Newton Motor Ability Test (Powell and Howe, 1939) was originally designed for high school girls but has been used with college women. Elementary-age children have been the focus of batteries of tests by Carpenter (1942) and Latchaw (1954).

McCloy (1954) revised the Brace Test, and it is now known as the Iowa Revision of the Brace Test. The Iowa-Brace Test has been used for elementary, junior high, and high school boys and girls.

An example of a general motor ability test will not be presented in this text. However, Table 13.2 lists the items of several of the most used tests, and inducates the types of items included in such tests.

Table 13.2 General Motor Ability Test Batteries

Barrow Motor AbilityTest (Men)
*Standing long jump
Softball throw for distance
*Zigzag run
Wall pass using basketball
*Six pound medicine ball put
60-yard dash
*Indoor battery
Cozens General Athletic AbilityTest (Men)
Baseball throw for distance
Football punt for distance
Bar snap (parallel bars)
Standing long jump
Dips (parallel bars)
Dodging run
Quarter-mile run
Scott Motor Ability Test(Women)
Basketball throw for distance
Four-second dash
Wall pass using basketball
Standing long jump
Obstacle run
Newton Motor AbilityTest
Standing long jump
Hurdle run
Scramble (agility run)

Larson Motor Ability Test(Men)

Indoor Battery	*Outdoor Battery*
Chins (pull ups)	Chins(pull-ups)
Vertical jump	Bar snap
Dips	Vertical jump
Dodging run	Baseball throw for distance
Bar snap	

Latchaw Motor AchievementTest (Elementary Children)

Basketball wall pass
Volleyball wall volley
Vertical jump
Standing long jump
Shuttle run
Soccer wall volley
Softball repeated throws

PHYSICAL FITNESS/MOTOR FITNESS

The concept of fitness has been studied at length by members of the physical education profession throughout the world. In the United States, emphasis on physical fitness, or at least components thereof, began with the scientific era of measurement in the 1860s. Interest in developing and maintaining physical fitness was a major reason in the establishment of the first professional organization in physical education, now the AAHPER, in 1885. As mentioned in Chapter 2, physical fitness has received renewed interest periodically because of the rejection of draftees in World War I and World War II for health reasons, the success of fitness programs of the armed services, and the famous Kraus-Weber Tests of Minimum Muscular Fitness, which gave impetus to the establishment of the President's Council on Youth Fitness in 1956.

Agreement has been reached that physical fitness is a goal of physical education programs. However, agreement on a definition of physical fitness and the components that comprise it is somewhat difficult to achieve. Two definitions will be presented here to exemplify what is currently accepted as physical fitness.

Physical fitness is the ability to carry out daily tasks vigorously and alertly without undue fatigue, and with ample energy to enjoy leisure time pursuits and to meet unforeseen emergencies (Clarke, 1976).

Physical fitness is the capacity to carry out reasonably vigorous physical activities and includes qualities important to the individual's health and well-being in general, as opposed to characteristics that relate to performance of specific motor skills (Johnson et al., 1975).

The lack of agreement of what actually comprises physical fitness is exemplified by the great variety of tests, all of which purport to measure it. Clarke (1976) identifies three components.

Muscular strength

Muscular endurance

Circulorespiratory endurance

Johnson and Nelson (1979) and Johnson et al. (1975) also include flexibility as a component of physical fitness. Other attempts to identify physical fitness have been all-encompassing, including the four traits already mentioned plus coordination, agility, balance, power, and speed; these conceptions go beyond the definitions of physical fitness presented in this text. Coordination, agility, balance, power, and speed are traits that enhance specific motor performance but are not really necessary to achieve and maintain physical fitness. The term "motor fitness" was developed to describe a broader concept than physical fitness — this extensive term means the ability to perform basic motor skills efficiently and effectively. However the term "physical fitness" and "motor fitness" are often used interchangably. In most situations the physical educator is more concerned about the broader concept; that is, the development and measurement of motor fitness. Its measurement and evaluation can be accomplished by using a standard motor fitness test battery such as the AAHPER Youth Fitness Test. This widely used test is easily administered, and national norms for each item have been developed. A second alternative is to develop a motor fitness test battery for local use. Each basic performance trait that composes motor fitness has been discussed separately in the previous chapter. Instructors can choose the items they believe are most relevant to be included in a local fitness test battery. Norms could be developed for the local situation using the unique test items.

Similar procedures could be followed if physical fitness as defined earlier in this discussion is the major objective of the program rather than motor fitness. Either a published test battery that measures muscular strength, muscular endurance, cardiorespiratory endurance, and flexibility can be utilized or separate items that measure each trait can be developed and used in a test battery.

Tests of physical fitness and motor fitness can be used for a variety of reasons. The first, and probably most important, use is to ascertain the level of fitness of an individual. Once the fitness level has been evaluated, methods of conditioning to develop or maintain fitness can be used. Another use of these tests in the class situation is as an instrument to evaluate whether or not behavioral objectives are achieved. Such test batteries can also be utilized as classification techniques to determine homogeneous groups for conditioning methods. Still other uses of such tests are as motivational devices in formative and summative evaluation and as a criterion for evaluating the local physical education program.

Fitness has been measured in a number of different ways including (1) by cardiorespiratory endurance tests: (2) by test batteries that measure cardiorespiratory endurance, muscular strength, muscular endurance and flexibility; (3) by motor fitness tests. Some of these tests obviously measure different traits; the disagreement about what is included in physical fitness is the major reason for the variations.

Physical fitness according to exercise physiologists, is best measured by tests of aerobic capacity. Such cardiorespiratory tests usually require the subject to perform maximal or submaximal work on a treadmill or bicycle ergometer. The individual's expired air is collected and analyzed to determine the amount of oxygen utilized. These tests, although extremely valid, are not practical for measuring fitness in school situations. Because of their high validity, however, tests of aerobic capacity have been utilized as criteria to establish validity of such practical tests as endurance runs. Distance runs and step tests are measures of aerobic capacity that are less exacting but administratively feasible in a physical education class situation. Both of these classroom tests have been discussed in the previous chapter. There are few test batteries that measure only cardiorespiratory endurance, muscular strength, muscular endurance, and flexibility. Johnson and Nelson (1979) have attempted to develop test batteries that primarily measure these traits. The U.S. Army Physical Fitness Test, U.S. Navy Physical Fitness Test, and the McCloy Strength Test also primarily measure these four traits. Since each individual trait has been discussed earlier in this chapter, perhaps it is most advisable to develop test batteries for local situations. Valid and reliable tests have been developed for each trait. The physical educator needs only to decide which specific test items are administratively feasible.

The most widely used measure of youth fitness has been the AAHPER Youth Fitness Test. The test was first purlished in 1958 and was developed by the AAHPER in response to the results of the Kraus-Weber Tests of Minimum Muscular Fitness, which reported that American children were not nearly as fit as European children.

The AAHPER Youth Fitness Test originally contained seven items (now six) designed to measure motor fitness traits. The battery includes items that are administratively feasible indoors and outdoors, are appropriate for boys or girls in grades 5 through 12, require little or no equipment, and are reasonably familiar.

The original items in the battery, to be administered in a two-day period, were as follows

First Day	*Second Day*
Pull-ups (Boys)	50-yard dash
Flexed-arm hang (Girls)	Softball throw for distance
Sit-ups	600-yard run-walk
Shuttle run	
Standing long jump	

Correlations between the test items were found to be low, indicating different traits were being tested. Since the original test with norms was published in 1958, two additional national surveys have been conducted with the most recent norms dated 1975. The flexed leg sit-up has been substituted for the straight leg sit-up because it has been found to be a more accurate measure of the efficiency of abdominal muscles. The softball throw has been eliminated because it tests skill to a great extent rather than a basic fitness trait. Both the softball throw and the straight leg sit-up had drawn criticism from teachers and measurement experts because of injuries incurred by students during testing. The 600-yard run-walk has been modified to include two optional runs: the 1-mile or 9-minute run for ages 10 to 12 and the 1½ mile or 12-minute run for ages 13 and older. This change has been made because of the vast amount of aerobic research, which indicates that 600 yards is too short a distance to measure cardiorespiratory endurance. Other items of the test have received criticism because they measure traits that are primarily motor fitness rather than physical fitness traits. However the broad concept of physical fitness has been maintained in the present test battery. By intention, the present items measure the traits shown in Figure 13.3.

Table 13.3 AAHPER Youth Fitness Tests: Revised Items and Traits That Items Measure

	Item	*Trait Measured*
1.	Pull-up (boys) or flexed-arm hang (girls)	Strength and endurance of arm and shoulder girdle
2.	Flexed-leg sit-up abdominal and hip flexion muscles	Strength and endurance of
3.	Shuttle run	Speed and agility
4.	Standing long jump	Explosive power of leg extensors
5.	50-yard dash	Speed
6.	600-yard run with options of 1 mile or 9 minutes, ages 10-12, or 1½ miles or 12 minutes, ages 13 and older	Cardiorespiratory endurance

Since this test battery is the most widely used test of fitness by schools in the United States, the entire test will be presented including the most recent norms for each item. Currently, there is an AAHPER committee studying the AAHPER Youth Fitness Test; dramatic changes in test items may be suggested. The new test which is to be published in the fall of 1979 will include four tests all of which emphasize health-related fitness. The items include: sit-up test; sit and reach test; a 9 min. or 1 mile run and skinfold measurement to assess body composition.

AAHPER Youth Fitness Test

Measurement Objective To assess fitness through test items measuring muscular strength and endurance, cardiorespiratory endurance, agility, and speed. *Test Qualities* Content validity is accepted. Intercorrelations between items are low, indicating that they measure separate traits.
Test Applications Male and female, grades 5 through 12, also college.
Equipment and Materials Presented with each item. Items are designed to require little or no equipment.
Procedure Flexibility in terms of testing areas and equipment is possible. Refer to each item.
Scoring Refer to each item.
Norms Percentile norms for ages 9 to 17 and over are found in Tables 13.4 through 13.19.*

Pull-Up (Boys)

Materials A metal or wooden bar approximately 1½ inches in diameter is preferred. A doorway gym bar can be used and, if no regular equipment is available, a piece of pipe or even the rungs of a ladder can serve the purpose (Figure 13.2).
Procedure The bar should be high enough so that the pupil can hang with his arms and legs fully extended and his feet free of the floor. He should use the overhand grasp (Figure 13.3). After assuming the hanging position, the pupil raises his body by his arms until his chin can be placed over the bar and then lowers his body to a full hang as in the starting position. The exercise is repeated as many times as possible.

Figure 13.2. Improvised equipment for pull-up – doorway gym bar in background, ladder in foreground.

Figure 13.3. Starting position for pull-up.

Rules 1. Allow one trial unless it is obvious that the pupil has not had a fair chance.

2. The body must not swing during the execution of the movement. The pull must in no way be a snap movement. If the pupil starts swinging, check this by holding an extended arm across the front of the thighs.

3. The knees must not be raised, and kicking of the legs is not permitted.

Scoring Record the number of completed pull-ups to the nearest whole number.

Flexed-Arm Hang (Girls)

Materials A horizontal bar approximately 1½ inches in diameter is preferred. A doorway gym bar can be used; if no regular equipment is available, a piece of pipe can serve the purpose. A stopwatch is needed.

Figure 13.4. Starting position for flexed-arm hang.

Procedure The height of the bar should be adjusted so it is approximately equal to the pupil's standing height. The pupil should use an overhand grasp (Figure 13.4). With the assistance of two spotters, one in front and one in back, the pupil raises her body off the floor to a position where the chin is above the bar, the elbows are flexed, and the chest is close to the bar (Figures 13.5). The pupil holds this position as long as possible.

Figure 13.5. Flexed-arm hang.

Rules 1. The stopwatch is started as soon as the subject takes the hanging position.
2. The watch is stopped when (a) pupil's chin touches the bar, (b) pupil's head tilts backwards to keep chin above the bar, (c) pupil's chin falls below the level of the bar.
Scoring Record in seconds to the nearest second the length of time the subject holds the hanging position.

Flexed-leg Sit-Up (Boys and Girls)

Materials Clean floor, mat or dry turf, and stopwatch.
Procedure The pupil lies on his or her back with the knees bent, feet on the floor, and heels not more than 12 inches from the buttocks. The angle at the knees should be less than 90 degrees. The pupil puts his or her hands on the back of the neck with fingers clasped and places elbows squarely on the mat, floor, or turf. The feet are held by the partner to keep them in touch with the surface (Figure 13.6). The pupil tightens his or her abdominal muscles and brings the head and elbows forward as he or she curls up, finally touching elbows to knees (Figure 13.7). This action constitutes one sit-up. The pupil returns to the starting position with the elbows on the surface before performing the sit-up again. The timer gives the signal "ready-go,.' and the sit-up performance is started on the word "go." Performance is stopped on the word "stop." The number of correctly executed sit-ups performed in 60 seconds shall be the score.

Figure 13.6. Starting position for flexed-leg sit-up.

Rules 1. Only one trial shall be allowed unless the teacher believes the pupil has not had a fiar opportunity to perform.
2. No resting is permitted between sit-ups.
3. No sit-ups shall be counted in which the pupil DOES NOT: (a) keep the fingers clasped behind the neck; (b) bring both elbows forward in starting to sit up without pushing off the floor with an elbow; or (c) return to starting position with ELBOWS FLAT ON THE SURFACE before sitting up again.

Figure 13.7. Flexed-leg sit-up.

Scoring Record the number of correctly executed sit-ups the pupil is able to do in 60 seconds. A foul nullifies the count for that sit-up. The watch is started on the word "go" and stopped on the word "stop."

Shuttle Run (Boys and Girls)

Materials Two blocks of wood, 2 inches by 2 inches by 4 inches, and stopwatch. Pupils should wear sneakers or run barefooted.
Procedure Two parallel lines are marked on the floor 30 feet apart. The width of a regulation volleyball court serves as a suitable area. Place the blocks of wood behind one of the lines as indicated in Figure 13.8. The pupil starts from behind the other line. On the signal "Ready? Go!" the pupil runs to the blocks, picks one up, runs back to the starting line, and PLACES the block behind the line; he then runs back and picks up the second block, which he carries back across the starting line. If the scorer has two stopwatches or one with a split-second timer, it is preferable to have two pupils running at the same time. To eliminate the necessity of returning the blocks after each race, start the races alternately, first from behind one line and then from behind the other.

Figure 13.8. Starting the shuttle run.

Rules Allow two trials with some rest between.
Scoring Record the time of the better of the two trials to the nearest tenth of a second.

Standing Long Jump (Boys and Girls)

Materials Mat, floor, or outdoor jumping pit, and tape measure.

Procedure Pupil stands as indicated in Figure 13.9, with the feet several inches apart and the toes just behind the takeoff line. In preparation for jumping, the pupil swings the arms backward and bends the knees. The jump is accomplished by simultaneously extending the knees and swinging the arms forward.

Rules 1. Allow three trials.

2. Measure from the takeoff line to the heel or other part of the body that touches the floor nearest the takeoff line (Figure 13.9).

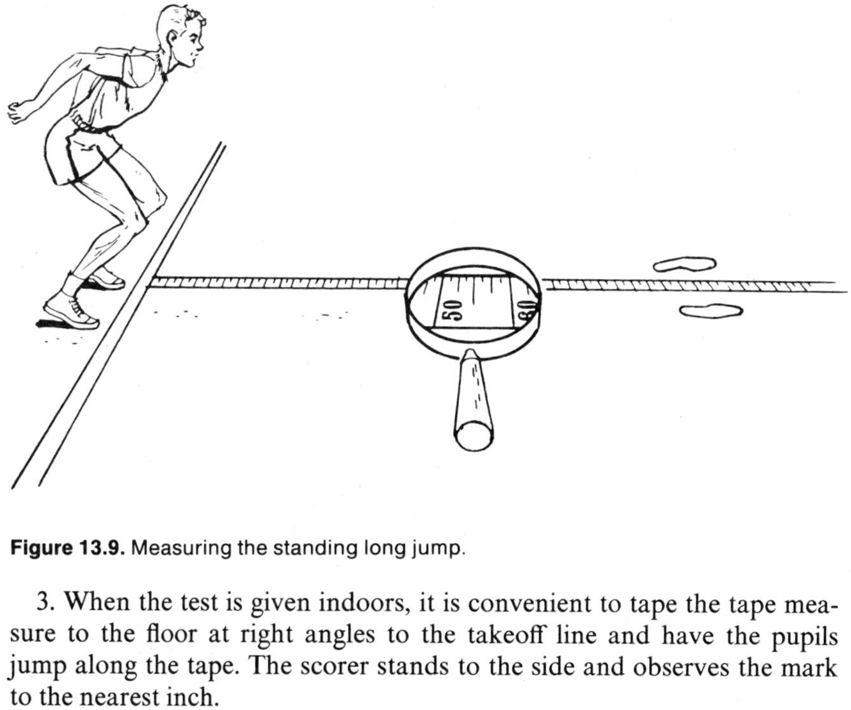

Figure 13.9. Measuring the standing long jump.

3. When the test is given indoors, it is convenient to tape the tape measure to the floor at right angles to the takeoff line and have the pupils jump along the tape. The scorer stands to the side and observes the mark to the nearest inch.

Scoring Record the best of the three trials in feet and inches to the nearest inch.

50-Yard Dash (Boys and Girls)

Materials Two stopwatches or one with a split-second timer.

Procedure It is preferable to administer this test to two pupils at one time. Have both take positions behind the starting line. The starter will use the commands "Are you ready?" and "Go!" The second instruction will be accompanied by a downward sweep of the starter's arm to give a visual signal to the timer, who stands at the finish line (Figure 13.10).

Figure 13.10. Starting the 50-yard dash.

Rules The score is the amount of time between the starter's signal and the instant the pupil crosses the finish line.
Scoring Record time in seconds to the nearest tenth of a second.

600-Yard Run (Boys and Girls)

Materials Track or area marked according to Figures 13.11, 13.12, or 13.13, and a stopwatch.
Procedure Pupil uses a standing start. At the signal "Ready? Go!" the pupil starts running the 600-yard distance. The running may be interspersed with walking. It is possible to have a dozen pupils run at one time by having the pupils pair off before the start of the event. Then each pupil listens for and remembers his partner's time as the pupil crosses the finish. The timer merely calls out the times as the pupils cross the finish line.
Rules Walking is permitted, but the object is to cover the distance in the shortest possible time.
Scoring Record time in minutes and seconds.

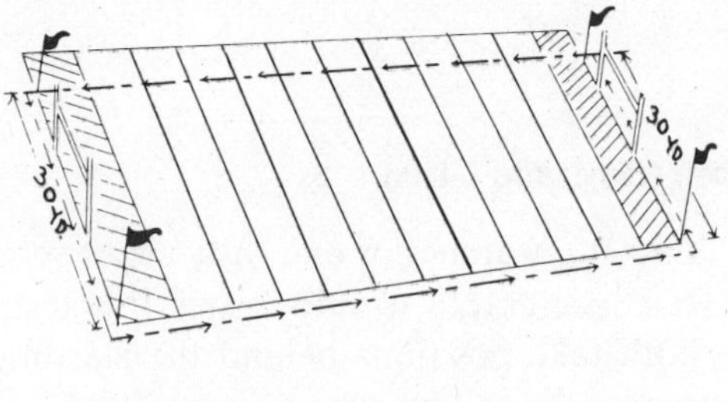

Figure 13.11. Using football field for 600-yard run.

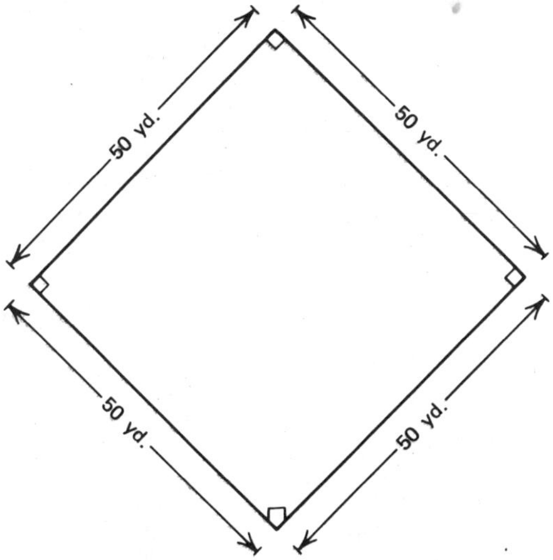

Options:
Ages 10–12, 1–mile or 9–minute run
Ages 13 or older, 1½–mile or 12–minute run

Figure 13.12. Using any open area for 600-yard run.

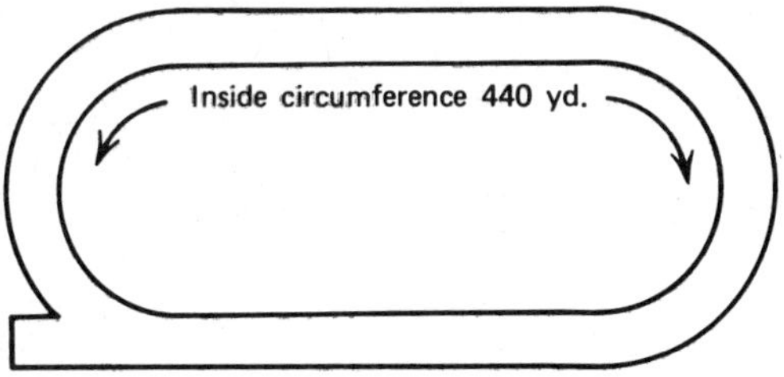

Figure 13.13. Using inside track for 600-yard run.

Table 13.4 Norms: Flexed-Arm Hang for Girls

Percentile Scores Based on Age/Test Scores in Seconds

	Age								
Percentile	*9-10*	*11*	*12*	*13*	*14*	*15*	*16*	*17+*	*Percentile*
100th	78	68	84	68	65	83	69	73	100th
95th	42	39	33	34	35	36	31	34	95th
90th	29	30	27	25	29	28	24	28	90th

85th	24	24	23	21	26	25	20	22	85th
80th	21	21	21	20	23	21	17	19	80th
75th	18	20	18	16	21	18	15	17	75th
70th	16	17	15	14	18	15	12	14	70th
65th	14	15	13	13	15	14	11	12	65th
60th	12	13	12	11	13	12	10	10	60th
55th	10	11	10	9	11	10	8	9	55th
50th	9	10	9	8	9	9	7	8	50th
45th	7	8	8	7	8	8	6	7	45th
40th	6	7	6	6	7	7	5	6	40th
35th	5	6	5	5	5	5	4	5	35th
30th	4	5	4	4	5	4	3	4	30th
25th	3	3	3	3	3	4	3	3	25th
20th	2	3	2	2	3	3	2	2	20th
15th	1	2	1	1	2	2	1	2	15th
10th	0	0	1	0	1	1	1	1	10th
5th	0	0	0	0	0	0	0	0	5th
0	0	0	0	0	0	0	0	0	0

Table 13.5 Norms: (Flexed-Leg Sit-Up for Girls

Percentile Scores Based on Age/Test Scores in Number of Sit-Ups Performed in 60 Seconds

	Age								
Percantile	9-10	11	12	13	14	15	16	17+	*Percentile*
100th	56	60	55	57	52	58	75	66	100th
95th	45	43	44	45	45	45	43	45	95th
90th	40	40	40	41	43	42	40	41	90th
85th	38	38	38	40	41	40	38	40	85th
80th	35	36	37	38	39	38	36	38	80th
75th	34	35	36	36	37	36	35	35	75th
70th	33	33	35	35	35	35	34	34	70th
65th	31	32	33	33	35	34	33	33	65th
60th	30	31	32	32	33	33	32	32	60th
55th	29	30	30	31	32	32	31	31	55th
50th	27	29	29	30	30	31	30	30	50th
45th	25	28	28	29	30	30	28	30	45th

40th	24	26	27	27	29	29	27	28	40th
35th	23	25	26	26	27	28	26	27	35th
30th	22	24	25	25	25	26	25	26	30th
25th	21	22	24	23	24	25	24	25	25th
20th	20	20	22	22	22	23	22	22	20th
15th	17	18	20	20	20	22	20	20	15th
10th	14	15	17	18	18	20	18	18	10th
5th	10	9	13	15	16	15	15	14	5th
0	0	0	0	0	2	2	0	1	0

Table 13.6 Norms: Shuttle Run for Girls
Percentile Scores Based on Age/Test Scores in Seconds and Tenths

	Age								
Percentile	9-10	11	12	13	14	15	16	17+	*Percentile*
100th	8.0	8.4	8.5	7.0	7.8	7.4	7.8	8.2	100th
95th	10.2	10.0	9.9	9.9	9.7	9.9	10.0	9.6	95th
90th	10.5	10.3	10.2	10.0	10.0	10.0	10.2	10.0	90th
8th	10.9	10.5	10.5	10.2	10.1	10.2	10.4	10.1	85th
80th	11.0	10.7	10.6	10.4	10.2	10.3	10.5	10.3	80th
75th	11.1	10.8	10.8	10.5	10.3	10.4	10.6	10.4	75th
70th	11.2	11.0	10.9	10.6	10.5	10.5	10.8	10.5	70th
65th	11.4	11.0	11.0	10.8	10.6	10.6	10.9	10.7	65th
60th	11.5	11.1	11.1	11.0	10.7	10.9	11.0	10.9	60th
55th	11.6	11.3	11.2	11.0	10.9	11.0	11.1	11.0	55th
50th	11.8	11.5	11.4	11.2	11.0	11.0	11.2	11.1	50th
45th	11.9	11.6	11.5	11.3	11.2	11.1	11.4	11.3	45th
40th	12.0	11.7	11.5	11.5	11.4	11.3	11.5	11.5	40th
35th	12.0	11.9	11.7	11.6	11.5	11.4	11.7	11.6	35th
30th	12.3	12.0	11.8	11.9	11.7	11.6	11.9	11.9	30th
25th	12.5	12.1	12.0	12.0	12.0	11.8	12.0	12.0	25th
20th	12.8	12.3	12.1	12.2	12.1	12.0	12.1	12.2	20th
15th	13.0	12.6	12.5	12.6	12.3	12.2	12.5	12.5	15th
10th	13.8	13.0	13.0	12.8	12.8	12.6	12.8	13.0	10th
5th	14.3	14.0	13.3	13.2	13.1	13.3	13.7	14.0	5th
0	18.0	20.0	15.3	16.5	19.2	18.5	24.9	17.0	0

Table 13.7 Norms: Standing Long Jump for Girls
Percentile Scores Based on Age/Test Scores in Feet and Inches

	Age								
Percentile	9-10	11	12	13	14	15	16	17+	*Percentile*
100th	7′11″	7′ 0″	7′ 0″	8′ 0″	7′ 5″	8′ 0″	7′ 7″	7′ 6″	100th
95th	5′10″	6′ 0″	6′ 2″	6′ 5″	6′ 8″	6′ 7″	6′ 6″	6′ 9″	95th
90th	5′ 8″	5′ 9″	6′ 0″	6′ 2″	6′ 5″	6′ 3″	6′ 3″	6′ 6″	90th
85th	5′ 5″	5′ 7″	5′ 9″	6′ 0″	6′ 3″	6′ 1″	6′ 0″	6′ 3″	85th
80th	5′ 2″	5′ 5″	5′ 8″	5′10″	6′ 0″	6′ 0″	5′11″	6′ 2″	80th
75th	5′ 2″	5′ 4″	5′ 6″	5′ 9″	5′11″	5′10″	5′ 9″	6′ 0″	75th
70th	5′ 0″	5′ 3″	5′ 5″	5′ 7″	5′10″	5′ 9″	5′ 8″	5′11″	70th
65th	5′ 0″	5′ 2″	5′ 4″	5′ 6″	5′ 8″	5′ 8″	5′ 6″	5′10″	65th
60th	4′10″	5′ 1″	5′ 2″	5′ 5″	5′ 7″	5′ 6″	5′ 6″	5′ 9″	60th
55th	4′ 9″	5′ 0″	5′ 1″	5′ 4″	5′ 6″	5′ 6″	5′ 4″	5′ 7″	55th
50th	4′ 8″	4′11″	5′ 0″	5′ 3″	5′ 4″	5′ 5″	5′ 3″	5′ 5″	50th
45th	4′ 7″	4′10″	4′11″	5′ 2″	5′ 3″	5′ 3″	5′ 2″	5′ 4″	45th
40th	4′ 6″	4′ 8″	4′10″	5′ 1″	5′ 2″	5′ 2″	5′ 1″	5′ 3″	40th
35th	4′ 5″	4′ 7″	4′ 9″	5′ 0″	5′ 1″	5′ 1″	5′ 0″	5′ 2″	35th
30th	4′ 3″	4′ 6″	4′ 8″	4′10″	4′11″	5′ 0″	4′10″	5′ 0″	30th
25th	4′ 1″	4′ 4″	4′ 6″	4′ 9″	4′10″	4′11″	4′ 9″	4′11″	25th
20th	4′ 0″	4′ 3″	4′ 5″	4′ 8″	4′ 9″	4′ 9″	4′ 7″	4′ 9″	20th
15th	3′11″	4′ 2″	4′ 3″	4′ 6″	4′ 6″	4′ 7″	4′ 6″	4′ 7″	15th
10th	3′ 8″	4′ 0″	4′ 2″	4′ 3″	4′ 4″	4′ 5″	4′ 4″	4′ 4″	10th
5th	3′ 5″	3′ 8″	3′10″	4′ 0″	4′ 0″	4′ 2″	4′ 0″	4′ 1″	5th
0	1′ 8″	2′10″	3′ 0″	3′ 2″	3′ 0″	3′ 0″	2′ 8″	3′ 3″	0

Table 13.8 Norms: 50-Yard Dash for Girls
Percentile Scores Based on Age/Test Scores in Seconds and Tenths

	Age								
Percentile	9-10	11	12	13	14	15	16	17+	*Percentile*
100th	7.0	6.9	6.0	6.0	6.0	6.0	5.6	6.4	100th
95th	7.4	7.3	7.0	6.9	6.8	6.9	7.0	6.8	95th
90th	7.5	7.5	7.2	7.0	7.0	7.0	7.1	7.0	90th
85th	7.8	7.5	7.4	7.2	7.1	7.1	7.3	7.1	85th
80th	8.0	7.8	7.5	7.3	7.2	7.2	7.4	7.3	80th
75th	8.0	7.9	7.6	7.4	7.3	7.4	7.5	7.4	75th

70th	8.1	7.9	7.7	7.5	7.4	7.5	7.5	7.5	70th
65th	8.3	8.0	7.9	7.6	7.5	7.5	7.6	7.5	65th
60th	8.4	8.1	8.0	7.7	7.6	7.6	7.7	7.6	60th
55th	8.5	8.2	8.0	7.9	7.6	7.7	7.8	7.7	55th
50th	8.6	8.3	8.1	8.0	7.8	7.8	7.9	7.9	50th
45th	8.8	8.4	8.2	8.0	7.9	7.9	8.0	8.0	45th
40th	8.9	8.5	8.3	8.1	8.0	8.0	8.0	8.0	40th
35th	9.0	8.6	8.4	8.2	8.0	8.0	8.1	8.1	35th
30th	9.0	8.8	8.5	8.3	8.2	8.1	8.2	8.2	30th
25th	9.1	9.0	8.7	8.5	8.3	8.2	8.3	8.4	25th
20th	9.4	9.1	8.9	8.7	8.5	8.4	8.5	8.5	20th
15th	9.6	9.3	9.1	8.9	8.8	8.6	8.5	8.8	15th
10th	9.9	9.6	9.4	9.2	9.0	8.8	8.8	9.0	10th
5th	10.3	10.0	10.0	10.0	9.6	9.2	9.3	9.5	5th
0	13.5	12.9	14.9	14.2	11.0	15.6	15.6	15.0	0

Table 13.9 Norms: 600-Yard Run for Girls

Percentile Scores Based on Age/Test Scores in Minutes and Seconds

	Age								
Percentile	9-10	11	12	13	14	15	16	17+	*Percentile*
100th	2′ 7″	1′52″	1′40″	1′43″	1′33″	1′41″	1′45″	1′39″	100th
95th	2′20″	2′14″	2′ 6″	2′ 4″	2′ 2″	2′ 0″	2′ 8″	2′ 2″	95th
90th	2′26″	2′21″	2′14″	2′12″	2′ 7″	2′10″	2′15″	2′10″	90th
85th	2′30″	2′25″	2′21″	2′16″	2′11″	2′14″	2′19″	2′14″	85th
80th	2′33″	2′30″	2′23″	2′20″	2′15″	2′18″	2′21″	2′20″	80th
75th	2′39″	2′35″	2′26″	2′23″	2′19″	2′22″	2′26″	2′24″	75th
70th	2′41″	2′39″	2′31″	2′27″	2′24″	2′25″	2′29″	2′26″	70th
65th	2′45″	2′42″	2′35″	2′30″	2′29″	2′28″	2′32″	2′30″	65th
60th	2′43″	2′45″	2′39″	2′34″	2′32″	2′30″	2′36″	2′35″	60th
55th	2′51″	2′48″	2′43″	2′37″	2′36″	2′34″	2′39″	2′38″	55th
50th	2′56″	2′53″	2′47″	2′41″	2′40″	2′37″	2′43″	2′41″	50th
45th	2′59″	2′55″	2′51″	2′45″	2′44″	2′40″	2′47″	2′45″	45th
40th	3′ 1″	2′59″	2′56″	2′49″	2′47″	2′45″	2′49″	2′48″	40th
35th	3′ 8″	3′ 4″	3′ 0″	2′55″	2′51″	2′50″	2′54″	2′53″	35th
30th	3′11″	3′11″	3′ 6″	2′59″	2′56″	2′55″	2′58″	2′56″	30th

25th	3′15″	3′16″	3′13″	3′ 6″	3′ 1″	3′ 0″	3′ 3″	3′ 2″	25th
20th	3′21″	3′24″	3′31″	3′12″	3′ 8″	3′ 5″	3′ 9″	3′ 9″	20th
15th	3′25″	3′30″	3′27″	3′20″	3′16″	3′12″	3′18″	3′19″	15th
10th	3′38″	3′44″	3′36″	3′30″	3′27″	3′26″	3′30″	3′30″	10th
5th	4′ 0″	4′15″	3′59″	3′49″	3′49″	3′28″	3′49″	3′45″	5th
0	5′48″	5′10″	6′ 2″	5′10″	5′ 0″	5′58″	5′ 5″	6′40″	0

Table 13.10 Norms: 9-Minute/1-Mile Run for Girls Ages 10-12

Percentile Scores Based on Age/Test Scores in Yards/Time

	9-Minute Run Girls			*1-Mile Run Girls*			
		Age			*Age*		
	10	*11*	*12*	*10*	*11*	*12*	
Percentile		*Yards*			*Time*		*Percentile*
100th	2157	2180	2203	6:13	5:42	5:08	100th
95th	1969	1992	2015	7:28	6:57	6:23	95th
90th	1867	1890	1913	8:09	7:38	7:04	90th
85th	1801	1824	1847	8:33	8:02	7:28	85th
80th	1746	1769	1792	8:57	8:26	7:52	80th
75th	1702	1725	1748	9:16	8:45	8:11	75th
70th	1658	1681	1704	9:31	9:00	8:26	70th
65th	1622	1645	1668	9:51	9:20	8:46	65th
60th	1583	1606	1629	10:02	9:31	8:57	60th
55th	1550	1573	1596	10:15	9:44	9:10	55th
50th	1514	1537	1560	10:29	9:58	9:24	50th
45th	1478	1501	1524	10:43	10:12	9:38	45th
40th	1445	1468	1491	10:56	10:25	9:51	40th
35th	1406	1429	1452	11:07	10:36	10:12	35th
30th	1370	1393	1416	11:27	10:56	10:22	30th
25th	1326	1349	1372	11:42	11:11	10:37	25th
20th	1282	1305	1328	12:01	11:30	10:56	20th
15th	1227	1250	1273	12:25	11:54	11:30	15th
10th	1161	1184	1207	12:49	12:18	11:44	10th
5th	1059	1082	1105	13:30	12:59	12:24	5th
0	871	894	917	14:45	14:14	:40	0

Source. Texas Physical Fitness-Motor Ability Test.

Table 13.11 Norms: 12-Minute/1.5 Mile Run for Girls, Ages 13 and Over
Percentile Scores Based on Age/Test Scores in Yards/Time

	12-Minute Run	*1.5-Mile Run*	
Percentile	Yards	Time	*Percentile*
100th	2693	10:20	100th
95th	2448	12:17	95th
90th	2318	13:19	90th
85th	2232	14:00	85th
80th	2161	14:34	80th
75th	2100	15:03	75th
70th	2050	14:26	70th
65th	2000	15:50	65th
60th	1950	16:14	60th
55th	1908	16:34	55th
50th	1861	16:57	50th
45th	1815	17:19	45th
50th	1772	17:39	40th
35th	1722	18:03	35th
30th	1672	18:27	30th
25th	1622	18:50	25th
20th	1561	19:19	20th
15th	1490	19:53	15th
10th	1404	20:34	10th
5th	1274	21:36	5th
0	1030	23:33	0

Source. Texas Physical Fitness-Motor Ability Test.

Table 13.12 Norms: Pull-Up for Boys
Percentile Scores Based on Age/Test Scores in Number of Pull-Ups

	Age								
Percentile	*9-10*	*11*	*12*	*13*	*14*	*15*	*16*	*17+*	*Percentile*
100th	19	16	18	17	27	20	26	23	100th
95th	9	8	9	10	12	15	14	15	95th
90th	7	6	7	9	10	12	12	13	90th

85th	5	5	6	7	9	11	11	12	85th
80th	4	5	5	6	8	10	10	11	80th
75th	3	4	4	5	7	9	10	10	75th
70th	3	4	4	5	7	9	9	10	70th
65th	2	3	3	4	6	8	8	9	65th
60th	2	3	3	4	5	7	8	8	60th
55th	1	2	2	3	5	7	7	7	55th
45th	1	1	1	2	4	5	6	6	45th
40th	1	1	1	2	3	5	6	6	40th
35th	1	1	1	2	3	4	5	5	35th
30th	0	1	0	1	2	4	5	5	30th
25th	0	0	0	1	2	3	4	4	25th
20th	0	0	0	0	1	2	3	3	20th
15th	0	0	0	0	1	1	3	2	15th
10th	0	0	0	0	0	1	2	1	10th
5th	0	0	0	0	0	0	1	0	5th
0	0	0	0	0	0	0	0	0	0

Table 13.13 Norms: Flexed-Leg Sit-Up for Boys

Percentile Scores Based on Age/Test Scores in Number of Sit-Ups Performed in 60 Seconds

	Age								
Percentile	9-10	11	12	13	14	15	16	17+	*Percentile*
100th	70	60	62	60	73	72	76	66	100th
95th	47	48	50	53	55	57	55	54	95th
90th	44	45	48	50	52	52	52	51	90th
85th	42	43	45	48	50	50	50	49	85th
80th	40	41	43	47	48	49	49	47	80th
75th	38	40	42	45	47	48	47	46	75th
70th	36	39	40	43	45	46	45	45	70th
65th	36	38	39	42	44	45	44	43	65th
60th	35	37	38	41	43	44	43	42	60th
55th	33	35	37	40	41	43	42	42	55th
50th	31	34	35	38	41	42	41	41	50th
45th	30	33	34	37	40	41	40	40	45th

40th	29	31	33	35	38	40	40	39	40th
35th	28	30	32	34	37	39	38	38	35th
30th	27	28	30	32	35	38	37	37	30th
25th	25	26	30	30	34	37	35	35	25th
20th	23	24	28	29	32	35	34	34	20th
15th	21	22	26	27	21	34	32	32	15th
10th	19	19	23	24	27	30	30	30	10th
5th	13	15	18	20	24	28	28	26	5th
0	2	0	0	2	6	4	12	1	0

Table 13.14 Norms: Shuttle Run for Boys
Percentile Scores Based on Age/Test Scores in Seconds and Tenths

	Age								
Percentile	9-10	11	12	13	14	15	16	17+	*Percentile*
100th	9.2	8.7	6.8	7.0	7.0	7.0	7.3	7.0	100th
95th	10.0	9.7	9.6	9.3	8.9	8.9	8.6	8.6	95th
90th	10.2	9.9	9.8	9.5	9.2	9.1	8.9	8.9	90th
85th	10.4	10.1	10.0	9.7	9.3	9.2	9.1	9.0	85th
80th	10.5	10.2	10.0	9.9	9.5	9.3	9.2	9.1	80th
75th	10.6	10.4	10.2	10.0	9.6	9.4	9.3	9.2	75th
70th	10.7	10.5	10.3	10.0	9.8	9.5	9.4	9.3	70th
65th	10.8	10.5	10.4	10.1	9.8	9.6	9.5	9.4	65th
60th	11.0	10.6	10.5	10.2	10.0	9.7	9.6	9.5	60th
55th	11.0	10.8	10.6	10.3	10.0	9.8	9.7	9.6	55th
50th	11.2	10.9	10.7	10.4	10.1	9.9	9.9	9.8	50th
45th	11.5	11.0	10.8	10.5	10.1	10.0	10.0	9.9	45th
40th	11.5	11.1	11.0	10.6	10.2	10.0	10.0	10.0	40th
35th	11.7	11.2	11.1	10.8	10.4	10.1	10.1	10.1	35th
30th	11.9	11.4	11.3	11.0	10.6	10.2	10.3	10.2	30th
25th	12.0	11.5	11.4	11.	10.7	10.4	10.5	10.4	25th
20th	12.2	11.8	11.6	11.3	10.9	10.5	10.6	10.5	20th
15th	12.5	12.0	11.8	11.5	11.0	10.8	10.9	10.7	15th
10th	13.0	12.2	12.0	11.8	11.3	11.1	11.1	11.0	10th
5th	13.1	12.9	12.4	12.4	11.9	11.7	11.9	11.7	5th
0	17.0	20.0	22.0	16.0	18.6	14.7	15.0	15.7	0

Table 13.15 Norms: Standing Long Jump for Boys
Percentile Scores Based on Age/Test Scores in Feet and Inches

	Age								
Percentile	9-10	11	12	13	14	15	16	17+	*Percentile*
100th	6′ 5″	8′ 5″	7′ 5″	8′ 6″	9′ 0″	9′ 0″	9′ 2″	9′10″	100th
95th	6′ 0″	6′ 2″	6′ 6″	7′ 1″	7′ 6″	8′ 0″	8′ 2″	8′ 5″	95th
90th	5′10″	6′ 0″	6′ 3″	6′10″	7′ 2″	7′ 7″	7′11″	8′ 2″	90th
85th	5′ 8″	5′10″	6′ 1″	6′ 8″	6′11″	7′ 5″	7′ 9″	8′ 0″	85th
80th	5′ 6″	5′ 9″	6′ 0″	6′ 5″	6′10″	7′ 3″	7′ 6″	7′10″	80th
75th	5′ 4″	5′ 7″	5′11″	6′ 3″	6′ 8″	7′ 2″	7′ 6″	7′ 9″	75th
70th	5′ 3″	5′ 6″	5′ 9″	6′ 2″	6′ 6″	7′ 0″	7′ 4″	7′ 7″	70th
65th	5′ 1″	5′ 6″	5′ 8″	6′ 0″	6′ 6″	6′11″	7′ 3″	7′ 6″	65th
60th	5′ 1″	5′ 5″	5′ 7″	6′ 0″	6′ 4″	6′10″	7′ 2″	7′ 5″	60th
55th	5′ 0″	5′ 4″	5′ 6″	5′10″	6′ 3″	6′ 9″	7′ 1″	7′ 3″	55th
50th	4′11″	5′ 2″	5′ 5″	5′ 9″	6′ 2″	6′ 8″	7′ 0″	7′ 2″	50th
45th	4′10″	5′ 2″	5′ 4″	5′ 7″	6′ 1″	6′ 6″	6′11″	7′ 1″	45th
40th	4′ 9″	5′ 0″	5′ 3″	5′ 6″	5′11″	6′ 5″	6′ 9″	7′ 0″	40th
35th	4′ 8″	4′11″	5′ 2″	5′ 5″	5′10″	6′ 4″	6′ 8″	6′10″	35th
30th	4′ 7″	4′10″	5′ 1″	5′ 3″	5′ 8″	6′ 3″	6′ 7″	6′ 8″	30th
25th	4′ 6″	4′ 8″	5′ 0″	5′ 2″	5′ 6″	6′ 1″	6′ 6″	6′ 6″	25th
20th	4′ 5″	4′ 7″	4′10″	5′ 0″	5′ 4″	5′11″	6′ 4″	6′ 4″	20th
15th	4′ 2″	4′ 5″	4′ 9″	4′10″	5′ 2″	5′ 9″	6′ 2″	6′ 2″	15th
10th	4′ 0″	4′ 3″	4′ 6″	4′ 7″	5′ 0″	5′ 6″	5′11″	5′10″	10th
5th	3′10″	4′ 0″	4′ 2″	4′ 4″	4′ 8″	5′ 2″	5 5″	5′ 3″	5th
0	3′ 1″	3′ 0″	3′ 2″	3′ 3″	2′ 0″	2′ 0″	3′ 4″	3′ 0″	0

Table 13.16 Norms: 50-Yard Dash for Boys
Percentile Scores Based on Age/Test Scores in Seconds and Tenths

	Age								
Percentile	9-10	11	12	13	14	15	16	17+	*Percentile*
100th	7.0	6.3	6.3	5.8	5.9	5.5	5.5	5.4	100th
95th	7.3	7.1	6.8	6.5	6.2	6.0	6.0	5.9	95th
90th	7.5	7.2	7.0	6.7	6.4	6.2	6.2	6.0	90th
85th	7.7	7.4	7.1	6.9	6.5	6.3	6.3	6.1	85th
80th	7.8	7.5	7.3	7.0	6.6	6.4	6.4	6.3	80th
75th	7.8	7.6	7.4	7.0	6.8	6.5	6.5	6.3	75th
705h	7.9	7.7	7.5	7.1	6.9	6.6	6.5	6.4	70th
65th	8.0	7.9	7.5	7.2	7.0	6.6	6.6	6.5	65th
60th	8.0	7.9	7.6	7.3	7.0	6.8	6.6	6.5	60th

55th	8.1	8.0	7.7	7.4	7.1	6.8	6.7	6.6	55th
50th	8.2	8.0	7.8	7.5	7.2	6.9	6.7	6.6	50th
45th	8.4	8.2	7.9	7.5	7.3	6.9	6.8	6.7	45th
40th	8.6	8.3	8.0	7.6	7.4	7.0	6.8	6.8	40th
35th	8.7	8.4	8.1	7.7	7.5	7.1	6.9	6.9	35th
30th	8.8	8.5	8.2	7.9	7.6	7.2	7.0	7.0	30th
25th	8.9	8.6	8.3	8.0	7.7	7.3	7.0	7.0	25th
20th	9.0	8.7	8.5	8.1	7.9	7.4	7.1	7.1	20th
15th	9.2	9.0	8.6	8.3	8.0	7.5	7.2	7.3	15th
10th	9.5	9.1	9.0	8.7	8.2	7.6	7.4	7.5	10th
5th	9.9	9.5	9.5	9.0	8.8	8.0	7.7	7.9	5th
0	11.0	11.5	11.3	15.0	11.1	11.0	9.9	12.0	0

Table 13.17 Norms: 600-Yard Run for Boys

Percentile Scores Based on Age/Test Scores in Minutes and Seconds

	Age								
Percentile	*9-10*	*11*	*12*	*13*	*14*	*15*	*16*	*17+*	*Percentile*
100th	1′52″	1′47″	1′38″	1′26″	1′27″	1′20″	1′21″	1′20″	100th
95th	2′ 5″	2′ 2″	1′52″	1′45″	1′39″	1′36″	1′34″	1′32″	95th
90th	2′ 9″	2′ 6″	1′57″	1′50″	1′44″	1′40″	1′38″	1′35″	90th
85th	2′11″	2′ 9″	2′ 0″	1′54″	1′47″	1′42″	1′40″	1′38″	85th
80th	2′15″	2′12″	2′ 4″	1′57″	1′50″	1′45″	1′42″	1′41″	80th
75th	2′17″	2′15″	2′ 6″	1′59″	1′52″	1′46″	1′44″	1′43″	75th
70th	2′20″	2′17″	2′ 9″	2′ 1″	1′55″	1′48″	1′46″	1′45″	70th
65th	2′27″	2′19″	2′11″	2′ 3″	1′57″	1′50″	1′48″	1′47″	65th
60th	2′30″	2′22″	2′14″	2′ 5″	1′58″	1′52″	1′49″	1′49″	60th
55th	2′31″	2′25″	2′16″	2′ 7″	2′ 0″	1′54″	1′50″	1′50″	55th
50th	2′33″	2′27″	2′19″	2′10″	2′ 3″	1′56″	1′52″	1′52″	50th
45th	2′35″	2′30″	2′22″	2′13″	2′ 5″	1′57″	1′54″	1′53″	45th
50th	2′40	2′34″	2′24″	2′15″	2′ 7″	1′59″	1′56″	1′56″	40th
35th	2′42″	2′37″	2′28″	2′20″	2′10″	2′ 1″	1′58″	1′57″	35th
30th	2′49″	2′41″	2′32″	2′24″	2′12″	2′ 5″	1′59″	1′59″	30th
25th	2′53″	2′47″	2′37″	2′27″	2′16″	2′ 8″	2′ 1	2′ 2″	25th
20th	2′59″	2′54″	2′42″	2′32″	2′22″	2′11″	2′ 4″	2′ 6″	20th
15th	3′ 7″	3′ 2″	2′48″	2′37″	2′30″	2′15	2′ 9″	2′12″	15th
10th	3′14″	3′14″	2′54″	2′45″	2′37″	2′23″	2′17″	2′22″	10th
5th	3′22″	3′29″	3′ 6″	3′ 0″	2′51″	2′30″	2′31″	2′38″	5th
0	4′48″	6′20″	4′10″	4′ 0″	6′ 0″	4′39″	4′11″	5′10″	0

Table 13.18 Norms: 9-Minute/1-Mile Run for Boys
Percentile Scores Baseed on Age/Test Scores in Yards/Time

	9-Minute Run Boys			*1-Mile Run Boys*			
	Age			*Age*			
	10	*11*	*12*	*10*	*11*	*12*	
Percentile	Yards			Time			*Percentile*
100th	2532	2535	2578	5:07	4:44	4:21	100th
95th	2294	2356	2418	5:55	5:32	5:09	95th
90th	2166	2228	2290	6:38	6:15	5:52	90th
85th	2081	2143	2205	7:06	6:43	6:20	85th
80th	2011	2073	2135	7:29	7:03	6:40	80th
75th	1952	2014	2076	7:49	7:26	7:03	75th
70th	1902	1964	2026	8:05	7:42	7:19	70th
65th	1853	1915	1977	8:22	7:59	7:36	65th
60th	1804	1866	1928	8:38	8:15	7:52	60th
55th	1762	1824	1886	8:52	8:29	8:06	55th
50th	1717	1779	1841	9:07	8:44	8:21	50th
45th	1672	1734	1796	9:22	8:59	8:36	45th
40th	1630	1692	1754	9:32	9:13	8:50	40th
35th	1581	1643	1705	9:52	9:29	9:06	35th
30th	1532	1594	1656	10:09	9:46	9:23	30th
25th	1482	1544	1606	10:25	10:02	9:39	25th
20th	1423	1485	1547	10:35	10:22	9:59	20th
15th	1353	1415	1477	11:08	10:45	10:22	15th
10th	1268	1330	1392	11:36	11:13	10:50	10th
5th	1140	1202	1264	12:19	11:56	11:33	5th
0	901	924	927	14:07	13:44	13:21	0

Source. Texas Physical Fitness-Motor Ability Test.

Table 13.19 Norms: 12-Minute/1.5-Mile Run for Boys, Age 13 and Older
Percentile Scores Based on Age/Test Scores in Yards/Time

	12-Minute Run	*1.5-Mile Run*	
Percentile	Yards	Time	*Percentile*
100th	3590	7:26	100th
90th	3297	8:37	95th
91th	3140	9:15	90th

85th	3037	9:40	85th
80th	2952	10:01	80th
75th	2879	10:19	75th
70th	2819	10:34	70th
65th	2759	10:48	65th
60th	2699	11:02	60th
55th	2648	11:15	55th
50th	2592	11:29	50th
45th	2536	11:42	45th
40th	2485	11:55	40th
35th	2425	12:10	35th
30th	2365	12:24	30th
25th	2305	12:39	25th
20th	2232	12:56	20th
15th	2147	13:17	15th
10th	2044	13:42	10th
5th	1888	14:20	5th
0	1594	15:32	0

Source. Texas Physical Fitness-Motor Ability Test.

There are many other examples of physical fitness test currently in use. Mny of them measure motor fitness rather than physical fitness per se. Examples of such tests are the Texas Physical Fitness-Motor Ability Test, the Fleishman Physical Fitness Battery, the JCR Test, the Oregon Motor Fitness Test, the Kirchner Physical Fitness Test for Elementary School Children, and the California Physical Performance Tests. Table 13.20 lists the items included in several of these batteries.

Information about these and other tests designed to measure physical and motor fitness can be found in Baumgartner and Jackson (1975), Fleishman (1969), Hockey (1977), Johnson and Nelson (1979), Johnson et al. (1975), and Safrit (1973).

Table 13.20 Motor Fitness Test Batteries

JCR Test (Phillips)
1. Vertical jump (J)
2. Chins (C)
3. Shuttle run (R)

Kirchner Physical Fitness Test (Ages 6-12)
1. Standing long jump
2. Bench push-up
3. Curl-ups (bent-knee sit-up)
4. Squat jump
5. 30-yard dash

Fleishman's Basic Fitness Battery (Fleishman)
1. Twist and touch
2. Bend, twist, and touch
3. Softball throw for distance
4. Shuttle run
5. Grip strength
6. Pull-ups
7. Leg lift
8. Cable-jump test
9. Balance
10. 600-yard run-walk

Oregon Motor Fitness Test

(Boys, grades 4-6)
1. Standing long jump
2. Floor push-ups
3. Sit-ups

(Boys, grades 7-12)
1. Pull-ups
2. Vertical jump
3. 160-yard agility race

(Girls, grades 4-12)
1. Standing long jump
2. Flexed-arm hang
3. Cross-arm curl-ups (sit-up)

California Physical Performance Tests (Ages 10-18)
1. Standing long jump
2. Pull-up (boys), modified push-ups (girls)
3. Bent-knee sit-up
4. 50-yard dash
5. Softball throw for distance

NSWA (NAGWS) Physpical Performance Test
1. Standing long jump
2. Basketball throw for distance
3. Potato race
4. Sit-ups
5. Modified push-up
6. Modified pull-ups
7. Squat thrusts, 10 seconds, 30 seconds

Summary

Multiple performance traits include physical fitness, motor fitness, and motor ability. Physical fitness includes the basic performance traits of muscular strength, muscular endurance, cardiorespiratory endurance, and flexibility.

Motor fitness comprises the four basic performance traits plus speed, power, agility, and balance.

Motor ability, the most general of the three terms, includes all of the traits of motor and physical fitness plus coordination.

Many test batteries have been developed to measure the multiple performance traits. Tests of physical fitness and motor fitness have maintained their popularity. A good example of a motor fitness test, popularly thought of as a test of physical fitness, is the AAHPER Youth Fitness Test. General motor ability, once a dominant concept in physical education measurement, has been negated by several studies and, therefore, general motor ability test batteries have lost much of their popularity.

Study Questions

1. Which basic performance traits are included in physical fitness? Motor fitness? Motor ability?
2. Locate a test battery measuring multiple performance traits. Does it measure physical fitness? Motor fitness? Motor Ability?
3. Compose a test battery that measures physical fitness. Motor fitness. General motor ability.
4. Why has the term general motor ability lost its popularity?

CHAPTER 14

The Domains of Behavior

After you have read and studied this chapter you should be able to:

1. *Summarize the uses of measurement of cognitive, affective, and psychomotor abilities and skills.*
2. *Locate and use published tests (Appendix A) as a resource for developing teacher-made tests in each domain of behavior.*
3. *Identify and critique the most common ways utilized to measure psychomotor skill.*

The domains of behavior have been discussed in detail in Chapter 6. However, measurement in the *cognitive domain* (knowledge tests), *affective domain* (attitudes and interests), and the *psychomotor domain* (sport and dance skills) is crucial to the total evaluation process. Therefore, a discussion of measurement in each area is included in this chapter.

COGNITIVE DOMAIN

The cognitive domain primarily includes recall or recognition of information and the development of intellectual abilities and skills. Tests of the cognitive domain are vitally important in physical education. The knowledge or interpretive-cortical objective has always been considered one of the major objectives of physical education. Even though much of the content in physical education is activity-oriented, the acquisition of knowledge serves as a base for successful performance in the gymnasium or on the athletic field. Understanding why certain warm-up methods, strategies, techniques, conditioning methods, and skills are beneficial often motivates students to utilize them.

Teacher-made cognitive tests may be either objective or subjective. The various types of test items used in such a test were discussed in Chapter 7. The test must relate specifically to the objectives of the instruction, and is a basis for evaluation and additional instruction.

Many knowledge tests in physical education have measured only recall of knowledge. This can be seen from an examination of the major levels of Bloom's *Taxonomy of Educational Objectives* (1956).

The major levels of the domain are:

1.00 Knowledge
2.00 Comprehension
3.00 Application
4.00 Analysis
5.00 Synthesis
6.00 Evaluation

It is quite apparent that course objectives include most of the major levels of the domain. However, published tests have failed to measure intellectual abilities and skills of the domain's higher levels. Consequently, standardized tests of cognitive ability in physical education are often not directly applicable to the local situation. Such tests often do not include questions that represent the behavioral objectives for the specific class and therefore are better used as guides for developing teacher-made tests. The use of a detailed set of behavioral objectives for each course gives the teacher much insight into the numbers of questions needed for each level of the domain. Also, since many classes in physical education are offered on different levels (i.e., beginning, intermediate, advanced), the use of behavioral objectives allows teacher-made test items to be commensurate with the level of the class.

Once a cognitive test is constructed by a teacher, the specific items can also be analyzed for their difficulty and for their ability to discriminate among students — some who know the material and some who do not. This process, called item analysis, should be conducted whenever a test is used for the first time and was discussed in Chapter 7. The validity and reliability of the test should also be evaluated by using procedures discussed in Chapter 5.

Tests of cognitive abilities and skills can be used for a variety of reasons. First, such tests can evaluate student achievement during and after instruction. The test results can help determine grades at the end of a teaching unit. Cognitive tests can also be used as motivational devices to stimulate learning. In research, these tests have helped to determine which of several methods of instruction is the most effective. They also serve, if given at the beginning of a teaching unit, to determine what information should be taught during that unit. For example, if the majority of students know basic rules, strategies, and the like, more time can be spent on advanced techniques and strategies of the particular activity.

There are numerous published tests of cognitive abilities and skills in physical education. Because of the many cognitive areas that may be tested, no specific example of a test will be given. Instead, a comprehensive bibliography of cognitive tests presented alphabetically according to activities is included in Appendix A. In addition, several publishers have printed knowledge tests for a wide variety of physical activities. Two firms who print knowledge tests in conjunction with physical activity texts are Wadsworth Publishing Company, Belmont, California, and the William C. Brown Company, Dubuque, Iowa.

AFFECTIVE DOMAIN

Physical educators have always attempted to develop students physically, mentally, socially, and emotionally through physical activities. Thus, general objectives of physical education have included social efficiency or emotional-impulsive development. Most of the components of these objectives are included in what is called the affective domain. The taxonomy of the affective domain developed by Krathwohl and others in 1964 provides a continuum for understanding such affective terms as interests, appreciations, attitudes, values, and adjustments. Chapter 6 discussed the affective domain in detail and indicated ways of developing behavioral objectives and evaluation instruments for affective behavior.

Emphasis on measuring affective domain components in physical education began in the 1920s and 1930s although even now, relatively few measuring instruments are available.

Self-report instruments measuring attitude generally include statements to which the student expresses favorable or unfavorable feelings toward some activity, person, or idea. Alternatives for response range from two choices (agree-disagree) to several choices (strongly agree-agree-undecided-disagree-strongly disagree) with some scales utilizing as many as 11 alternatives.

These scales are useful primarily when the student has little reason for distorting the results because they reflect only what an individual is willing to relate about his or her attitude.

If the instructor desires to evaluate attitudes of students, the best procedure is to use direct observation methods in which evidence is gathered through anecdotal records, rating scales, and checklists.

In addition to attitude, the other major category of the affective domain includes such aspects as character, self-concept, leadership, ethics, values, interests, and adjustments. Various instruments have been developed to measure each of these attributes. Several sociopsychological instruments not intended for use specifically in physical education have been applied — the Tennessee Self-Concept Scale and the Semantic Differential Scale, for example. Information about these and all standardized instruments measuring affective behavior can be found in the *Mental Measurements Yearbooks*. A discussion about locating such tests was found in Chapter 10.

Notice that a standardized instrument of the affective domain rarely represents the affective behavioral objectives of a particular class. Such instruments, however, provide good resources for developing instruments that do measure achievement of specific behavioral objectives.

Attitude scales and other instruments measuring the affective domain can be utilized for several reasons. Most important is that results of such measurement serve as a basis for evaluating whether the affective behavioral objectives of specific instruction have been attained. A second related use is to determine the effectiveness of the teaching methods used during instruction. Other specific uses include evaluating such attributes as leadership, self-concept, adjustment, and character.

Because of the many affective areas in which instruments have been developed and also because very few of these instruments relate specifically to behavioral objectives of a particular class, no examples of affective tests will be given. However, a bibliography of sources containing such instruments is presented in Appendix A for resource information.

PSYCHOMOTOR DOMAIN

One of the general objectives of physical education is the development of neuromuscular skills. Indeed, the major goal of many physical education programs is to develop various psychomotor skills in students. In Chapter 6, Jewett's taxonomy of the motor domain was given; the model of this domain includes a taxonomic presentation of movement and skill. Harrow's model of the psychomotor domain, *A Taxonomy of the Psychomotor Domain* (1972), includes fundamental movements and abilities and such traits as endurance, strength, flexibility, and agility as well as a taxonomic classification of skill. This discussion considers the psychomotor domain similar to Jewett's presentation or the upper levels of Harrow's taxonomy. In other words, the psychomotor domain in physical education includes the functional performance of sport and dance skills. Because development of neuromuscular skill is such an important part of most physical education programs, it is important that valid and reliable tests measure these skills.

Tests should be selected or developed that measure achievement in psychomotor skills as identified by behavioral objectives. There have been many published tests in numerous sport and dance activities. In addition to such skill tests, rating scales and evaluation of actual performance can serve as criteria for assessing psychomotor skills.

Skill tests, whether selected or developed, must be administered in an environment as similar to the actual game or activity environment as possible. Some skill tests do not test practical skill. That is, they measure one certain aspect of the skill and not the ability to perform in a competitive situation using the skill. This has caused some physical educators to de-emphasize the use of skill tests. Particular attention should be given to the validity and reliability of published skill tests.

There are numerous uses of tests of psychomotor skills. The test's most important function is to assess the achievement of the psychomotor behavioral objectives of a prescribed unit of instruction. The results of these tests can be used, with other methods of evaluation, to determine grades. In addition, such tests can help evaluate the use of certain instructional methods. Tests of skill can be used in both formative (progress) and summative (achievement) evaluation. Such tests can also be used as motivational devices, for placement, diagnosis, and prediction.

Skills can be evaluated in several ways including: (1) accuracy measures, (2) timed measures, (3) distance measures, and (4) combinations thereof performed in either simulated conditions or game performance situations as identified in Chapter 7.

This classification is useful especially for the several new sport activities such as team handball that are being implemented into physical education programs. If a skill test is desired, the category can be consulted and a new skill test adapted for a specific use.

Accuracy Measures

Tests that measure accuracy of performance are frequently used by physical educators. Common examples of sports skills in which accuracy is a major component are the free throw in basketball, the penalty kick in soccer, and the pitched ball in baseball or softball. A target of some sort is usually used as the criterion. An example of an accuracy test is the French Short Serve Test.

French Short Serve Test (1943)

Measurement Objective To measure the ability to place accurately the low, short serve in badminton.

Test Qualities Validity coefficients range from .41 to .66 using tournament results as a criterion. Reliability is .51 to .96.

Test Application Male and female, junior high through college.

Equipment and Materials Doubles badminton court, shuttlecocks, racket, clothesline attached to standards 20 inches above net, and floor markings drawn as arcs at distances of 22, 30, 38, and 46 inches from the midpoint of the intersection of the center line and the short service line of the right service court. The arcs should be drawn 1½ inches wide (Figure 14.1).

Procedure Performer takes a comfortable position within the right service court and serves 20 shuttles diagonally to the opposite service court. Trials should be taken in groups of 5, 10, or 20. The performer attempts to serve the shuttles between the net and the rope into the areas of highest numerical value.

Scoring Zones are given numerical values of 5, 4, 3, 2, and 1 as shown in Figure 14.1. Each serve is scored according to the numerical value of the zone in which it first lands. Shuttles that land on a line are given the higher score value. Scorer should stand near the target but out of the way of the shuttles. Serves that do not pass between the rope and the net or that land out of play short or to the side of the right doubles service court score 0. Test score is total numerical score for 20 serves.

Norms Available in Scott and French (1959), Barrow and McGee (1971).

Tests that utilize accuracy as the sole criterion generally do not give the physical educator much insight into the causes of specific performance. For instance, identical accuracy scores on the French Short Serve Test could be at-

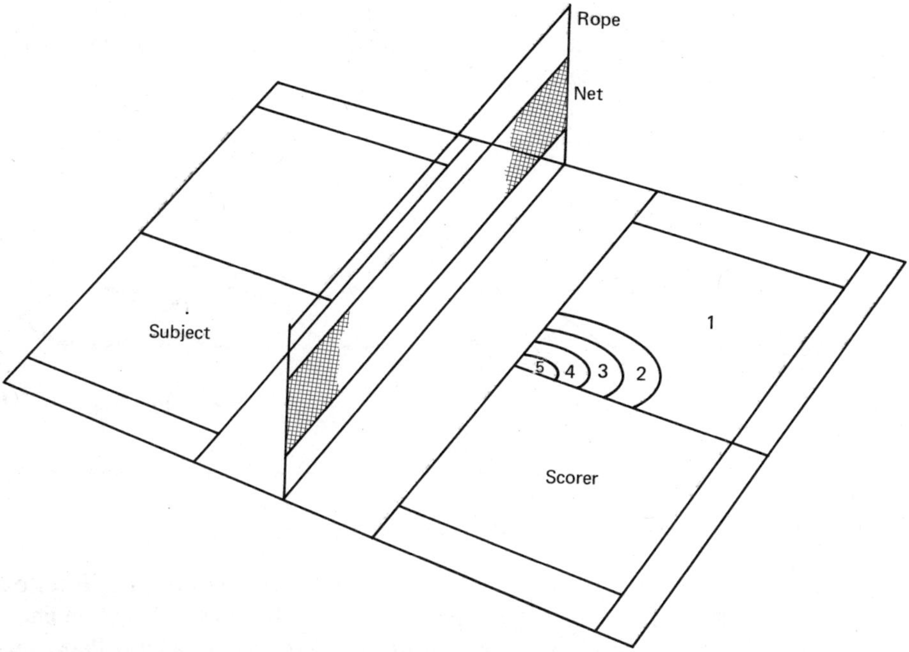

Figure 14.1. Specifications for French Short Serve Test.

tained by performers who serve at different trajectories and speeds. A more intricate target system such as one developed by Hale (1970) for badminton can increase the diagnostic capabilities of accuracy tests. A second alternative explained in Chapter 5 is to increase the reliability of the test by adding trials.

Timed Measures

Tests that utilize time elapsed as the criterion to evaluate the performance of a skill or the repetition of the same skill for a specified time are commonplace in physical education. The stopwatch or other timing device is often used to measure timed events such as track and swimming activities. It is also appropriate to use timed measures in sports in which the projectile remains on the playing surface such as floor hockey, ice hockey, and bowling. An example of a test item in which time is the sole criterion is the AAHPER Football Skills Test item — Ball Changing Zigzag Run.

AAPHER Football Skills Test — Ball Changing Zigzag Run (1965)

Measurement Objective To measure speed with which performer can run around obstacles while continuously changing football to outside arm.
Test Qualities Validity is .72. Reliability ranges from .84 to .93.

Test Application Males, junior high through college.
Equipment and Materials Five chairs each placed 10 feet apart, facing away from starting line (Figure 14.2) with first chair 10 feet from starting line; stopwatch, football.

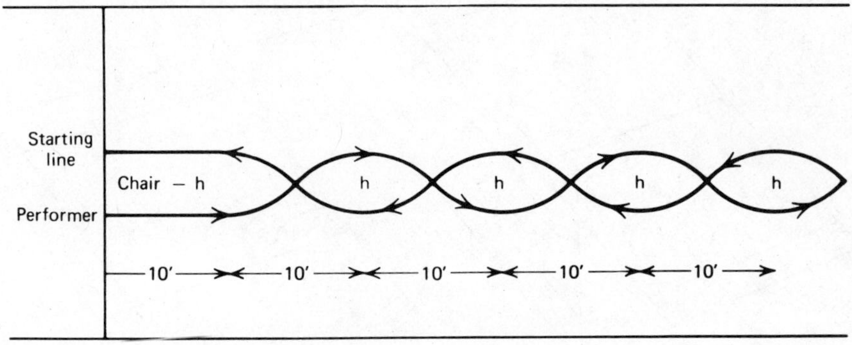

Figure 14.2. Diagram for Ball-Changing Zigzag Run Test (Football).

Procedure Performer holds football under right arm and starts from behind starting line at the signal "go." He runs to the right of the first chair, then changes ball to left arm as he runs to left of second chair. Performer continues zigzag pattern, changing position of ball to outside arm as he passes each chair. The inside arm should be extended as in stiff-arming. He circles around the end chair and continues the zigzag pattern back to the starting line. Performer is not allowed to hit the chairs.
Scoring Score is the elapsed time from the signal "go" until performer passes back over starting line. Test score is the better of two trials recorded to the nearest tenth of a second.
Norms Norms are available from the AAPHER for boys ages 10 to 18 and are also available in Johnson and Nelson (1979).

An example of a repetitive skill that is timed is the Racquetball Rally Test.

Racquetball Rally Test

Measurement Objectives To measure ability to hit and control a racquetball.
Test Qualities Validity is .81 when tournament results are used as criterion. Reliability is .91 with test-retest method.

Test Application Male and female, junior high through college.
Equipment and Facilities Racquetball racquet, official racquetballs, a watch, and a racquetball court or wall and floor with appropriate markings.
Procedure Performer begins test by taking a position anywhere behind the short line (20 feet from front wall). At the signal "go," the performer drops the ball to the floor and hits it continuously to the front wall for 30 seconds using any stroke. The ball may be hit on the volley or after it has bounced once or more, but the performer must remain behind the short line for a legal hit. If the ball does not return, the performer can advance to retrieve it, but must return behind the short line to hit the ball. If the ball goes out of control, another ball is handed to the performer by a partner. The test administrator gives the signal "stop" when 30 seconds have elapsed.
Scoring One point is scored for each time the ball contacts the front wall as a result of a legal stroke. Score is counted and verified by test administrator; it is the number of times ball legally hits front wall in 30 seconds for each of 3 trials. No points are given for balls that are hit from in front of the short line or otherwise are illegally hit. Test score is best of three trials although the average of the three trials can also effectively be used.
Norms Norms are not available.

Objectives have been raised regarding the validity of tests that require repeated executions of the same skill. First, in wall-volley tests the performer must receive his or her own volley. In the game of racquetball, for instance, the players never hit their own shots, which have rebounded from the front wall. Wall-volley tests, then, inject elements that are often atypical of actual game performance. A second objection is related. Faults other than how the ball is actually stroked may be responsible for poor scores. Also, a test in which speed is the major criterion often causes performers to disregard accuracy. Both speed and accuracy are important factors of skills. Physical educators should attempt to select or develop skill tests that use both factors as criteria for evaluating performance.

Distance Measures

Some of the more common kinds of skill tests used by physical educators measure the ability to throw, kick, or strike an object or to propel the body by jumping.

Several examples have been given in the previous chapter. Among these are:

Baseball Throw for Distance	Cozens General Athletic Ability Test
Softball Throw for Distance	California Physical Performance Test
	Fleishmans Basic Fitness Battery
	Barrow Motor Ability Test
Standing Long Jump	Barrow Motor Ability Test
	AAHPER Youth Fitness Test
	Scott Motor Ability Test
	Newton Motor Ability Test
	California Physical Performance Tests
Six Pound Medicine Ball Put	Barrow Motor Ability Test
Vertical Jump	Larson Motor Ability Test
	JCR Test
Basketball Throw for Distance	NSWA (NAGWS) Physical Performance Test

Other obvious examples can be given for ballistic sport activities. The football pass for distance, the soccer instep kick for distance, and the fungo hit in baseball all exemplify this category of tests. Usually such tests are reliable since the distance a projectile travels can be objectively measured. However, the speed at which a projectile is thrown, hit, or struck is sometimes used as a criterion.

Combinations

Velocity or speed reflects amount of force applied and is calculated by dividing distance by time and recorded in feet per second or miles per hour.

For example the speed of a pitched baseball can be calculated by dividing the distance traveled (approximately 60 feet 6 inches) by the time it takes for the ball to reach the catcher's glove (about 0.5 seconds).

Therefore the velocity of the ball is 60.5 feet/0.5 second or 121 feet per second.

Since 15 miles per hour = 22 feet per second, the baseball travels 82.5 mph. Generally, if velocity is calculated, there is also interest in accuracy of performance. A major league baseball pitcher usually must be fast and accurate to be successful. For optimum evaluation of skill in throwing, kicking, or stroking objects, measures of velocity and accuracy are required.

Velocity can be estimated by several other methods. Safrit (1973) identifies three ways of measuring velocity. Two additional methods involve the use of photocells to calculate time required for a projectile to travel a prescribed distance and the use of a Juggs radar gun to determine the approximate speed of a projectile.

Because there are so many sport and dance activities in which skill tests have been published and because most psychomoter skills can be measured in the ways mentioned in this discussion, examples of tests for each activity will not be given. However, as with the cognitive and affective domains, a comprehensive bibliography of sources is included in Appendix A.

Summary

Measurement in the cognitive, affective, and psychomotor domains is crucial in the total evaluation process. Tests in each domain have been used in formative and summative evaluation of student progress, in determination of grades, as motivation, for research, preassessment, and evaluation of teaching methods.

Tests in the psychomotor domain generally can be categorized into accuracy measures, timed measures, distance measures, and combinations thereof. Cognitive tests can be generally categorized as objective and subjective while most affective measures are self-report rating scales.

Published tests in the cognitive and psychomotor domains are quite common. A comprehensive bibliography of tests in each domain is included in Appendix A. This compilation can be used to locate published tests and they can be used directly or as guidelines for development of teacher-made tests.

Study Questions

1. What are the most common uses of cognitive tests? Affective tests? Psychomotor tests?
2. Develop a measuring instrument in one of the domains of behavior using a published test as a guide.
3. Psychomotor skill can be assessed in several categories of measurements. Which four categories contain the majority of skill tests? Give an example of a test in each category.
4. Cognitive, psychomotor, and affective measures have been criticized but for different reasons. Identify and compare criticisms of tests of each domain.

Selected References

AAHPER Skill Test Manuals, American Alliance for Health, Physical Education, and Recreation, Washington D.C., 1966, 1967, 1969.

AAHPER, Skills Test Manual: Football, American Association for Health, Physical Education, Recreation, Washington, D.C., 1965.

AAHPER Youth Fitness Test Manual, Revised 1976 Edition, American Alliance for Health, Physical Education, and Recreation, Washington, D.C., 1976.

Alexander, Howard W., "The Estimation of Reliability When Several Trials are Available," *Psychometrika, 12:* 79-99, June, 1947.

American Educational Research Association, *Technical Recommendations for Achievement Tests*, AERA, Washington, D.C., 1955, p. 16.

Ammons, Robert, "Effects of Knowledge of Performance: A Survey and a Tentative Theoretical Formulation," *Journal of General Psychology, 54:* 279-299, 1956.

Anastasi, A., "The Concept of Validity in The Interpretation of Test Scores," *Educational and Psychological Measurement, 10:* 67-78, 1950.

Anmerman, H. L., and W. H. Melching, *The Derivation, Analysis and Classification of Instructional Objectives*, George Washington University, Alexandria, VA., 1966.

Baker, Eva L., and W. James Popham, *Expanding Dimensions of Instructional Objectives*, Prentice-Hall, Inc., Englewood Clifs, N.J., 1973.

Barrow, Harold M. and Rosemary McGee, *A Practical Approach to Measurement in Physical Education*, Second Edition, Lea and Febiger, Philadelphia, 1971.

Bass, Ruth I., "An Analysis of the Components of Tests of Semi-circular Canal Function and of Static and Dynamic Balance," *Research Quarterly, 10:* 33-52, May, 1939.

Baumgartner, Ted. A., "The Applicability of the Spearman-Brown Prophecy Formula When Applied to Physical Performance Tests," *Research Quarterly, 39:* 847-856, December, 1968.

Baumgartner, Ted, A., "Estimating Reliability When All Test Trials are Administered on the Same Day," *Research Quarterly, 40:* 222-225, March, 1969.

Baumgartner, Ted, A., "Stability of Physical Performance Test Scores," *Research Quarterly, 40:* 257-261, May, 1969.

Baumgartner, Ted, A., and A. S. Jackson, *Measurement for Evaluation in Physical Education*, Houghton Mifflin Company, Boston, 1975.

Beall, Elizabeth, "Essential Qualities in Certain Aspects of Physical Education with Ways of Measuring and Developing Same," unpublished master's thesis, University of California, 1925.

Bechtoldt, H. E., "Construct Validity: A Critique," *American Psychologist, 14:* 619-629, 1959.

Behnke, Albert R. and Jack H. Wilmore, *Evaluation and Regulation of Body Build and Composition*, Prentice-Hall, Inc., Englewood Cliffs, N. J., 1974.

Blair, G. M., R. S. Jones, and R. H. Simpson, *Educational Psychology*, Fourth Edition, Macmillan Publishing Co., Inc., New York, 1975, Chapter 19.

Blanchard, B. E., Jr., "A Behavior Rating Scale for the Measurement of Character and Personality in Physical Education Classroom Situations," *Research Quarterly, 7:* 56-66, May, 1936.

Bliss, J.C., *Basketball*, Lea and Febriger, Philadelphia, 1929.

Bloom, Benjamin S., Ed., *Taxonomy of Educational Objectives Handbook I: Cognitive Domain,* David McKay Co., Inc., New York, 1956.

Bloom, Benjamin, S. J., Thomas Hastings, and George F. Madaus, *Handbook on Formatime and Summative Evaluation of Student Learning*, McGraw-Hill Book Company, New York, 1971.

Bookwalter, Karl W., and Carolyn W. Bookwalter, *A Measure of Motor Fitness for College*, Bulletin of School of Education, Indiana University, 19 September, 1943.

Bovard, John F., Frederick W. Cozens, and E. Patricia Hagman, *Tests and Measurements in Physical Education*, Third Edition, W. B. Saunders Company, Philadelphia, 1950.

Brace, David K., *Measuring Motor Ability*, A. S. Barnes and Co., New York, 1927.

Brace, David K., "Testing Basketball Technique," *American Physical Education Review 29:* 159-165, April, 1924.

Brandhorst, Ted., "ERIC, Reminders of How it Can Help You," *Phi Delta Kappan 58:* 627-630, April, 1977.

Brouha, Lucian, "The Step Test: A Simple Method of Measuring Physical Fitness for Muscular Work in Young Men," *Research Quarterly, 14:* 31-36, March, 1943.

Brozek, Josef Howard Alexander, "Components of Variation and Consistency of Repeated Measurements," *Research Quarterly, 18:* 152-166, May, 1947.

Brubacher, John S., *Modern Philosophies of Education*, Third Edition, McGraw-Hill Book Company, New York, 1962.

Buros, Oscar K., Ed., *The Third Mental Measurements Yearbook,* Gryphon Press, Highland Park, N.J., 1947.

Buros, Oscar K., Ed., *The Fourth Mental Measurement Yearbook*, Gryphon Press, Highland Park, N.J., 1953.

Buros, Oscar K., Ed., *The Fifth Mental Measurements Yearbook*, Gryphon Press, Highland Park, N.J., 1965.

Buros, Oscar K., Ed., *The Sixth Mental Measurements Yearbook*, Gryphon Press, Highland Park, N.J., 1965.

Buros, Oscar K., Ed., *The Seventh Mental Measurement Yearbook*, Gryphon Press, Highland Park, N.J., 1972.

Buros, Oscar K., Ed., *The Eighth Mental Measurements Yearbook*, Gryphon Press, Highland Park, N.J., 1978.

Buros, Oscar K., Ed., *The Nineteen Thirty Eight Mental Measurements Yearbook*, Gryphon Press, Highland Park, N.J., 1938 (reissued 1972).

Buros, Oscar K., Ed., *The Nineteen Forty Mental Measurements Yearbook*, Gryphon Press, Highland Park, N.J., 1941 (reissued 1972).

Buros, Oscar K., Ed., *Tests in Print II*, Gryphon Press, Highland Park, N.Y., 1973.

California Physical Performance Tests, Bureau of Health Education, Physical Education, and Recreation, California State Department of Education, 1962.

Campbell, D. T., "Recommendations for APA Test Standard Regarding Construct, Trait, or Discriminant Validity," *American Psychologist, 15:* 546-553, 1960.

Carpenter, Aileen, "Strength Testing in the First Three Grades," *Research Quarterly, 13:* 328-335, October, 1942.

Carter, J. E. Lindsay, *The Heath-Carter Somototype Method*, San Diego State University, San Diego, California, Revised Edition, 1975.

Cattell, Raymond B., "Validity and Reliability, A Proposed More Basic Set of Concepts," *Journal of Educational Psychology, 55:* 1-22, February, 1964.

Clarke, David H., "Adaptations in Strength and Muscular Endurance Resulting from Exercise," in *Exercise and Sport Sciences Reviews*, Jack H. Wilmore, Ed., Academic Press, New York, 1974.

Clarke, H. Harrison, *Application of Measurement to Health and Physical Education*, Fifth Edition, Prentice-Hall, Inc., Englewood Cliffs, N.J., 1976.

Clarke, H. Harrison, "Comparision of Instruments for Recording Muscle Strength," *Research Quarterly 25:* 398-411, December, 1954.

Clarke, H. Harrison, *Physical and Motor Tests in the Medford Boys' Growth Study*, Prentice-Hall, Inc., Englewood Cliffs, N.J., 1971.

Commission on the Reorganization of Secondary Education, *Cardinal Principles of Secondary Education*, Bureau of Education Bulletin *35*, Washington, D.C., 1918.

Completed Research in Health, Physical Education, and Recreation, American Alliance for Health, Physical Education, and Recreation, Washington, D.C.

Consolazio, C. F., R. E. Johnson, and L. J. Pecors, *Physical Measurements of Metabolic Function in Man*, McGraw-Hill Book Company, New York, 1963.

Cooper, Kenneth H., *The Aerobics Way*, M. Evans and Company, Inc., New York, 1977.

Cooper, Kenneth H., *The New Aerobics*, Bantam Books, Inc., New York, 1970.

Cowell, Charles C., "Validating an Index of Social Adjustment for High School Use," *Research Quarterly 29:* 7-18, March, 1958.

Cozens, F. W., *The Measurement of General Athletic Ability for College Men*, University of Oregon Press, Eugene, Oregon, 1929.

Cureton, E. E., "Validity," in *Educational Measurement*, E. F. Linquist, Ed., American Council in Education, Washington, D.C., 1951, pp. 621-694.

Cureton, Thomas K., Jr., "Flexibility as an Aspect of Physical Fitness," *Supplement to the Research Quarterly, 12:* 388-389, May. 1941.

Cureton, Thomas K., *Physical Fitness Appraisal and Guidance*, C. V. Mosby Company, St. Louis, 1947.

Current Index to Journals in Education, Macmillan Information, New York.

Doppelt, J. E., "How Accurate is a Test Score?" in *Readings in Measurement and Evaluation*, N. Gronlund, Ed., The Macmillan Company, New York: 203-207, 1968.

Downie, N. M., *Fundamentals of Measurement*, Second Edition, Oxford University Press, New York, 1967.

DuBois, P. H., *A History of Psychological Testing*, Allyn and Bacon, Inc., Boston, 1970.

Durost, Walter N., *The Characteristics, Use, and Computation of Stanines*, Harcourt, Brace, and Jovanovich, Inc., New York, 1961.

Dyer, Joanna T., "The Backboard Test of Tennis Ability," *Supplement to the Research Quarterly 6:* 63-74, March, 1935.

Ebel, Robert L., Ed., *Encyclopedia of Education Research*, Fourth Edition, The Macmillan Company, 1969.

Ebel, Robert L., "Estimation of the Reliability of Ratings," *Psychometrika, 16:* 407-424, December, 1951.

Ebel, Robert L., "Must All Tests Be Valid?" *American Psychologist, 16:* 640-647, 1961.

Ebel, Robert L., "Obtaining and Reporting Evidence on Content Validity," *Educational and Psychological Measurement, 16:* 269-282, Autumn, 1956.

Ebel, Robert L., *Essentials of Educational Measurement*, Prentice-Hall, Inc., Englewood Cliffs, N.J., 1972.

Edington, D. W., and V. R. Edgerton, *The Biology of Physical Activity*, Houghton Mifflin Company, Boston, 1976.

Educational Policies Commission, *The Central Purpose of American Education*, National Education Association, Washington, D.C., 1961.

Educational Policies Commission, *Purposes of Education in American Democracy*, National Education Association, Washington, D.C., 1938.

Espenshade, Anna S., "Restudy of Relationships Between Physical Performance of School Children and Age, Height, and Weight," *Research Quarterly, 34:* 144-153, May, 1963.

Fabricius, Helen, "Grading in Physical Education," *Journal of Health, Physical Education, and Recreation, 38:* 34-49, May, 1967.

Feldt, Leonard S., and Mary Ellen McKee, "Estimation of the Reliability of Skill Tests," Research Quarterly, 29: 279-293, October, 1958.

Ferguson, George R., *Statistical Analysis in Psychology and Education*, Fourth Edition, McGraw Hill Book Company, New York, 1976.

Fiske, D. W., and L. Rice, "Intra-Individual Reponse Variability," *Psychological Bulletin, 52:* 217-250, 1955.

Fleishman, Edwin A., *The Structure and Measurement of Physical Fitness*, Prentice-Hall, Inc., Englewood Cliffs, N.J., 1969.

French, Esther L., "The Construction of Knowledge Tests on Selected Professional Courses in Physical Education, *Research Quarterly 14:* 406-424, December, 1943.

Gates, Donald P., and R. P. Sheffield, "Tests of Change of Direction as Measurement of Different Kinds of Motor Ability in Boys of 7th, 8th, and 9th Grades," *Research Quarterly, 11:* 36-47, October, 1940.

Getchell, Bud, *Physical Fitness A Way of Life*, Second Edition, John Wiley and Sons, Inc., New York; 1979.

Ghiselli, E. E., "The Validation of Selection Tests in the Light of the Dynamic Character of Criteria," *Personnel Psychology, 12:* 225-231, 1960.

Green, John A. *Teacher-made Tests*, Harper and Row, Publishers, New York, 1963.

Gronlund, Norman E., *Improving Marking and Reporting in Classroom Instruction*, MacMillan Publishing Co., Inc., New York, 1974.

Gronlund, Norman E., *Measurement and Evaluation in Teaching*, Third Edition, Macmillan Publishing Co., Inc., New York, 1976.

Gulliksen, H., "Intrinsic Validity," *American Psychologist, 5:* 511-517, 1950.

Hale, P. A., "Construction of a Long Serve Test for Beginning Badminton Players," unpublished master's thesis, University of Wisconsin, Madison, 1970.

Hanson, Dale L., "Grading in Physical Education," *Journal of Health, Physical Education, and Recreation, 38:* 34-39, May, 1967.

Harris, Margaret L., "A Factor Analytic Study of Flexibility," *Research Quarterly, 40:* 62-67, May, 1969.

Harrow, Anita J., *A Taxonomy of the Psychomotor Domain, A Guide for Developing Behavioral Objectives*, David McKay Co., Inc., New York, 1972.

Haskins, Mary Jane, *Evaluation in Physical Education*, William C. Brown Company, Publishers, Dubuque, Iowa, 1971.

Henry, Franklin M., "Coordination and Motor Learning," *59th Annual Proceedings*, College Physical Education Association, 1956, pp. 68-75.

Henry, Franklin M., "Reliability Measurement Error and Intra-Individual Difference," *Research Quarterly, 30:* 21-25, March, 1959.

Henry, Franklin M., "Specificity vs. Generality in Learning Motor Skills," *61st Annual Proceedings*, College Physical Education Association, 1958, pp. 126-128.

Henry, Franklin M., and Donald E. Rodger, "Increased Response Latency for Complicated Movements and a 'Memory Drum' Theory of Neuromotor Reaction," *Research Quarterly, 31:* 448-458, 1960.

Hewitt, Jack E., "Hewitt's Tennis Achievement Test," *Research Quarterly, 37:* 231-240, May, 1966.

Hockey, Robert V., *Physical Fitness, The Pathway to Healthful Living*, C. V. Mosby Co., St. Louis, 1977.

Hodgkins, Jean, "Reaction Time and Movement Time in Males and Females of Various Ages," *Research Quarterly, 34:* 335-343, October, 1963.

Horn, John L., "Integration of Concepts of Reliability and Standard Error of Measurement," *Educational and Psychological Measurement, 31:* 57-74, Spring, 1971.

Hoyt, C. J., "Reliability," in *Encyclopedia of Research*, C. H. Harris, ed., The Macmillan Company, New York, 1960.

Huddleston, Edith M., "Test Development on the Basis of Content Validity," *Educational and Psychological Measurement, 16:* 283-293, Autumn, 1956.

Humiston, Dorothy A., "A Measurement of Motor Ability in College Women," *Research Quarterly, 8:* 181-185, May, 1937.

Hyde, Edith I., "An Achievement Scale in Archery," *Research Quarterly 8:* 109-116, May, 1937.

Jackson, R. W. B., "Studies on Reliabilities of Tests," Bulletin No. 12, Department of Educational Research, University of Toronto, 1941.

Jewett, Ann E., L. Sue Jones, Sherry M. Luneka, and Sarah M. Robinson, "Educational Change Through A Taxonomy for Writing Physical Education Objectives," *Quest* XV, 1971, pp. 32-38.

Johnson, Barry L., and John Leach, "A Modification of the Bass Test of Dynamic Balance," (unpublished study, East Texas State University, 1968).

Johnson, Barry L., and Jack K. Nelson, *Practical Measurements for Evaluation in Physical Education*, Third Edition, Burgess Publishing Company, Minneapolis, Minn., 1979.

Johnson, M. Clemens, *A Review of Research Methods in Education*, Rand McNally College Publishing Company, Chicago, 1977.

Johnson, Marion Lee, "Construction of Sportsmanship Attitude Scales," *Research Quarterly, 40:* 312-316, May, 1969.

Johnson, Perry B. et al., *Sport Exercise and You*, Holt, Rinehart and Winston, Inc., New York, 1975.

Katch, Frank I., and William D. McArdle, *Nutrition, Weight Control and Physical Conditioning*, Houghton Mifflin Company, Geneva, Ill., 1977.

Kenyon, Gerald S., "Six Scales for Assessing Attitude Toward Physical Activity," *Research Quarterly 39:* 566-574, October, 1968.

Kibler, Robert J., Larry L. Barker, and David T. Miles, *Behavioral Objectives and Instruction*, Allyn and Bacon, Inc., Boston, 1970.

Kibler, Robert J., Donald I. Cegala, Larry L. Barker, and David T. Miles, *Objectives for Instruction and Evaluation*, Allyn and Bacon, Inc., Boston 1974.

Kirchner, Glen, *Physical Education for Elementary School Children*, William C. Brown Company, Publishers, Dubuque, Iowa, 1970.

Kirchner, Glenn, and Don Glines, "Comparative Analysis of Eugene, Oregon Elementary School Children Using the Kraus-Weber Test of Minimum Muscular fitness," *Research Quarterly, 28:* 16-25, March, 1957.

Krathwohl, David R., Benjamin S. Bloom, and Bertram B. Masia, *Taxonomy of Educational Objectives Handbook II:* Affective Domain, David McKay Co., Inc., New York, 1964.

Krathwohl, David A., and D. A. Payne, "Defining and Assessing Educational Objectives" in *Educational Measurement*, Robert L. Thorndike, ed., American Council on Education, Washington, D.C., 1971.

Kraus, Hans, and Ruth P. Hirshland, "Minimum Muscular Fitness in School Children," *Research Quarterly 25:* 177-188, May, 1954.

Kretschmer, E., *Physique and Character*, Harcourt, Brace and Co., New York, 1925.

Kroll, Walter, "A Note on the Coefficient of Intraclass Correlation as an Estimate of Reliability," *Research Quarterly, 33:* 313-316, May, 1962.

Kroll, Walter, "Reliability Theory and Research Decision in Selection of a Criterion Score," *Research Quarterly, 38:* 412-419, October, 1967.

Kropp, R. P., H. W. Stoker, and W. L. Bashaw, "The Validation of the Taxonomy of Educational Objectives, *Journal of Experimental Education, 34:* 69-76, Spring, 1966.

Kuder, G. F., and M. W. Richardson, "The Theory of Estimation of Test Reliability," *Psychometrika, 2:* 151-160, 1937.

Larson, Leonard A., "A Factor Analysis of Motor Ability Variables and Tests, with Tests for College Men," *Research Quarterly, 12:* 499-517, October, 1941.

Larson, Leonard A., and Rachael D. Yocom, *Measurement and Evaluation in Physical Education and Recreation*, C. V. Mosby Co., St. Louis, 1951.

Latchaw, Marjorie, "Measuring Selected Motor Skills in Fourth, Fifth, and Sixth Grades," *Research Quarterly, 25:* 439-449, December, 1954.

Leighton, Jack R., "An Instrument and Technique for the Measurement of Range of Joint Motion," *Archives of Physical Medicine and Rehabilitation, 36:* 571-578, September, 1955.

Lennon, Roger T., "Assumptions Underlying the Use of Content Validity," *Educational and Psychological Measurement, 16:* 294-304, Autumn, 1956.

Liba, Marie, "A Trend Test as a Preliminary to Reliability Estimation," *Research Quarterly, 33:* 245-248, May, 1962.

Lindeman, Richard H., *Educational Measurement*, Scott Foresman and Company, Glenview, Ill., 1967.

Linden, K. W., and J. D. Linden, *Modern Mental Measurement: A Historical Perspective*, Houghton Mifflin Company, Boston, 1968.

Lindquist, E. F., *Design and Analysis of Experiments*, Houghton Mifflin Company, Boston, 1956.

Lord, Fredric M., "Tests of the Same Length Do Have the Same Standard Error of Measurement," *Educational and Psychological Measurement, 19:* 233-239, Summer, 1959.

Mager, Robert F., *Preparing Instructional Objectives*, Fearon Publishers, Inc., Palo Alto, Calif., 1962.

Marteniuk, Ronald G., "Individual Differences in Intra-Individual Variability," *Journal of Motor Behavior, 1:* 307-316, December, 1969.

Mathews, Donald K. *Measurement in Physical Education*, Fifth Edition, W. B. Saunders Co., Philadelphia, 1978.

Mathews, Donald K., and E. L. Fox, *The Physiological Basis of Physical Education and Athletics,* Second Edition, W. B. Saunders, Philadelphia, 1976.

Mayer, Jean, *Overweight: Cause, Cost and Control*, Prentice-Hall, Inc., Englewood Cliffs, N. J., 1968.

McCloy, Charles H., "Character Building Through Physical Education," *Research Quarterly 1:* 41-61, October, 1930.

McCloy, Charles H., and Norma Young, *Tests and Measurements in Health and Physical Education*, Third Edition, Appleton-Century Crofts, Inc., New York, 1954.

Mehrens, William A., and Irvin J. Lehmann, *Measurement and Evaluation in Education and Psychology*, Holt, Rinehart and Winston, Inc., New York, 1973.

Melograno, Vincent J., and James E. Klinzing, *An Orientation to Total Fitness*, Kendall/Hunt Publishing Company, Dubuque, Iowa, 1974.

Meredith, Howard V., "A Physical Growth Record for Use in Elementary and High Schools," *American Journal of Public Health, 39:* 878-885, July, 1949.

Meyers, Carlton R., and T. Erwin Blesh, *Measurement in Physical Education*, Ronald Press Co., New York, 1962.

Montoye, Henry J., *An Introduction to Measurement in Physical Education*, Allyn and Bacon, Inc., Boston, Mass., 1978.

Mood, Dale, "Test of Physical Fitness Knowledge: Construction, Administration, and Norms," *Research Quarterly, 42:* 423-430, December, 1971.

Mosier, Charles I., "A Critical Examination of the Concepts of Face Validity," *Educational and Psychological Measurement, 7:* 191-205, Summer, 1947.

Mosier, Charles I., "Problems and Design of Cross Validation," *Educational and Psychological Measurement, 11:* 5-11, Spring, 1951.

Motor Fitness Tests for Oregon Schools, State Department of Education, Salem, Oregon, 1962.

National Center for Health Statistics: NCHS Growth Charts, 1976 *Monthly Vital Statistics Report, 25*, Supp (HRA) 76-1120, Rockville, Md., Health Resources Administration, June 22, 1976.

Neilson, N. P., and Frederick W. Cozens, *Achievement Scales in Physical Education Activities for Boys and Girls in Elementary and Junior High School*, A. S. Barnes and Company, New York, 1934.

Neilson, N. P., and Clyne R. Jensen, *Measurement and Statistics in Physical Education*, Wadsworth Publishing Co., Inc., Belmont, Calif., 1972.

Nelson, Fred, B., "The Nelson Reaction Timer," Instruction Leaflet, Lafayette, Louisiana.

Phillips, B. E., "The JCR Test," *Research Quarterly, 18:* 12-29, March, 1947.

Popham, W. James, *Criterion-Referenced Instruction*, Fearon Publishers, Belmont, California, 1973.

Popham, W. James, and Eva L. Baker, *Systematic Instruction,* Prentice-Hall, Inc., Englewood Cliffs, N.J., 1970.

Popham, W. James, and Kenneth A. Sirotnik, *Educational Statistics, Use, and Interpretation*, Second Edition, Harper and Row, Publishers, New York, 1973.

Powell, Elizabeth, and E. C. Howe, "Notor Ability Tests for High School Girls," *Research Quarterly, 10:* 81-88, December, 1939.

Psychological Abstracts, The American Psychological Association, Inc., Washington, D. C.

Remmers, H. H. et al., *A Practical Introduction to Measurement and Evaluation*, Harper and Row, Publishers, New York, 1965.

Research in Education, U. S. Government Printing Office, Washington, D.C.

Rogers, Frederick R., *Physical Capacity Tests in the Administration of Physical Education*, New York, Teachers College, Columbia University, 1925.

Roscoe, John T., *The Funstat Package in Fortran IV*, Holt, Rinehart and Winston, Inc., New York, 1973.

Roscoe, John T., *Fundamental Research Statistics for the Behavioral Sciences*, Holt, Rinehart and Winston, Inc., New York, 1975.

Russell, Naomi, and Elizabeth Lange, "Achievement Tests in Volleyball for Junior High School Girls," *Research Quarterly 11:* 33-41, December, 1940.

Safrit, Margaret J., *Evaluation in Physical Education*, Prentice-Hall, Inc., Englewood Cliffs, N. J., 1973.

Sage, George H., *An Introduction to Morot Behavior: A Neuropsycholgoical Approach*, Second Edition, Reading, Mass., 1977

Sargent, D. A., "Intercollegiate Strength Tests," *American Physical Education Review, 2:* 108, 1897.

Sargent, D. A., "The Physical Test of Man," *American Physical Education Review 26:* 188-194, April, 1921.

Schneider, E. C., "A Cardiovascular Rating as a Measure of Physical Fatigue and Efficiency," *Journal of American Medical Association, 74:* 1507, 1920.

Scott, N. Gladys, "The Assessment of Motor Abilities of College Women Through Objective Tests," *Research Quarterly, 10:* 63-89, October, 1939.

Scott, M. Gladys, "Measurement of Kinesthesis," *Research Quarterly, 26:* 324-341, October, 1955.

Scott, M. Gladys, and Esther French, *Measurement and Evaluation in Physical Education*, William C. Brown Company, Publishers, Dubuque, Iowa, 1959.

Seymour, Emery W., "Classification of Emory University Male Freshmen in Physical Education Classes," *Research Quarterly, 24:* 459-462, December, 1953.

Sheldon, William, C. W. Dupertuis, and Eugene McDermott, *Atlas of Man*, Harper and Brothers, New York, 1954.

Sheldon, William H., S. S. Stevens, and W. B. Tucker, *The Varieties of Human Physique*, Harper and Brothers, New York, 1940.

Simpson, E. J., *The Classification of Educational Objectives, Psychomotor Domain*, Vocational and Technical Education Grant, Contract No. OE 5-85-104, Office of Education, U. S. Department of Health, Education and Welfare, May, 1966.

Singer, Robert H., "Grading in Physical Education," *Journal of Health, Physical Education, and Recreation, 38:* 34-39, May, 1967.

Singer, Robert N., *Motor Learning and Human Performance*, Sound Edition, Macmillan Publishing Company, Inc., New York, 1975.

Singer, Robert N., and Walter Dick, *Teaching Physical Education, A Systems Approach*, Houghton Mifflin Company, Boston, 1974.

Siri, William E., "Gross Composition of the Body," *Advance in Biological and Medical Physics*, IV, J. H. Lawrence and C. A. Tobias, Eds., Academic Press, Inc., New York, 1956.

Smith, Fred M., and Sam Adams, *Educational Measurement for the Classroom Teacher*, Harper and Row, Publishers, New York, 1966.

Solley, William H., "Grading in Physical Education," *Journal of Health, Physical Education, and Recreation, 38:* 34-39, May, 1967.

Sonstroem, Robert J., "Attitude Testing Examining Certain Psychological Correlates of Physical Activity," *Research Quarterly, 45:* 93-103, May, 1974.

Stanley, J. C., "Reliability," in *Educational Measurement*, Second Edition, R. L. Thorndike, Ed., American Council on Education, Washington, D. C., 1971.

Stanley, J. C., "Reliability of Test Scores and Other Measurements," in *Encyclopedia of Education*, L. C. Deighton, Ed., The Macmillan Company, New York, 1971.

Symonds, P. M., "Factors Influencing Test Reliability," *Journal of Educational Psychology, 19:* 73-87, 1928.

Tenbrink, Terry D., *Evaluation: A Practical Guide for Teachers*, McGraw-Hill Book Company, New York, 1974.

Terwilliger, J. S., *Assigning Grades of Students*, Scott Foresman and Co., Glenview, Ill., 1971.

Texas Governor's Commission on Physical Fitness, "Physical Fitness Motor Ability Test," The Commissioner, Austin, Texas, 1973.

Thomas, R. Murray, "Records and Reports," *Encyclopedia of Educational Research*, Fourth Edition, Macmillan Publishing Company, Inc., New York, 1969.

Thorndike, Robert L., "Marks and Marketing Systems," in *Encyclopedia of Educational Research*, Fourth Edition, Robert L. Ebel, Ed., Macmillan Publishing Company, Inc., New York, 1969.

Thorndike, R. L., "Reliability," in *Educational Measurement*, E. F. Lindquist, Ed., American Council on Education, Washington, D. C., 1951, 560-620.

Thorndike, Robert L., and Elizabeth Hagen, *Measurement and Evaluation in Psychology and Education*, Fourth Edition, John Wiley and Sons, Inc., New York, 1977.

Tuttle, Waid, W., "The Use of the Pulse-Ratio Test for Rating Physical Efficiency," *Research Quarterly 2:* 5-17, May, 1931.

VanDalen, Deobold, and Bruce Bennett, *A World History of Physical Education*, Second Edition, Prentice-Hall, Inc., Englewood Cliffs, N. J., 1971.

Vanier, Maryhelen, and Hollis Fait, *Teaching Physical Education in Secondary Schools*, Fourth Edition, W. B. Saunders Co., 1975.

Wear, Carlos, "Construction of Equivalent Forms of An Attitude Scale," *Research Quarterly, 26:* 113-119, March, 1955.

Wesman, A. G., "Reliability and Confidence," in *Readings in Measurement and Evaluation*, Norman Gronlund, Ed., The Macmillan Company, New York, 1968, 208-214.

West, Charlotte, and Jeanelle Thorpe, "Construction and Validation of an Eight-Iron Approach Test," *Research Quarterly, 30:* 1115-1120, December, 1968.

Wetzel, Norman G., "The Treatment of Growth Failure in Children," National Education Association Service, Cleveland, Ohio, 1948.

Wiebe, Vernon R., "A Study of Tests of Kinesthesis," *Research Quarterly, 25:* 222-230, May, 1954.

Willgoose, Carl E., *Evaluation in Health Education and Physical Education*, McGraw-Hill Book Co., Inc., New York, 1961.

Wilmore, Jack H., and Albert R. Behnke, "An Anthropometric Estimation of Body

Density and Lean Body Weight in Young Men," *Journal of Applied Physiology, 27:* 25-31, July, 1969.
Wilmore, Jack H., and Albert R. Behnke, "An Anthropometric Estimation of Body Density and Lean Body Weight in Young Women," *American Journal of Clinical Nutrition, 23:* 267-274, March, 1970.

APPENDIXES

A. Sources for Tests in Physical Education

- A.1 Cognitive Tests
- A.2 Affective Tests
- A.3 Psychomotor (Sports Skill) Tests

B. Percentage of Total Areas Under the Normal Curve Between the Mean and Ordinate Points at any Given Standard Deviation Distance from the Mean

C. Metric Units

D. Common Metric Conversions

E. Grouped Data Organizational and Computational Procedures

F. Computer Programs

- F.1 Means and Standard Deviations by Groups
- F.2 Standard Scores Program
- F.3 Pearson Product Moment Correlation Matrix
- F.4 Item Analysis for Objective Tests

APPENDIX A

Sources for Tests in Physical Education

A.1 COGNITIVE TESTS

Archery

Ley, Katherine L., "Constructing Objective Test Items to Measure High School Levels of Achievement in Selected Physical Education Activities," (doctoral dissertation on Microcard, University of Iowa, 1960).

Snell, Catherine, "Physical Education Knowledge Tests," *Research Quarterly, 6:* 83-86, October, 1935.

Badminton

Fox, Katherine, "Beginning Badminton Written Examinations," *Research Quarterly, 24:* 135-146, May, 1953.

French, Esther, "The Construction of Knowledge Tests in Selected Professional Courses in Physical Education," *Research Quarterly, 14:* 406-424, December, 1943.

Goll, Lillian M., "Construction of Badminton and Swimming Knowledge Tests for High School Girls," master's thesis on Microcard, Illinois State Univeristy, 1956, pp. 65-75).

Hennis, Gail M., "Construction of Knowledge Tests in Selected Physical Education Activities for College Women," *Research Quarterly, 27:* 301-309, October, 1956.

Hooks, Edgar W., Jr., "Hooks' Comprehensive Knowledge Test in Selected Physical Education Activities for College Men,'. *Research Quarterly, 37:* 506-514, December, 1966.

Ley, Katherine L., "Constructing Objective Test Items to Measure High School Levels of Achievement in Selected Physical Education Activities," (doctoral dissertation on Microcard, University of Iowa, 1960).

Phillips, Marjorie, "Standardization of a Badminton Knowledge Test for College Women," *Research Quarterly, 17:* 48-63, March, 1946.

Scott, Gladys M., "Achievement Examination in Badminton," *Research Quarterly, 12:* 242-253, May, 1941.

Baseball

Goldberg, Isidor H., "The Development of Achievement Standards in Knowledge of Physical Education Activities," (doctoral dissertation on Microcard, New York University, 1953).

Hemphill, Fay, "Information Tests in Health and Physical Education for High School Boys," *Research Quarterly, 3:* 82, December, 1932.

Rodgers, E. G., and Marjorie L. Heath, "An Experiment in the Use of Knowledge and Skill Tests in Playground Baseball," *Research Quarterly, 2:* 128-130, December, 1931.

Snell, Catherine, "Physical Education Knowledge Tests," *Research Quarterly, 7:* 87-91, May, 1936.

Basketball

Bliss, J. G., *Basketball*, Lea and Febiger, Phildelphia, 1929.
Fisher, Rosemary B., "Tests in Selected Physical Education Service Courses in a College," (doctoral dissertation on Microcard, State University of Iowa, 1950, pp. 158-181).
French, Esther, "The Construction of Knowledge Tests in Selected Professional Courses in Physical Education," *Research Quarterly, 14:* 406-424, December, 1943.
Goldberg, Isidor H., "The Development of Achievement Standards in Knowledge of Physical Education Activities," (doctoral dissertation on Microcard, New York University, 1953.
Hemphill, Fay, "Information Tests in Health and Physical Education for High School Boys," *Research Quarterly, 3:* 82, December, 1932.
Hennis, Gail M., "Construction of Knowledge Tests in Selected Physical Education Activities for College Women," *Research Quarterly, 27:* 301-309, October, 1956.
Ley, Katherine L., "Constructing Objective Test Items to Measure High School Levels of Achievement in Selected Physical Education Activities," (doctoral dissertation on Microcard, University of Iowa, 1960).
Schwartz, Helen, "Knowledge and Achievement Tests in Girls' Basketball on the Senior High Level," Research Quarterly, *8:* 153-156, March, 1937.
Snell, Catherine, "Physical Education Knowledge Tests" *Research Quarterly, 7:* 79-82, March, 1936.

Body Mechanics

French, Esther, "The Construction of Knowledge Tests in Selected Progessional Courses in Physical Education," *Research Quarterly, 14:* 406-424, December, 1943.

Bowling

Hennis, Gail M., "Construction of Knowledge Tests in Selected Physical Education Activities for College Women," *Research Quarterly, 27:* 301-309, October, 1956.
Ley, Katherine L., "Constructing Objective Test Items to Measure School Levels of Achievement in Selected Physical Education Activities," (doctoral dissertation on Microcard, University of Iowa, 1960).

Canoeing

French, Esther, "The Construction of Knowledge Tests in Selected Professional Courses in Physical Education," *Research Quarterly, 14:* 406-424, December, 1943.

Dance and Rhythm

French, Esther, "The Construction of Knowledge Tests in Selected Professional Courses in Physical Education," *Research Quarterly, 14:* 406-424, December, 1943.

Murry, Josephine K., "An Appreciation Test in Dance," (unpublished master's thesis, University of California, 1943).

Stockard, Sara, "The Development and Evaluation of an Information Test in Beginning Modern Dance for Undergraduate College Students," *LAHPER* Journal, Fall Issue, 1972 p. 29.

Field Hockey

Dietz, Dorthea, and Beryl Frech, "Hockey Knowledge Test for Girls," *Journal of Health, Physical Education, Recreation, 11:* 366, June, 1940.

French, Esther, "The Construction of Knowledge Tests in Selected Professional Courses in Physical Education," *Research Quarterly, 14:* 406-424, 1943.

Grisier, Gertrude J., "The Construction of an Objective Test of Knowledge and Interpretation of the Rule of Field Hockey for Women," *Research Quarterly Supplement, 5:* 79-81, March, 1943.

Hennis, Gail M., "Construction of Knowledge Tests in Selected Physical Education Activities for College Women," *Research Quarterly, 27:* 301-309, October, 1956.

Kelley, Ellen D., and Jane E. Brown, "The Construction of a Field Hockey Test for Women Physical Education Majors," *Research Quarterly, 23:* 322-329, October, 1952.

Snell, Catherine, "Physical Education Knowledge Tests," *Research Quarterly, 6:* 86-89, October, 1935.

Football

Goldberg, Isidor H., "The Development of Achievement Standards in Knowledge of Physical Education Activities," (doctoral dissertation on Microcard, New York University, 1953).

Hamphill, Fay, "Information Tests in Health and Physical Education for High School Boys," *Research Quarterly, 3:* 82, December, 1932.

Fundamentals

Snell, Catherine, "Physical Education Knowledge Tests," *Research Quarterly, 6:* 79-83, October, 1935.

Golf

French, Esther, "The Construction of Knowledge Tests in Selected Professional Courses in Physical Education," *Research Quarterly, 14:* 406-424, 1943.

Ley, Katherine L., "Constructing Objective Test Items to Measure High School Levels of Achievement in Selected Physical Education Activities," (doctoral dissertation on Microcard, University of Iowa, 1960).

Snell, Catherine, "Physical Education Knowledge Test," *Research Quarterly, 7:* 79-80, May, 1936.

Waglow, I. F., and C. H. Rehling, "A Golf Knowledge Test," *Research Quarterly, 24:* 463-470, December, 1953.

Gymnastics

Fisher, Rosemary B., "Tests in Selected Physical Education Service Courses in a College," (doctoral dissertation on Microcard, State University of Iowa, 1950, pp. 145-156).

French, Esther, "The Construction of Knowledge Tests in Selected Professional Courses in Physical Education," *Research Quarterly, 14:* 406-424, December, 1943.

Gershon, Ernest, "Apparatus Gymnastics Knowledge Test for College Men in Professional Physical Education," *Research Quarterly, 28:* 332, December, 1957.

Nipper, John, "A Knowledge Test of Tumbling and Gymnastics," (unpublished study, Northeast Louisiana University, 1966).

Handball

Phillips, Bernath E., *Fundamental Handball,* A. S. Barnes and Company, New York, 1937.

Horseback Riding

Snell, Catherine, "Physical Education Knowledge Tests," *Research Quarterly, 7:* 80-84, May, 1936.

Physical Fitness

Mood, Dale, "Tests of Physical Fitness Knowledge: Construction, Administration and Norms," *Research Quarterly, 42:* 423-430, December, 1971.

Stradtman, Alan D., and T. K. Cureton, "A Physical Fitness Knowledge Test for Secondary School Boys and Girls," *Research Quarterly, 21:* 53-57, March, 1950.

Recreational Sports

Fisher, Rosemary B., "Tests in Selected Physical Education Service Courses in a College," (doctoral dissertation on Microcard, State University of Iowa, 1950, pp. 285-319).

French, Esther, "The Construction of Knowledge Tests in Selected Professional Courses in Physical Education" *Research Quarterly, 14:* 406-424, December, 1943.

Soccer

Fisher, Rosemary B., "Tests in Selected Physical Education Service Courses in a Col-

lege," (doctoral dissertation on Microcard, State University of Iowa, 1950, pp. 123-143).
French, Esther, "The Construction of Knowledge Tests in Selected Professional Courses in Physical Education," *Research Quarterly, 14:* 406-424, December, 1943.
Heath, Marjorie, L., and E. G. Rodgers, "A Study in the Use of Knowledge and Skill Tests in Soccer," *Research Quarterly, 3:* 33-53, October, 1932.
Knighton, Marian, "Soccer Questions," *Journal of Health and Physical Education, 1:* 29, October, 1930.
Ley, Katherine L., "Constructing Objective Test Items to Measure High School Levels of Achievement in Selected Physical Education Activities," (doctoral dissertation on Microcard, University of Iowa, 1960).
Snell, Catherine, "Physical Education Knowledge Tests," *Research Quarterly, 7:* 76-79, March, 1936.

Softball

Fisher, Rosemary B., "Tests in Selected Physical Education Service Courses in a College," (doctoral dissertation on Microcard, State University of Iowa, 1950, pp. 254-270).
French, Esther, "The Construction of Knowledge Tests in Selected Professional Courses in Physical Education," *Research Quarterly, 14:* 406-424, December 1943. Construction of Knowledge Tests in Selected Physical Education Activities for College Women," *Research Quarterly, 27:* 301-309, October, 1956.
Hooks, Edgar W., Jr., "Hooks' Comprehensive Knowledge Test in Selected Physical Education Activities for College Men," *Research Quarterly, 37:* 506-514, December, 1966.
Ley, Katherine L., "Constructing Objective Test Items to Measure High School Levels of Achievement in Selected Physical Education Activities," (doctoral dissertation on Microcard, University of Iowa, 1960).
Waglow, I. F., and Fay Stephens, "A Softball Knowledge Test," *Research Quarterly, 26:* 234-237, May, 1955.

Swimming

Fisher, Rosemary B., "Tests in Selected Physical Education Service Courses in a College," (doctoral dissertation on Microcard, State University of Iowa, 1950, pp. 182-253).
French, Esther, "The Construction of Knowledge Tests in Selected Professional Courses in Physical Education," *Research Quarterly, 14:* 406-424, December, 1943.
Goll, Lillian M., "Construction of Badminton and Swimming Knowledge Tests for High School Girls," (master's thesis on Microcard, Illinois State University, 1956).
Scott, M. Gladys, "Achievement Examinations for Elementary and Intermediate Swimming Classes," *Research Quarterly, 11:* 104-111, May, 1940.

Tennis

Broer, Marion B., and Donna M. Miller, "Achievement Tests for Beginning and Intermediate Tennis," *Research Quarterly, 21:* 303-313, October, 1950.

Fisher, Rosemary B., "Tests in Selected Physical Education Service Courses in a College," (doctoral dissertation on Microcard, State University of Iowa, 1950, pp. 271-284).

French, Esther, "The Construction of Knowledge Tests in Selected Professional Courses in Physical Education" *Research Quarterly, 14:* 406-424, December, 1943.

Hennis, Gail M., "Construction of Knowledge Tests in Selected Physical Education Activities for College Women," *Research Quarterly, 27:* 301-309, October, 1956.

Hewitt, Jack E., "Hewitt's Comprehensive Tennis Knowledge Test," *Research Quarterly, 35:* 149-154, May, 1964.

———, "Comprehensive Tennis Knowledge Test," *Research Quarterly, 8:* 74-84, October, 1937.

Hooks, Edgar W., Jr., "Hooks' Comprehensive Knowledge Test in Selected Physical Education Activities for College Men," *Research Quarterly, 37:* 506-514, December, 1966.

Miller, Wilma K., "Achivement Levels in Tennis Knowledge and Skill for Women Physical Education Major Students," *Research Quarterly, 24:* 81-89, March, 1953.

Scott, M. Gladys, "Achievement Examination for Elementary and Intermediate Tennis Classes," *Research Quarterly, 12:* 43-49, March, 1941.

Snell, Catherine, "Physical Education Knowledge Tests," *Research Quarterly, 7:* 84-87, May, 1936.

Track and Field

French, Esther, "The Construction of Knowledge Tests in Selected Professional Courses in Physical Education," *Research Quarterly, 14:* 406-424, December, 1943.

Volleyball

Fisher, Rosemary B., "Tests in Selected Physical Education Service Courses in a College," (doctoral dissertation on Microcard, State University of Iowa, 1950, pp. 82-122).

French, Esther, "The Construction of Knowledge Tests in Selected Professional Courses in Physical Education," *Research Quarterly, 14:* 406-424, December, 1943.

Hennis, Gail M., "Construction of Knowledge Tests in Selected Physical Education Activities for College Women," *Research Quarterly, 27:* 301-309, December, 1957.

Hooks, Edgar W., Jr., "Hooks' Comprehensive Knowledge Test in Selected Physical Education Activities for College Men," *Research Quarterly, 37:* 506-514, December, 1966.

Langston, Dewey F., "Standardization of a Volleyball Knowledge Test for College Men Physical Education Majors," *Research Quarterly, 26:* 60-66, March, 1955.

Ley, Katherine L., "Constructing Objective Test Items to Measure High School Levels of Achievement in Selected Physical Education Activities, (doctoral dissertation on Microcard, University of Iowa, 1960).

Snell, Catherine, "Physical Education Knowledge Tests," *Research Quarterly, 7:* 73-76, March, 1936.

A.2 AFFECTIVE TESTS

Adams, R.S., "Two Scales for Measuring Attitudes Toward Physical Education," *Research Quarterly, 34:* 635-643, March, 1963.

Alderman, K. B., "A Sociopsychological Assessment of Attitudes Toward Physical Activity in Championship Athletes," *Research Quarterly, 41:* 1-9, March, 1970.

Barrow, Harold M., and Rosemary McGee, *A Practical Approach to Measurement in Physical Education,* Second Edition, Lea and Febiger, Philadelphia, 1971, Chapter 12.

Baumgartner, Ted A., and Andrew S. Jackson, *Measurement for Evaluation in Physical Education,* Houghton Mifflin Company, Boston, 1975, Chapter 9.

Blanchard, B. E., "A Behavior Frequency Rating Scale for the Measurement of Character and Personality in Physical Education Classroom Situations," *Research Quarterly, 6:* 56-66, May, 1936.

Breck, Sabrina June, "A Sociometric Measurement of Status in Physical Education Classes," *Research Quarterly, 21:* 75-82, May, 1950.

Campbell, Donald E., "Students' Attitudes Toward Physical Education," *Research Quarterly, 39:* 456-462, October, 1968.

Campbell, Donald E., "Wear Attitude Inventory Applied to Junior High School Boys," *Research Quarterly, 39:* 888-893, December, 1968.

Cowell, Charles C., "Validating an Index of Social Adjustment for High School Use, "*Research Quarterly, 29:* 7-18, March, 1958.

Edington, Charles W., "Development of an Attitude Scale to Measure Attitudes of High School Freshmen Boys Toward Physical Education," *Research Quarterly, 39:* 505-512, October, 1968.

Johnson, Barry L., and Jack K. Nelson, *Practical Measurements for Evaluation in Physical Education,* Second Edition, Burgess Publishing Co., Minneapolis, Minn., 1974, Chapter 20.

Johnson, Marion L., "Construction of Sportmanship Attitude Scales," *Research Quarterly, 40:* 312-316, May, 1969.

Kenyon, Gerald S., "A Conceptual Model for Characterizing Physical Activity," *Research Quarterly, 39:* 96-105, October, 1968.

Kenyon, Gerald S., "Six Scales for Assessing Attitudes Toward Physical Activity," *Research Quarterly, 39:* 566-574, October, 1968.

Keogh, Jack, "Extreme Attitudes Toward Physical Education," *Research Quarterly, 34:* 27-33, March, 1963.

Keogh, Jack, "Analysis of General Attitudes Toward Physical Education," *Research Quarterly, 33:* 239-248, May, 1962.

Kirkendall, Don R., "Physical Education Effects in the Affective Domain," *75th Proceedings of the National College Physical Education Association for Men,* 1972.

Kneer, Marion E., "Kneer Attitude InventorV and Diagnostic Statements in Barrow and McGee," *A Practical Approach to Measurement in Physical Education,* Second Edition, Lea and Febiger, Philadelphia, 1971, pp. 439-539.

Lakie, William L., "Expressed Attitudes of Various Groups of Athletes Toward Athletic Competition, *Research Quarterly, 35:* 497-503, December, 1964.

NcCloy, Charles H., "Character Building Through Physical Education," *Research Quarterly, 1:* 41-61, October, 1930.

McCue, Betty F., "Constructing an Instrument for Evaluating Attitude Toward Intensive Competition in Team Games," *Research Quarterly, 24:* 205-209, March, 1953.

McPherson, B. D., and Yubasz, M. S., "An Inventory for Assessing Men's Attitude Toward Exercise and Physical Activity," *Research Quarterly, 39:* 218-219, March, 1968.

Mercer, Emily L., "Mercer Attitude Scale in Barrow and McGee," *A Practical Approach to Measurement in Physical Education*, Second Edition, Lea and Febiger, Philadelphia, 1971.

Nelson, Dale O., "Leadership in Sports," *Research Quarterly, 37:* 268-275, May, 1966.

Richardson, Charles E., "Thurstone Scale for Measuring Attitude of College Students Toward Physical Fitness and Exercise," *Research Quarterly, 31:* 638-643, December, 1960.

Richardson, Deane E., "Ethical Conduct in Sport Situations," 66th Annual Proceedings of the National College Physical Education for Men Association, 1962, pp. 98-104.

Sonstroem, Robert J., "Attitude Testing Examining Certain Psychological Correlates of Physical Activity," *Research Quarterly, 45:* 93, May, 1974.

Wear, Carlos L., "Construction of Equivalent Forms of an Attitude Scale," *Research Quarterly, 26:* 113-119, March, 1955.

A.3 PSYCHOMOTOR (SPORTS SKILL) TESTS

Archery

AAHPER Skills Test Manual: Archery, American Association for Health, Physical Education, and Recreation, Washington, D. C., 1967.

Bohn, Robert W., "An Achievement Test in Archery," (unpublished master's theses, University of Wisconsin, 1962).

Hyde, Edith I., "An Achievement Scale in Archery," *Research Quarterly, 8:* 109, May, 1937.

Zabik, Roger M., and Andrew S. Jackson, "Reliability of Archery Achievement," *Research Quarterly, 40:* 254-255, March 1969.

Badminton

Davis, Phillis R., "The Development of a Combined Short and Long Badmonton Service Skill Test," (unpublished master's thesis, University of Tennessee, 1968).

French, Esther, and Evelyn Stalter, "Study of Skill Tests in Badminton for College Women," *Research Quarterly, 20:* 257-272, October, 1949.

Gray, Charles A., and Wayne B. Brumbach, "The Effect of Daylight Projection of Film Loops on Learning Badminton," *Research Quarterly, 38:* 562-569, December, 1967.

Greiner, M. R., "Construction of a Short Serve Test for Beginning Badminton Players,"

master's thesis, University of Wisconsin, Madison, 1964 (Microcard PE 670, University of Oregon, Eugene).
Hale, Pat A., "Construction of a Long Serve Test for Beginning Badminton Players (Singles)," master's thesis, University of Wisconsin, Madison, 1970 (Microcard PE 1133, University of Oregon, Eugene).
Hicks, J. V., "The Construction and Evaluation of a Battery of Five Badminton Skill Tests," unpublished doctoral dissertation, Texas Women's University, Denton, 1967.
Johnson, Rose Marie, "Determination of the Validity and Reliability of the Badminton Placement Test," (unpublished master's thesis, University of Oregon, 1967).
Kowert, Eugene A., "Construction of a Badminton Ability Test for Men," (unpublished master's thesis, University of Oregon, 1967).
Kowert, Eugene A., "Construction of a Badminton Ability Test for Men," (unpublished master's thesis, University of Iowa, 1968).
Lockhart, Aileene, and Frances A. McPherson, "Development of a Test of Badminton Playing Ability," *Research Quarterly, 20:* 402-405, December, 1949.
Lucey, Mildred A., "A Study of the Components of Wrist Action as They Relate to Speed of Learning and the Degree of Proficiency Attained in Badminton," (unpublished doctoral dissertation, New York University, 1952).
McDonald, E. Dawn, "The Development of a Skill Test for the Badminton High Clear," (unpublished master's thesis, Southern Illinois University, 1968).
Miller, Frances A., "A Badminton Wall Volley Test," *Research Quarterly, 22:* 208-213, May, 1951.
Poole, James, *Badminton,* Goodyear Publishing Company, Pacific Palisades, Calif., 1969, pp. 30-32.
Poole, James, and Jack Nelson, "Construction of a Badminton Skills Test Battery," (unpublished study, Louisiana State University, 1970).
Scott, M. Gladys, Aileen Carpenter, Esther French, and Louise Kuhl, "Achievement Examinations in Badminton," *Research Quarterly, 12:* 242-53, May, 1941.
Scott, M. Gladys, and Esther French, *Measurement and Evaluation in Physical Education,* William C. Brown Company, Publishers, Dubuque, Iowa, 1959, Chapter VI.
Thorpe, Joanne, and Charlotte West, "A Test of Game Sense in Badminton," *Perceptual and Motor Skills, 28:* 159-169, February, 1969.
Washington, Jean, "Construction of a Wall Volley Test for the Badmonton Short Serve, and the Effect of Wall Practice on Court Performance," (unpublished master's thesis, North Texas State University, 1968).

Basketball

AAHPER Skills Test Manual: Basketball for Boys, American Association for Health, Physical Education, and Recreation, Washington D.C., 1966.
AAHPER Skills Test Manual: Basketball for Girls, American Association for Health, Physical Education, and Recreation, Washington D.C., 1966.
Barrow, Harold M., "Basketball Skill Test," *Physical Educator, 16:* 26-27, March, 1959.
Bonner, Donald A., "A Comparative Study of the Ability of High School Basketball

Players to Perform Basic Skills at Three Stages of the Season," (unpublished master's thesis, North Carolina Central University, 1963).

Cunningham, Phyllis, "Measuring Basketball Playing Ability of High School Girls, (unpublished doctoral dissertation, University of Iowa, 1964).

Edgren, H. D., "An Experiment in the Test of Ability and Progress in Basketball," *Research Quarterly, 3:* 159-171, March, 1932.

Elbel, E. R., and Forrest C. Allen, "Evaluating Team and Individual Performance in Basketball," *Research Quarterly, 5:* 538-55, October, 1941.

Harrison, Edward R., "A Test to Measure Basketball Ability for Boys," (unpublished master's thesis, University of Florida, 1969.)

Gilbert, Raymond R., "A Study of Selected Variables in Predicting Basketball Players," (unpublished master's thesis, Springfield College, 1968).

Jacobson, Theodore V., "An Evaluation of Performance in Certain Physical Ability Tests Administered to Select Secondary School Boys," (unpublished master's thesis, University of Washington, 1960).

Johnson, L. William, "Objective Test in Basketball for High School Boys," (unpublished master's thesis, State University of Iowa, 1934).

Jones, Edith, "A Study of Knowledge and Playing Ability in Basketball for High School Girls," (unpublished master's thesis, State University of Iowa, 1941).

Kay, H. Kenner, "A Statistical Analysis of the Profile Technique for the Evaluation of Competitive Basketball Performance," (unpublished master's thesis, University of Alberta, 1966).

Knox, Robert D., "Basketball Ability Tests," *Scholastic Coach, 17:* 45-47, November, 1947.

Lambert, A. R., "A Basketball Skill Test for College Women," (unpublished master's thesis, University of North Carolina, Greensboro, 1969).

Latchaw, Marjorie, "Measuring Selected Motor Skills in Fourth, Fifth, and Sixth Grades," *Research Quarterly, 25:* 439-449, December, 1954.

Lehsten, Nelson, "A Measure of Basketball Skills in High School Boys," *The Physical Educator, 5:* 103-109, December, 1948.

Leilich, Avis, "The Primary Components of Selected Basketball Tests for College Women," (unpublished doctoral dissertation, Indiana University, 1952).

Matthews, Leslie, E., "A Battery of Basketball Skills Test for High School Boys," (unpublished master's Thesis, University of Oregon, 1963).

Niller, Wilma K., "Achievement Levels in Basketball Skills for Women Physical Education Majors," *Research Quarterly, 25:* 450-455, December, 1954.

Mortimer, Elizabeth M., "Basketball Shooting," *Research Quarterly, 22:* 234-243, May, 1951.

Nelson, Jack K., "The Measurement of Shooting and Passing Skills in Basketball," (unpublished study, Louisiana State University, 1967).

Peters, Gerald V., "The Reliability and Validity of Selected Shooting Tests in Basketball," (unpublished master's thesis, University of Michigan, 1964).

Pimpa, Udom, "A Study to Determine the Relationship Between Bunn's Basketball Skill Test and the Writer's Version of that Test," (unpublished master's thesis, Springfield College, 1968).

Plinke, John F., "The Development of Basketball Physical Skill Potential Test Batteries by Height Categories," (unpublished doctoral dissertation, Indiana University, 1966).

Schwartz, Helen, "Achievement Tests in Girls Basketball at the Senior High School Level," *Research Quarterly, 8:* 143-156, March, 1937).

Stroup, Francis, "Relationship Between Measurement and Field of Motion Perception and Basketball Ability in College Men," *Research Quarterly, 28:* 72-76, Narch, 1950.

Stubbs, Helen C., "An Explanatory Study of Girls Basketball Relative to the Measurement of Ball Handling Ability," (unpublished master's thesis, University of Tennessee, 1968).

Thornes, Ann B., "An Analysis of a Basketball Shooting Test and Its Relation to Other Basketball Skill Tests," (unpublished master's thesis, University of Wisconsin, 1963).

Voltmer, E. F., and Ted Watts, "A Rating Scale for Player Performance in Basketball," *Journal of Health and Physical Education, 2:* 94-95, February, 1947.

Walton, Ronald J., "A Comparison Between Two Selected Evaluative Techniques for Measuring Basketball Skill," (unpublished master's thesis, Western Illinois University, 1968).

Wilbur, Carol D., "Construction of a Simple Skills Test," in *Basketball Guide — 1959-60,* American Association for Health, Physical Education and Recreation, Washington, D.C., 1959, pp. 30-33.

Young, Genevieve, and Helen Moser, "A Short Battery of Tests to Measure Playing Ability in Women's Basketball," *Research Quarterly, 5:* 3-23, May, 1934.

Bowling

Johnson, Norma Jean, "Tests of Achievement in Bowling for Beginning Girl Bowlers," (unpublished master's thesis, University of Colorado, 1962).

Martin, Joan L., "A Way to Measure Bowling Success," *Research Quarterly, 31:* 113-116, March, 1960.

Martin, Joan, and Jack Keogh, "Bowling Norms for College Students in Elective Physical Education Classes," *Research Quarterly, 35:* 325-327, October, 1964.

Olson, Janice, and Marie R. Liba, "A device for Evaluating Spot Bowling Ability," *Research Quarterly, 38:* 193-201, May, 1967.

Phillips, Marjorie, and Dean Summers, "Bowling Norms and Learning Curves for College Women," *Research Quarterly, 21:* 377-385, December, 1950.

Dance and Rhythm

Ashton, Dudley, "A Gross Motor Rhyming Test," *Research Quarterly, 24:* 253-260, October, 1953.

Benton, Rachel Jane, "The Measurement of Capacities for Learning Dance Movement Techniques," *Research Quarterly, 15:* 137-140, May, 1944.

Shambaugh, Mary E., "The Objective Measurement of Success in the Teaching of Folk Dancing to University Women," *Research Quarterly, 6:* 33-58, March, 1935.

Waglow, I. F., "An Experiment in Social Dance Testing," *Research Quarterly, 24:* 97-101, March, 1953.

Fencing

Bower, M. G., "A Test of General Fencing Ability," (unpublished master's thesis, University of Southern California, Los Angeles, 1961).

Cooper, C. K., "The Development of a Fencing Skill Test for Measuring Achievement of Beginning Collegiate Women Fencers in Using the Advance, Beat, and Lunge," (unpublished master's thesis, Western Illinois University, Macomb, 1968).

Fein, J. T., "Construction of Skill Tests for Beginning Collegiate Women Fencers," (unpublished master's thesis, University of Iowa, Iowa City, 1964).

Safrit, M. J., "Construction of a Skill Test for Beginning Fencers," (unpublished master's thesis, University of Wisconsin, Madison, 1962).

Schutz, H. J., "Construction of an Achievement Scale in Fencing for Women," (unpublished master's thesis, University of Washington, Seattle, 1940).

Wyrick, W., "A Comparison of the Effectiveness of Two Methods of Teaching Beginning Fencing to College Women," (unpublished master's thesis, The Women's College of the University of North Carolina, Greensboro, 1958).

Field Hockey

Friedel, J. W., "The Development of a Field Hockey Skill Test for High School Girls," master's thesis, Illinois State Normal University, Normal, 1956 (Microcard PE 289, University of Oregon, Eugene).

Illner, J. A., "The Construction and Validation of a Skill Test for the Drive in Field Hockey," master's thesis, Southern Illinois University, Carbondale, 1968, (Microcard, PE 1075, University of Oregon, Eugene).

Perry, E. L., "An Investigation of Field Hockey Skills Tests for College Women," (unpublished master's thesis, Pennsylvania State University, University Park, Penn.).

Schmithals, Margaret, and Esther French, "Achievement Tests in Field Hockey for College Women," *Research Quarterly, 11:* 84-92, October, 1940.

Strait, C. J., "The Construction and Evaluation of a Field Hockey Skills Test," (unpublished master's thesis, Smith College, Northampton, Mass., 1960).

Football

American Association for Health, Physical Education and Recreation, *Football Skills Test Manual*, American Association for Health, Physical Education and Recreation, Washington, D.C., 1966.

Borleske, S. E., "Achievement of College Men in Touch Football," in F. W. Cozens, "Ninth Annual Report of the Committee on Curriculum Research of the College Physical Education Association," *Research Quarterly, 8:* 73-78, May, 1937.

Brace, David K., "Validity of Football Achievement Tests as Measures of Learning as a Partial Basis for the Selection of Players, ' *Research Quarterly, 14:* 372, December, 1943.

Cowell, C. C., and A. H. Ismail, "Validity of a Football Rating Scale and its Relationship to Social Integration and Academic Ability," *Research Quarterly, 33:* 461-67, December, 1961.

Lee, Robert C., "A Battery of Tests to Predict Football Potential," (unpublished master's thesis, University of Utah, 1965).

Golf

Bowen, Robert T., "Putting Errors of Beginning Golfers Using Different Points of Aim," *Research Quarterly, 39:* 31-55, March, 1968.
Brown, H. S., "A Test Battery for Evaluating Golf Skills," *Texas Association for Health, Physical Education and Recreation Journal,* May, 1969, pp. 4-5, 28-29.
Bevett, Melvin A., "An Experiment in Teaching Methods of Golf," *Research Quarterly, 2:* 104-106, December, 1931.
Cochrane, June F., "The Construction of an Indoor Golf Skills Test as a Measure of Golfing Ability," (unpublished master's thesis, University of Minnesota, 1960).
Cotten, Doyice J., Jerry R. Thomas, and Thomas Plaster, "A Plastic Ball Test for Golf Iron Skill," (paper presented at AAHPER National Convention, Houston, Texas, March 24, 1972).
Green, Kenneth N., "The Development of a Battery of Golf Skill Tests for College Men," (doctoral dissertation, University of Arkansas, 1974).
McKee, Mary E., "A Test for the Full-Swing Shot in Golf," *Research Quarterly, 21:* 40-46, March, 1950.
Nelson, Jack, "An Achievement Test for Golf," (unpublished study, Louisiana State University, 1967).
Reece, Patsy A., "A Comparison of the Scores Made on an Outdoor and the Scores Made on an Indoor Golf Test by College Women," (unpublished master's thesis, University of Colorado, 1960).
Vanderhoof, Ellen R., "Beginning Golf Achievement Tests," (unpublished master's thesis, State University of Iowa, 1956).
Watts, Harriet, "Construction and Evaluation of a Target on Testing the Approach Shot in Golf," (unpublished master's thesis, University of Wisconsin, 1942).
West, Charlotte, and Jo Anne Thorpe, "Construction and Validation of an Eight-Iron Approach Test," *Research Quarterly, 39:* 1115-1120, December, 1968.)

Gymnastics

Amateur Athletic Union (AAU), *Gymnastics Guide,* AAU, 231 W. 58th St., New York (publication updated regularly).
Bowers, Carolyn O., "Gymnastic Skill Test for Beginning to Low Intermediate Girls and Women," (unpublished master's thesis, Ohio State University, 1965).
Division of Girls' and Women's Sports (DGWS), *Gymnastic Guide,* American Association for Health, Physical Education, and Recreation, Washington, D.C. (publication updated regularly).
Faulkner, John and Newt Loken, "Objectivity of Judging at the National Collegiate Athletic Association Gymnastic Meet: A Ten-year Follow-up Study," *Research Quarterly, 33:* 485-6, October, 1962.
Harris, J. Patrick, "A Design for a Proposed Skill Proficiency Test in Tumbling and Apparatus for Male Physical Education Majors at the University of North Dakota," (unpublished master's thesis, University of North Dakota, 1966).

Johnson, Barry L., "A Screening Test for Pole Vaulting and Selected Gymnastic Events," *Journal of Health, Physical Education and Recreation, 44:* 71-72, May, 1973.

Johnson Barry L., and Patricia Duncan Boudreaux, *Basic Gymnastics for Girls and Women*, Appleton-Century-Crofts, Inc., New York, 1971, pp. 122-125.

Landers, Daniel M., "A Comparison of Two Gymnastic Judging Methods," (unpublished master's thesis, University of Illinois, 1965).

National Collegiate Athletic Association (NCAA), *Official Gymnastics Rules*, NCAA, 394 E. Thomas Rd., Phoenix, Ariz. (publication updated regularly).

Schwartzkoph, Robert J., "The Iowa-Brace Test as a Measuring Instrument for Predicting Gymnastic Ability," (unpublished master's thesis, University of Washington, 1962).

United States Gymnastic Federation (USGF), *Age Group Workbook*, USGF, P.O. Box 4699, Tucson, Ariz. (publication updated regularly).

Handball

Cornish, Clayton, "A Study of Measurement of Ability in Handball, *Research Quarterly, 20:* 215-222, May, 1949.

Griffith, Malcolm A., "An objective Method of Evaluating Ability in Handball Singles," (unpublished master's thesis, University of North Carolina, 1949).

McCachren, James R., "A Study of the University of Florida Handball Skill Test," (unpublished master's thesis, University of North Carolina, 1949).

Montoye, H. J., and J. Brotzman, "An Investigation of the Validity of Using the Results of a Doubles Tournament as a Measure of Handball Ability," *Research Quarterly, 22:* 214-18, May, 1951.

Pennington, G. Gary, James A. P. Day, John N. Drowatsky, and John F. Hanson, "A Measure of Handball Ability," *Research Quarterly, 38:* 247-253, May, 1967.

Tyson, Kenneth W., "A Handball Skill Test for College Men," (unpublished master's thesis, University of Texas, Austin, 1970).

Ice Hockey

Merrifield, H. H., and G. A. Walford, "Battery of Ice Hockey Skill Tests," *Research Quarterly, 40:* 146-52, March, 1969.

Ice Skating

Carriere, D. L., "An Objective Figure Skating Test for Use in Beginning Classes," (unpublished master's thesis, University of Illinois, Urbana, 1969).

Leaming, T. W., "A Measure of Endurance of Young Speed Skaters," (unpublished master's thesis, University of Illinois, Urbana, 1959).

Recknagel, D., "A Test for Beginners in Figure Skating," *Journal of Health and Physical Education, 168:* 91-92, February, 1945.

Lacrosse

Hodges, C. V., "Construction of an Objective Knowledge Test and Skill Tests in Lacrosse for College Women," master's thesis, University of North Carolina, Greensboro, 1967 (Microcard PE 1074, University of Oregon, Eugene).
Lutze, M. C., "Achievement Tests in Beginning Lacrosse for Women," (unpublished master's thesis, State University of Iowa, Iowa City, 1963).
Wilke, B. J., "Achievement Tests for Selected Lacrosse Skills of College Women," (unpublished master's thesis, University of North Carolina, Greensboro, 1967).

Racquetball / Paddleball

Keeley, Steve, *The Complete Book of Racquetball*, Follett Publishing Co., Chicago, 1976.
Leve, Chuck, *Inside Racquetball*, Henry Regnery Company, Chicago, 1973.
Reznik, John W., *Championship Racquetball*, Leisure Press, Cornwall, N.Y., 1976.
Reznik, John W., David O. Matthews, and James Peterson, *Racquetball for Men and Women*, Stipes Publishing Company, Champaign, Illinois, 1972, Chapter XI.

Skiing

Rogers, H. M., "Construction of Objectively Scored Skill Tests for Beginning Skiers," (unpublished master's thesis, University of Colorado, Boulder, 1960).
Wolfe, J. E., and H. H. Merrifield, "Predictability of Beginning Skiing Success from Basic Skill Tests in College Age Females," (paper presented at the National American Association for Health, Physical Education and Recreation Convention in Detroit, Michigan, April, 1971).

Soccer and Speedball

Bontz, Jean, "An Experiment in the Construction of a Test for Measuring Ability in Some of the Fundamental Skills Used by Fifth and Sixth Grade Children in Soccer," (unpublished master's thesis, State University of Iowa, 1942).
Buchanan, Ruth E., "A Study of Achievement Tests in Speedball for High School Girls," (unpublished master's thesis, State University of Iowa, 1942).
Crew, Vernon N., "A Skill Test Battery for Use in Service Program Soccer Classes at the University Level," (unpublished master's thesis, University of Oregon, 1968).
Johnson, Joseph R., "The Development of a Single-Item Test as a Measure of Soccer Skill," (master's thesis on Microcard, University of British Columbia, 1963).
MacKenzie, John, "Evaluation of a Battery of Soccer Skill Tests as an Aid to Classification of General Soccer Ability," (unpublished master's thesis, University of Massachusetts, 1968).
McDonald, Lloyd G., "The Construction of a Kicking Skill Test as an Index of General Soccer Ability," (unpublished master's thesis, Springfield College, 1951).
Mitchell, J. Reid, "The Modification of the McDonald Soccer Skill Test for Upper Elementary School Boys," (unpublished master's thesis, University of Oregon, 1963).
Schaufele, Evelyn F., "The Establishment of Objective Tests for Girls of the Ninth and

Tenth Grades to Determine Soccer Ability," (unpublished master's thesis, State University of Iowa, 1940).

Smith, Gwen, "Speedball Skill Tests for College Women," (unpublished study, Illinois State University, 1947).

Streck, Bonnie, "An analysis of the McDonald Soccer Skill Test as Applied to Junior High School Girls," (unpublished master's thesis, Fort Hayes State College, 1961).

Weiss, Raymond A., and Marjorie Phillips, *Administration of Tests in Physical Education*, C. V. Mosby Company, St. Louis, 1954, pp. 253-257.

Softball and Baseball

AAHPER, *Skills Test Manual: Softball for Boys*, American Association for Health, Physical Education, and Recreation, Washington, D.C., 1966.

AAHPER, *Skills Test Manual: Softball for Girls*, American Association for Health, Physical Education, and Recreation, Washington D.C., 1966.

Cole, Audrey A., "The Investigation and Analysis of Softball Skill Tests for College Women," (unpublished master's thesis, University of Maryland, 1962).

Elrod, Joe M., "Construction of a Softball Skill Test Battery for High School Boys," (unpublished master's thesis, Louisiana State University, 1969).

Everett, Peter W., "The Prediction of Baseball Ability," *Research Quarterly, 23:* 15-19, March, 1952.

Finger, Margaret N., "A Battery of Softball Skill Tests for Senior High School Girls," (unpublished master's thesis, University of Michigan, 1961).

Fox, Margaret G., and Olive G. Young, "A Test of Softball Batting Ability," *Research Quarterly, 25:* 26-27, March, 1954.

Hardin, Donald H., and John Ramirez, "Elementary School Performance Norms," *AAHPER Journal*, February, 1972, pp. 8-9.

Hooks, G. Eugene, "Prediction of Baseball Ability Through Analysis of Measures of Strength and Structure," *Research Quarterly, 30:* 38-43, March, 1959.

Kehtel, Carmen H., "The Development of a Test to Measure the Ability of a Softball Player to Field a Ground Ball and Successfully Throw it at a Target," (unpublished master's thesis, University of Colorado, 1958).

Kelson, Robert E., "Baseball Classification Plan for Boys," *Research Quarterly, 24:* 304-309, October, 1953.

O'Donnell, Doris J., "Validation of Softball Skill Tests for High School Girls," (unpublished master's thesis, Indiana University, 1950).

Shick, Jacqueline, "Battery of Defensive Softball Skills Tests for College Women," *Research Quarterly, 41:* 82-87, March 1970.

Swimming and Diving

Arrasmith, Jean L., "Swimming Classification Test for College Women," (unpublished doctoral dissertation, University of Oregon, 1967).

Bennett, LaVerne M., "A Test of Diving for Use in Beginning Classes," *Research Quarterly, 13:* 109-115, March, 1942.

Burris, Barbara J., "A Study of the Speed-Stroke Test of Crawl Stroking Ability and Its

Relationship to Other Selected Tests of Crawl Stroking Ability," (unpublished master's thesis, Temple University, 1964).
Durrant, Sue M., "An Analytical Method of Rating Synchronized Swimming Stunts," *Research Quarterly, 35:* 126-134, May, 1964.
Fox, Margaret G., "Swimming Power Test," *Research Quarterly, 28:* 233-237, October, 1957.
Hewitt, Jack E., "Swimming Achievement Scale Scores for College Men," *Research Quarterly, 12:* 282-289, December, 1948.
———, "Achievement Scale Scores for High School Swimming," *Research Quarterly, 20:* 170-179, May, 1949.
Kilby, Emelia Louise J., "An Objective Method of Evaluating Three Swimming Strokes," (unpublished doctoral dissertation, University of Washington, 1956).
Munt, Marylin R., "Development of an Objective Test to Measure the Efficiency of the Front Crawl for College Women," (unpublished master's thesis, University of Michigan, 1964).
Rosentsweig, Joel, "A Revision of the Power Swimming Test," *Research Quarterly, 39:* 818-819, October, 1968.
Scott, M. Gladys, and Esther French, *Measurement and Evaluation in Physical Education*, William C. Brown Company, Publishers, Dubuque, Iowa, 1959, Chapter VI.
Wilson, Marcia R., "A Relationship Between General Motor Ability and Objective Measures of Achievement in Swimming at the Intermediate Level for College Women," (unpublished master's thesis, University of North Carolina, 1962).

Table Tennis

Mott, Jane A., and Aileen Lockhart, "Table Tennis Backboard Test," *Journal of Health and Physical Education, 17:* 550-52, November 1946.

Tennis

Benton, R., "Teaching Tennis by Testing," in *Selected Tennis and Badminton Articles*, D. Davis, Ed. Division of Girl's and Women's Sports, AAHPER, 1963.
Broer, Marian R., and Donna Mae Miller, "Achievement Tests for Beginning and Intermediate Tennis," *Research Quarterly, 21:* 303-321, October, 1950.
Cobane, Edith, "Test for the Service," in AAHPER, *Tennis and Badminton Guide*, June 1962-June 1964, American Association for Health, Physical Education, and Recreation, pp. 46-47, Washington, D.C.
Cotten, Doyice J., and Jane Nixon, "A Comparison of Two Methods of Teaching the Tennis Serve," *Research Quarterly, 39* 929-931, December, 1968.
DiGennaro, Joseph, "Construction of Forehand Drive, Backhand Drive, and Serve Tennis Tests," *Research Quarterly, 40:* 496-501, October, 1969.
Dyer, Joanna T., "Revision of the Backboard Test of Tennis Ability," *Research Quarterly, 9:* 25-31, March, 1938.
Edwards, Janet, "A Study of Three Measures of the Tennis Serve," (unpublished master's thesis, University of Wisconsin, 1965).

Fonger, Sandra J., "The Development of a Reliable Objective and Practical Tennis Serve Test for College Women," (unpublished master's thesis, University of Michigan, 1963).

Hewitt, Jack E., "Classification Tests in Tennis," *Research Quarterly, 39:* 552-555, October, 1968.

———, "Revision of the Dyer Backboard Tennis Test," *Research Quarterly, 36:* 153-157, May, 1965.

———, "Hewitt's Tennis Achievement Test," *Research Quarterly, 37:* 231-237, May, 1966.

Hubbell, Nancy C., "A Battery of Tennis Skill Tests for College Women," (unpublished master's thesis, Texas Woman's University, 1960).

Johnson, Joann, "Tennis Serve of Advanced Women Players," *Research Quarterly, 28:* 123-131, May, 1957.

Jones, Shirley K., "A Measure of Tennis Serving Ability," (unpublished master's thesis, University of California, 1967).

Kemp, Joann, and Marilyn F. Vincent, "Kemp-Vincent Rally Test of Tennis Skill," *Research Quarterly, 29:* 1000-1004, December, 1964.

Malinak, Nina R., "Thc Construction of an Objective Measure of Accuracy in the Performance of the Tennis Serve," (unpublished master's thesis, University of Illinois, 1961).

Recio, Michael, and Charles Prestidge, "The Overhead Smash Test Utilizing the Johnson Tennis and Badminton Machine," (unpublished study, Northeast Louisiana University, 1972).

Ronning, Hilding E., "Wall Tests for Evaluating Ability," (unpublished master's thesis, Washington State University, 1959).

Scott, M. Gladys, "Achievement Examinations for ElementarV and Intermediate Tennis Players," *Research Quarterly, 12:*y40-49, March, 1941

Timmer, Karen L., "A Tennis Test to Determine Accuracy in Playing Ability," (unpublished master's thesis, Springfield College, 1965).

Volleyball

AAHPER, *Skills Test Manual: Volleyball*, American Association for Health, Physical Education, and Recreation, 1969, Washington, D.C.

Blackman, Claudia J., "The Development of a Volleyball Test for the Spike," (unpublished master's thesis, Southern Illinois University, 1968).

Brady, George F., "Preliminary Investigations of Volleyball Playing Ability," *Research Quarterly, 16:* 14-17, March, 1945.

Camp, Billie Ann, "The Reliability and Validity of a Single-Hit Repeated Volleys Test in Volleyball and the Relationship of Height to Performance on the Test," (unpublished master's thesis, University of Colorado, 1963).

Chaney, Dawn S., "The Development of a Test of Volleyball Ability for College Women," (unpublished master's thesis, Texas Woman's University, 1966).

Clifton, Marguerite A., "Single Hit Volley Test for Women's Volleyball," *Research Quarterly, 33:* 208-211, May, 1962.
Crogan, Corrinne, "A Simple Volleyball Classification Test for High School Girls," *Physical Educator, 4:* 34-37, October, 1943.
Cunningham, Phyllis, and Joan Garrison, "High Wall Volley Test for Women's Volleyball," *Research Quarterly, 39:* 480-490, October, 1968.
French, Esther L., and Bernice I. Cooper, "Achievement Tests in Volleyball for High School Girls," *Research Quarterly, 8:* 150-157, May, 1937.
Helmen, R. M., "Development of Power Volleyball Skill Tests for College Women," (paper presented at the Research Section of the 1971 American Association for Health, Physical Education, and Recreation National Convention, Detroit, Michigan).
Jackson, Patricia, "A Rating Scale for Discriminating Relative Performance of Skilled Female Volleyball Players," (unpublished master's thesis, University of Alberta, 1967).
Johnson, Judith A., "The Development of a Volleyball Skill Test for High School Girls," (unpublished master's thesis, Illinois State University, 1967).
Jones, Richard N., "The Development of a Volleyball Skills Test for Adult Males," (unpublished master's thesis, California State College, 1968).
Kessler, Adrian A., "The Validity and Reliability of the Sandefur Volleyball Spiking Test," (unpublished master's thesis, California State College, 1968).
Kronquist, Roger A., and Wayne B. Brumbach, "A Modification of the Brady Volleyball Skill Test for High School Boys," *Research Quarterly, 39:* 116-120, March, 1968.
Lamp, Nancy A., "Volleyball Skills for Junior High School Students as a Function of Physical Size and Maturity," *Research Quarterly, 25:* 189-200, May, 1954.
Liba, Marie R., and Marylin R. Stauff, "A Test for the Volleyball Pass," *Research Quarterly, 34:* 56-63, March, 1963.
Lopez, Delfina, "Serve Test," in Division of Girls' and Women's Sports (DGWS), *Volleyball Guide — 1957-1959,* American Association for Health, Physical Education, and Recreation, Washington, D.C., 1957, pp. 29-30.
Michalski, Rosalie A., "Construction of an Objective Skill Test for the Underhand Volleyball Serve," (unpublished master's thesis, University of Iowa, 1963).
Mohr, Dorothy R., and Martha V. Haverstick, "Repeated Volleys Test for Women's Volleyball," *Research Quarterly, 26:* 179-184, May, 1955.
Petry, Kathryn, "Evaluation of A Volleyball Serve Test," (unpublished master's thesis, Los Angeles State College, 1967).
Russell, Naomi, and Elizabeth Lange, "Achievement Tests in Volleyball for Junior High School Girls," *Research Quarterly, 11:* 33-41, December, 1940.
Ryan, Mary F., "A Study of Tests for the Volleyball Serve," (unpublished master's thesis, University of Wisconsin, 1969).
Shaw, John H., "A Preliminary Investigation of a Volleyball Skill Test," (unpublished master's thesis, University of Tennessee, 1967).
Shavely, Marie, "Volleyball Skill Tests for Girls," in Division of Girls' and Women's Sports (DGWS), *Selected Volleyball Articles,* American Association for Health, Physical Education, and Recreation, Washington, D.C., 1960, pp. 77-78.

APPENDIX B

Percentage of Total Area Under the Normal Curve Between the Mean and Ordinate Points at any Standard Deviation Distance from the Mean

$\frac{X-\bar{X}}{s} =$ z	.00	.01	.02	.03	.04	.05	.06	.07	.08	.09
0.0	00.00	00.40	00.80	01.20	01.60	01.99	02.39	02.79	03.19	03.59
0.1	03.98	04.38	04.78	05.17	05.57	05.96	06.36	06.75	07.14	07.53
0.2	07.93	08.32	08.71	09.10	09.48	09.87	10.26	10.64	11.03	11.41
0.3	11.79	12.17	12.55	12.95	13.31	13.68	14.06	14.43	14.80	15.17
0.4	15.54	15.91	16.28	16.64	17.00	17.36	17.72	18.08	18.44	18.79
0.5	19.15	19.50	19.85	20.19	20.54	20.88	21.23	21.57	21.90	22.24
0.6	22.57	22.91	23.24	23.57	23.89	24.44	24.54	24.86	25.17	25.49
0.7	25.80	26.11	26.42	26.73	27.04	27.34	27.64	27.94	28.23	28.52
0.8	28.81	29.10	29.39	29.67	29.95	30.23	30.51	30.78	31.06	31.33
0.9	31.59	31.86	32.12	32.38	32.64	32.90	33.15	33.40	33.65	33.89
1.0	34.13	34.38	34.61	34.85	35.08	35.31	35.54	35.77	35.99	36.21
1.1	36.43	36.65	36.86	37.08	37.29	37.49	37.70	37.90	38.10	38.30
1.2	38.49	38.69	38.88	39.07	39.25	39.44	39.62	39.80	39.97	40.15
1.3	40.32	40.49	40.66	40.82	40.99	41.15	41.31	41.47	41.62	41.77
1.4	41.92	42.07	42.22	42.36	42.51	42.65	42.79	42.92	43.06	43.19
1.5	43.32	43.45	43.57	43.70	43.83	43.94	44.06	44.18	44.29	44.41
1.6	44.52	44.63	44.74	44.84	44.95	45.05	45.15	45.25	45.35	45.45
1.7	45.54	45.64	45.73	45.82	45.91	45.99	46.08	46.16	46.25	46.33
1.8	46.41	46.49	46.56	46.64	46.71	46.78	46.86	46.93	46.99	47.06
1.9	47.13	47.19	47.26	47.32	47.38	47.44	47.50	47.56	47.61	47.07
2.0	47.72	47.78	47.83	47.88	47.93	47.98	48.03	48.08	48.12	48.17
2.1	48.21	48.26	48.30	48.34	48.38	48.42	48.46	48.50	48.54	48.57
2.2	48.61	48.64	48.68	48.71	48.75	48.78	48.81	48.84	48.87	48.90
2.3	48.93	48.96	48.98	49.01	49.04	49.06	49.09	49.11	49.13	49.16
2.4	49.18	49.20	49.22	49.25	49.27	49.29	49.31	49.32	49.34	49.36
2.5	49.38	49.40	49.41	49.43	49.45	49.46	49.48	49.49	49.51	49.52
2.6	49.53	49.55	49.56	49.57	49.59	49.60	49.61	49.62	49.63	49.64
2.7	49.65	49.66	49.67	49.68	49.69	49.70	49.71	49.72	49.73	49.74
2.8	49.74	49.75	49.76	49.77	49.77	49.78	49.79	49.79	49.80	49.81
2.9	49.81	49.82	49.82	49.83	49.84	49.84	49.85	49.85	49.86	49.86
3.0	49.87									
3.5	49.98									
4.0	49.997									
5.0	49.99997									

APPENDIX C

Metric Units

Quantity	*Common Units*	*Symbol*	*Acceptable Equivalent*	*Symbol*
Length	kilometer	km		
	hectometer	hm		
	meter	m		
	centimeter	cm		
	millimeter	mm		
Area	square kilometer	km^2		
	square hectometer	hm^2	hectare	ha
	square meter	m^2		
	square centimeter	cm^2		
	square millimeter	mm^2		
Volume	cubic meter	m^3		
	cubic decimeter	dm^3	liter[a]	L
	cubic centimeter	cm^3	milliliter[a]	mL
Velocity	meter per second	m/s		
	kilometer per hour	km/h		
Acceleration	meter per second squared	m/s^2		
Frequency	megahertz	MH_z		
	kilohertz	kH_z		
	hertz	H_z		
Mass	megagram	Mg	metric ton	†
	kilogram	kg		
	gram	g		
	milligram	mg		
Density	kilogram per cubic meter	kg/m^3	gram per liter	g/L
Force	kilonewton	kN		
	newton	N		
Pressure	kilopascal	kPa		
Energy, work, or quantity of heat	megajoule	MJ		
	kilojoule	kj		
	joule	J		
	kilowatt-hour	kW•h		

Power or heat flow rate	kilowatt	kW
	watt	W
Temperature	kelvin	K
	degree Celsius	°C
Electric current	ampere	A
Quantity of electricity	coulomb	C
	ampere-hour	A•h
Electromotive force	volt	V
Electric resistance	ohm	Ω
Luminous intensity	candela	cd

[a] To be used for fluids (both gases and liquids) and for dry ingredients in recipes. Do not use any prefix with "liter" except "milli."

APPENDIX D

Common Metric Conversions

	If You Know *U.S. Customary Unit*		*Multiply By*	*To Find* *Metric Unit*
Length	inches	X	25.4	= millimeters
	inches	X	2.54	= centimeters
	feet	X	0.305	= meters
	yards	X	0.914	= meters
	miles	X	1.609	= kilometers
Area	square inches	X	6.452	= square centimeters
	square feet	X	0.093	= square meters
	square yards	X	0.836	= square meters
	acres	X	0.405	= hectares
Volume	fluid ounces	X	29.573	= milliliters
	quarts (1q)	X	0.946	= liters
	cubic yards	X	0.765	= cubic meters
Mass	ounces (avdp)	X	28.350	= grams
	pounds (avdp)	X	0.454	= kilograms
Temperature	degrees Fahrenheit	X	5/9 (after subtracting 32)	= degrees Celsius

	If You Know *Metric*		*Multiply By*	*To Find* *U.S. Customary Unit*
Length	millimeters	X	0.039	= inches
	centimeters	X	0.394	= inches
	meters	X	3.281	= feet
	meters	X	1.094	= yards
	kilometer	X	0.621	= miles
Area	square centimeters	X	0.155	= square inches
	square meter	X	10.764	= square feet
	square meters	X	1.196	= square yards
	hectares	X	2.471	= acres
Volume	millimeters	X	0.034	= fluid ounces
	liters	X	1.056	= quarts (1q)
	cubic meters	X	1.308	= cubic yards

Mass	grams	X	0.035	= ounces (avdp)
	kilograms	X	2.205	= pounds (avdp)
Temperature	degrees Celsius	X	9/5 (then add 32)	= degrees Fahrenheit

APPENDIX E

Grouped Data Organizational and Computational Procedures

ORGANIZING DATA USING GROUPED PROCEDURES

Another method of organizing test scores is called the *grouped method.* Grouping data has been the traditional procedure for organizing test scores to facilitate interpretation and analysis. In addition to tradition, the other primary reason for including the grouped procedures in this text is the value in interpretation of scores from larger groups. The teacher can sometimes save time by grouping the data when class size exceeds 40 or 50 students. Also use of the grouped method produces a compact frequency table. With large groups, scores often cover a large range making an ungrouped presentation of data bulky. A grouped method of presentation can give a better concept of the shape of the distribution of scores.

When grouping data the scores are organized into a frequency table as shown in Table E.2. The raw scores that are used in the frequency table are shown in Table E.1.

Table E.1 Raw Scores for Golf Instructional Unit ($N = 50$)

80	59	75	70	40	71
37	42	68	68	46	63
57	48	51	57	53	64
45	56	53	57	48	70
58	47	61	49	59	60
60	56	42	64	57	54
67	40	56	72	52	68
81	62	61	65	50	72
		67	55		

A frequency table is simply a distribution of the scores arranged into arbitrarily defined groupings to reduce the number of classes. The scores in Table E.2. have been grouped into classes called *step intervals.*

Table E.2 Frequency Table of Scores from a Golf Skills Test ($N = 50$)

Step Intervals	*Tallies*	*Frequencies*
81-83	1	1
78-80	1	1
75-77	1	1
72-74	11	2
69-71	111	3
66-68	~~1111~~	5
63-65	1111	4
60-62	~~1111~~	5
57-59	~~1111~~ 11	7
54-56	~~1111~~	5
51-53	1111	4
48-50	1111	4
45-47	111	3
42-44	11	2
39-41	11	2
36-38	1	1

A step interval is an arbitrarily selected small range of scores utilized to provide compactness for the list of test scores. In constructing a frequency table the first problem confronted is how to determine the size of the step interval. This is a decision that must be made by the teacher. There is, however, a "rule of thumb" that might be applied. Select a step interval of such a size that between 10 and 20 intervals will cover the entire range of measures. If, for example, the lowest measure in the distribution is 37, and the highest is 81, a step interval of 3 would be appropriate and would result in a frequency table with 16 intervals. This can be seen in Table E.2. Other step intervals might also be selected resulting in frequency tables with differing numbers of intervals.

To compute the size of the step interval divide the range by the approximate number of intervals desired. This will determine the actual limits of the step interval, which will indirectly determine the number of intervals in the frequency table. For example, the teacher might choose 15 as the desired number of step intervals with which to work. The *range* must first be determined. The range is defined as the high score minus the low score plus 1. From Table E.1. we see that the high score on the skill test is 81, and the low score is 37. Using the formula

$$R = H - L + 1$$

where

R = range
H = high score
L = low score

Therefore

$$R = 81-37 + 1$$

$$R = 45$$

By dividing the range of 45 by 15, the resulting nearest whole number is 3. Therefore, 3 is the step interval in this sample and will be utilized throughout the remainder of this discussion.

With 3 as the step interval the frequency table is constructed as shown in Table E.2. Notice that the bottom interval contains the lowest score and the upper interval contains the highest score. In the example 36 was chosen as the starting number. It would have been equally valid to begin with 35 or 37 although a multiple of the step interval is often recommended. Either of these scores could have been used as a beginning point for the lowest step interval since they would have met the criterion of having the first step contain the lowest score.

Once the frequency distribution is determined, the raw scores of the golf skills test found in Table E.1 are placed in the proper step interval. The first score under skill application is 80, and it is placed in the step interval 78-80. The scores are usually recorded as tallies (*T*) first and are then transformed to a total in the frequency column (*F*). This procedure is repeated until all raw scores are placed in the frequency table.

With this grouping process some of the precision found in the ungrouped frequency distribution is lost. For example, the identities of the individual scores are lost within each step interval. With a normal group there is no reason to anticipate that any one score within the interval will occur more often than another so it is assumed that the scores are evenly distributed. The slight inaccuracies introduced by the grouped method are more than made up for in the time and labor saved in later computation.

The Limits of a Step Interval

In a frequency distribution the limits of step intervals are written as test scores. For example the first interval in Table E.2 is presented as 36-38. The test score, however, actually represents the midpoint of a distance that extends one-half a unit below and one-half a unit above the actual score value. Thus, a score of 37 extends from 36.5 to 37.5 and a score of 38 from 37.5 to 38.5. These limits of each score are called the real limits of the score. Therefore, the step interval also has lower and upper real limits that extend ½ unit below the lowest actual score in the interval to ½ unit above the highest score respectively. These real limits are essential to certain statistical computations that will be demonstrated later in this discussion. Generally the step intervals are presented as score limits, called the *actual limits* for convenience. The upper and lower actual limits are merely the highest and lowest numbers in each step interval. Notice that real limits are established one place value beyond the actual limits. For example if the actual score obtained was .196, the upper and lower real limits of the score would be .1955 and .1965 respectively.

The Midpoint of the Step Interval

Another essential computation relative to the frequency table is the midpoint of the step interval. It is defined as one-half of the step interval added to the lower real limit. The midpoint is necessary in computing percentiles, the median, the mean, and the quartile deviation. An example for computing the midpoint from the step interval 36-38 is shown. One-half of the step interval is 1.5, and the lower real limit of the step interval is 35.5. Therefore the midpoint is 35.5 + 1.5 or 37. All other midpoints for each interval are computed in a similar manner. It is usually advantageous to use an odd number for the size of a step interval since the midpoint of each step interval will then be a whole number.

GRAPHIC PRESENTATION OF TEST SCORES

Occasionally the teacher may desire to study the distribution of scores more carefully or may wish to present a clearer picture of the distribution to others. A graphic presentation with either the histogram (bargraph) or the frequency polygon (linegraph) may be used very satisfactorily to accomplish this purpose.

The Histogram

Possibly the most commonly used graphic presentation of frequency distributions is the histogram. It presents the data in a series of adjacent rectangular columns or bars. The base of each column represents the actual limits of the step interval and the height of each column indicates the frequency of scores falling within that interval. An analogy might be to picture the students whose scores occur in each interval standing directly on the shoulders of the students beneath them to form a human column. Figure E.1 is a histogram showing the scores from the golf skills test discussed earlier in this chapter.

To prepare an accurate histogram, obtain common graph paper. Draw a horizontal line (x-axis) to represent the skill test scores and a vertical line (y-axis) to represent the frequencies. Identify an appropriate scale for both skill test scores and frequency. The step intervals are placed equidistantly along the horizontal base line and the possible frequencies are placed equidistantly along the vertical line. For each step interval the corresponding frequency is noted, and a short horizontal line is drawn the width of the interval. The histogram is completed by joining the ends of the short horizontal lines to the corresponding ends of the intervals on the horizontal axis. Notice that the horizontal and vertical lines or axes must be appropriately labeled. An interpretation of the graph should also accompany the presentation. In a histogram the frequencies are represented as being equally distributed over the whole range of the step interval.

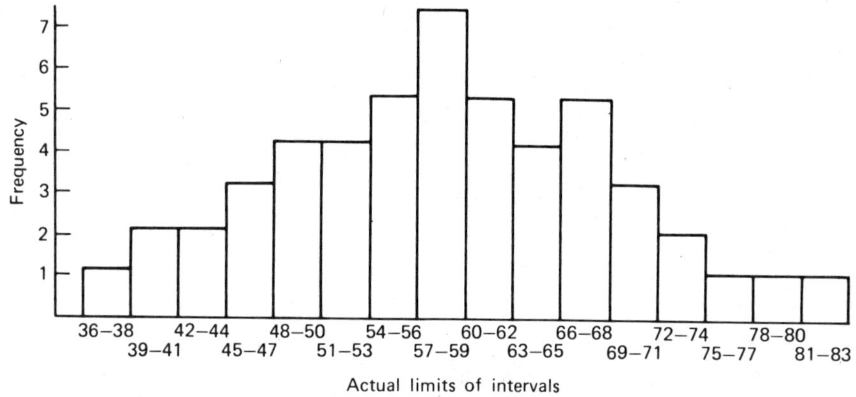

Figure E.1. Histogram of scores from a golf skills test.

The Frequency Polygon

Another method of graphically representing test scores is by constructing a frequency polygon or linegraph as shown in Figure E.2. In a frequency polygon it is assumed that all cases in each interval are concentrated at the midpoint of each interval. The development of this type of presentation is somewhat similar to the development of the histogram. However, instead of drawing a horizontal line the full width of the step interval, a dot is placed above the midpoint of each interval at a level equal to the appropriate frequency. Usually an extra interval is added at each end of the horizontal scale to demonstrate a starting and finishing point for the graph, which has frequencies equal to zero.

The frequency polygon and the histogram are simply different graphical presentations of the same data. Figure E.2 shows the same information in polygon form as the histogram does in rectangular form. Rarely would a teacher use both forms, and the choice appears to be purely a matter of personal choice.

COMPUTATION OF THE MEASURES OF CENTRAL TENDENCY

The measures of central tendency that will be computed by using grouped data procedures are the *mode, median*, and *mean*. The defenition and interpretations for the measures were presented in Chapter 3.

Computation of the Mode From Grouped Data

The grouped scores for the golf skills test are found in Table E.2. It is indicated

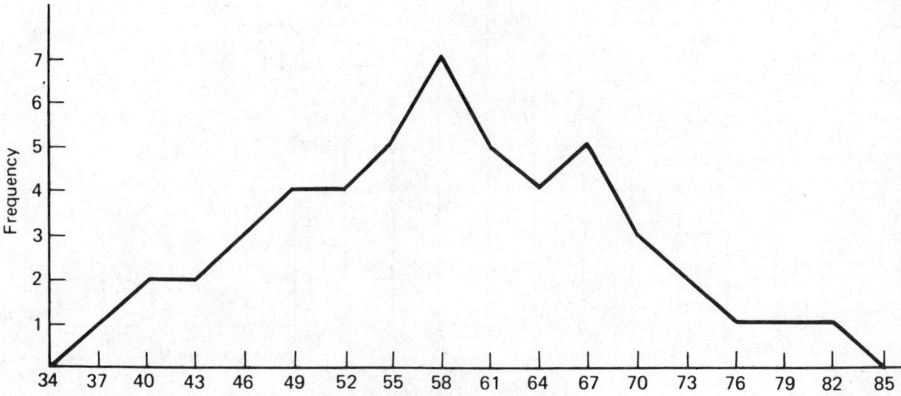

Figure E.2. Frequency Polygon of scores from a golf skills test.

that the interval that occurs most often is 57-59, which contains seven scores. The midpoint of that interval is found to be 58, which is the mode of the skill test scores when grouped data are considered. We see that the mode for the grouped data is 58, whereas the mode from the ungrouped list of raw scores is 57. This is an example of losing accuracy through the grouping process. This is due, of course, to the loss of identity of the specific measures within the step interval.

Computation of the Median from Grouped Data

In computing the median from grouped data the problem is to compute the point such that half the scores fall above and half the scores fall below the value. The problem is amplified by the loss of the identities of the scores within the intervals of the frequency table.

The procedures for computing the median from the frequency table are similar to the ungrouped procedures but with some adjustments because of the grouping of the scores within the intervals. The basic procedure involves counting upward from the lowest interval to the interval containing the middle score. Then by interpolation the precise location of the median is located within the step interval. A step-by-step procedure of computing the median using the data in Table E.3 is presented below.

Table E.3 Measures of Central Tendency Computed from Grouped Golf Skills Test Scores ($N = 50$)

Step Interval	*Frequency*	x'	fx'	fx'^2
81-83	1	8	8	64
78-80	1	7	7	49
75-77	1	6	6	36
72-74	2	5	10	50

69-71	3	4	12	48
66-68	5	3	15	45
63-65	4	2	8	16
60-62	5	1	5/71	5
57-59	7			
54-56	5	−1	−5	5
51-53	4	−2	−8	16
48-50	4	−3	−12	36
45-47	3	−4	−12	48
42-44	2	−5	−10	50
39-41	2	−6	−12	72
36-38	1	−7	−7/66	49

$$\text{Mdn} = LL + \frac{\left(\frac{N+1}{2} - cf\right)}{fi} SI$$

$$\text{Mdn} = 56.5 + \frac{\left(\frac{50+1}{2} - 21\right)}{7} 3 = 58.43$$

where

LL = lower real limit of the step interval that contains the median
N = total number scores
cf = cumulative frequency of all scores below the step interval that contains the median
fi = frequency in the step interval that contains the mdn.
SI = size of the step interval

1. Divide the total number (N) of measures plus 1 by 2 ($50 + 1 \div 2 = 25.5$).
2. Find the step interval in which the score in Step 1 is located and determine the lower real limit (LL) of that interval (57-59). The lower real limit (LL) is 56.5.
3. Beginning at the lower end of the frequency table (Table E.3), sum the scores (cumulative frequency) for each step interval until the interval containing the median is reached but not included. This number is the cumulative frequency used later in the computation ($1 + 2 + 2 + 3 + 4 + 4 + 5 = 21$).
4. Subtract the cf found in Step 3 from the number required to reach the median found in Step 1 ($25.5 - 21 = 4.5$).
5. Determine the amount of the step interval that contains the median, which is to be added to its lower real limit by dividing $(N + 1)/2 - cf$ found in Step 4 by the frequency (fi) of the median interval. This result is then multiplied by the size of the step interval: (SI) ($5\frac{1}{2} - 21/7$) $= .64 \times 3 = 1.93$.
6. Add the number obtained in Step 5 to the lower real limit (LL) of

the median interval that was found in Step 2. This sum is the median (56.5 + 1.93 = 58.43).

Computation of the Mean From Grouped Data

The computation of the mean from grouped data utilizes a few modifications of the procedures and formulas used in the ungrouped computation. The grouped procedure may appear complicated but is greatly simplified by following the steps listed below. The mean is also computed from the golf test scores shown in Table E.3.

$$\overline{X} = AM + \left(\frac{\Sigma fx'}{N}\right) SI$$

$$\overline{X} = 58 + \frac{(5)3}{50}$$

where

X = mean
AM = assumed mean
$\Sigma fx'$ = sum of the frequencies multiplied by x'
N = total number scores
SI = size of the step interval

1. Arbitrarily select an interval as a starting point. It is suggested that this interval be located near the middle of the distribution and be clearly marked on the frequency table. The midpoint of this interval is called the assumed mean (AM) and is designated as 0 in the deviation (x') column (AM = 58).
2. Identify the next highest interval in the deviation x') column as +1, the one above that as +2, and so on, and the corresponding intervals below the assumed mean as −1, −2, and so on. (For the interval 60-62 the deviation score is +1, the interval 63-65 is +2, and so on, as shown in the x' column in Table 4.5).
3. Compute the fx' column by multiplying the number of scores (f) in each interval by the number in the corresponding x' column. (For the interval 60-62, fx' is 5 x 1 = 5; for the interval 63-65, fx' is 4 x 2 = 8, and so on).
4. Sum the products in the fx' column; remember the plus and minus signs. It is recommended that the plus entries and minus entries be added separately and then be summed together to give the final total ($\Sigma fx'$). (71-66 = 5).

5. Obtain the total sum of the frequencies (N). The sum of all frequencies in the example is 50.
6. Divide the sum of fx' by the total number of frequencies ($\Sigma fx'/N$) to obtain the average deviation from the assumed mean ($5/50 = .1$).
7. Multiply the result in Step 6 by the size of the interval (SI) in score units ($.1 \times 3 = .3$).
8. Add the result obtained in Step 7 to the assumed mean (AM) found in Step 1 ($58 + .3 = 58.3$). The sum of this final addition is the mean ($\overline{X}$) of the set of scores.

COMPUTATION OF THE MEASURES OF VARIABILITY

The measures of variability that will be computed using grouped data procedures are the *quartile deviation* and *standard deviation*. The definition and interpretations for these measures were presented in Chapter 3.

Computation of the Quartile Deviation From Grouped Data

The formula for computing quartile deviation from grouped data is the same as for ungrouped data. The only difference in the procedure is that the 1st and 3rd quartiles must be computed from the frequency table, which requires an additional formula. The formulas and computations of the quartile deviation from the data in Table E.3 are shown below.

$$Q_D = \frac{Q_3 - Q_1}{2}$$

$$Q_3 = LL + \left(\frac{3N/4 - cf}{fi}\right) SI$$

$$Q_1 = LL + \left(\frac{N/4 - cf}{fi}\right) SI$$

where

LL = the lower real limit of the interval that contains the 1st or 3rd quartile
N = total number of scores
cf = cumulative frequency of all scores below the step interval that contains the 1st or 3rd quartile
fi = frequency in the step interval that contains the 1st or 3rd quartile
SI = size of the step interval
Q_D = quartile deviation
Q_3 = 3rd quartile
Q_1 = 1st quartile
2 = constant

Therefore

$$Q_3 = 65.5 + \left(\frac{3(50)/4 - 37}{4}\right)3$$

$$Q_3 = 65.5 + .375 = 65.875$$

$$Q_1 = 50.5 + \left(\frac{50/4 - 12}{4}\right)3$$

$$Q_1 = 50.5 + .375 = 50.875$$

$$Q_D = \frac{65.875 - 50.875}{2} = 7.5$$

Computation of the Standard Deviation from Grouped Data

The standard deviation is quite easy to compute from the grouped data found in Table E.3. Again as with the mean, the formula for computing standard deviation from grouped data is similar to the formula used in the ungrouped procedure. Certain modifications have to be made since the specific deviation scores cannot be obtained from grouped data. The formula and computations are presented below

$$s = SI\sqrt{\frac{\Sigma fx'^2}{N} - \left(\frac{\Sigma fx'}{N}\right)^2}$$

where

s = standard deviation
SI = step interval
Σ = summation
fx'^2 = the product of the frequency (f) of each step interval and the deviation (x') squared
N = number of scores
fx' = the product of the frequency and the deviation

Therefore

$$s = 3\sqrt{\frac{589}{50} - \left(\frac{5}{50}\right)^2}$$

$$s = 3\sqrt{11.78 - .01}$$

$$s = 3\sqrt{11.77}$$

$$s = 3 \times 3.43$$

$$s = 10.29$$

The following steps will help the student work logically through the computational procedures of the standard deviation for grouped data.

1. Prepare the column headed fx'^2. Each number in this column is the product of the frequency (f) times the square of the deviation $(x')^2$. The actual procedure is to multiply the numbers in the last two columns of the frequency table (x' x fx').
2. From the frequency table, obtain the sum of the fx'^2 column. All values are positive so that the entire column may be summed ($fx'^2 =$ 589).
3. Divide the sum of fx'^2 ($\Sigma fx'^2$) by the number of scores ($\Sigma fx'^2/N$)
4. From the frequency table, obtain the sum of the fx' column. This has usually been done in the computation of the mean ($\Sigma fx'/N$).
5. Divide the sum of the fx' column by the number of scores ($\Sigma fx'/N$).
6. Square the result obtained in Step 5 $(fx')^2/N$.

$$\frac{\Sigma fx'^2}{N} - \left(\frac{\Sigma fx'}{N}\right)^2$$

7. Subtract the value obtained in Step 6 from that obtained in Step 4.
8. Compute the square root of the value obtained in Step 7.

$$\left(\sqrt{\frac{\Sigma fx'^2}{N} - \frac{(\Sigma fx'^2)}{N}}\right)$$

9. Multiply the value obtained in Step 8 by the size of the step interval.

$$SI\sqrt{\frac{\Sigma fx'^2}{N} - \left(\frac{(\Sigma fx')}{N}\right)^2}$$

COMPUTATION OF PERCENTILES

The computations for percentiles will be presented in this section. Definitions and interpretations for this measure were presented in Chapter 4.

Calculation of Percentiles

It is often convenient to group data when the number of students exceed 40 or 50. The method for determining percentiles from grouped data is similar to that of ungrouped data but somewhat more complicated. The information utilized for calculating percentiles for ungrouped data according to the discussion in Chapter 4 is presented in Table E.4.

Table E.4 Frequency Distribution for Physical Fitness Knowledge Test (N = 30)

Class Interval	*Frequency*	*Cumulative Frequency*
29–30	3	30
27–28	2	27
25–26	3	25
23–24	5	22
21–22	5	17
19–20	2	12
17–18	4	10
15–16	2	6
13–14	2	4
11–12	1	2
9–10	1	1

The formula used for calculating any percentile with grouped data is

$$P_x = LL + SI\left(\frac{Px(N) - cf}{fi}\right)$$

where

P_x = desired percentile
LL = lower real limit of interval containing P_x
SI = size of the step interval in the frequency table
N = total number of scores
cf = cumulative frequencies below LL
fi = frequency of step interval containing P_x

To calculate P_{20}, estimate where the desired percentile will lie by using the formula for ungrouped data. $P_x = n(x)$. The estimate is that P_{20} will be in the interval that contains the sixth score. Using this information in the formula, P_{20} can be calculated as follows.

From Table E.4 for P_{20}, $LL = 14.5$, $SI = -2, P_x = .20$, $N = 30$, $cf = 4$, and $fi = 2$

$$P_{20} = 14.5 + 2\,\frac{(.20 \times 30 - 4)}{2}$$

$$P_{20} = 14.5 + 2 = 16.5$$

APPENDIX F COMPUTER PROGRAMS*

APPENDIX F.1 MEANS AND STANDARD DEVIATIONS BY GROUPS

This program identifies each data card as belonging to a given group or sample (as many as 15 groups are allowed) and reports the mean and standard deviation for one or more (up to 80) variables for each group. The standard deviation is calculated using n_j (the number of individuals in the jth group) rather than $N_j - 1$ in the denominator. For a discussion of the methods of calculating the standard deviation, the reader is directed to chapter eight of *Fundamental Research Statistics for the Behavioral Sciences*.

The first user card is the title card. The second user card is a control card reporting the number of variables in columns 4-5 and the number of groups in columns 9-10. The maximum number of variables is 80, and the maximum number of groups is 15. The third user card is the data format. Data cards, one for each subject, must correspond to the data format. The first variable (the group or sample number) is recorded in integer mode, and the remaining variables are recorded in floating point mode. The data deck must be followed by an END-OF-FILE marker.

*John T. Roscoe, The Funstat Package in Fortran IV, HOH, Rinehart and Winston, Inc., New York, 1973, pp. 36-50. Reprinted by permission.

```
C MEANS AND STANDARD DEVIATIONS BY GROUPS
C     IDENTIFIES EACH SUBJECT AS BELONGING TO ONE OF UP TO 15 GROUPS
C     AND COMPUTES MEAN AND STANDARD DEVIATION ON EACH OF UP TO 80
C     VARIABLES BY GROUPS.
C FIRST USER CARD IS TITLE CARD.
C 2ND USER CARD IS CONTROL CARD REPCRTING NV (# VARIABLES) IN COLUMNS
C     4-5 AND NG (# GROUPS) IN COLUMNS 9-10.
C 3RD USER CARD IS DATA FORMAT.
C     EXAMPLE:  (I5,15F5.0)
C DATA FOLLOW CONFORMING TO DATA FORMAT.
C     1ST VARIABLE IS GROUP NUMBER (INTEGER MODE).
C     REMAINING VARIABLES ARE SCORES (ALL FLOATING POINT MODE).
C FOLLOW DATA WITH END OF FILE MARKER.
      DIMENSION TITLE(20), X(80), SLM(15,80), SS(15,80), N(15), IFMT(20)
      IR = 5
      IP = 6
    1 FORMAT (20A4)
    5 FORMAT (16I5)
   21 FORMAT ('1',132('*')//5X,'TITLE:  ',20A4,'  N =',I5//1X,132('*')/
     -5X,'DATA FORMAT:  ',20A4/1X,132('*'))
   22 FORMAT (1X,'GROUP NO.',2X,15(4X,I2,2X))
   23 FORMAT (/1X,'VAR. NO.', I3)
   24 FORMAT (8X, 'MEAN', 15(1X, F7.2))
   25 FORMAT (8X, 'STDV', 15(1X, F7.2))
   26 FORMAT (1X, 132('*') / 11X, 'N', 15(2X, I5, 1X))
   99 FORMAT (1X, 132('*'))
C READ TITLE, CONTROL, DATA FORMAT, ZERU STORAGE.
  100 READ (IR,1) TITLE
      READ (IR,5) NV, NG
      READ (IR,1) IFMT
      NT = 0
      DO 110 I=1,NG
      N(I) = 0
      DO 110 J=1,NV
      SUM(I,J) = 0.0
  110 SS(I,J) = 0.0
C READ DATA, ACCUMULATE SUMS, RAW SUMS OF SQUARES, AND N'S.
  120 READ (IR,IFMT,END=200) I, (X(J), J=1,NV)
      IF ((I.LT.1).CR.(I.GT.NG)) GO TO 200
      NT = NT + 1
      N(I) = N(I) + 1
      DO 13C J=1,NV
      SUM(I,J) = SUM(I,J) + X(J)
  130 SS(I,J) = SS(I,J) + X(J)**2
      GO TO 120
  200 WRITE (IP,21) TITLE, NT, IFMT
      WRITE (IP,22) (J, J=1,NG)
      WRITE (IP,99)
C CALCULATE MEANS AND STDV'S, PRINT CUT ONE VARIABLE AT A TIME.
      DO 300 J=1,NV
      DO 250 I=1,NG
      IF (N(I).EQ.0) GO TO 250
      FN = N(I)
      SS(I,J) = SQRT((SS(I,J) - SUM(I,J)**2/FN) / FN)
      SUM(I,J) = SUM(I,J) / FN
  250 CONTINUE
      WRITE (IP,23) J
      WRITE (IP,24) (SUM(I,J), I=1,NG)
  3CC WRITE (IP,25) (SS(I,J), I=1,NG)
      WRITE (IP,26) (N(I), I=1,NG)
      WRITE (IP,99)
      STOP
      END
```

```
************************************************************************************************************
    TITLE:  DATA FROM FUNDAMENTAL RESEARCH STATISTICS PAGE 234. X2=X1+10 AND X3=X1+100,ETC.    N =    23

************************************************************************************************************
    DATA FORMAT:  (3X,I2,15F5.0)
************************************************************************************************************
GROUP NC.          1          2          3          4
************************************************************************************************************

VAR. NC.  1
        MEAN     6.00       4.00       7.00       0.00
        STDV     1.94       1.50       1.20       0.00

VAR. NC.  2
        MEAN    16.00      14.00      17.00       0.00
        STDV     1.94       1.50       1.20       0.00

VAR. NO.  3
        MEAN   106.00     104.00     107.00       0.00
        STDV     1.94       1.50       1.20       0.00

VAR. NC.  4
        MEAN  1006.00    1004.00    1007.00       0.00
        STDV     1.94       1.50       1.25       0.00

VAR. NO.  5
        MEAN     0.00       0.00       0.00       0.00
        STDV     0.00       0.00       0.00       0.00
************************************************************************************************************
           N        8          8          7          0
************************************************************************************************************
```

APPENDIX F.2 STANDARD SCORES PROGRAM

This program produces a frequency distribution, percentile ranks, linear *z*-scores, plus normally distributed *z*-scores, and stanines from a real variable that may include both positive and negative scores with or without one or two decimal places. For a discussion of the various score systems reported, the reader is directed to chapters three, nine, and eleven of *Fundamental Research Statistics for the Behavioral Sciences*. The normalizing procedure is an algebraic approximation adopted from Hastings in *Approximations for Digital Computers* published by Princeton University Press in 1955. It provides three-decimal accuracy.

The first user card is the title card. The second user card is a control card reporting. The minimum score of the raw score distribution in columns 1-5, the maximum score in columns 6-10, and the number of decimal places in column 15. The values of the minimum and maximum scores may be either negative or positive and may or may not have decimal places; however, the minimum value must be algebraically smaller than the maximum. The number of decimal places may be zero, one, or two. A data format card must precede the data cards. Only one entry on each data card is read, and it is in floating point mode. Scores may be either negative or positive and may have as many as two decimal places. They must not, however, exceed the range of scores (minimum to maximum) reported on the control card. An END-OF-FILE marker should follow the last data card.

```
C STANDARD SCORES PROGRAM
C     PRODUCES FREQUENCY DISTRIBUTION, PERCENTILE RANKS, LINEAR AND
C     NORMAL Z-SCORES, T-SCORES, AND STANINES.
C FIRST USER CARD IS TITLE CARD.
C 2ND USER CARD IS CONTROL CARD IN I5 REPORTING XMIN, XMAX, AND NDECI.
C     XMIN IS LOWEST SCORE IN DISTRIBUTION, XMAX IS HIGHEST.
C     NDECI IS NUMBER OF DECIMAL PLACES IN RAW SCORES (OPTIONAL).
C 3RD USER CARD IS DATA FORMAT.
C DATA FOLLOW CONFORMING TO DATA FORMAT.
C     ONE SCORE (FLOATING POINT MODE) PER CARD.  SCORES MAY BE NEGATIVE
C     OR POSITIVE, AND MAY BE INTEGERS OR NOT.  PRINTOUT REPORTS RAW
C     SCORES WITH TWO DECIMAL PLACES.
C FOLLOW DATA WITH END OF FILE MARKER.
      DIMENSION TITLE(20), FREQ(6001), IFMT(20)
      IR = 5
      IP = 6
    1 FORMAT (20A4)
    6 FORMAT (2F5.0, I5)
   21 FORMAT ('1',120('*')//5X,'TITLE:  ',20A4,'  N =',I5//1X,120('*')/
     -5X,'DATA FORMAT:  ',20A4/1X,120('*'))
   22 FORMAT (6X,'RAW        SCORE      PERCENTILE   LINEAR',3(6X,'NORMAL'
     -)/5X,'SCORE    FREQUENCY      RANK',6X,2('Z-SCORE',5X),'T-SCORE
     = STANINE'/1X,120('*'))
   51 FORMAT (/2X, F8.2, 5X, I6, 4(6X,F6.2), 7X, I2)
   52 FORMAT(/1X,120('*')/5X,'MEAN =',F8.3,5X,'STDV =',F8.3/1X,120('*'))
C READ TITLE, CONTROL, DATA FORMAT, ZERO STORAGE.
  100 READ (IR,1) TITLE
      READ (IR,6) XMIN, XMAX, NDECI
      READ (IR,1) IFMT
      N = 0
      SUM = 0.0
      SS = 0.0
      D = 10.0**NDECI
      XMIN = XMIN * D
      XMAX = XMAX * D
      KK = XMAX - XMIN + 1
      DO 110 J=1,KK
  110 FREQ(J) = 0.0
C READ DATA, COUNT N, BUILD FREQUENCY DISTRIBUTION.
  120 READ (IR,IFMT,END=200) X
      X = X * D
      IF ((X.LT.XMIN).OR.(X.GT.XMAX)) GO TO 200
      N = N + 1
      SUM = SUM + X/D
      SS = SS + X*X
      J = X - XMIN + 1.0
      FREQ(J) = FREQ(J) + 1.
      GO TO 120
  200 WRITE (IP,21) TITLE, N, IFMT
      WRITE (IP,22)
      FN = N
      STDV = SQRT((SS - SUM**2/FN) / FN)
      AMEAN = SUM / FN
C CALCULATE PERCENTILE RANKS AND LINEAR Z-SCORES.
      CF = FN
      DO 300 K=1,KK
      J = KK - K + 1
      X = (J + XMIN - 1.0) / D
      IFREQ = FREQ(J)
      PR = (100./FN) * ( CF- FREQ(J)/2.)
      Z = (X - AMEAN) / STDV
C CALCULATE NORMAL Z-SCORES, T-SCORES, AND STANINES.
      IF (PR.EQ.50.0) PR = 50.00001
      A = SQRT(ALOG(1.0 / (0.5 - ABS(50.0 - PR) * 0.01)**2))
      A=A-(2.5155+.80285*A+.0103*A*A)/(1.+1.4328*A+.1893*A*A+.0013*A**3)
      ZND = ((PR - 50.0) / ABS(PR - 50.0)) * A
      T = 10.0 * ZND + 50.0
      STAN = 2. * ZND + 5.499
      ISTAN = STAN
      IF (ISTAN.LT.1) ISTAN = 1
      IF (ISTAN.GT.9) ISTAN = 9
      CF = CF - FREQ(J)
  300 WRITE (IP,51) X, IFREQ, PR, Z, ZND, T, ISTAN
      WRITE (IP,52) AMEAN, STDV
      STOP
      END
```

TITLE: DATA FROM FUNDAMENTAL RESEARCH STATISTICS PAGES 14 AND 19. N = 120

DATA FORMAT: (4X,F2.0)

RAW SCORE	SCORF FREQUENCY	PERCENTILE RANK	LINEAR Z-SCORE	NORMAL Z-SCORE	NORMAL T-SCORE	NORMAL STANINE
20.00	1	99.58	2.24	2.64	76.39	9
19.00	2	98.33	1.99	2.13	71.29	9
18.00	3	96.25	1.74	1.78	67.81	9
17.00	6	92.50	1.49	1.44	64.40	8
16.00	7	87.08	1.24	1.13	61.30	7
15.00	6	81.67	0.99	0.90	59.03	7
14.00	8	75.83	0.74	0.70	57.01	6
13.00	10	68.33	0.49	0.48	54.77	6
12.00	12	59.17	0.24	0.23	52.31	5
11.00	13	48.75	-0.01	-0.03	49.69	5
10.00	10	39.17	-0.27	-0.27	47.25	4
9.00	9	31.25	-0.52	-0.49	45.12	4
8.00	9	23.75	-0.77	-0.71	42.86	4
7.00	8	16.67	-1.02	-0.97	40.33	3
6.00	4	11.67	-1.27	-1.19	38.08	3
5.00	6	7.50	-1.52	-1.44	35.60	2
4.00	3	3.75	-1.77	-1.78	32.19	1
3.00	2	1.67	-2.02	-2.13	28.71	1
2.00	0	0.83	-2.27	-2.39	26.06	1
1.00	1	0.42	-2.52	-2.64	23.61	1

MEAN = 11.058 STDV = 3.992

APPENDIX F.3 PEARSON PRODUCT-MOMENT CORRELATION MATRIX

This program produces a correlation matrix of all possible correlations among as many as 80 variables recorded on a given group of subjects. It also produces the mean and standard deviation for each variable. The standard deviation is calculated using N (the total number of subjects) rather than N − 1 in the denominator. One of the unique features of the program is a coding operation in which the scores on the first subject are used as an assumed mean. To the extent that the scores of this individual are typical of the collection, the rounding errors characteristic of most correlation matrix programs are greatly reduced. Generally, this coding feature will improve the accuracy even with an atypical first subject. A discussion of the methods of coding and of calculating the standard deviation will be found in Chapter 8 of *Fundamental Research Statistics for the Behavioral Sciences*. Formulas for calculating the Pearson product-moment correlation coefficient will be found in chapter twelve of the same text.

If the data are ranks, ranging from 1 to N for each variable, the Spearman rank coefficient and the Pearson coefficient are mathematically equivalent. Similarly, if one (or both) of two variables is dichotomous, the point biserial coefficient (or the Phi coefficient) is mathematically equivalent to the Pearson. Thus, this one computer program can conveniently be used for calculating several kinds of correlation coefficients.

The first user card is the title card. The second user card is a control card reporting the number of variables in columns 4-5. The third user card is the data format. Data cards, one for each subject, must correspond to the data format. All variables are in floating point mode. An END-OF-FILE marker should follow the last data card.

```
C PEARSON PRODUCT MOMENT CORRELATION MATRIX
C FIRST USER CARD IS TITLE CARD.
C 2ND USER CARD IS CONTROL CARD REPORTING NV IN COLUMNS 4-5.
C    NV IS # OF VARIABLES ON EACH DATA CARD.
C 3RD USER CARD IS DATA FORMAT.
C    EXAMPLE:  (5X,15F5.0)
C DATA (ALL FLOATING POINT MODE) FOLLOW, CONFORMING TO DATA FORMAT.
C FOLLOW DATA WITH END OF FILE MARKER.
      DIMENSION TITLE(20),X( 80),SUM( 80),SS( 80, 80)
      DIMENSION STDV( 80), C( 80), IFMT(20)
      IR = 5
      IP = 6
    1 FORMAT (20A4)
    5 FORMAT (16I5)
   21 FORMAT ('1',132('*')//5X,'TITLE:  ',20A4,'  N =',I5//1X,132('*')/
     -5X,'DATA FORMAT:  ',20A4/1X,132('*'))
   22 FORMAT (2X,'VAR.NO.', 15(5X,I3) / 1X,132('*'))
   23 FORMAT (/5X, I3, 3X, 15F8.4)
   24 FORMAT (/1X, 132('*')  / 3X, 'MEANS', 3X, 15F8.3)
   25 FORMAT (/3X, 'STDV.', 3X, 15F8.3)
   99 FORMAT (1X, 132('*'))
C READ TITLE, CONTROL, DATA FORMAT, ZERO STORAGE.
  100 READ (IR,1) TITLE
      READ (IR,5) NV
      READ (IR,1) IFMT
      N = 0
      DO 110 J=1,NV
      SUM (J) = 0.0
      DO 110 I=1,NV
  110 SS(I,J) = 0.0
      READ (IR,IFMT,END=200) (C(J), J=1,NV)
      N = 1
  120 READ (IR,IFMT,END=200) (X(J), J=1,NV)
      N = N + 1
      DO 125 J=1,NV
      X(J) = X(J) - C(J)
  125 SUM(J) = SUM(J) + X(J)
      DO 130 J=1,NV
      DO 130 I=1,NV
  130 SS(I,J) = SS(I,J) + X(I) * X(J)
      GO TO 120
  200 FN = N
C CALCULATE CORRECTED SS, THEN MEANS AND STDVS, THEN CORRELATIONS.
      DO 240 I = 1,NV
      DO 240 J=1,NV
  240 SS(I,J) = SS(I,J) - (SUM(I) * SUM(J) / FN)
      DO 250 J=1,NV
      SUM(J) = SUM(J) / FN    + C(J)
  250 STDV(J) = SQRT (SS(J,J) / FN) + 0.000001
      DO 260 I=1,NV
      DO 260 J=1,NV
  260 SS(I,J) = SS(I,J) / (FN * STDV(I) * STDV(J))
C WRITE OUT CORRELATIONS, MEANS, AND STANDARD DEVIATIONS IN MATRIX FORM.
      JJ = 1
      MM = (NV - 1) / 15 + 1
      DO 280 M=1,MM
      WRITE (IP,21) TITLE, N, IFMT
      JJJ = M * 15
      WRITE (IP,22) (J, J=JJ,JJJ)
      JJJ = JJ + 14
      IF (NV.LE.JJJ) JJJ = NV
      DO 270 I=1,NV
  270 WRITE (IP,23) I, (SS(I,J), J=JJ,JJJ)
      WRITE (IP,24) (SUM(J), J=JJ,JJJ)
      WRITE (IP,25) (STDV(J), J=JJ,JJJ)
  280 JJ = JJ + 15
      WRITE (IP,99)
      STOP
      END
```

TITLE: DATA FROM FUNDAMENTAL RESEARCH STATISTICS PAGES 74-75. N = 10

DATA FORMAT: (4CF2.0)

VAR.NC.	1	2	3	4	5	6	7	8	9	10	11	12	13	14	15
1	1.0000	0.8833	0.9833	-0.8500	0.9778	-0.0667	0.0000								
2	0.8833	1.0000	0.9000	-0.8750	0.8833	-0.0500	0.0000								
3	0.9833	0.9000	1.0000	-0.8500	0.9833	-0.0750	0.0000								
4	-0.8500	-0.8750	-0.8500	1.0000	-0.8167	0.1000	0.0000								
5	0.9778	0.8833	0.9833	-0.8167	1.0000	0.0000	0.0000								
6	-0.0667	-0.0500	-0.0750	0.1000	0.0000	1.0000	0.0000								
7	0.0000	0.0000	0.0000	0.0000	0.0000	0.0000	0.0000								
MEANS	5.000	5.000	5.000	5.000	5.000	5.000	0.000								
STDV.	3.000	2.000	2.000	2.000	3.000	2.000	0.000								

APPENDIX F.4 ITEM ANALYSIS FOR OBJECTIVE TESTS

This is a program designed to provide item analyses and certain other statistics for multiple-choice, true-false, and matching tests. It produces the following information.

(1) Proportion of examinees getting the correct answer to each item. This is sometimes called the index of item difficulty.

(2) The correlation of the item score (where a correct answer is scored 1 and a wrong answer scored 0) with the total score (the sum of the correct answers). This is an index of item consistency with the total test content, and it is sometimes used as an index of item validity where content validity is to be established.

(3) The number of examinees selecting each response (a maximum of nine responses to each question is permitted). Test constructors often use this information to determine the usefulness of the distractor responses.

(4) The mean, standard deviation, and the number of scores in the distribution.

(5) Several different eatimates of test reliability, including Kuder-Richardson formula 20, Kuder-Richardson formula 21, the correlation of the odd item scores with the even item scores, and the odd-even correlation corrected for attenuation by the Spearman-Brown prophecy formula.

The calculations and their logic are discussed in chapter fifteen of *Fundamental Research Statistics for the Behavioral Sciences*.

The first user card is the title card. The second user card is a control card reporting the number of items on the test in columns 4-5 and the maximum number of the response to a test item in column 10. The maximum number of test items is 75, and the maximum number of responses may range as high as 9. If the latter figure is left blank, it will be set equal to 9. The third user card is an answer key. The word "KEY" may be placed in the first three columns to identify the card, and the correct responses to the various items on the test should follow in order beginning in column 4. The fourth user card is the data format. Data cards, one for each examinee, must correspond to the data format. The data are integers recorded in floating point mode. Typically, the examinee's identification number will be recorded in columns 1-3, and the responses to the various questions will follow in order beginning in column 4. An END = OF-FILE marker should follow the last data card.

```
C ITEM ANALYSIS FOR OBJECTIVE TESTS
C    FOR MULTIPLE-CHOICE, TRUE-FALSE, AND MATCHING TESTS (MAXIMUM = 9
C    RESPONSES).  PRODUCES PROPORTION PASSING ON EACH ITEM, CORRELATION
C    OF ITEM SCORE WITH TOTAL SCORE, AND NUMBER OF EXAMINEES CHOOSING
C    RESPONSE TO EACH ITEM.  ALSO PRODUCES KR20, KR21, AND ODD-EVEN
C    RELIABILITY ESTIMATES.  ODD-EVEN IS REPORTED WITH AND WITHOUT
C    SPEARMAN-BROWN CORRECTION.
C FIRST USER CARD IS TITLE.
C 2ND USER CARD IS CONTROL CARD REPORTING NV IN COLUMNS 4-5 AND NC
C    IN COLUMN 10.  NV IS # OF ITEMS ON EACH DATA CARD.  NC IS MAXIMUM
C    RESPONSE TO TEST ITEMS (DEFAULT = 9).
C 3RD USER CARD IS KEY.  FORMAT (3X,75I1).  PLACE 'KEY' IN COLUMNS 1-3.
C 4TH USER CARD IS DATA FORMAT.
C    EXAMPLE:  (10X,70I1)
C DATA (ALL INTEGERS) FOLLOW, CONFORMING TO DATA FORMAT.
C    DATA CARDS (ONE FOR EACH EXAMINEE) REPORT RESPONSE TO EACH QUESTION
C FOLLOW DATA WITH END OF FILE MARKER.
      DIMENSION TITLE(20), IX(75), X(75), KEY(75), SUMX(75), SSX(75)
      DIMENSION SP(75), MATRX(75,10), IFMT(20)
      IR = 5
      IP = 6
    1 FORMAT (20A4)
    2 FORMAT (3X, 75I1)
    5 FORMAT (16I5)
   21 FORMAT ('1',120('*')//5X,'TITLE:  ',20A4,'  N =',I5//1X,120('*')/
     -5X,'DATA FORMAT:  ',20A4/1X,120('*'))
   22 FORMAT (2X,'ITEM    RIGHT    PROPORTION    CORRELATION    NUMBER GIVIN
     -G EACH RESPONSE'/3X,'NO.     ANS.    RIGHT ANS.     WITH TOTAL       0
     =',9(7X,I1)/1X,120('*'))
   23 FORMAT (/3X, I2, 6X, I1, 7X, F6.4, 7X, F7.4, 1X, 10(4X,I4))
   24 FORMAT(1X,120('*')/40X,'MEAN =',F8.3,5X,'STDV =',F8.3/1X,120('*'))
   25 FORMAT (5X,'RELIABILITY:',5X,'KR20 =',F7.4,5X,'KR21 =',F7.4,5X,
     - 'UNCORRECTED ODD-EVEN =',F7.4,5X,'CORRECTED ODD-EVEN =',F7.4/
     = 1X,120('*'))
C READ TITLE, CONTROL, DATA FORMAT, ZERO STORAGE, NC+1 FOR NO RESPONSE.
  100 READ (IR,1) TITLE
      READ (IR,5) NV, NC
      READ (IR,2) (KEY(I), I=1,NV)
      READ (IR,1) IFMT
      IF (NC.EQ.0) NC = 9
      NCO = NC + 1
      FNV = NV
      N = 0
      SUMY = 0.0
      SSY = 0.0
      SUMOD = 0.0
      SSODD = 0.0
      SUMEV = 0.0
      SSEVN = 0.0
      UNCOR = 0.0
      SUMPQ = 0.0
      DO 110 I=1,NV
      SUMX(I) = 0.0
      SSX(I) = 0.0
      SP(I) = 0.0
      DO 110 J=1,10
  110 MATRX(I,J) = 0
C READ DATA, COUNT N, BUILD RESPONSE MATRIX; SUM TOTAL, ODD-EVEN SCORES.
  120 READ (IR,IFMT,END=200) (IX(I), I=1,NV)
      N = N + 1
```

```
      SCORE = 0.0
      DO 130 I=1,NV
      X(I) = 0.0
      IF (IX(I).EQ.KEY(I)) X(I) = 1.0
      SCORE = SCORE + X(I)
      J = IX(I) + 1
  130 MATRX(I,J) = MATRX(I,J) + 1
      ODD = 0.0
      EVEN = 0.0
      DO 135 I=2,NV,2
      J=I-1
      ODD = ODD + X(J)
  135 EVEN = EVEN + X(I)
      SUMOD = SUMOD + ODD
      SUMEV = SUMEV + EVEN
      SSODD = SSODD + ODD**2
      SSEVN = SSEVN + EVEN**2
      UNCOR = UNCOR + ODD * EVEN
      SUMY = SUMY + SCORE
      SSY = SSY + SCORE**2
      DO 140 I=1,NV
      SUMX(I) = SUMX(I) + X(I)
      SSX(I) = SSX(I) + X(I)**2
  140 SP(I) = SP(I) + SCORE * X(I)
      GO TO 120
  200 FN = N
      WRITE (IP,21) TITLE, N, IFMT
      WRITE (IP,22) (J, J=1,9)
C CALCULATE CORRELATION ITEM WITH TOTAL, PRINT ITEM ANALYSIS.
      SSY = SSY - SUMY**2 / FN
      DO 210 I=1,NV
      SSX(I) = SSX(I) - SUMX(I)**2 / FN
      SP(I) = SP(I) - SUMX(I) * SUMY / FN
  210 SUMX(I) = SUMX(I) / FN
      DO 300 I=1,NV
      R = SP(I) / (SQRT(SSX(I) * SSY) + 0.0000001)
      SUMPQ = SUMPQ + SUMX(I) - SUMX(I)**2
  300 WRITE (IP,23) I, KEY(I), SUMX(I), R, (MATRX(I,J), J=1,NCO)
C CALCULATE MEAN, STDV, AND RELIABILITY ESTIMATES AND PRINT.
      YMEAN = SUMY / FN
      VAR = (SSY / FN ) + 0.0000001
      STDV = SQRT (VAR)
      WRITE (IP,24) YMEAN, STDV
      FKR20 = (FNV/(FNV-1.0)) * ((VAR-SUMPQ)/VAR)
      FKR21 = (FNV*VAR - YMEAN*(FNV-YMEAN)) / ((FNV-1.0)*VAR)
      SSODD = SSODD - SUMOD**2/FN
      SSEVN = SSEVN - SUMEV**2/FN
      UNCOR = UNCOR - SUMOD*SUMEV/FN
      UNCOR = UNCOR / (SQRT(SSODD * SSEVN) + 0.0000001)
      CORR = 2.0*UNCOR / (1.0 + UNCOR)
      WRITE (IP,25) FKR20, FKR21, UNCOR, CORR
      STOP
      END
```

```
TITLE:  DATA FOP TESTING ITEM ANALYSIS PROGRAM                    N =  20

DATA FORMAT:  (3X,77I1)
```

ITEM NO.	RIGHT ANS.	PROPORTION RIGHT ANS.	CORRELATION WITH TOTAL	NUMBER GIVING EACH RESPONSE 0	1	2	3	4	5	6	7	8	9
1	5	0.5000	0.3602	0	2	2	2	4	10				
2	2	0.4500	0.5752	0	1	9	4	2	4				
3	3	0.3000	0.4745	0	2	10	6	1	1				
4	1	0.3500	0.6810	0	7	4	5	2	2				
5	4	0.4500	0.6556	0	6	2	3	9	0				
6	4	0.6500	0.4377	1	1	1	4	13	0				
7	3	0.4000	0.4194	0	0	6	8	5	1				
8	1	0.3500	0.3175	0	7	4	5	2	2				
9	5	0.4000	0.3104	0	2	2	3	5	8				
10	2	0.5500	0.6583	0	2	11	0	2	5				
11	3	0.3500	0.6251	1	1	8	7	3	0				
12	3	0.4000	0.2832	2	2	5	8	1	2				
13	5	0.2500	0.7471	4	3	1	4	3	5				
14	4	0.3000	0.7656	11	0	2	0	6	1				
15	2	0.2500	0.5931	12	1	5	1	1	0				

```
MEAN =    5.950     STDV =    3.748

RELIABILITY:    KR20 = 0.8108    KR21 = 0.7976    UNCORRECTED ODD-EVEN = 0.7412    CORRECTED ODD-EVEN = 0.8514
```

Author Index

Subject Index